ROARING CENTURY

QUEEN VICTORIA AT WINDSOR

A hitherto unpublished photograph, taken in 1894. With the Queen in the Oak Room at Windsor Castle are her daughter and son-in-law, Princess Beatrice and Prince Henry of Battenberg, with three of their children; (*right to left*) Princess Victoria Eugenie (later Queen of Spain), Prince Alexander of Battenberg (now Marquess of Carisbrooke) and Prince Leopold of Battenberg (later Lord Leopold Mountbatten).

ROARING CENTURY

1846 - 1946

BY

R. J. CRUIKSHANK

HAMISH HAMILTON
LONDON

First published 1946
Second impression December 1946

Printed in Great Britain by Jarrold & Sons, Ltd., Norwich and London

FOREWORD

FIRST, a word on how this book began.

In the raw morning hours of 21 January 1846, Charles Dickens carried home the first copy of a daily newspaper. He was its editor. The name of the newspaper was the *Daily News*.

Gilbert Chesterton, who wrote well on many themes, but best of all on the theme of Charles Dickens, once besought the newspaper never to forget " its semi-divine origin." It was in remembrance of this semi-divine origin that its bound copies for the year 1846 were brought up from their long sleep in the vaults. In the centenary year, of all years, one felt it a duty to repair to Kipling's " Kensal Green of greatness called the Files."

The beginning of this book was a reading of those newspapers of a hundred years ago. At first sight, those files looked remote and faded. On opening them, the names that stared from the headlines seemed forgotten names, or at best half-forgotten. The crowds coming from the Odeon on a Saturday night or going down to Epsom on a June morning wouldn't make much of them, one fancied. What has all this to do with our aching post-war cares ? they might ask. With the atomic bomb ? Or with the struggle of the world to find everlasting peace and security ? But that feeling did not last long. It was the origins of our life and our times, the elements that have shaped and fostered us, that the explorer found embodied here.

The records of 1846 set one brooding over the way the world went then and over the many changes that have since taken place— 1846 provided many points of departure. The writer found himself caught up, for example, in that long debate as to the true nature of Progress which ran through the century and has not yet reached an end. Our forefathers in 1846 were greatly concerned over the relationship of man and the machine, though in a different manner from us. They contended hotly about the conflicting rights of the individual and the rights of the community. They pondered over man's duty to God and his neighbour ; over man's place in a universe that even then had become frighteningly vast.

The world that we live in today—both its physical setting and the weather of the mind—was largely shaped by the middle years of last century. The conflict of ideas that took place in that age of intellectual vigour has sensibly influenced not only the modern Briton, but the modern American, and the modern European. Men pass ; great happenings are forgotten ; machines become out of date. But the ideas that were expressed through men, events and machines have their own life and evolution, surviving their temporary forms of expression and taking other shapes.

For this writer, there was much more than the rustling of dead laurels, the turning over of faded pages, in these centenary labours. In the first place, the year 1846 came to cast a spell over his imagination. The London of that time became as visible and tangible a city as the London of 1946. He watched the unfolding of its panorama of opulence and grime. The ill-paved streets were rowdy with the clatter of hooves. But through the rumble of the horse omnibuses and the coaches of the quality pierced the whistle of the railway locomotive—that friendly monster which so perfectly represented Progress, the Age of Machines and the glorious Future. The city had a smell that our nostrils would find unbearable—a smell compounded of bad drains, cesspools, horse dung, and rookeries, each with a polluted ditch at its heart. The lighted windows in the great squares showed a triumphant middle-class feasting a slightly bewildered aristocracy. Twemlow, the gentleman, had become the oldest friend of Veneering the bounder. Looking in at the windows stood Poor Jo !

If, in the pages that follow, there may seem to some readers an excessive preoccupation with Charles Dickens, then the blame must entirely rest on Charles Dickens. For such is the power of that genius that it is impossible to look at scenes and aspects of London life in 1946 without saying, " That, of course, belongs to *Bleak House*," or " This is *Our Mutual Friend*." How, then, can one expect to escape that mighty influence in going back to 1846 ? It is easy to get completely lost in that past, becoming a fugitive in the fantastic London of shadows and strange lights that is built up, stone by stone, and street by street, in the novels of Dickens. The force of the illusion is so great that in turning back to 1846 one sees the politicians and the railway trains, the bankers, the gutter snipes, and the women of the slums in the wild poetic lightnings of his vision. But something more is here than the power of a narrative poet who can give a house front the physiognomy of an evil old witch or can invest Micawber with the splendour of an archangel. Besides the pure descriptive magic—the creation of thronged streets of crazy houses with Gothic characters, stretching their heads out of the windows, like gargoyles, there is the building up of a city of moral ideas, a true City of God. Under the wavering gaslight of the streets of 1846, amid the dirt, the huddle and the smells, it is this that one grasps, not boastfully as with a discovery made, but in a decent humility of spirit, as with a revelation granted. It is the growth and influence of these ideas in the subsequent hundred years that matters most and creates a tradition to live for rather than a strange dream to remember. If, as one friendly critic who looked at these pages in manuscript remarked, King Charles Dickens's head is forever tumbling into them, that is because, in one's broodings over all the years between, he turned out to be the most representative man of his century. In his life he was thought to be a brilliant topical writer ; we now see him to be a broodingly prophetic one. " Who touches this book, touches a man," wrote Whitman. Who touches Dickens touches a century.

There is a modern school of critics who, having discovered that Dickens had considerable faults as a man, proceed to denounce Pickwick as a humbug and David Copperfield as a villain. This is an order of moral snobbery even worse than the social snobbery of those Baconians who argue that Shakespeare could not have written sublime poetry because he was born a poor boy, and that it would take at least a Lord Chancellor to compose *Antony and Cleopatra*. But the mystery of genius is of a piece with the mystery of religion. The wind of the spirit blows where it lists. The domestic troubles and the money troubles of Dickens, his treatment of newspaper proprietors and publishers, his vanity and his touchiness, make interesting material for a biographer, but they have as much relevance to *Little Dorrit* or *Hard Times* as the fact that he wore diamond studs and liked claret. What attaches one to him in these days are the living parts of his genius, the intuitive and mediumistic elements in him that foresaw the perils of our machine civilisation and forecast the dilemma of this modern age. According to one theory of immortality only the best qualities of a man survive, and his baser parts crumble to nothingness with his dust. That would seem, at least, to apply to Dickens. For through this hundred years, the noblest part of him, his writing, has not only survived, but quickened in vitality and deepened in influence. He started his newspaper at the beginning of the modern Liberal State ; it was his protest on behalf of the utterly abandoned and disinherited that in the end modified the whole conception in the minds of his million readers of what the Liberal State should be. Under the pressure of a genius that moved by instinct rather than by the aid of any dialectic, Marxian or Hegelian, the emphasis of politics slowly but irresistibly changed from property rights to human rights, from the sacredness of things to the sacredness of personality. All the blind, unconscious power that was in him—the dreaming thing that lay underneath the worldly man and the brilliant reporter—affirmed the brotherhood of man. He was a propagandist, a frank and shameless propagandist, as indeed most great writers have been. He exerted his powers as a popular novelist to protect the weak and to redress abuses. He rejoiced at the prospect of running a newspaper because that seemed to offer an enormous extension of his propagandist scope. There was never any doubt as to where he stood on liberty, and it is plain enough that the author of *Bleak House* shared to the full Rouncewell's views on equality. But, in the end, what he cared most about was fraternity. It was the impulse towards brotherhood which lay at the deepest springs of his genius; with him it was that force below the conscious mind which makes a writer write better than he knows; and it is the movement towards fraternity, towards the recognition of social responsibility, that gives the century its finest significance.

This book was originally planned to mark an interesting centenary. Its pretensions were modest and its limitations obvious. But it proved to be rather like a ship that is pulled out of its course by a magnetic mountain. Some may even complain that the nails in the ship flew out from the force of the attraction. So it cannot fairly claim to be a comprehensive record of the hundred years life of the newspaper which Dickens began. Even less does it pretend to be the history of a crowded century. One might put it this way—that in wandering about the streets of that Victorian city, gaslit, malodorous, proud, with the cheer of the lighted windows, and the human scarecrows in the shadows, one could not help speculating how it would all turn out. What would be the fate of the children of Progress? Would their faith in salvation through the machine be justified? What chance would there be for compassion and tenderness in an age of iron and gold? So it comes about that these chapters represent little more than a long reverie, a brooding over Then and Now, the imagination being stirred by those lamps and shadows of certain streets a hundred years ago. The starting point of these explorations was always 1846. And the point of return was 1846. For it was by every reckoning an extraordinary year.

But, why, asks the sceptic, do you set up two such arbitrary fences as 1846 and 1946 and call the field between a century? Isn't that playing hob with history? An unfinished manuscript by Mr. Geoffrey Crowther (from which he permits this writer to quote) provides as strong a shield against the wrath of the historians as any amateur could wish. "Those who like to amuse themselves with historical parallels," writes Mr. Crowther, "may reflect that in modern history the great dividing lines have occurred round about the middle of the calendar centuries, not at their beginnings. It is in the 'forties or 'fifties of each century, not in the oo's, that the great decisions have been reached which have sent Western civilisation off on a new tack. . . . New men and new ideas get control in the 'forties and 'fifties, and, for a few decades, work out the new pattern." That was most certainly true of the middle years of the last century.

R. J. C.

CONTENTS

ILLUSTRATIONS

ACKNOWLEDGMENTS

Acknowledgments are due to the following for permission to quote: John Murray, *The Life of Disraeli* (Moneypenny and Buckle) ; Mrs. George Bambridge, *The Lesson*, from *The Five Nations* (Rudyard Kipling) ; Messrs. Methuen & Co., Ltd., *My Own Times* (Lady Dorothy Neville) ; Messrs. Gerald Duckworth & Co., Ltd., *Collected Poems* (Hilaire Belloc) ; Messrs. Cassell & Co., Ltd., *The Life of George Cadbury* (A. G. Gardiner) ; Messrs. G. Routledge & Sons, Ltd. *Rough Islanders* (H, W. Nevinson) and Messrs. Macmillan & Co., Ltd., *Gladstone* (John Morley).

Thanks are also due to the proprietors of *Punch, The Illustrated London News* and *The Autocar* for permission to reproduce " The British Lion, 1850 ", " The Reform Club Banquet, 1846 " and " The Man With The Red Flag ", and to Messrs. Boosey & Hawkes, Ltd., for " The Excursion Train Galop " ; to Messrs. B. Feldman & Co., Ltd., for the words of the parody " The Moon Shines Bright on Charlie Chaplin ", and to the Publishers of " We Don't Want to Fight but By Jingo if We Do " for permission to include the chorus of that song.

CHAPTER I

IT WAS A HUNDRED YEARS AGO

O N the table rest the first files of the *Daily News*, January to December 1846 — brought up from the vaults — peaceful Victorian survivors from our mad times of H.E.s, fly bombs, rockets.

Looking at the panorama of that year, its splendours and its despairs, one is tempted to apply to it the famous opening lines of *A Tale of Two Cities* : " It was the best of times, it was the worst of times, it was the age of wisdom, it was the age of foolishness, it was the epoch of belief, it was the epoch of incredulity, it was the season of Light, it was the season of Darkness, it was the spring of hope, it was the winter of despair, we had everything before us, we had nothing before us, we were all going direct to Heaven, we were all going direct the other way. . . ."

Yet to the Time traveller from 1946 it is the gusto of that year which makes the strongest impression. The achievements of the men and women of that year were remarkable, their energies were unwearying. They had a great faith in their own powers and a great faith in the future of their country. It is a good tonic to spend some time in their cheerful company. Many evil and cruel things were done in those days, but there were strong voices to put a name to evil and cruelty ; the general tone of the age was one of buoyant optimism. We were on our way to the sunny uplands !

It was, of course, a notable year in our political history. In January Sir Robert Peel, the Prime Minister, declared for the Repeal of the Corn Laws, shattering the Conservative Party in the process, altering the balance of power in English society, and bringing in that length of years during which Free Trade became as much a religion as an economic system. That summer was an arch through which gleamed an untravelled world of riches, and pride, and might. In the June of that year Peel's Government fell, and Russell's Cabinet sat in its place, coming in with all the radiant hope of Victorian Liberalism.*

" This is a year of wonders," said the men of the cities.

" Peel has betrayed his party and ruined his country," said the country squires. " God save us from what will happen next. What's to become of the farm lands ? "

* Among the distinguished men born in this year was that incomparable defender of Liberal ideals, C. P. Scott of the *Manchester Guardian*. F. H. Bradley, whose *Appearance and Reality* was the noblest product of English philosophy in the nineteenth century, was born in 1846.

There was gloom in the manors, that June ; joy in Manchester. Power was passing from the country house to the counting house, from Sir Leicester Dedlock to Mr. Rouncewell, the manufacturer. The long reign of the mercantile middle-classes had begun.

(Just one year short of the century, in June 1945, another great Conservative leader, Mr. Churchill, met defeat in his hour of triumph, and a Labour Government came in.)

The roaring 'forties were also the hungry 'forties, the 'forties of the potato blight and the mildewed corn. The country was on the eve of such an expansion of trade as it had never known, but phantoms were in the streets. The failure of the potato crop brought misery to millions ; many starved to death in Ireland ; in the end it decided the issue of Repeal. Famine shadowed men's minds in 1846 as it shadows them in 1946.

" Rotten potatoes have done it all ; they put Peel in his damned fright," growled the Duke of Wellington. In our relations with the Irish we have been a long time paying the price of those rotten potatoes. On the day Repeal was carried in the House of Lords, Peel was overthrown in the Commons on a Bill to deal with crimes in Ireland. " For upwards of a hundred years," wrote the *Daily News*, " ministers and legislators have had to repress outrage in Ireland by coercive laws levelled indiscriminately against all classes." The effort was a vain one, sighed the newspaper. But for another seventy-five years successive Governments were to pursue the policy of alternate repression and conciliation. Ireland was the sphinx of the century, continually propounding her riddle to English politicians, and destroying them when they gave the wrong answer.

The great migration began in that summer of 1846. The precise figure of Ireland's population that year is not known, but it is commonly put at around 8,500,000. Within ten years at least 2,000,000 had fled to America to escape starvation. Many did not survive the journey. To quote Mr. J. L. Garvin's brilliant shorthand note of history—America gave Ireland the potato on which a large population was reared ; from America came the blight which destroyed the potato ; and it was America which provided a sanctuary for the victims.

It was the year when Income Tax was 7d. in the £ instead of nine shillings. It was the year when Britain and the United States came near to war over the Oregon boundary line.

To the men of that age, as to later generations, 1846 was a memorable year for other reasons than its politics. It was the year, for example, of " the great Railroad Mania." Quite suddenly, the British public became fully aware of what might be made of this new method of moving about the globe—and of the fortunes that would spring from it. The little sporadic, unconnected lines began to be linked up into systems, unifying the country and making internal communication and trade infinitely easier.   On the maps of the time the spider is seen to be working with a furious diligence, criss-crossing the country with his threads, until the web comes to look very much as it appears to-day in Bradshaw or the A.B.C.   These great-grandfathers of ours had the same feeling about the railways that their great-grandsons have about air transport.   " It is becoming a small world," they said.   " It is becoming one world."   Good-bye to the romanticism of coaches and the coaching inns !   Farewell, Mr. Pickwick !

Fast transport—easy communications—free trade and the new machines to accelerate that free exchange of goods—all this was opening up the globe and bringing its peoples closer, ever closer. The vision of a world in which all men would be prosperous and happy, with war become as absurd an anachronism as the clash of knights in armour, shone before the eyes of an optimistic generation.   On the waters, the change from sailing ships to steam ships, from wood to iron was going on rapidly. A sense of good times coming was in the air. Trade was marching well ahead of the flag. The Repealers foretold that prosperity would soon come roaring in like a Cornish tide. The British were plainly the favourite sons of Destiny.

1846 was the year when the Electric Telegraph Company was formed in London to exploit commercially the invention of the " magnetic telegraph " ; the Post Office did not take the system over until 1870. The first public telegram had been handled by the Great Western Railway in 1838, but the invention was still young enough not to have lost its savour of witchcraft.   Soon, wherever the iron road was laid, the bare telegraph trees would follow, and a new sound would be brought into the countryside, the sleepy drone of the wires. That summer the *Daily News* recorded how, through the agency of the magnetic telegraph, a thief running across the platform at Cambridge and leaping on a train had been picked up by the police on reaching London. The newspaper noted the striking detail that the warning message from Cambridge had taken less than half a minute to speed to London. Here was Ariel in the service of the Law, wearing a Bobby's tall beaver hat. Inspector Bucket had found a new ally in the detection of crime. Nearly seventy years later an even more astonishing device of the scientists, wireless, was employed by Bucket's successor, Inspector Dew, to capture the murderer Crippen at Quebec.*

* The first telegraph message used in tracking a murderer described him as " a man in the garb of a kwaker," there being no Q in the code. That was in 1839.

In this January of 1846, Michael Faraday, who is one of the germinal minds of the century, was lecturing to the Royal Institution on his experiments with electricity. The professor, said the newspapers, gave " the first experimental demonstration of his recent important discoveries in Magnetism and Light." With the sparkles and flashes at the tips of his fingers, Faraday appeared a benevolent sorcerer. The electric age would soon be upon Britain. All the curious and searching brains of '46 were being stirred by the boundless hopes of science. Many of the inventions which have changed man's daily habits have sprung from Faraday's researches or his intuitions—telegraphy, ocean cables, wireless, electric power and light, the telephone, among them. There was a buoyant faith abroad in 1846 that invention and human happiness were inseparable, that science was the all-bountiful mother, that physical progress must inevitably increase the sum of virtue. No shadow of atomic bombs crossed the sunshine of those cheerful Victorians.

This was the year when ether was first used in operations, and, for the rest of the century, human kind was spared an infinity of suffering and pain. Working men of London, aware through their daily lives that there were other abuses besides the Corn Laws crying for redress, formed an association to draw attention to the sorry state of housing and health in the slums. The Chartists were in a constant eruption this year, calling great crowds together on moor and common, rolling up petitions and crying a plague on Whig and Tory. Men of property were in high alarm at the spread of Chartism. A German merchant's son, Friedrich Engels, had lately been in Lancashire, dissecting the dumb miseries of the victims of the Industrial Revolution. Engels' *The Working Classes in England*, published in 1844, had wakened but small notice. Podsnap was our tutelary deity in those days, and of foreigners he said, " They do, sir—they do—I am sorry to be obliged to say it—*as* they do."

But there were writers at home to prod the fat ribs of complacency. Disraeli's *Sybil, or the Two Nations*, brought out in 1845, had displayed the rhetorician of the Young Tories, the man who shot Peel full of arrows, as a pioneer in the novel of social significance. " I was told that an impassable gulf divided the Rich from the Poor ; I was told that the Privileged and the People formed Two Nations, governed by different laws, influenced by different manners, with no thoughts or sympathies in common ; with an innate inability of mutual comprehension."

Thomas Carlyle, the Scot " with a rat gnawing inside him," is represented in the *Daily News* of 1846 by a long review of his *Oliver Cromwell*, one of his obeisances to the great man theory of history, a theory which has added considerably to the woes of the world since then. But it was Carlyle's virtue that he cried out, like Elijah born again, against the sins of self-satisfaction, the corruptions of contentment ; prophesying, not without sombre relish, the fire that must fall upon the city of man's pride. " England is full of wealth, of multifarious produce, supply for human want in every kind ; yet England is dying of inanition. With unabated bounty, the land of England blooms and grows ; waving with yellow harvests ; thick-studded with workshops, industrial imple- ments, with fifteen millions of workers understood to be the strongest, the cunningest and the willingest Earth ever had. . . . Of these successful, skilful workers some two millions, it is now counted, sit in workhouses, Poor-Law prisons or have outdoor relief flung over the wall to them." Where is our wealth ? We are all enchanted, Carlyle cries. A terrible spell lies upon us.

1846 was the year when her Majesty graciously gave assent to the first Public Baths and Washhouses Bill. It would soon be possible for the begrimed navvy to cleanse his body for twopence. Elegant and refined persons were even willing to concede the existence of drains in that blazing hot summer of 1846. One of the most useful contributions made to human progress this year was Mr. Doulton's invention of a new drain-pipe.

In 1846 an Act was passed turning disreputable Battersea Fields into a Royal Park. Out of that Act sprang one of London's loveliest parks—and the movement to furnish playing fields for the million —the reaching out towards sport and the open air—which has been one of the great social betterments of the century.

This was a year of note in literature. In the *Daily News* for 30 December, appears the announcement that the first part of *Vanity Fair—Pen and Pencil Sketches of English Society* will be published next day, price one shilling. The author's name is given as W. M. Thackeray (Titmarsh). Michael Angelo Titmarsh—what a pen-name for a master ! In the spring of this year there crept out a small volume of poems by Currer, Ellis and Acton Bell, of which scant notice was taken beyond an indifferent review in the *Athenaeum* for 4 July 1846.

Its fate is a monument to critical blindness, for the contributions made by Ellis Bell included poems that are likely to endure so long as the English-speaking world has a care for poetry. Ellis Bell happened to be Emily Brontë. The masculine cape of Currer Bell enfolded Charlotte, and behind Acton Bell hid Anne. The *Daily News* was the only paper in which Charlotte would advertise the poems. Frozen by the neglect of their verse in this spring of 1846, the sisters turned to the novel : Charlotte produced *The Professor*,

which all the publishers of the day returned with scant regrets ;
Anne wrote *Agnes Grey* ; while from Emily, in dying, came an
unmatched thing in English letters, that splendour of darkness,
Wuthering Heights.

Yet another major novelist made an odd first appearance in 1846.
A young woman from Coventry who had revolted against the
evangelicalism of her upbringing this year produced a translation
of Strauss' *Leben Jesus*. Strauss' critical treatment of the New
Testament caused much horror and disgust among the orthodox.
His translator was Miss Mary Anne Evans, to become later known
as George Eliot, one of the great ethical influences of the Victorian
age. This unconciliating entry was characteristic of the author of
Adam Bede and *Middlemarch*.

It was on 12 September 1846, that Robert Browning
eloped with Elizabeth Barrett from Wimpole Street, a romance
blessed and magnified long afterwards by Mr. Samuel Goldwyn.
The *Annual Register* for this year showed its taste by reprinting
" How They Brought the Good News from Ghent to Aix," from
Bells and Pomegranates.

Browning was the son of an officer of the Bank of England. The
son of the respected principal partner of the sherry importers,
Ruskin, Telford and Domecq, this year produced the second volume
of *Modern Painters*. In 1846 Edward Lear was giving drawing
lessons to Queen Victoria. He also gave the world in this year the
first edition of his *Book of Nonsense*. Landor's *Hellenic Studies* was
published in 1846, and the first volume of Grote's *History of Greece*
appeared.

Although this beginning year of our century seems in the pages
of the newspapers to be wholly concerned with the clash of economic
forces, with material progress and with scientific advance, there
was a spiritual restlessness that puzzled newspapers and politicians.
Lord Melbourne's view that the Church should not interfere in a
gentleman's private affairs was respectfully accepted by most
churchmen. But certain passionate remonstrances were beginning
to break the old moulds. The Oxford Movement, the High Church
revival, had been one such reawakening of the spirit of men. On
the Low Church side, Lord Ashley (to be better known as Shaftesbury) was led by his evangelical faith and by that sensitive spirit,
which never knew any peace from the burden of wronged innocence,
to agitate constantly against the employment of little children in
mines, mills and factories. There is no more disinterested character
in our period than this aristocrat who refused office and preferment
the better to plead the cause of the friendless.

One marks the growing political influence of the Dissenters.

Their ministers were familiar figures on the platforms of the Anti-Corn Law League. Methodism, in particular, was a strong force in the social stirrings of provincial England. This warm and ardent evangel, that made men and women feel they were in an intensely personal way the sons and daughters of the Creator, gave the under-dog something more than hope, it gave him self-respect. Here was a spiritual dynamic for the new Trade Union movement. Farm labourers and town workers drew from it sense of the dignity of the human soul. If even the poorest and more degraded wretch could by his own election become a child of God and the fellow of princes, then it was plain that it was a sin against the light to treat human beings with less thought than was given to a horse or an ox. From this came that precise hue and impulse of British Labour which has set it off from the secular Socialism of the rest of Europe.

In the city of Nottingham in 1846 a youth of 17 had lately become a Wesleyan local preacher—William Booth. Three years later he came to London to preach in slum streets—and finding Methodism too limited for " the divine incendiarism " of his spirit was to become the great guerrilla warrior of nineteenth-century Christianity—General Booth, who would not let the Devil steal all the merry tunes, and who bore the blood-red Flag and the Glory Song into streets where policemen would venture only in pairs.

It was in February, 1846, that John Henry Newman left Oxford, not to return for thirty years to that city he loved so dearly. He had made his submission to Rome in October 1845. The crossing of Newman from the Church of England to the Catholic faith left a mark on Victorian England that was not effaced for a great while. " An event of calamitous importance," was Gladstone's description, and a few years later Disraeli said the Church was still reeling from the blow.

Many men and women in that age suffered tortures of the mind over change of faith or loss of faith. The tender and pensive music in which Newman resolved his spiritual conflict haunted the minds of his contemporaries ; " Lead kindly Light, amid the encircling gloom, lead Thou me on." Doubt—the " melancholy, long, withdrawing roar " of the sea of faith—drew forth its own piercing strain of poetry :—

> " Nor certitude, nor peace, nor help for pain ;
> And we are here as on a darkling plain
> Swept with confused alarms of struggle and flight
> Where ignorant armies clash by night."

Charles Darwin was represented in 1846 by the publication of

his *Geological Observations on South America*. And while the Commons
was sitting late in tug-of-war on the Corn Laws he was collating the
data for *The Origin of Species* to be published in 1859. On 11
January 1844, Darwin had written to Hooker, " At last gleams
of light have come, and I am almost convinced (quite contrary to
the opinion I started with) that species are not (it is like confessing
a murder) immutable." Murder would not be out until fifteen
years later. The theory of evolution was to create an extraordinary
ferment in the life of the century. (It was, by the way, on
3 December 1846 that H.M.S. *Rattlesnake* left England for
tropical seas with a young biologist named Thomas Henry Huxley
aboard.) The old stage thunder of that age rattles around our
heads again when we read of Disraeli, in his black velvet shooting-
coat and wideawake hat, declaiming at Oxford in 1860, " What
is the question now placed before society with an assurance the
most astounding ? The question is this—Is man an ape or an angel?
My Lord, I am on the side of the angels."

It is now possible to talk of these things—of Newman's conversion,
of Arnold's doubts, of the effect of the theory of evolution—without
heat or without giving mortal offence. These accounts (men say)
are closed. But there can be few Britons of mature age who have
not been influenced, through their parents, by the strong religious
passions of the Victorian age. They are in the bone and the blood,
and they come out sometimes in strange forms. The Prayer Book
debate in the House of Commons in 1928 astonished many foreign
observers, but, less directly, one can trace the religious emotions of
a century ago in the politics of our own time.

The wider world on which John Bull looked out in 1846 bore few
resemblances to the world he sees today. In the year that the *Daily
News* began, France was a monarchy. Louis Philippe, the Citizen
King, had narrowly escaped two attempts on his life. In May,
Prince Louis Napoleon—afterwards Napoleon III, " Napoleon the
Little "—that mild forerunner of the Fascist dictators of our
times had escaped from his fortress prison at Ham. The knowing
ones laughed at him as a seedy adventurer who had made himself
absurd by walking out in a workman's smock, carrying a plank,
and would not be heard of again. In six years' time he became
Emperor of the French.

Germany was a medley of small kingdoms and duchies. Among
the insignificant items of news in 1846 was the appointment of a
Prussian aristocrat of 31, Otto von Bismarck to be *Deichhauptmann*,
which meant that he was put in charge of those dykes by which
the country around the River Elbe was spared from inundations.
It was a quarter of a century later that the German Empire was

proclaimed at Versailles. What dykes Bismarck erected then! The world saw the waters pour over them in the spring of 1945.

Italy was in chains, as fair and hapless a captive as ever prayed to St. George. The Pope held temporal power. Pius IX was elected this year—a progressive pontiff who signalised his response to the Free Trade lead of England by lowering the tariff of the Papal States. His Holiness was reported, too, as exhibiting a lively interest in the development of railways in his dominions. When temporal power was lost in 1870, this Pope became the first prisoner of the Vatican. Japan was sealed to the outer world. Seven years were to pass before Commodore Perry was to break open that box of curses. The United States in 1846 was at war with Mexico ; denounced by the *Daily News* as a bully but praised for reducing its tariff. There were 3,000,000 Negro slaves in the Southern States, and the institution seemed unassailable. Russia was being depicted by the cartoonists as a marauding and clumsy bear with a crown ; by good Liberals the Czar Nicholas was feared as an aggressor and hated as a despot. The emancipation of the serfs lay seventeen years ahead. An emperor reigned in Brazil. There was a Maori war. Canada was alarmed at the Mother Country's lowering of tariffs. There was trouble in India. The first Sikh war was costing the British severe losses, the Sikhs being the bravest fighters in India. The war ended with the Treaty of Lahore signed on 11 March 1846.

What glittering empires of the clouds have risen, and filled the skies, then crumbled utterly away since 1846. The century of the newspaper's life has seen the upbuilding and fall of the Hohenzollern Empire and of Hitler's Reich ; it has seen the breaking up of the Austro-Hungarian Empire and the passing of the Hapsburgs ; the unification of Italy and its ruin by Mussolini ; the Russian revolution ; the collapse, in turn, of the Orleanist monarchy, the Second Republic, the Second Empire and the Third Republic in France ; the expulsion of the once-mighty, once-dreaded Turk from Europe ; the change of Japan from a hermit state to an aggressor, from a rising sun to a sun that has set ; the coming into the world of that new design in world relations, the British commonwealth ; the swinging march of the United States to a place of dominating economic power—and, at the end, the freeing of atomic energy.

In the outcome, the wonders of mechanical progress which the ardent characters of 1846 saw ahead outran their prophecies. It became the century of the motor car, as well as the railway. Of wireless as well as the telegraph. Of the plane as well as the balloon. From the swoop and flutter of the Wright Brothers' machine at Kitty Hawk to jet propulsion is a long, long flight.

Man invented a series of extraordinary machines—his ingenuity was unending—and he came near to destroying himself in so doing. But—to vindicate the optimistic spirits of 1846—in all the centuries that went before there were no such conquests made over disease, pain and death as in this century. The life force and the death force are seen in spectacular conflict all through that hundred years. One sees, too, during the period the social conscience in man struggling hard to draw level with his mechanical genius and his material triumphs. Each advance in technological progress brought fresh human problems crowding in upon a perplexed and out-of-breath generation. The human environment was constantly being shaken violently, broken down, then built up again to a fresh design. Men and women had to adjust themselves rapidly to new material conditions, and then, in turn, to adjust themselves to the social consequences of those material changes. It is not surprising that justice as well as mercy sometimes lagged in this race, and that cruel things were done by naturally well-disposed men in a hurry, men buffeted, spinning, and dizzy from the pelting pace of their world.

It was in the closing year that invention, which had dominated the century, presented mankind with the atomic bomb. This was the strange crown of a century filled with the triumphs of physical science. Faraday's researches into electricity were dwarfed ; and Kelvin's discoveries ; and Edison's. The report of the bombing of Hiroshima in the newspapers of 7 August 1945, made the old problem of reconciling the moral sense with the machine no longer a subject for philosophic essays. It was the clamouring issue of survival. What must a world do to be saved ?

There came back to one a troubling remembrance of reading that Alfred Nobel, so long ago as the 'sixties, when he invented dynamite, refused to believe that men would ever use it for blowing each other to bits. Their moral sense would forbid. Dynamite would be an agent of peace—helping the miner, blasting quarries, tearing holes out of mountains, so that the railway engineers could more easily link people to people. As the smoke from the two atom bombs that were dropped on Japan rises up in our imagination, the cloud appears to take the shape of a query mark. It is this tremendous ? that hangs over the coming century. The answer to it must be found before 2046.

On a fair and windless Sunday morning in July 1846, travellers on the Channel packets caught their breath at a singular spectacle. From the coast of France were rising myriads upon myriads of white butterflies. This shimmering snowstorm of summer, that whirled or floated high in the air, but never fell, drifted at last towards England. No one could guess the numbers of the butterflies, for they spread out on each hand as far as the eye could measure. " Hundreds of yards of them," men said. " Heaped-up millions of them." They composed the only clouds that moved in the July sky. At noon they quite darkened the air, drawing shadows or tracing glimmerings like moonlight over the mirror of the Channel, until they vanished at last over the South Downs. Superstitious travellers, gaping at this fantasy, sought to read the omen. A promise from heaven ? But no great change came to Britain or mankind. If there was any meaning for the travellers, it was that there are inexplicable elements in the world and that nature has her wayward phantoms of beauty. Or one might have taken it to mean that poetry would always be breaking into that assured and respectable world.

CHAPTER II

WHEN DICKENS WAS EDITOR

I

POLICY AND PRINCIPLES

THIS advertisement appeared in *Punch* on 27 December 1845 :—

NEW MORNING PAPER
TO COMMENCE AT THE OPENING OF PARLIAMENT.

PRICE FIVEPENCE.

THE DAILY NEWS
A MORNING NEWSPAPER OF LIBERAL POLITICS AND

THOROUGH INDEPENDENCE.

The new paper, the first really Liberal daily newspaper to be attempted in London, was in itself a sign of those bustling times. It sought to bring into an effective alliance the radical spirit, of which Chartism was the extreme form, and the liberalism of the progressive middle-classes to whom Government by Whig earls was not much more pleasing than Government by Tory dukes. All things were working together for change in this year 1846. The cry for cheap bread rising from the factory workers in the new industrial centres and from the farm labourers was growing too strong to be denied.

In the leading article that Charles Dickens, its editor, wrote in the first issue of the newspaper he promised that " the principles advocated by the *Daily News* will be principles of progress and improvement ; of education, civil and religious liberty and equal legislation ; principles such as its conductors believe the advancing spirit of the time requires ; the condition of the country demands, and justice, reason and experience legitimately sanction. Very much has to be done, and must be done towards the bodily comfort, mental elevation and general contentment of the English people."

Then Dickens significantly added that the paper held it to be impossible to consider the true interests of the people as a class question, or to separate them from the interests of the merchant and manufacturer. It would be no part of its function to widen the breach between employer and employed but rather " to show their true relations or mutual independence and their mutual power of adding to the sum of general happiness and prosperity. The Liberals of that day were worried over the excesses of the Chartists.

It was like Mr. Rouncewell, the manufacturer in *Bleak House*, expressing his view of life with composure and firmness to Sir Leicester Dedlock, not blinking the fact that Mr. Rouncewell's mother was Sir Leicester's housekeeper. Like Mr. Rouncewell, Dickens was eager to demonstrate the dignity of the new order. Here was to be no flame-throwing journal of Jacobinism. " Its Parliamentary reports, its Law Reports, and every other item of such matter, will be furnished by gentlemen of the highest qualification."

Delane of *The Times* was the Dedlock whom Rouncewell-Dickens had in mind. The new paper was a direct defiance to the Jove of Printing House Square. To the interest excited by a journalistic departure was added the zest of a sporting event, and that steel-on-flint shower of sparks between eminent persons which the town enjoys. Delane was the despot of public opinion ; Dickens was the most popular writer of his day. Both had courage and gusto. It should prove a spirited fight.

Men noted the challenge of the price—5d. *The Times* was 7d.

As the *Daily News* was to be the advocate in the Press of the Free Trade age and the Railway age, it was appropriate that the financial support for the paper should be furnished by Joseph Paxton and Bradbury and Evans, the owners of *Punch*.

Paxton, in his inventiveness, industry and unorthodoxy was as fine a type of the new man in public affairs as could be found between Lombard Street and the High Peak of Derbyshire. He was a Samuel Smiles hero, demonstrating throughout a crowded career the prized Victorian virtue of self-help. Starting life as gardener to the Duke of Devonshire, he had become a prosperous man of business, making a considerable fortune in the railway boom. In the supreme undertaking of his life, the building of the Crystal Palace for the Great Exhibition of 1851, Paxton displayed the originality and the courage of genius. In an age bemused by bogus Gothic, he produced a design that was unlike anything else the Victorians had seen. Employing ideas of construction first worked out in building the conservatory at Chatsworth to house the giant Victoria Regia lily, Paxton gave this age the high temple of its pride. Rising in glittering bubbles of glass above the trees of Hyde Park, it looked as dream-like as the stately pleasure dome which Kubla Khan decreed in Xanadu. It seemed so frail that many people were sure the first hailstorm would shatter it. It lasted for

85 years, until that autumn night of 1936 when fire destroyed it. This design of iron and glass, combining airy grace with massive strength, was so far ahead of its times that it was sixty years and more before architecture caught up with it. That Paxton should have conceived it in that age of Pugin, who had a passion for Gothic, and Barry, who dreamed of filling London with Renaissance palaces, such as the Reform Club, was astonishing. That they should have let him build it at all is a tribute to the power of the Victorians to master their own prejudices and conventions.

It was this original mind, nearly breaking down under the load of its many enthusiasms, that took up one more enthusiasm in the founding of the *Daily News*. The first agreement, now in the possession of Miss Violet Markham, Paxton's grand-daughter, provided that £50,000 should be subscribed to start the paper ; Paxton took up £25,000 ; Bradbury and Evans jointly £22,500 ; and Richard Wright £2,500. It was modest enough capital by modern tests. Not twenty times that sum would suffice to launch a daily newspaper in 1946.

The association of Paxton with the new venture was a powerful stimulus to Dickens. He wrote in a letter at this time :—

" Paxton has command of every railway influence in England and abroad, except the Great Western, and he is in it heart and purse. One other large shareholder is to come in ; and that is to be a house which has the power of bringing a whole volley of advertisements upon the paper always. The commercial influence that will come down on it with the whole might of its aid and energy ; not only in the City of London, but in Liverpool, Manchester, Bristol and Yorkshire, is quite stunning. I am trying to engage the best people right and left." (The other large share-holder was, of course, Bradbury and Evans.)*

So it came about that the radicalism of *Punch*—for *Punch* was far to the Left of centre in those days—and the liberalism of the new Nabobs of transport combined to create the *Daily News*.

The *Punch* of the 'forties was the *Punch* of Hood's *Song of the Shirt* ; the satirist of ducal landlords and plutocratic bishops ; the journal that was in a constant fury against the inhumanity of the Work-houses and the Game Laws. The Duke of Wellington, invested in the almost legendary glory of Waterloo, was Peel's chief ally in the House of Lords. Of him this disrespectful *Punch* wrote, " The old Duke should no longer block up the great thoroughfare of civilisation—he should be quietly and respectfully eliminated. For the future, let us have him and admire him—in history." One can detect the accent of Douglas Jerrold in that, as in a later comment

* Miss Violet Markham's *Paxton and the Bachelor Duke.*

in the *Daily News* on the old Duke's " belaurelled and befuddled brows."

In its early years, the *Daily News* shared writers as well as proprietors with *Punch*. Mark Lemon, *Punch's* editor, and Douglas Jerrold were among them. *Punch* writers were pluralists in those days. The most illustrious in this gallery of satirists, Thackeray, was already contributing to *The Times*. Suppose that he had been free ? . . . No—it couldn't have been. No mortal newspaper was large enough to contain both Dickens and Thackeray. Of his rival, Thackeray said, " I may quarrel with his art a thousand and a thousand times. I delight and wonder at his genius," and came to the conclusion that one of them must be wrong as to what constitutes a novel. There was, too, the ambiguous comment he made in America that Mr. Dickens was an admirable writer for children. To say that they were both novelists was as imprecise a description as saying that they were both Englishmen. There was a difference of kind rather than degree. Chesterton put it with characteristic wit when he said that all Thackeray's books might be gathered under the title *Vanity Fair*, and that in the same way the whole of Dickens might be called *Great Expectations*.

II

THE MAN AND THE SETTING

It was in an atmosphere of political combat, social ferment and intellectual liveliness that the *Daily News* was born.

To the strains of *Rule Britannia*, the curtain rises on a thronged and busy stage, filled with optimistic politicians and cheerful inventors ; a rout of company promoters, showering railway scrip, passes across the boards ; there are redcoat survivors from Waterloo ; a bonnet and shawl ballet of sylph-like girls ; a procession of hungry scarecrows crying, " Bread " ; a *pas de deux* of the over-fed and the under-fed ; with drum and fife and shaken fists, the Chartists cross over ; an eighteenth-century coach, gilded and en-scrolled, rolls across the stage, with an eighteenth-century Milor's sceptical smile glimpsed at the window ; there are policemen in tall hats, and Jeames Yellowplush, well-powdered, and with swelling calves. The dying flourish of a coaching horn is heard off, and in the centre of the carnival a gigantic locomotive lifts its trumpet-shaped funnel, snorting steam, coughing flame, and spitting cinders—the Great God Locomotive around which the whole crowd—peers, policemen in tall hats, stock-jobbers, M.P.s,

Sairey Gamp, Mrs. Todgers, Pecksniff, Stiggins, steamboat captains, Chancery judges, chimney sweep's boys, pastry cooks and clerks—join hands and circle at last in a wild, uproarious dance.

Among the characters in that ballet of 1846, many are recognisably the creations of a writer of genius. At the age of 33, Charles Dickens was one of the chief forces of the period. His choice as editor of a new daily paper, which was designed to stand for all that was fresh and progressive in this expanding age, was thought to be a timely stroke, if an unexpected one.

It is worth trying to recapture something of the feeling which his contemporaries had for him.

He was admired as no novelist since Scott had been admired, though for far different reasons. He was prized, as those writers alone are prized who can touch the springs of laughter in their generation. The glorious high spirits of his earlier novels had seemed to men and women to liberate their own spirits from the heaviness of the times. *Pickwick* was the *youngest* masterpiece ever written. In its heavenly length, the England of the " dark, satanic mills " and the invading locomotive was quite transformed. An unsullied countryside stretched out before the travelling reader in the sparkling freshness of a June morning. When Mr. Pickwick put his head out of the lattice window at Dingley Dell in the freshness of that morning, sighing, " Pleasant, pleasant country," all Englishmen put their heads out of the window with him and saw how fair a land they owned. " The rich, sweet smell of the hayricks rose to his chamber window ; the hundred perfumes of the little flower-garden beneath scented the air around ; the deep-green meadows shone in the morning dew that glistened on every leaf as it trembled in the gentle air ; and the birds sang as if every sparkling drop were a fountain of inspiration to them. Mr. Pickwick fell into an enchanting and delicious reverie." So did his readers.

Yet to the grave, religious mind of Shaftesbury, brooding over the intolerable cruelties of his world, Dickens was endowed by God with his half-miraculous talents so that he might awaken the conscience of his generation. To Shaftesbury his genius was a kind of trumpet of the resurrection to quicken dead souls, to sound the reveillé over the mills, factories, sweat-shops, slums.

The poor people thought of Dickens as their friend, the gallant leader of an eternal opposition which never seemed to get represented in the House of Commons. The liberal middle classes saw reflected in him their own favourite image of themselves as the men and women of goodwill. He had a comic invention so rich that it created a fairy-tale world which existed side by side with the sober world of Peel's tariff schedules and Prince Albert's scientific researches, and sometimes spilled over into it, Pickwick being often seen on Ludgate Hill. In the profuse and rioting April of his imagination Dickens went on budding and budding characters —gnomes and ogres and princesses ; unicorns like Pecksniff and dragons like Mrs. Gamp.

A happy man, they said, to give such happiness. Glorious were the streams and fountains of humour that flowed in this world of the imagination and never dried up. Dickens was unique in this, that all his life he attracted a feeling of gratitude from all sorts and conditions of men such as no other writer has commanded. They were grateful for that great gift of laughter, and thought of him as the chief public benefactor of his times.

But on its tragic side, its midnight side, his mind had a comprehension of the power of evil which was present from *Oliver Twist* onwards, deepening as he grew older, so that in the last novels the comic characters seem to be crouching together in a hut on the barren moor against the storm and the lightnings. There was in him, too, a singular imaginative faculty which—as one reads— suddenly transforms long stretches in a novel to the texture and quality of dreaming, so that one says there could be nothing more irrelevant than to complain of the unreality of his figures when tested say, by realist Trollope's, because they are true to all that the mind can recall of dream states.   Jonas Chuzzlewit on his errand of murder drives through the closed atmosphere and scenery of a nightmare. That is an everlasting nightmare, too, through which shapes of evil, like Fagin or Quilp pursue us—dwarfs with tremendous shadows.

The queer runic rhythms of his style—the repetitions of a key-word, and the sense of a voice chanting the phrases like an incantation in one's ear—as though he were striving to exert his mesmeric powers after death through the printed page—increase the supernatural effect. At the end, the opening of the unfinished *Edwin Drood* conveys a frightening sense of the whole solid Victorian world crumbling into the waters of an opium dream. " An ancient English Cathedral Tower ? How can the ancient English Cathedral tower be here ? The well-known massive grey square tower of its old Cathedral ? How can that be here ! There is no spike of rusty iron in the air, between the eye and it, from any point of the real prospect. What is the spike that intervenes, and who has set it up ? Maybe it is set up by the Sultan's orders for the impaling of a horde of Turkish robbers, one by one. It is so, for cymbals clash, and the Sultan goes by to his palace in long procession. Ten thousand scimitars flash in the sunlight, and thrice ten thousand

dancing-girls strew flowers. Then follow white elephants caparisoned
in countless gorgeous colours and infinite in numbers and attendants.
Still, the Cathedral Tower rises in the background, where it cannot
be and still no writhing figure is on the grim spike. Stay ! Is the
spike so low a thing as the rusty spike on the top of a post of an
old bedstead that has tumbled all awry ? "

That was a far different vision from Mr. Pickwick's when he
looked at the summer morning from his lattice window, but Jasper
was implicit in Dickens from the start, for *Oliver Twist* was being
written before *Pickwick* was finished.

There was another unusual thing about him which helps to
explain his influence over his contemporaries. The wild and
unearthly quality of poetry that surged up in Dickens was linked
to a journalist's flair for the topical and an impatience for reform
as powerful as Carlyle's own. If he was a dreamer, he was also an
agitator for the redress of such grimly real abuses as the workhouse
and the debtors' prison. If he was poet, he was also a first-class
reporter who sped about the country to gather his copy freshly,
producing his early novels as though they were, in truth, enormous
newspapers. Even *Pickwick*, the most care-free and happiest of his
books, contained a rattling assault on the Law, and the stench of
the prison rises at the end to sully the freshness of the June morning.
" ' There is no air here,' said the sick man faintly. ' The place
pollutes it.' "   *Oliver Twist*, the dark dream of the charity boy,
brought the inhumanity of the new Poor Law to the warm chestnut-
roasting hearths of the comfortable, as though it were a tale for
All Hallows Eve, making the nervous look over their shoulders.
The comic ogre Bumble towered to a prodigious height in the
imagination of Dickens' readers—and he has remained there since ;
and skulking in the shadows at the back of the collective mind is
Bill Sikes. Then, in *Nicholas Nickleby*, the novelist had brought a
shudder to his public by showing them what private schools could
be like in that age of enlightenment and progress. Everybody's
business was nobody's business. Because people were indifferent,
Dotheboys Hall could clutch its prey, breaking the bodies and
torturing the minds of boys, as though it were Bluebeard's Castle.
The cannibal leer of Wackford Squeers, crying, " There's richness
for you " haunted the dreams of the sensitive.

He had written his tracts for the times in the form of ghost
stories. It was the union of the special correspondent, the leader-
writer and the wild enchanter in him that gave Dickens his
unrivalled power over his contemporaries. It was because the eye
of a visionary had received the training of a reporter—in those
years when he had whirled about the country in stage-coaches for

the *Morning Chronicle*—that it saw more clearly into the heart of reality than most eyes.   It saw, for example, behind the shiny optimism of the age of mechanical progress the shapes of greed and oppression ; and those eternal problems of human wickedness for which Free Trade, *laissez-faire* and scientific invention were not to provide the answer.   This searching eye looked at the elegant new model of a workhouse, which so greatly pleased the utilitarians, and saw in it the foulness of a dungeon.   Where the neat lawns and shrubbery of the Victorian mansions left off, the jungle began. Sometimes, indeed, the monsters peeped through the laurel bushes and the euonymus of the Norwood or Hampstead gardens— not merely golliwogs like Tulkinghorn, but tigers like Carker and Fascination Fledgeby, and boa constrictors like Bounderby and Gradgrind.

What did the first editor look like at the time of his adventure into daily journalism ?

In the absurd pencil sketches of the 'thirties he had the appearance of a Disraeli hero rather than of a Charles Dickens hero.   He looks like a friend of Coningsby rather than a friend of Copperfield. A cascade of hair falls around an empty face.   The photographs of the 'forties have a grimmer cast.   One is caught by the worn, burnt-out, disenchanted look.   It is the face of a man who has grown mature too soon.   The mouth suggests sensitiveness to pain rather than easy laughter.   One understands well enough that this old-young man has been David Copperfield, has been Pip, has been Oliver.

But he was like Miss Mowcher, a volatile creature.   What is missing from the photographs is the sense of animated smallness, of rapid play of expression, which is given in Carlyle's description of him after their first meeting.   " He is a fine little fellow—Boz, I think ; clear blue intelligent eyes that he arches amazingly, large, protrusive rather loose mouth, a face of the most extreme *mobility*, which he shuttles about—eyebrows, eyes, mouth and all—in a very singular manner while speaking.   Surmount these with a coil of common-coloured hair, and set it on a small compact figure very small and dressed *à la* D'Orsay, rather than well —this is Pickwick.   For the rest, a quiet, shrewd-looking little fellow, who seems to guess pretty well what he is and what others are."

He had discovered powers of mesmerism in himself which he exercised on individuals—and, in his later years, on audiences. Justin McCarthy wrote of him, " His very manner and voice had something inspiriting.   Younger people who did not know Charles Dickens can have little idea of the moving power of his words, his appeals, his very presence over men. The mere thrill of his wonderful voice had a magic of persuasion in it."

The fastidious were somewhat repelled by the costume à la D'Orsay. It was felt that the waistcoats were a little too dazzling—red, green or yellow—and the cravats a little too loud, and the diamond studs a little too sparkling.

This small figure crackled with nervous energy. " It may be doubted if ever any man's mental effort cost him more," wrote John Forster. " His habits were robust, but not his health." During the latter part of 1845, while planning the newspaper, he worked in a frenzy. He was often prostrated by giddiness, headaches and a general malaise. Spasms of pain in his side warned him how severely he was taxing his strength. Forster, the crusty and the faithful, grumbled at his taking on so wearisome and so hazardous a task as starting a daily newspaper.

In his reply Dickens wrote that Forster's remonstrance weighed with him heavily. But, he added, " I think I descry in these times greater stimulants to such an effort ; greater chance of some fair recognition of it ; greater means of persevering in it, or retiring from it unscratched by any weapon one should care for, than at any other period. And most of all I have, sometimes, that possibility of failing health or fading popularity before me, which beckons me to such an adventure when it comes within my reach. At the worst, I have written to little purpose, if I cannot *write myself right* in people's minds, in such a case as this."

Fading popularity at 33 ! The most popular writer of his time was ridden by a sense of failure. He had been deeply wounded by the inexplicable falling off in the sales of his latest novel, *Martin Chuzzlewit*, while *A Christmas Carol*, written to repair the loss, had proved a financial disappointment.

To Dickens the new paper was a new career. Harassed by bills, he needed a fresh source of income, and he also needed the assurance of a fresh kind of success to restore his faith in his powers. He busied himself with the smallest details of management as well as with large designs of policy. He was energetic in recruiting staff and appointing foreign correspondents ; in projects for distribution by special trains and in negotiations with the printers. To Paxton he wrote on 1 December 1845, " I intend going to Liverpool myself in a week to blow vague trumpets for the *Daily News*." It was a capital staff he built up. In addition to the men from *Punch*, already mentioned, Dickens drew in W. J. Fox, M.P., the finest orator of the Corn Law League, and John Forster as leader-writers. Eyre Crowe was wooed from the *Morning Chronicle* to be Paris correspondent and Thomas Hodgkinson was seduced from the

Economist. William Hazlitt, the son of the essayist, Leigh Hunt, R. H. Horne, the author of that forgotten epic, *Orion*,* and Father Prout, the witty Irish priest, who wrote *The Bells of Shandon*, were among the captures. Charles Mackay was engaged to put the principles of the paper into metrical form. He set the note in his verses, " The Wants of the People," in the first number :—

> *What do we want ? Our daily bread ;*
> *Leave to earn it by our skill ;*
> *Leave to labour freely for it ;*
> *Leave to buy it where we will.*

Lady Blessington, whose alliance with Count D'Orsay was a lion-hunting partnership—most famous men, but no respectable matrons, attended her salon at Gore House, Kensington—was engaged for a fee of £500 to furnish six months' exclusive social intelligence. One traces her hand in a complaint in the newspaper that Lord Wilton has introduced a dangerous innovation into dinner parties by distributing his guests at small tables.

The editor drew a salary of £2,000 a year at a time when £1,000 was thought very handsome. A great stir was caused among newspapermen by the salaries paid to reporters by the new paper. At that time the standard rate was £5 a week. Dickens, with his eye on the debates on the Corn Laws which lay ahead, sought to build up a fine House of Commons gallery team. So he captured a number of *The Times* Parliamentary reporters by offering £7 a week. He himself had been an expert Parliamentary reporter at the age of nineteen, and had journeyed all over England by coach to report the orations of eloquent bores, transcribing his notes in exquisite discomfort on the return journey, his coat covered with candle drippings. He placed his feckless father, John Dickens, in charge of the reporters. The character of Wilkins Micawber preserves some part of the elder Dickens. Or it would be more true to say that some flashing grains from that statue of pure gold, Micawber, were visible in the rosy portliness of John Dickens. A fat, amiable little man, puffing like Panks, the human tug-boat ; losing his silk handkerchief each afternoon in Fleet Street to the boy pickpockets, the brood of Fagin, who swarmed in the street, and too corpulent to run after them. His trottings between the editorial rooms and the case room had the mild pathos of a stout little man trying to catch up with the unforgiving minute rather than the sublime majesty of Micawber waiting for something to turn up. In

---

* Horne published his epic at a farthing. Hence the story of the boy who went to the bookseller's counter and asked for "a pennorth of Orions." Horne was engaged by Dickens at eight guineas a week and travelling expenses.

The Times office they said that John Dickens would be no match for the resolute Delane in the assembling of news. They were right.

There were raised eyebrows over nepotism in the newspaper's arrangements, for Dickens' father-in-law, George Hogarth, was made music and dramatic critic at five guineas a week, and his uncle John Henry Barrow was brought in as a sub-editor. All his life he was passing rich in poor relations.

The Times office exhibited something of the peculiar excitement which affects " The Laburnums " when a new family is moving into " Mon Repos." There was a constant trembling of the curtains at the front parlour window. Glimpsed through the potted fernery, the new family certainly appeared unusual neighbours. Bohemianism was suspected. But of all the inevitable gossip, the piece that irritated the new editor most was the report that all proofs were to be served to him on a silver tray by a footman.

III

THE DOUBLE DRAMA

The editor, they said, would kill himself before the paper could be brought out. He must moderate his pace.

But Dickens was essentially an immoderate man. His idea of curing himself of nervous exhaustion was to go galloping after fresh excitement. Was the newspaper proving too much for him ? Then plainly the thing to do was to add to the day's labour the traffic of the stage. Only Dickens would have thought of engaging simultaneously in two of the occupations which make the greatest drain upon the nervous energies. The eve of the first appearance of the *Daily News* found its editor, and part of his staff, absorbed in a theatrical production almost too elaborate to be called an amateur one. On 3 January 1846, he appeared at the Royalty Theatre in Fletcher's comedy, *The Elder Brother*, followed by a farce, *Comfortable Lodgings*—for in those days theatrical bills, like hotel menus, were generously full. The performance was for the benefit of Miss Kelly, who, in her bewitching youth, had acted with Siddons and Kean—and had declined Charles Lamb's offer of marriage.

The company that Dickens directed was bold in its pretensions and distinguished by its literary talents, though professional actors, such as Macready, found a sorry lack of art in their performances. Dickens was the martinet manager, who sustained leading parts, incessantly busied himself with details of production, the box office, the newspaper puffs and even the seating plan. Grease paint and printer's ink became weirdly mixed in that January. Thomas Britton, the first publisher of the newspaper, recalled in after years seeing the actors assembling in the *Daily News* office at 90, Fleet Street, to " run through their parts," while the birth-pangs of the paper were taking place. Britton was also summoned to attend Dickens, Jerrold and Mark Lemon at the Royalty Theatre while they were preparing the theatre for their performance. They took off their coats and set about putting the dress circle and boxes in order, and numbering the seats. " The pockets of the puce-coloured waistcoat of velvet texture—a favourite article of dress with the immortal Boz—served on the occasion as a receptacle for the bradawl and tin tacks, Dickens himself going about with hammer in hand. Mr. Jerrold's work was confined to the stage. . . . He saw to the scenery, and had to prepare a fire, in theatrical fashion, with slacked lime and red tinsel. Having completed the latter task, Mr. Jerrold rose from his stooping position, and called ' Lemon, how will that do ? ' to which the editor of *Punch* replied, ' The smoke is all right, but a little more tinsel would improve the fire.' This was done, and the effect approved of. So far so good, and Mr. Jerrold soon vacated the boards, and made his appearance in the front of the house—suggesting some refreshment to the toilers in the boxes, which was readily agreed to." It was an odd prelude to the launching of the *Daily News*.*

For a man seeking an escape from failing health and fading popularity, Dickens was trying Providence a little high. During a great part of his life he had a suppressed desire to manage a theatre, and act in it ; to be, in short, what Irving was to become later in the century. In this year 1846 he was possessed by a restlessness that nothing could still. It was a restlessness that pursued him to the end. In a vivid phrase that he used in a later crisis of the nerves, his head would burst like a cannon ball if he could not do something new.

The Elder Brother and *Comfortable Lodgings* were acted to warm enthusiasm. Dickens, who loved nothing so much as applause, and the tide of sympathy flowing out from an audience, was, for a moment, happy.

As for that other drama in which Dickens played lead, the Birth of a Newspaper, Britton records that " altogether the first night was creditable as far as the mechanical work was concerned ; and as there were no newspaper trains or post office collecting vans at 3.40 a.m. in those days, the despatch of No. 1 of the paper did not materially suffer by being a little late."

Any journalist will mark a certain sub-acidity in that cautious note of the publisher.

Each craft has its endearing smell. The smell of his craft is

* Quoted from the Jubilee Book of the *Daily News*.

sweeter in the nostrils of the craftsman than burnt offerings or the roses of Persia. The smell of lead is a good smell, even though it be a perilous one, and the minute-to-minute affairs of a news-paper office have an unholy fascination. The smell of the theatre is a grand smell, compounded of dust, gas, paint, wardrobe mustiness ; and the glow of footlights when they light up is one of the miracles that never loses its miraculousness. But it is not permitted by the gods that a man shall snuff up double incense, even though he is Charles Dickens.

By the time the night came for the first production of the paper, the editor was sucked dry of zeal and inspiration. In Forster's stately phrase, " his editorial work began with such diminished ardour that its brief continuance could not but be looked for." He was at the office all night. Before going home on that Wednesday morning, he scribbled a note to Forster saying, " they had been at press three-quarters of an hour," and were out before *The Times*. (A defensive glance at the publisher, here.)

On the starry threshold of Jove's Court in Printing House Square forebodings changed to relief—and a malicious joy. An anxious watcher in *The Times* office, W. H. Russell (" Crimea " Russell) wrote of the rival's appearance, " The 21st January, 1846, came at last, and there was a wild rush for the first number. At the sight of the outer sheet, hope at once lighted up the gloom of Printing House Square, the Strand and Shoe Lane. The *Daily News* No. 1 was ill-printed on bad paper and ' badly made up,' and despite the brilliant Picture from Italy by Dickens was a fiasco. There were reports that there had been a saturnalia among the printers. I am not sure that there were not social rejoicings that night in the editorial chambers which had been so long beset by dread."*

It is true that in the early hours of that Wednesday morning, when the new paper, after considerable travail, had at last been brought out, its compositors and writers gathered around the composing room stone—the stone being that sacrificial table on which the columns of type are finally assembled—to drink the health of the enterprise. Dickens spoke, but, as the Jubilee Book of the *Daily News* chronicles, " a more express record has remained of a word spoken by Douglas Jerrold. His was a fit figure for such a scene. As he stood by the ' stone,' short of stature, frail of build, with eager eyes, aquiline face, and with hair flying from his forehead down to his shoulders, he brought his fist down with a bang as he told the men, with an emotion which was long remembered among them, how he had worked his way up through stony-hearted London."

* Violet Markham's *Paxton and the Bachelor Duke*.

It was not quite the saturnalia that they imagined at *The Times*.
Jerrold was an unusual character who in himself would make a
good subject for a sympathetic biography. He had risen with
hard struggles from a poverty that was probably bitterer than
any Dickens had known. But while Dickens had genius to aid him,
Jerrold had but talent and so his fight was always harder. His best
remembered book, *Mrs. Caudle's Curtain Lectures*, had just been
published. It exploited a theme that was of unstaling appeal to
Victorian readers, the sufferings of a henpecked husband. *Mrs.
Caudle* should properly be read as a companion piece to Mill on
The Subjection of Women. In the 'forties, Jerrold was as fierce a
radical as was to be found at *Punch's* round table. The dukes and
the bishops had no more resolute foe. By the 'fifties, he had become
a fierce Nationalist, which was the curious fate of a number of the
Radicals of that time.

On 22 January the editor wrote from his home in Devonshire
Terrace, " I am delighted to say that we have a capital paper
to-day. I sat at the Stone and made it." Less than three weeks
later, on the night of Monday, 9 February, Dickens wrote
Forster a note saying that being " tired to death and quite
worn out," he had resigned his editorship. With many groans and
mutterings, Forster agreed to succeed him. Not long afterwards
Dickens approached a leading member of the Government with a
view to being appointed a Metropolitan magistrate. There was
a distinguished literary precedent for this ; Henry Fielding had
been the Bow Street magistrate in the eighteenth century ; but
none who knew Dickens could conceive of him finding satisfaction
in such employment. Luckily for his fame, authority was cold to
his offer.

He was wise enough to take his family to Lausanne that summer
and there, said he, he found " roses enough to smother the whole
Daily News establishment in." Faith in his powers as a novelist
came back to him. " Dealings with the firm of *Dombey and Son*,
Wholesale, Retail and For Exportation " began to take shape. Mr.
Carker, that forerunner of the managerial revolution was evolving.

IV

A MAN OF OUR TIMES

He had come in with great expectations. He had acted with
great energy. He had created a staff of uncommon talents. His
hopes had been high. Now, within so short a time, all was over.

The street with the little shop at the corner was a street he could never walk down again.

One speculates as to what those Victorian readers thought of it all. They were granted no explanation. Forster touches the episode as gingerly as he touched the story of Dickens' relationship with Ellen Ternan. Contemporary writers turned their eyes away from the aberrations of genius.

It was a stormy ending. The letter that Dickens wrote to Evans about his partner Bradbury on 26 February 1846, is shrill with recriminations. Of Bradbury, he declares, " I consider that his interposition between me and almost every act of mine at the newspaper office was as disrespectful to me as injurious to the enterprise. And I entertain so strong a sentiment on this point, that I have already informed my successor in the Editorship that I would, on no account, attend any meeting of Proprietors at which he was likely to be present."

Dickens quotes two of the trivial incidents that galled him—then goes on, " And to these I must add, with great pain, that I have not always observed Mr. Bradbury's treatment of my father (than whom there is not a more zealous, disinterested, or useful gentleman attached to the paper) to be very creditable to himself, or delicate towards me."   Poor Micawber !

Bradbury, declaims Dickens, is a man " possessed of the idea that everyone receiving a salary in return for his services is his natural enemy and should be suspected and mistrusted accordingly."

So it goes on. The fury with which the conscientious Bradbury is pursued is magnificent. But as an explanation of the editor's abandonment of his child before it was a month old, this hardly seems adequate. In looking through the letters of the time, one suspects that the interventions of Bradbury were an excuse that Dickens used to extricate himself from a situation which had become intolerable to him for other and deeper reasons.

The Nonesuch Press edition of Dickens' letters, published in 1938, has greatly extended our knowledge of him, and Dame Una Pope-Hennessy's excellent life, the first to appear since the Nonesuch issue, presents a far more complex character than the earlier biographers revealed. With the extension of knowledge, the enigma grows.

The trouble is that the more light that is shed on Dickens the less clearly one is able to see the Dickens one is most curious about. He tends to vanish in a dazzle of neon lighting. The essential Dickens, the Dickens who matters in life as well as in letters, is to be found in his books from *Pickwick* to *Edwin Drood*. A student who had never read any of the biographies from John Forster onwards would be able to trace his spiritual Odyssey through the novels and the occasional papers. The public Dickens, the oratorical Dickens who delighted in presiding at banquets, who loved to stand on a platform above a lake of spellbound faces, who was an insatiable diner-out and a profuse letter-writer, who challenged Macready on the boards, and would have been a baronet had he lived a few weeks longer, is less important, even in a public reckoning, than the Dickens who described the fog in Chancery in the opening of *Bleak House* and the social habits of the Veneerings in *Our Mutual Friend*.

There is a sense in which the novels present the inner life of the century as well as the inner life of Charles Dickens.

Chesterton said of Dickens that he was not by any means naturally fitted for the position of editor. " He was the best man in the world for founding papers ; but many people wished that he could have been buried under the foundations, like the first builder in some pagan or prehistoric pile."

To that one might add that he was in truth buried, but buried as an acorn is buried in the earth. It was the hiding away of the germinal force which in the end thrusts up and becomes the tree.

Taking the novels as the best guide to what Dickens was like, one hazards the guess that the real trouble was that Dickens was too far ahead of his times to make a success of a job in which he was expected to keep abreast of the times rather than be ahead of them. Russell of *The Times* suggested that his lack of political understanding and his ignorance of foreign affairs disqualified him as editor. The truth is he understood politics only too well. He saw them in terms of human suffering and human happiness rather than in terms of schedules, Blue Books and Commissioner's reports. He was a better democrat than Brougham, who had rejoiced in the efficiency of the new Poor Laws in gathering up the scarecrows from the countryside and clapping them into workhouses, because Dickens saw those places through the eyes of a child. He had a truer sense of freedom than Bright, for Bright, blinded by the philosophy of *laissez-faire*, believed that freedom meant the right to employ young children in mills and workshops for long hours and under cruel conditions. Carlyle kept asking, " What is your wealth, gentlemen ? Where is it ? "—while Dickens kept asking, " What is freedom ? " In his eyes, whatever freedom was, it could not be oppression. If Bright thought it meant Gradgrind and Bounderby then Bright must think again. Freedom must be something that Poor Jo could enjoy as well as Mr. Merdle.

In a letter from Lausanne he exhibited his disquiet over the newspaper's enthusiasm for railways and doubted if its proprietors would " bruise their foreheads by running against a bold idea."

The difference between Dickens and most of his eminent contemporaries seems to be this, that they thought of progress as an inevitable mechanical process, more trains, faster trains, swifter looms, while he thought of it as a development of human sensibility. He could not be a successful editor in 1846 because he was thinking then as many men were beginning to think in 1896, and most men are thinking in 1946. One cannot expect a major prophet to be an altogether satisfactory leader-writer.

In this year 1846 Dickens contended with Macaulay over the ethics of hanging. It is a pity that they did not debate the larger issue—" What is Progress ? " for that would have been the most thrilling debate of the century. Macaulay, the cocksurest man who ever lived, was the supreme exponent of the theory of inevitable progress and the beauties of a material civilisation. He translated the principles of Gradgrind and Bounderby, of Merdle and Podsnap into a scintillating and ringing Macaulayese which he imposed with all the force of a new religion upon his age. He made complacency seem as exciting as adventure. What possible dissolvent of this hard, brilliant thing could there have been except the spirit, compounded in equal parts of compassion and wrath, which animated the novels of Charles Dickens. *Our Mutual Friend* was written after Macaulay was dead. Some there are who think this novel the greatest of them all in social penetration and political understanding. In its dark mirror the pagoda of prosperity and material progress which Macaulay described in his glittering pages is now reflected back as a towering dust-heap, with the Golden Dustman as the king of the castle, and the Veneerings, the Lammles, the Podsnaps and the rest pecking about on the lower slopes for vendible scraps and pieces.

In the spring of 1846 they were saying that Dickens had been a failure. The rocket had come down without even exploding its colours in the air. But he was not a failure. His success was to be all the greater because it was retarded. His guesses turned out to be the right guesses. The chronicle of the next hundred years was to exhibit the continuous growth of conscience and sensibility, the gradual acceptance of the ideas about children, prisons, workhouses, charity, crime and punishment and social relationships which Dickens championed. In particular, the whole evolution of the Liberal spirit in Britain, using Liberal in its widest sense, has made him a leader as well as a prophet. That steady shift of emphasis to humane values gives a unity to the century.

The average English democrat of today is very like Dickens in his view of society. He is not in the least like Macaulay. It was Dickens' misfortune in 1846 to be a century in front of many of his fellows. It is his good fortune in 1946 to be an almost precise contemporary in the essentials of the spirit, if not in outward dress.

CHAPTER III

GREAT EXPECTATIONS

I

PEEL VERSUS DISRAELI

THERE were columns on columns in the first number about the Corn Laws. The eve of the session ! One gets a breathless impression of Taper and Tadpole dashing madly from Westminster to Carlton House Terrace and back again ; of Boots and Brewer flying wildly around in cabs. Of the Coodles and Doodles conspiring in shadowy corners of Pall Mall. Of the Buffys and Cuffys hatching plots in Brooks'. An impression of a vast disturbed beehive with the Parliamentary bees droning in clouds around it, bees zooming out banging into bees bumbling in. Always hustle, bustle, and an immense busy-ness and buzz on the crowded stage. What would the Queen's Speech say ? What would Johnny Russell do ? Oh, there was no doubt what would be said and done. The Corn Laws would be done with. Hard times were hammering at the door. The gentlemen of England would hearken. A part of them—a larger part than was at first thought likely—would stand in the last ditch against their leader Peel, against the Duke, against the spirit of the times. An exotic character would become the orator of their dumb resentments, the curled and oriental Disraeli—as strange an assumption of leadership, thought the Peelites, as the appearance of a flame-coloured cockatoo from Brazil directing a meeting of rooks in the rectory elms. The House of Lords ? All would be well there. The Duke of Wellington himself would lead the hedgers against the ditchers. The Iron Duke would cry, "Lords ! Atten-shun ! " and the Lords would be marched into the Repeal Lobby. The hero of Waterloo had a romantic, indeed, a mystical faith, that he must sustain the young Queen, and the Queen's Government. So it would be, " Lords ! Eyes right ! "

The columns in this first number are tightly packed, the type teases the eye. There is a four-and-a-half column report in tightest type of a debate on Repeal taking place the evening before at Norwich between Mr. Cobden and Mr. Wodehouse. Mr. Cobden, that orator who was so effective because he avoided all the oratorical devices of his age and was an early exponent of the modern conversational style of political speaking, had won a signal success. Five thousand men and women were there. Through the grey shell of the columns bursts the triumph of the Anti-Corn Law League.

What was the explosive they used ? It was a relatively new force in the world. It was the force of propaganda. Wilberforce, in his inspired campaigning against slavery, had invented the method of reaching people, rallying people, exciting people in the tranquillity of their parlours so that they said, " We must go out and do something about this before we can sink back among the cushions again." But the seven men of Manchester who set out to overthrow the Corn Laws had taken the old sword of Wilberforce and had hammered it, and sharpened it, until it became the short, hacking blade of modern propaganda. How they worked ! All the energy that went into the furnace-building, the mine-delving, the market-hunting of the early Victorians was now concentrated on this single end. In eight years the seven men of Manchester achieved a result which to their contemporaries seemed worthy of seven giants in a Grimm story. At the start it was as improbable as if the seven men had said they were coming up from Manchester to pull the Monument down and topple it in London River. The Corn Laws and the general protectionist system were far older than the Monument, they had survived two Civil Wars and a Revolution, and they were intrinsic to the English fabric. Yet the seven men changed them in eight years, mightily helped, of course, by those allies, blighted corn and black potatoes. They had issued tracts by the ton-load. Ten million of them. That was an astonishing total for those days, and would be remarkable in these. The Protectionist squires found themselves lost in a blinding snowstorm of pamphlets and leaflets. The League held their meetings wherever meetings could be held, and made it a rule that in each large city there must be a gathering once a week to renew the ardour of the faithful and to make fresh conversions. At the corner of Fleet Street and Whitefriars Street a blue plaque records that this was the site of the London offices of the Anti-Corn Law League from 1844 to 1846. From here the missionaries of Cobden and Bright sped into the country. Their labours showed the results that could be achieved through the persistent agitation of a small band of resolute men. Canning possibly had been the first Minister to invoke public opinion in support of his policies against hostile colleagues. Now public opinion had grown up and was conscious of its powers. It came pressing through the doors of Parliament to bear upon Ministers.

The night came when, in a House of Commons roaring with excitement, Peel, white and scornful as a stone image—self-destroyed as a Minister in destroying the Corn Laws—rose from the Treasury Bench and uttered his noble farewell : " But it may be that I shall be sometimes remembered with expressions of goodwill in those places which are the abodes of men whose lot it is to labour and earn their daily bread by the sweat of their brow ; in such places, perhaps, my name may be remembered with expressions of goodwill, when they who inhabit them recruit their exhausted strength with abundant and untaxed food, the sweeter because no longer leavened with a sense of injustice." The Parliamentary report ends: "Loud and long-continued cheering, during which Sir Robert Peel resumed his seat." The watch of the seven men of Manchester was over. The single-mindedness of Cobden and the silver tongue of Bright had conquered.

It is, by the way, well worth comparing the debates on Repeal with the debates in our current Parliament. Legislation that would have engaged the time of a whole session a century ago now goes through in a few days. Parliament spent many exhausting weeks over the Corn Laws ; the House sat late ; and the Herbert Morrisons and Anthony Edens of that time were expected to deliver speeches of four or five hours length. There is certainly nothing in our modern politics to compare with the sustained invective of Disraeli against Peel which made the Repeal debates more exciting than a play to the men of that time. In reading them to-day one gets the curious feeling that this was one of the most desperate flings that ever came off. It is like seeing a man with his bare hands starting to claw down a marble statue. It is plainly impossible— the image-breaker will do no more than break his hands. But, then, before one's eyes the marble begins to scale and crack ; an ear breaks off ; next, an arm ; then the whole image topples. How on earth was it done ? How could it happen that Peel, who for decade after decade had commanded that peculiar respect which the House gives to its acknowledged masters—a kind of totem worship—could come to be so derided and humiliated in those noisy scenes which accompanied the third reading of the Corn Bill on 15 May 1846 ? Men who had followed and adulated the great Minister for many a year now jeered, catcalled and cocked snooks at him. It is difficult for an age like ours, far less given to worshipping heroes, to comprehend the solemnity of respect which the Victorians accorded their leading statesmen. With the exception of Gladstone, no Minister in the entire century had evoked the sense of awe which surrounded Peel. And without any exception at all, no man ever made a more unfortunate entry into politics than Disraeli. His Radical past was against him, his looks were against him, his origins were against him, his affected voice and theatrical mannerisms, his novel-writing, his epigrams, his clever- ness, his incredible clothes were all against him. If ever there was a creation of ambiguous artifice likely to be repellent to the rosy- faced squires from the English counties who sat on the Tory benches, those honest men of beef, ale and the hunting field, it must surely have been Disraeli. If ever there was a Parliamentary manager who was so made by Providence that his genius could only express itself in the House of Commons, and if ever there was an incarnation of the solid virtues of the Conservative tradition, it was Peel. He had saved the Tory tradition from decay by creating the new Conservative party. He had come back in 1841 fortified by such a prestige and authority that to have opposed him from his own side would have seemed less a political misdemeanour than a brawling in church. Yet in these debates on the Corn Bill he was confronted by the spectacle of the despised Harlequin who, not so many years before, had been laughed down by the House, now leading the men of beef and broad acres against him. It was a fantastic affair, as fantastic as if in that earlier crisis of Peel's fortunes —the political struggle over the Ladies of the Queen's Bedchamber —the great Whig duchesses and countesses had been led by a ballet dancer. The party conflict of 1846 is fascinating not only because of the clash of economic forces, the struggle for supremacy between an old class against a new class, but because it prevents one from forgetting that in politics the power of the individual intelligence and the incalculable vagaries of genius can be factors almost as potent as economic interests and mass movements. If Peel had given Disraeli office when he asked for office in 1841, the whole political history of Britain in this century might have been different. One can be reasonably sure that the brilliant soldier of fortune would have devoted his talents to Repeal. Then, presumably, like the rest of that distinguished company, the Peelites, including Gladstone, he would ultimately have joined the Whigs and Radicals in creating the Liberal party. Perhaps the speculation is a little frivolous, but one cannot help wondering what would have happened if Disraeli and Gladstone had contended for the leadership of Victorian Liberalism.

By supplying a dumb opposition with a voice in 1846—and what a voice !—Disraeli accomplished the destruction of Peel. When he sat down after his speech on the third reading of the Corn Bill, the country gentlemen in the House were beside themselves with a cruel joy. Some might say that this delight, and the rudeness which Peel met with when he rose, were identical with the relief that is felt in primitive communities when the old man of the tribe is challenged by the young chieftain. Disraeli's speech is in large part a young man's indictment of an old man. It is filled with the eternal complaint of the young that the old are unoriginal and absorb their vitality from others. Listen to Disraeli on the subject of Peel. " His life has been a great appropriation clause. He is a burglar of others' intellect. . . . There is no statesman who has committed political petty larceny on so great a scale. . . . These political pedlars that bought their party in the cheapest market and sold us in the dearest." Stroke after stroke, so phrase falls on phrase ; phrases that must have been forged and burnished in many a session under the midnight lamp before the House heard them. " I know, sir, that we appeal to a people debauched by public gambling, stimulated and encouraged by an inefficient and a short-sighted Minister. I know that the public mind is polluted with economic fancies—a depraved desire that the rich may become richer without the interference of industry and toil."

The leader writers of the *Daily News* were filled with indignation and scorn over the paradoxes and sophistries of Mr. Disraeli.

II

THE THINGS THAT INTERESTED DICKENS

The Corn Law Repeal League expiring in its hour of triumph, left behind it a habit of assembly and agitation which the British have cherished ever since. To form committees, to fill halls, to array platforms with talent, to organise deputations, to spread pamphlets, to storm Bastilles became from henceforward one of the engrossing activities of the public-minded. It came to be as readily accepted a part of the democratic process as a General Election. Exeter Hall (destroyed in the blitz) served for decades as a home for those countless causes which one Victorian group or another espoused and agitated.

The leading article on Repeal in that first issue of the newspaper was written by W. J. Fox, the spell-binder of the Anti-Corn Law League. A mesmerist, this William Johnson Fox. Like Dickens, he could draw the soul out of an audience and bind it to his will. Once in addressing a meeting in the Free Trade Hall, Manchester, he produced an uncanny effect by his description of Protection as a serpent around which the League had at last got its hand and which it would surely squeeze to death. As he turned this metaphor into a solemn pantomime of hands and shoulders and head—his eyes scintillating like a magician's—his long mane flaring out like a comet—numbers of men and women were seen to rise from their seats, lift their hands in the air and with gasps and cries bring them slowly together as though impelled by an irresistible impulse to go through the motions of strangling invisible serpents. Sweat stood out on their brows—their faces were transfigured. That, as the circus men say, was the 'fluence. One speculates as to how the wizards of this school of oratorical hypnotism would have accommodated themselves to the aloof medium of broadcasting.

Were audiences more susceptible, or were spell-binders in possession of stronger spells in those days ? There comes back to one, from the records of the earlier years of the nineteenth century, the description of Edmund Kean's entry as Sir Giles Overreach, with the whole pit rising and recoiling as one man at that flaming apparition. One recalls, too, reports of the effect of Charles Dickens' public and private readings of the murder of Nancy from *Oliver Twist*. At the rehearsals, Dickens was besought by some of his friends not to pile on that agony as they feared hysteria in his audiences.

If there were columns on columns about the Corn Laws in this first issue of a hundred years ago, there were also columns on columns about the railways. Now it is one of the interesting and peculiar features of this first issue of the paper that Dickens chose to contribute to it, under his name, a piece of writing in which he rejoices with a boyish gusto in the exhilaration of a journey by coach across France to Italy. In the hour of the railway mania, he had gone back to Pickwick.

Travelling Letters—Written on the Road. It was the first of the series of sketches of travel afterwards published in book form as *Pictures from Italy*, and it was the one contribution to the newspaper which, in Russell's jaundiced eye, redeemed it, though it doubtless also confirmed his belief that the editor lacked political understanding. The writing is in Dickens' vein of swiftest impressionism—the rapid notation of a pair of eyes that take in everything, but that are especially alert for the smiles, the gesticulations and the tricks of speech which illuminate character. These pages in which the flash of the sunshine and the whirl of the white dust make the very type dance under one's eyes are swifter than watercolour sketches—they are a series of instantaneous photographs. The words almost fly off the page ; the characters—the Courier, the Postillion, the Landlord—gleam like fishes just out of the water.

To the faithful reader of that first issue who had absorbed thirty or forty thousand solid words of political intelligence and railway information it must have been a little dizzying to be whisked out of London by Dickens and to be carried at breakneck speed in a coach along a country road in France, with the sun in his eyes and dust in his throat, and adventure—or a collision, at the next bend of the road.

Take, for example, this passage describing the arrival at the Inn, and contrast it with Disraeli on Peel or Gladstone on the Broad Gauge : " As if the equipage were a great firework, and the mere sight of a smoking cottage chimney had lighted it, instantly it begins to crack and splutter, as if the very devil were in it. Crack, crack, crack, crack. Crack-crack-crack. Crick-crack. Crick-crack. Helo ! Hola ! Vite ! Voleur ! Brigand ! Hi hi hi ! En r-r-r-r-r-route ! Whip, wheels, driver, stones, beggars, children, crack, crack, crack ; helo ! hola ! charité pour l'amour de Dieu ! crick-crack-crick-crack ; crick, crick, crick ; bump, jolt, crack, bump, crick-crack ; round the corner, up the narrow street, down the paved hill on the other side ; in the gutter ; bump, bump ; jolt, jog, crick, crick, crick ; crack, crack, crack ; into the shop windows on the left-hand side of the street, preliminary to a sweeping turn into the wooden archway on the right ; rumble, rumble, rumble ; clatter, clatter, clatter, crick, crick, crick ; and here we are in the yard of the Hotel de l'Ecu d'Or ; used up, gone out, smoking, spent, exhausted ; but sometimes making a false start unexpectedly, with nothing coming of it—like a firework to the last!"

It was as though on that crowded and humming stage where Taper chaffered with Tadpole and the stock jobbers and company promoters danced deliriously around the Great God Locomotive Charles Dickens had suddenly appeared in Pickwick's coach, and then, in a flourish of dust and trampling of horses, had whirled off in grand defiance.

The Travelling Letters—the travels, incidentally, had taken place in 1844—went on appearing in the paper for weeks after Dickens had left it. There were to be other pieces, too, to preserve his association.

To the issue of 14 February, he contributed one of his rare efforts in verse—a *Hymn of the Wiltshire Labourers*. He was an adept versifier, as he was an adroit after-dinner speaker, but one feels it was the public man, the prose part of him that really found expression in his verses, while the poetry that was in him, a poetry as democratic as Walt Whitman's, could only express itself through the incantations of his prose. This hymn was prompted by some words of Lucy Simpkins, a poor labouring woman who spoke against protection with homely eloquence at open-air meetings of the agricultural labourers. She had said, " They do say we be purtected. If we be purtected, we be staarved." Lucy Simpkins' question, " Don't you all think that we have a great need to cry to our God to put it in the hearts of our gracious Queen and her Members of Parliament to grant us free bread ? " was the text of Dickens' verses. The hymn began,

> Oh God, Who by Thy Prophet's hand
> Didst smite the rocky brake,
> Whence water came, at Thy command,
> Thy people's thirst to slake ;

THE BRITISH LION IN 1850 ;
or, the Effects of Free Trade.
(A Cartoon from *Punch* in 1846.)

Strike now upon this granite wall,
Stern, obdurate, and high
And let some drops of pity fall
For us, who starve and die.

Farm labourers were gathering on commons before dawn that winter, meeting by the light of torches and lanterns to cry, " Repeal ! "

During March, Dickens contributed to the paper a sympathetic article on the newly-formed Ragged Schools. This was one of the interests he shared with Miss Burdett-Coutts (Baroness Burdett-Coutts) that great Victorian heiress who devoted her fortune and her talents to philanthropy. It was not the least among Miss Burdett-Coutts' virtues that she considered benevolence to be one of the high and difficult arts, demanding the dedication and study of a lifetime, and the constant cultivation of both sense and sensibility. She turned to an artist rather than to a professional philanthropist to advise her, and the long friendship between her and Dickens, and their conspiracies of kindness, make one of the pleasantest chapters in his life story—and one of the few quite unruffled by storms.

Then there were the three long *Letters on Capital Punishment* which Dickens wrote for the *Daily News*. In these he argued with a smoky glow of eloquence that hanging does not stop crime, but increases it through making heroes of the criminals. In those days men and women were still hanged in public. It was not until 1868 that public executions were abolished.

One of the most telling passages in these letters is that in which Dickens draws the portrait of a silly, vain youth of the period led to do murder by the notoriety which public hanging gave the criminal. This boy, Thomas Hocker, thirsted for fame, and could find no shorter cut to it than the gallows. " Come, Tom, get your name up ! " wrote Dickens. " Let it be a dashing murder that shall keep the wood-engravers at it for the next two months. You are the boy to go through with it and interest the town. The miserable wretch, inflated by this lunatic conceit, arranges his whole plan for publication and effect." . . .

The boy goes through the squalid drama with bravado and easy insolence, playing lead with a smirk in each scene : in " the Court, where Thomas Hocker, with his dancing-master airs, is put upon his trial and complimented by the Judge," and in public, where " at the condemned sermon, he deports himself as becomes the man whose autographs are precious, whose portraits are innumerable ; in memory of whom, whole fences and gates have been borne away in splinters from the scene of murder. He knows that the eyes of Europe are upon him ; but he is not proud, only graceful. He bows, like the First Gentleman in Europe, to the turnkey who brings him a glass of water." It is not until the last dreadful moment that the poor wretch is deflated. Then he faints on the scaffold in front of the gaping mob, and, a limp bundle of bones and clothes, is hanged like a dog.

Those letters on capital punishment bring out something that is important to the understanding of Dickens as editor and journalist, and of his influence upon his age. In particular, they raise the whole issue of his sentimentality which has been debated for the best part of this century. He was as fascinated by crime and punishment, by criminals and jailers as two other major novelists of the century, Balzac and Dostoievsky. He knew as well as any man of his time the circles of Inferno ; the muddy ways of the Victorian underworld ; the habits, and the *argot* of thieves and cut-throats—and creatures of a much baser sort. When *Oliver Twist* came out, the genteel were repelled by the graphic particularity with which Fagin's den and Sikes' haunts were described. "Who wants to read about such people ? " asked Lord Melbourne petulantly. Dickens cultivated the friendship of detectives ; on those interminable night rambles through the streets of London he would turn up at the police office to consult Inspector Field ; and Field would become translated into Inspector Bucket, the great-grandfather of hundreds of police officers of British and American detective fiction.* It became common form with his critics to gird at his preoccupation with criminals and their hunting down ; with violence and violent men ; with prisons—and, most of all, with murder. There are many pages in Dickens in which the atmosphere is heavy with the load of blood-guiltiness, and it was not unfitting that the pen should drop at last from an over-driven hand leaving the mystery of Edwin Drood unsolved.

He never belonged either by his talents or his circumstances to any of the accepted divisions of society, and so all classes were of equal interest to his restlessly inquisitive mind. That freedom from social blinkers enabled him to enter into the soul of the gentle, faded little aristocrat Mr. Twemlow as successfully as into the fierce, hungry soul of Abel Magwitch, the convict.

It is a curious fact that the kind of people who rebuked Dickens in his life for knowing too much about human nature reproached him after his death for not knowing anything about it

---

* The coat of a genius, after his death, is always divided. There is a parallel here between Dickens and Balzac, for one of the coat buttons of Balzac provided material for a whole library of French crime and detection novels.

at all. The type of mind that condemned him as too brutal a realist in 1846 condemns him to-day as the sweetly sentimental creator of angelic young women menaced by pantomime dragons while weaving daisy chains. It is not necessary to probe very deeply into Dickens' world to discover an interesting thing about the way society treated its artists. The force of convention was so powerful in the Victorian age that a great novelist like Dickens, and, a very different kind of great novelist, like Thackeray could not put down upon paper one half of what they knew about the world they lived in. Mrs. Grundy, Mr. Podsnap (scanning the cheek of the Young Person for a blush), Mrs. General, driving the Proprieties in spanking style like a coach and four, and, yes, indeed, Mrs. Caudle, formed a Board of Censorship from which there was no appeal. It was not merely that Dickens and Thackeray were forbidden to call a spade a spade. They were often not allowed even to toy with an agricultural implement. No, said Podsnap and Mrs. General, you must confine yourself to sugar-tongs, soup ladles, syrup spoons ; at a pinch you may even take up the fire irons ; but agricultural implements—NO, emphatically, NO. In a Parliamentary report or a Blue Book, perhaps, because nobody reads such literature, but in a popular novel spread around by circulating libraries—NO ! We must spare the cheek of the Young Person.

There were no two observers of the human tragi-comedy who had a clearer vision of what a spade really was than Dickens and Thackeray, though they had so little else in common. But in *Vanity Fair* it is almost pathetic to see Thackeray's efforts to tell the truth about Becky Sharp and her *milieu* without more than hinting that there are such things as agricultural implements in the world. (How he must have envied Balzac in Paris writing reams about spades during the year when *Vanity Fair* was being written.) And in the sombre novels of Dickens' middle years, *Bleak House* and *Little Dorrit*, there is a similar muffled and blinded power, as of a noble statue which has had a sack drawn over its head by Podsnap. The artist, thus swaddled, is forced to resort to strange circumlocutions to express his emotions and his vision ; and, with Dickens, the commonest of these circumlocutions is his sentimentality.

It is true that there were times, many times, when he deliberately played to the gallery for tears as he never played to the gallery for laughs. Then the writing rasps ; the voice breaks on a false note. But it is also true that there are many other times when what is deplored as his sentimentality is the stammering struggle of a frustrated man of exceeding sensitiveness trying to " write himself *right*" about subjects which Mrs. General had decided were not subjects which should be written about at all.

The crowning irony of that highly ironic book, *Little Dorrit*, is that Charles Dickens, the writer of it, suffers even more from the ordinances of the Circumlocution Office than Arthur Clennam who was only its hero. On that haunted night, that night of witches and hobgoblins, when Little Dorrit is shut out from the Marshalsea, and is forced to wander the streets of London until morning in company with poor, feeble-minded Maggy, Dickens contrives by a twisting of the shadows of the street lamps, the swirl of the black river at the piers and the mysterious whisperings and rustlings in alley ways to symbolise the crouching evil that Podsnap and Mrs. Grundy would not let him exhibit. He who had so often wandered those London streets from midnight to " the ghastly dying of the night " now follows in a sweat of anxiousness the wanderings of Little Dorrit and Maggy. " Three o'clock, and half-past three, and they had passed over London Bridge. . . . They had shrunk past homeless people, lying coiled up in nooks. They had run from drunkards. They had started from slinking men, whistling and signing to one another at by-corners, or running away at full speed. . . . And more than once some voice, from among a knot of brawling or prowling figures in their path, had called out to the rest to ' let the woman and the child go by.' So the woman and the child had gone by, and gone on, and five had sounded from the steeples. They were walking slowly toward the east, already looking for the first pale streak of day when a woman came after them. . . ."

We can only surmise from the criminal records of the period how gross were the jeopardies of the midnight side of London and how great was the need of a strong ray of publicity to shock the citizens into action. Any appraisement of Dickens must go wildly wrong that does not take this into account. His laughter is of the gods, and is universal, but his sentimentality cannot fairly be judged from the screened fireplaces of a comfortable drawing-room.

By those who have lived sheltered lives by southern walls where the figs ripen, Dickens has often been chided for inventing improbable heroines of unearthly innocence. Oddly, that is a criticism one seldom hears from working-class readers of Dickens, or very poor readers who may be presumed to know more of the thistles than the figs of life. It is a safe generalisation that the poorer a man is, not only in this country but in Europe and America, the more ready he is to accept Charles Dickens' reading of life. The longer the time one spends over the old files and with contemporary records, the more likely it comes to seem that Dickens created these characters out of a desperate necessity of his genius and of the times. Amid the sultry murk of the lower depths of society, it was needful to make this affirmation that goodness and innocence did exist in order to save one's sanity, certainly to prevent society from falling to pieces from its own corruptions. To one who had looked into the face of evil, and had seen how victorious was the look on that face, the single saving grace to cling to was the existence of the pure in heart.

He himself never escaped, even at the peak of his fame and wealth, from a dreadful feeling of insecurity. He never recovered from the wounds which he had suffered when as a child (and a child of great pride, conscious talents, and a very considerable ego) he had been betrayed to the blacking factory, and the world he had trusted crumbled around him. Some critics are repelled by Dickens because of the exaggerated resentment and bitterness he cherished all his life against the world ; because of the self-pity manifest in *David Copperfield*. It explains, they say, his neurotic restlessness, his selfishness, his quarrels with loyal and honourable friends. He always feared that he was going to be betrayed again—or that he *had* been betrayed. But while that dread of insecurity may have flawed him as a man, it was his salvation as a novelist, keeping fresh in him the springs of pity, tenderness and wonder on other men's account. It saved him from Thackeray's fate of becoming brittly cynical, dried up, and too wordly wise. It saved him from George Eliot's fate of becoming prosy and pedantic as in *Felix Holt* or *Theophrastus Such*. The child who never died in him was a tormented and egotistic child, but he was a child of genius, and now he is the undying child, demanding for all men an assurance from the skies that goodness and not evil has the final word.

One dwells upon this aspect of his genius, because those intuitions of his, despite all the swaddling bands of Podsnappery, did communicate themselves to his own generation, and to the generations that came after, and influenced the minds and hearts of his countrymen as much as anything that was said or done in Parliament. They did, in fact, transform Coodle and Buffy and their parties. They were of particular importance to those who followed in the tradition of journalism which he had established and had received from his abounding vitality an impress they could never lose.

He was not, after all, buried in his newspaper's foundations. He *was* the foundation.

CHAPTER IV

THE ROAR OF THE RAILWAYS

I

"RINGING GROOVES OF CHANGE"

CARKER was the manager. Carker was the thief. Carker was the man with the wolf-like smile who pulled down the House of Dombey. To Dickens in 1846 the House of Dombey was the emblem of the pride of Victorian commerce—that more than Venetian pride which held the gorgeous East in fee, and the expanding West as well. Carker was pursued by the Furies. And the Furies were the railway trains now beginning to roar everywhere across the land.

Dickens was a master of nightmares. He always had an uncanny skill in describing the emotions of hunted men and haunted men. But there is no more frightening nightmare of a hunted man in all Dickens than Carker's last days on earth. Waking or sleeping, the fiery devils pursue him. " A trembling of the ground, and quick vibration in his ears ; a distant shriek ; a dull light advancing, quickly changed to two red eyes, and a fierce fire, dropping coals ; an irresistible bearing on of a great roaring and dilating mass ; a high wind, and a rattle—another come and gone, and he holding to a gate, as if to save himself ! He waited for another, and for another." The iron road, with the smoking cinders streaming in the track of the monster, draws him with a dreadful fascination. At night he goes to the window to watch the fiery devils rush through the valley leaving their wake of glare and smoke. So to the end, when, starting back to avoid Dombey, the man he has betrayed, he is caught and destroyed by the monster. " He heard a shout—another—saw the face change from its vindictive passion to a faint sickness and terror—felt the earth tremble—knew in a moment that the rush was come—uttered a shriek—looked round— saw the red eyes, bleared and dim in the daylight close upon him— was beaten down, caught up, and whirled away upon a jagged mill, that spun him round and round, and struck him limb from limb, and licked his stream of life up with its fiery heat, and cast his mutilated fragments in the air."

The fiery devils that rush and thunder through the novel, which Dickens began in 1846, took a less frightening shape in the news-

paper he began in 1846.* But the editor was just as obsessed as
the novelist. The prospectus of the paper gave pride of place to
the promise that " its scientific and in actual operation, in progress
or projected, will always be found to be complete." Dickens
appointed an engineer, Scott Russell, as Railway Editor, " allowing
him a very free hand in the conduct of his department." Russell
in after years assisted Brunel in building the *Great Eastern*—the ship
which laid the Atlantic cable—that magnificent ship, too big and too
bold for its time, and shunned by the superstitious because of the
legend of the phantom riveter who had been sealed up in it, and who
could be heard in the night watch tapping, tapping to be released.

The first number of the *Daily News* contains three close-packed
columns of railway news—a two-column report of a meeting of the
shareholders of the London and South Western Railway at Nine
Elms Station, Vauxhall—for Nine Elms was the terminus until
Waterloo was built—and one column of railway share prices. The
new paper espoused the railways with as warm a zeal as it espoused
Free Trade. Indeed, swift and easy communication was seen to be
indispensable to the free exchange of goods. The railways were the
exhilarating symbols of the spirit of progress. The mines, the mills,
the foundries, the whirring wheels of the factories were pouring out
their riches. Here was the genie with the iron wings who would
carry them about the country. It was like the opening up of a new
frontier. There was a winning of the West to be achieved in Britain
as well as in America. Small though the island was, it was still composed of isolated communities. To Dorset, Yorkshire was an
unknown land. (That feeling of Yorkshire being as remote as Van
Diemen's Land is vividly conveyed in the opening pages of Mrs.
Gaskell's *Life of Charlotte Bronte*.) Trade would increase our borders,
and the black curses of pauperism and hunger be diminished. British
skill and British capital would take the civilising invention of railways
to other lands, thus creating wider markets still for British goods.
Progress ! Who dare resist it ? To Dickens, the poet-novelist of
Dombey, the fiery devil was a frightening apparition ; he felt securer
in a coach. To Dickens, the editor, the railways were progress in its
most spectacular shape. The enemies of the railways were the
enemies of all political and social advances. It was the most crusted
member of the House of Commons who was most vocal in his
opposition to the new transport, Colonel Sibthorp of Lincoln—
vehement and witty, and pictured as a Don Quixote of these times
charging the fiery monster with his puny lance.

* Dickens and Ellen Ternan, returning from Paris, came near being killed in
the Staplehurst railway disaster of 1865. The shock is supposed to have contributed
to the novelist's physical breakdown.

Eton waved the Great Western away from its patrician shades and pointing to Slough said : " Thus far and no farther." It was complained that the Provost had confused the iron road with the primrose path. Oxford sternly refused to allow the accursed lines to draw any nearer the last enchantments of the Middle Ages than Didcot. Wordsworth lamented the doom of smoke, flame and cinders that would fall upon the Lake Country. The cathedral cities who resisted extension of the lines ; the lords of the manor who objected to their pheasants being disturbed ; the county squires who were outraged at the interference with fox-hunting ; the agricultural interests who were hostile to almost any project favoured by the commercial classes, smelling the ruin of England in it ; the traditionalists who clung to stage coaches as sentimentally as they had clung to the whimsical old customs of flogging soldiers and hanging men for stealing sheep—all these were ranged against the railways. They were recognised by progressive-minded men as their traditional foes, and so the railways naturally became identified with the expanding Liberalism of the age. All through the century mechanical developments and popular philosophy acted and reacted on each other, sometimes with queer effects. It is a process that never ends in the English-speaking world. The early leading articles on the railways have the same note of manifest destiny that one marks to-day in American writings on civil aviation.

Britain had invented the railway. It was a child of the Industrial Revolution. Originally it was the answer of the Northern and Midland industrialists to the problem of getting the coal away from the pit-heads—faster and faster to meet the clamorous calls of the furnaces and workshops. In the first stage labourers laid wooden tracks to speed the transport of coal along the broken, swampy roads. For a time horses were thought adequate enough to pull the trucks, then the locomotive won. There ensued another debate as to whether this fire-breathing monster should be allowed to progress along the King's highway or should be supplied with roads of its own. The verdict was for roads of its own, and slowly the looks of England began to change. The nation began to realise that this new form of haulage could be put to far wider uses than carting coal about. Why stop at coal ? There was nothing a train could not carry ; animal, vegetable or mineral. It could—dazzling thought !—even be used to take human beings about the country, more swiftly, more cheaply and more comfortably than the stage coaches.

Ten years before the birth of the *Daily News* the first Railway Boom took place. Then in 1845 came that great mania which continued to rage throughout 1846 until the collapse and money

"HOLD HARD, THERE!"

From an Engraving by J. H. Engleheart, 1855.

panic in October of that year. It was a " universal epidemic,"
a madness which seized all classes. Hundreds of companies were
floated to finance thousands of miles of new track. Prospectuses
swarmed at such a rate that the newspapers could not print them.
It was not unusual for the promoters to offer 14% or 15% interest.
The alleys around the Stock Exchange were choked with mobs of
chaffering speculators. Nothing like this had been seen in London
since the South Sea Bubble. The Wall Street boom of the 1920's
is the closest parallel to it that our times have known. The
Annual Register for 1846 noted the extraordinary diversity of
characters represented in those lists of railway shareholders which
Parliament had ordered to be printed. These returns presented
" a combination of peers and printers, vicars and vice-admirals,
spinsters and half-pays, M.P.s and steeple builders, professors and
cotton spinners, gentlemen's cooks and Queen's Counsellors,
attorney's clerks and college scouts, waiters at Lloyd's, relieving
officers and excise men, barristers and butchers, Catholic priests
and coachmen, editors and engineers, dairymen and dyers, braziers,
beer-sellers and butlers, domestic servants, footmen and mail
guards—with a multitude of other callings recorded in the Book
of Trades." 900 lawyers, 364 bankers, 257 clergymen and 157 M.P.s
were listed among the speculators. A *Punch* cartoon in 1846 showed
the Queen pressing the hand of an abashed Prince Consort, the
caption reading : " The Momentous Question—Tell me, oh, tell
me, dearest Albert, have you any railway shares ? "

Parliament, in the throes of the Corn Law Repeal debates, was
overwhelmed by Railway Bills—petitions *for* new lines, petitions
against new lines. In one of the early issues of the *Daily News*
there appears a list of 507 Railway Bills then before the Lords and
Commons. The Parliamentary lawyers were swamped with briefs.
It was a happy summer in the Temple. Appropriately enough, in
the Barrister's Dream in *The Hunting of the Snark*, " they threatened
its life with a railway share ; they charmed it with smiles and
soap."

The chief promoters of the Railway companies became the
Nabobs of that age. They lorded it in grand mansions in Belgravia.
The most magnificent of them all, George Hudson, was adulated as
the Railway King. Hudson, a linen draper from York, grew to be a
dark power in finance, industry, politics and society. He became
an M.P. He made a great fortune and gave great parties. He even
entertained the Queen and Prince Albert. It was told of him that,
presiding at a meeting of the Eastern Counties Railway he made
the insouciant remark that dividends might be paid out of capital
as that made people happy. This was not a financial principle

likely to commend itself for long to the early Victorians, but Hudson's tremendous brio carried even the cautious off their feet. The crash came. What else was to be expected ? The great Railway Mania ended in the great Railway slump. Large fortunes and little fortunes were lost. Hundreds of thousands suffered. *Punch*, turning savagely upon Hudson, wrote, in parody of " Toll for the Brave " :

> *Toll for a Knave*
> *A Knave whose day is o'er !*
> *All sunk—with those who gave*
> *Their cash, till they'd no more.*

Macaulay said crisply that he was Mammon and Belial rolled into one. Others compared him unfavourably with Moloch.

But Hudson was something more than a knave. He was one of those buccaneers who are the half-conscious embodiments of the spirit of their age and are driven forward, even to criminal folly, by a sense of obligation to it. He saw more clearly than most the economic and social possibilities of the railways. The Railway Mania brought misery to many who committed their savings to it, but it left behind a system whose main outlines remain little changed to this day. There could be no liquidation of its material and social consequences. No official receiver in bankruptcy could be appointed for the ideas liberated by the Hudson Boom. The railways were as powerful a force as Free Trade in hastening the urban and industrial developments of modern Britain. They were the pioneers of Britain's new frontiers. They were essential to the success of the grand design of cheap food and cheaply made goods.

In the conquering sweep of the railways the stage coaches were relegated to a place in the museum next to the sedan chairs. That was inevitable. But it was a pity the railway promoters used their wealth to cripple the canal and inland waterway system of the country which was one of its living assets. The development of that system was a monument to the engineering skill and mercantile enterprise of the eighteenth century. Its ruin was a general loss to the community ; its revival would be to the general gain.

In those early weeks of 1846, when no chill wind had yet touched the abounding confidence of the railroad promoters, it was plainly good journalism for the *Daily News* to devote so much space to the absorbing theme. There was such a diversity of interests bound up in the subject. There were animated discussions in and out of the House of Commons on the broad versus narrow gauge. The brilliant expert on railways in Peel's Cabinet, young Mr. Gladstone, had presided over a Committee which recommended a uniform gauge for all lines, and in the first issue of the newspaper he was recorded as receiving deputations on the subject of railroads in the Colonies.

It was in this birth year of ours, 1846, that the Act was passed ordaining a 4 ft. 8½ in. gauge for English and Scottish railways and 5 ft. 3 in. gauge for the Irish.

Accidents were frequent, and as the sub-editors of those days had a fondness for the adjectives " frightful " and " awful," the nervous newspaper-reader's hair must have been perpetually on end. The express trains on the Brighton line were averaging 37 m.p.h. ; on the Northern and Eastern 45 ; on the South Western and Birmingham line, 43 ; on the Great Western, 50. There was still much head-shaking over the breakneck speed of locomotives. There were very many who thought with the writer in the *Quarterly Review*—" we would as soon expect the people of Woolwich to suffer themselves to be fired off upon one of Congreve's ricochet rockets, as trust themselves to the mercy of such a machine going at such a rate." It was a prophetic analogy, for today men are talking of the rocket train.

Those journalists and members of Parliament who were unfriendly to the railways frequently drew attention to the exploitation of labour which they involved. The locomotive men worked very long hours under severe strain. Reports of railway accidents were common in the *Daily News* in its early years, and when they happened there was often a disposition to blame them upon the over-stretched nerves and sinews of the railwaymen. Aha ! growled the opposition, this shows you what devourers of men these railways are.

II

PURITANS

The railways inevitably aroused the hostility of that strong Sabbatarian spirit which marked the British throughout our century. In the first week of June 1846, the *Daily News* recorded the Bishop of London presenting a petition in the House of Lords from several clergymen in Essex concerning an accident which happened in that county on Easter Sunday, due to a train " going wrong on the rail." The petition prayed the Lords to adopt measures to " prevent pleasure trains from travelling on Sundays." The Bishop was thought by his noble listeners to be a little unfortunate in his phrasing, for he spoke of " a dreadful accident by which the lives of *so many* beasts, as well as of so many members of their Lordships' House had been endangered." As the *Daily News* pointed out, the prelate evidently ranked the peers a little lower than the beasts. The Bishop recalled with a swell of satisfaction that when he was in charge of the parish of Chesterton he had succeeded in putting a stop to the Sabbath desecration caused by peripatetics of the Jockey Club—" lords and gentlemen riding in their carriages to Newmarket and playing cards on the way." The scattering of cards on the road by these dashing players as they flew by—they included a Royal prince, the Duke of York—had a bad influence on the simple villagers. Now there had come the railways roaring through the countryside on a Sunday to unsettle their tranquil minds and corrupt their pastoral morals. Lord Fitzwilliam, the Whig, replying to the Bishop, said forthrightly that he thought that travelling for recreation and pleasure was the only kind of travelling which ought to be permitted on Sundays.

The *Daily News* leader-writer—it was surely the Bishop-baiting Jerrold—snorted like one of the new locomotives over the Bishop and his petition. He took up the phrase about trains " going wrong on the rail " with rare spirit. Hah ! Off the rail, indeed ! " How many divines have we seen lately running off the rail and running on very wrong lines ! " the editorial writer exclaimed. " How many frightful collisions with morality and the law of the land have amazed and shocked the community within the last three years ! " The homily ended with the advice to the Bishop to keep his eye fixed on the behaviour of his parsons instead of watching " the misgoings of locomotives."

The Puritan forces were, of course, resolutely behind the ban on smoking on the railways, not only in compartments but in waiting rooms or on station platforms. This was a period when men in middle-class homes had to repair to their own dens or snuggeries to smoke a pipe or cigar, attired in velvet coats and fezzes which sometimes made a mild banker in Belgravia look like the Terrible Turk. (Cigarettes, like beards, did not come into fashion until the late 'fifties. They were introduced by the soldiers who had fought in the Crimean war, Ruskin describing the habit " as enabling a man to do nothing without being ashamed of himself.") The reek of drains which haunted even fashionable streets did not appear to offend the fastidious sense of early Victorian matrons one half so much as the scent of tobacco. A chemical trace of the weed, caught in drawing-room velvets or bedroom hangings, led to unhappy domestic scenes, and many a Mr. Caudle was forced to cultivate the secret vice of smoking in his counting house. The drains at Windsor Castle were so primitive that the footmen in the pantry were always getting sore throats, but the Queen was far more exercised about the aroma of cigars. The English were always being shocked by the French in those days—as since—but these early Victorians found few things more scandalous than that Madame George Sand should smoke hideous black cigars in the drawing-rooms of Paris—and did so wearing trousers. They found her amours with Chopin and Alfred de Musset less shocking. . . . * During 1846 one enterprising line, the Eastern Counties Railway, advertised the startling novelty of " Smoking Saloons." But it took years of agitation for smoking compartments to become general.

There were constant complaints in the *Daily News* and other papers of the insolent manners of railway servants. " They herd the public like cattle into trucks and then treat them less kindly than cattle," was the burden of the grievance. A jaunty gentleman, with dyed side-whiskers, had a Havana snatched from his lips by the station-master as he waited on the platform of a West Country station for a carriage to take him to the Duke of Beaufort's. The traveller said nothing, did nothing, looked coolly unaware. When the station-master discovered that this insult had been offered to no less a man than the sublime Lord Palmerston, he hurried after him and flung himself at his feet. " Sir," said Palmerston magnificently, " I thought you were an honest Briton doing your job. Now I find that you are only a snob."

From the 'forties first-class compartments were well-cushioned and cosy, with ample space for long-legged travellers, but for many years third-class accommodation remained grimly uncomfortable. Coaches began as open trucks, begriming passengers, showering them with cinders ; they were roofed in during the 'thirties and 'forties, but the seats were just as hard and the travellers were as cramped. Until then the third-class passenger was treated as a very low form of life. Many companies declined to carry him at all, and those that did jolted him black and blue in cattle boxes without buffers. At the end of his journey, public scorn was invited to his lowly estate by the warning board inscribed, " The company's servants are strictly ordered not to *porter* for wagon passengers."

Just before the birth of the *Daily News*, Gladstone's Cheap Trains Act requiring each line to provide a minimum of one train a day with third-class fares at a penny a mile came into force. The strong group of railway directors in the House of Commons resisted the reform—against their own interests as it proved. During the century ahead these cheap fares brought the railways revenues of which even the sanguine Hudson never dreamed.

It took the companies a long time to grasp how popular the

* Harriet Martineau in the 'sixties smoked a cigar each night before going to bed, but explained that she did so on medical grounds as cigars were a cure for insomnia.

railways had become. The first underground line in London, the Metropolitan, was opened in January, 1863. The growth of the Underground and of the suburban railways modified the habits of Londoners and speeded the development of London. London, as late as 1860, was bounded by leafy Kensington in the west, Poplar with its forest of masts in the east, Regent's Park in the north and the cottages of Camberwell in the south. The City's workers and the City's Nabobs lived within three or four miles of their offices and workshops. Now the vast brick wastes of the inner suburbs began to be built ; London was spreading out. On the maps of the time the black spreads out over the green like a bottle of ink spilt on a baize cloth. But the pleasant cult of the suburban garden also began, and brought relief to the tedium of bricks.

Out of the growth of the railways came the rise of that British institution, the annual holiday by the sea. It is said that there are still Londoners to be found who have never seen the sea. A century ago the overwhelming mass of Londoners had not seen it. It was in the eighteenth century that sea-bathing was first recommended by doctors, though at the beginning there was some confusion as to whether a patient should swallow salt water or immerse in it. The development of our coast resorts was due first to the aristocracy —they turned the fishing village of Brighthelmstone into the Prince Regent's Brighton—then to the middle classes, and lastly to the patronage of the working people. The annual hegira widened, ever widened, through our century. The average town-dweller's memories of the seaside holiday seem now to be almost part of the race memory, with bright and dim mixed together. He sees through that luminous haze broken pictures and half-caught impressions. He remembers being a small child on his first journey to the sea, the bucket and spade on the rack ; and there sweeps over him the recollection of that most thrilling of all the *first* experiences life has to offer, the first scent of the sea. It is once again an azure afternoon, the train has curved sharply, noses are thrust out of the window to await that sacred moment of the track when, through the gap in the chalk cliffs, there comes quite suddenly the smell of the sea—at once piercing and caressing, and soothing and intoxicating—and he feels for the first time how glorious a thing it is to breathe—and all the stale dustiness of ordinary life falls away and vanishes in that large cleanness.

" I do like to be beside the seaside, I do like to be beside the sea," sang the pierrots in that pleasant stretch of years between the end of the Boer War and the beginning of the first German war— years towards which many a wistful backward look has been cast since. The memories are a jumble of glimpses of yellow sands and tawny cliffs—of Brighton rock and beach donkeys—of coloured minstrels, and the soubrette of the concert party singing, " I used to sigh for the silvery moon "—of the melancholy procession of the bath-chairs along the Marine Parade—of the fishermen brooding at the end of the pier—of the hardy bathers plunging into icy waters at Easter—of John Hassall's " so bracing " poster—of the grisly humours of boarding-houses—of sand-castles, starfish and shells picked up at low tide—of portly city men, white-waistcoated and purple-gilled, sunning themselves in deck-chairs among the geraniums, lobelias and marguerites of the front at Eastbourne—of the rows of Victorian bathing-machines and those trailing coils of seaweed that Victorian bathing dresses became in the water—of the pines above the Italian villas at Bournemouth, and the languid heat, and the days when Robert Louis Stevenson lived there at *Skerryvore*—of Thomas Hardy's Weymouth and the statue on the esplanade that recalls the heroic day when His Majesty George the Third descended into the sea to bathe while a band played encouragingly, " God Save the King "—of Charles Dickens at Broadstairs alternating between bouts of work and sleeping in the sun—of long and subtle disputations concerning the virtues of the air at Margate as opposed to the air at Ramsgate—of the Regency dignity of Hove, and the Edwardian hi-jinks of Brighton, and R. G. Knowles' mournfully chanting, " Brighton ! Brighton ! they do such things and they say such things, I won't go there any more "—of the high-shouldered, declivitous facade of Hastings, and its keen, sweet smell—of the Leas at Folkestone, and a young H. G. Wells trundling an infant Wells in a perambulator and imagining the tale of *The New Accelerator*—of a general sense of places where generations of ordinary people have found a simple happiness—and of the rueful look on the sunburnt faces of children packing into the train when the holidays were at an end—children going reluctantly home, decade after decade.

The first statutory August Bank Holiday was observed on the 7 August 1871. Sir John Lubbock, the author of the Bank Holidays Act, became quite properly canonised as Saint John Lubbock. The newspapers of the time recorded that the City offices nearly all took advantage of that first holiday, but that the West End shops with few exceptions kept open. Many thousands of liberated clerks swarmed to the railway stations and three or four times the usual number of excursion trains left for Margate, Ramsgate and Dover. The contemporary reporter wrote, " the commons of Chislehurst and Hayes ; the hills stretching from Reigate to

Guildford ; the parks of Richmond, Bushey and Windsor ; Kew, Hampton Court, Taplow, Maidenhead, Henley and other riverside towns, offering attractions to young men with aquatic propensities, were visited by thousands ; and nearer London, Hampstead and Highgate, the lanes beyond Willesden and Hendon, and the remains of Epping Forest were enlivened by picnic parties. In the east end of the town many of the manufactories were closed, and several of the great capitalists who give their workpeople an annual *treat* engaged fields in which the workmen, with their wives and families, were entertained and amused with outdoor sports. By rail and by river more than ten thousand Oddfellows of the North London District of the Manchester Unity went down to the North Woolwich Gardens to take part in a fête held for the benefit of the widows and orphans of the deceased members. On Monday night the great thoroughfares in the City leading from the railways— especially at Ludgate Hill, the Bank, and Gracechurch Street—were filled with holiday folks " homeward bound." Several schools gave a whole holiday to the pupils, and children of all ages formed part of most of the groups. Not a tipsy or ill-conducted person could be seen. The day had been glorious, and the sum of happiness and social and domestic enjoyment evidently conferred by this first Bank holiday in August testifies to the wisdom of the Legislature."

It is worth remembering that there was a time, not so long ago, when to be free to go to the seaside or to a common was a bewilderingly new kind of joy to millions.

III

GRIM AND GAY

The railways demanded even more space from the early *Daily News* than the columns it gave to the engineering and financial writings of the Railway Editor and to reports of the constant stir in Parliament over Railway Bills. The new transport brought with it new crimes. " Murder on the Line " in those days had the peculiar thrill that " Murder in the Stratosphere Airliner " would give readers of 1946. Macabre tales were recounted in the paper of passengers finding themselves shut up with lunatics. (The interior communication cord did not come into use until 1900. An outside cord that pulled a bell in the driver's cabin was introduced around 1870.) The old *Punch* joke about the conversational passenger on the Great Western saying to his travelling companion : " How plainly you can see the lights of Hanwell from the railway," and receiving the dark reply, " Not half so plain as the lights of the

GEORGE HUDSON
The Railway King.

train look from Hanwell," brought a shudder rather than a smile to our grandmothers.

After a particularly gruesome murder of a passenger by a man named Muller, one company installed spy holes between compartments as a protective device. But the Victorians valued privacy so highly that they were willing to risk getting their throats cut to keep it, and, after indignant protests from those who held that the Englishman's compartment was his castle, the spy holes were closed.

The pickpockets trained by the Fagins of the time discovered fresh scope for their talents among the crowds at London's new main stations. The forging of railway scrip and the malpractices of speculators added to the business of the courts. The correspondents of the *Daily News* in the provinces frequently record the stir caused by the arrest of some respectable merchant or other for railway fraud, respectable being an overworked epithet of that period.

The first issue of our paper advertises the *Iron Times*, " the only daily newspaper entirely devoted to railway information, price 5d." This enterprise did not last long, for one observes that by March the *Iron Times* was in liquidation. Composers wrote " Railway Overtures " for bands, with steam and piston effects—thus anticipating Honegger's study of an engine in music, " Pacific 231 " —while the earliest of a *genre* of popular songs that was to culminate in such minor classics as *Oh, Mr. Porter* were sung.

There lies on the table of the writer of these chapters some sheets of popular music of the period. Among them are railway polkas and railway quadrilles. *The Excursion Train Galop* has a gaily coloured cover, showing an open third-class compartment, like a coal truck, crowded with men in silk hats and women in bonnets. Here, next to the Galop, is a song of the early 'sixties—*The Railway Bell(e) and Railway Guard*. On the cover is a magnificent-looking guard, with an Old Testament beard of chestnut brown, conducting to an engaged compartment a charmer in a crinoline. At one side of the platform, dropping his umbrella in fright at this alliance, is her beaver-hatted beau. One learns from the song that she serves the twopenny buns at a first-class Refreshment Room on the Chatham and Dover Line, while her rejected suitor is a traveller in the pickling vinegar trade. The melancholy chorus goes :

> *I try to be merry, but it is no use,*
> *My case is very hard ;*
> *She left me as silly as a farmyard goose,*
> *When she married that railway Guard.*

c

Down to R. G. Knowles' song, *The Tuppeny Tube*—" From Shepherd's Bush unto the Bank and get there 'fore you're dead "— the railways were to be raw material for the music halls.

In Lewis Carroll and Edward Lear fantasy gleamed along the lines, a dancing marshlight ahead of the red glare. Down the wind of the years floats the tender and wistful music of Lear's lament:—

> *O my agéd Uncle Arly,*
> *Sitting on a heap of barley*
> *Thro' the silent hours of night—*
> *Close beside a leafy thicket :—*
> *On his nose there was a Cricket,—*
> *In his hat a Railway-Ticket :*
> *(But his shoes were far too tight.)*

It is the mark of a virile age to be able to make jokes about the things it takes most seriously, and the railways were an ever-playing fountain of fun to our ancestors in 1846. The professional humorists exploited them, as the motor-car was exploited fifty years afterwards by Mr. Harry Tate, senior. The *Illustrated London News* appointed Albert Smith, a wit of the time, to be its Railway Humorist, giving him a column called " Tracts for the Trains " in which to fantasticate the oddities of passengers—as though passengers were a separate race—the comedy of timetables, the quirks of guards, the flamboyance of station-masters. The nervous old lady with or without baggage, but usually with, flapped and fluttered in the comic drawings. In the 'sixties, the nice deportment of crinolines in crowded compartments provided as steady a source of fun as Mr. Robertson Hare's trousers in the 1940's. There was the endless friction over smoking. " I don't like pipes," says the old lady to the navvy. " Ho ! don't you, ma'am," says he, fortified by being in a smoker, " Then hout you get." *Punch* alternated between full-blooded burlesque, and fierce invective against Railway Directors for their lust for profits and their disregard of human life. Bradshaw was a constant source of copy for the comic writers. This guide and friend to puzzled travellers had first appeared in 1839. Quakers in the North of England, such as Pease of Darlington, had been pioneers of the railways, and Bradshaw was the creation of a Quaker who offered it as a piece of much-needed public service. For at least a hundred years it was to follow the Quaker custom of naming the months, First Month for January, Second Month for February and so on. At a time when scores of independent lines were sprouting, with great gaps between connections, the production of a guide was a miracle of patience. If Bradshaw had been edited jointly by Robert Browning and Thomas Carlyle, the humorous journalists could not have taken greater delight in its obscurities of style and its esoteric allusiveness. They were always professing to discover in it ghostly trains that set out but never arrived at any earthly terminus, trains that turned up from nowhere, third-class passengers who were swallowed up by the earth in Kent and first-class passengers for whom relief expeditions into wildest Wiltshire must be fitted out. The hands, daggers and other printing devices in which Bradshaw indulged suggested the warnings of a secret society. Bradshaw was the Black Hand. Comic Bradshaws were brought out to the further confusion of innocent minds. The gentle philanthropist must have been mildly perplexed at the Press he got—but Bradshaw survived to be an honoured British institution.

The discomforts of railway travel were partly redeemed by the pleasure that writers extracted from them. This was a humour of the masochist rather than the sadist. Windy and comfortless Mugby Junction, with its goods trains " gliding on like vast weird funerals " and the network of rails gleaming in the rain, took on endearing characteristics in the pages of Dickens. " I am the boy at what is called the Refreshment Room at Mugby Junction, and whats proudest boast is it never yet refreshed a mortal being. Up in a corner of the Down Refreshment Room at Mugby Junction, in the height of twenty-seven cross draughts (I've counted them while they brush the First-Class hair twenty-seven ways) behind the bottles, among the glasses, bounded on the nor'-west by the beer, stood pretty far to the right of a metallic object that's at times the tea-urn and at times the soup-tureen, according to the last twang imported to its contents which are the same groundwork, fended off from the traveller by a barrier of stale sponge-cakes erected atop of the counter, and lastly exposed sideways to the glare of Our Missis's eye—you ask a Boy so sitivated next time you stop in a hurry at Mugby, for anything to drink ; you take particular notice that he'll try to seem not to hear you, that he'll appear in a absent manner to survey the line through a transparent medium composed of your head and body, and that he won't serve you as long as you can possibly bear it. That's me."

An Englishman reared in the stage-coach era was astonished to find in 1846 that the iron giant could whirl him from Birmingham to London in less than three hours. Looking up on his arrival at the balloons floating over London from Cremorne Gardens, he would have been all the more likely to take gravely the prophecy that one day a man would be able to travel to the United States by air. An American story-teller—Edgar Allan Poe, no less—had hoaxed the public in 1844 with the story of a balloon named Victoria crossing the Atlantic from North Wales in 75 hours. That his fantasy was so widely reprinted as truth showed how willing the age was to accept it.

Faster, faster, was the cry of the century. We were on our way. On our way with a tearing wind ; and with tons of metal plunging through the night. These giants roaring and shrieking through the quiet counties, hurtling like meteors, and drawing after them a train of golden light gave the Victorians an exhilarating sense of urgent power. " Let the great world spin for ever down the ringing grooves of change," wrote Tennyson, inspired by the sight, though the poet was a little confused at the time as to how exactly railway trains ran, for grooves are one thing and rails another.

" What are we but coaches ? " moralising Mr. Pecksniff had asked not long before. " Some of us are slow coaches, some of us are fast coaches. . . . Our passions are the horses ; and rampant animals too. . . . Virtue is the drag. We start from *The Mother's Arms* and we run to *The Dust Shovel*."

Now the moralist could see himself in the likeness of a train. Power and speed !—that was Progress. Faster, faster, iron giant, thundering and flaring through the night. " The smoke alone is worth a thousand pounds a puff."

Hail the locomotive ! To the Victorians it was their dominion over nature. It was their drama. It was their promise. And then one remembers also a queer fragment from Charles Dickens' writings —in some occasional paragraphs which he called *Chips*—in which he half seems to anticipate the chapters on the machines in Butler's *Erewhon*. He suspects that the locomotives are not simply the iron slaves they look to be. They appear to him as sentient beings. He has observed that they show as many differences of character as horses, some being vicious, some gentle. He notices that one locomotive will do anything for Tom when he takes it out, but it jibs violently at Harry. Dickens is saying what Butler said in the 'seventies, " Proud man, don't be too sure you know everything about machines because you have made them."

It was only one part of the Railway Development that it expanded the home market, and helped foreign trade by rapid transport from production centres to ports. The social consequences of the railways were considerable ; the population became more fluid ; ideas as well as goods became more freely exchanged ; the railways were emancipators. There was a greater mixing of classes, and the hauteur of the aristocracy melted a little under the genial influences of a scramble on Paddington platform or a wait at Mugby Junction.

An example of the struggle to break through the fences around public information is provided by the efforts made by the *Daily News* in the first few days of its existence to carry the text of Peel's House of Commons speech on the Corn Laws to the country.   Trains were chartered to hurry the papers to every town on the lines. Local papers reprinted the Parliamentary report of the *Daily News* and congratulated the new journal on its enterprise. But underneath the plaudits one catches the rumbled undertone, " This must be costing them a pretty penny." A cross-Channel steamer was hired to carry the papers to France. French journals copied the report from the *Daily News*. M. Guizot, the Prime Minister, was impressed. A new commercial policy ! Britain had decided for Free Trade. That would set every Government in the world a conundrum. It is a pity that the bills for this enterprise have crumbled in the dust of years.   It would be worth knowing today just how pretty that penny was.

IV

ENTER THE MOTOR

It is amusing to close the file of 1846 upon all the excited rattle and clamour of the Railway Mania and open the file of fifty years later. There, in the *Daily News* of 30 January 1896, one discovers this paragraph demurely tucked away, almost out of sight :—

" The Question of Horseless Carriages.

" At the Tonbridge Police Court, Mr. Walter Arnold, the owner of a horseless carriage, was summoned on four informations with reference to using a horseless carriage on the highway. The first was for using a locomotive without a horse with no permit from the County Council, the second for having less than three persons in charge of the same, the third for going at a greater rate than two miles an hour, and the fourth for not having his name and address placed on the machine. The evidence was that the carriage was going at the rate of 8 miles an hour—Mr. Cripps, who defended contended that the machine was not one contemplated when the Locomotive Acts were passed, and said that these carriages had been used by Sir David Salomons and the Hon. Evelyn Ellis without any notice being taken. If the Bench considered that the carriage was a locomotive he asked for the imposition of a nominal penalty.—The Bench inflicted a penalty of 5s. and £2 os. 11d. costs for using the carriage without a locomotive horse, and 1s. and 9s. costs in each of the other three cases."

The next day this letter appeared in the *Daily News* :

" *Horseless Carriages.*

" Sir,—At the request of the president of the Self-Propelled Traffic Association (Sir David Salomons, Bart), I desire to bring under public notice the prosecution before the Tonbridge magistrates for using a horseless carriage. When it is generally agreed that an Act will shortly be passed to facilitate this class of traffic the issue of four summonses for one supposed breach of the law is shameful and calls for the attention of the Home Secretary. To do justice in the matter he should quash all the convictions but one,—I am, Sir, your obedient servant,

" ANDW. W. BARR, Hon. Sec.,
Self-Propelled Traffic Association,
40, Moorgate Street, E.C."

We were now at the beginning of the motor age ! There were not many who understood the significance of this apparition on the roads of which the Tonbridge magistrates took so poor a view. It was the kind of contraption that should be kept in gardens or private parks like a toy railway. On the highway it was a nuisance and a danger—and must be KEPT DOWN.

One recalls that in the early days of railways there was much debate as to whether trains should be run upon the public highway. In 1865 a Highways Act was passed restricting mechanical traction on the roads to a speed of four miles an hour and requiring a man to walk in front of any such vehicle carrying a red flag. The first motor-cars had been produced in Germany in 1885, but motoring languished in an unsympathetic atmosphere for eleven years. Tireless agitation by Sir David Salomons and his friends secured the amendment of the limiting Act in August, 1896. A parade of " mechanically propelled vehicles," created a stir which helped the motorist's cause in Press and Parliament. The amending measure was entitled " The Locomotives on Highways Act." (What youth of 1946 would recognise a Morris or Austin by the name of locomotive ?) The speed limit was raised to fourteen miles an hour, the man with the red flag lost his occupation, lighting regulations were imposed on these new monsters and it was ordained that every such locomotive " should carry a bell or other instrument capable of giving audible and sufficient warning of the approach or position of the carriage." There were some who said the rattle, chug-chug and fumes of the first motors made bells or gongs superfluous.

The motor car, like the railway train long before, became an image in a conflict of philosophies. The progressively-minded saw it

as a symbol of man's conquest of his environment, and to the young
it was a thrilling new form of mechanical excitement. The
traditionalists used against it the aesthetic arguments that
Wordsworth and Ruskin had brought against the railways.
Preachers were concerned again by the ethical problems of speed
and pleasure. A restless age was in a devouring hurry to move
on—faster, faster—but had it thought where it was going?

Kipling's story, *The Village that Voted the Earth was Flat*,
is charged with the moral rage which the early motorists felt
towards their persecutors—hostile magistrates in particular.
Significantly, it was a Liberal M.P., sitting as a country Justice of
the Peace, who was the object of revenge to Kipling's motorists.
Mechanical progress had ceased to be synonymous with Liberalism,
and with the turn of the century had become an attachment of
the imperialist mind. From now on, authoritarian ideas would
ride happily in the machine. It was uneasily felt that mechanical
progress and humanitarian advances were not brother and sister—
indeed, that their relationship might become that of the lady and
the Tiger. Kipling, the laureate of the jungle, was also the laureate
of the machines.

In the nineteen-hundreds the motor car was as profitable a
subject for popular humour as trains had been fifty years earlier.
Mr. Harry Tate's sketch *Motoring*, encrusted with all the rococo
ornaments of a comic genius, expressed much of the social criticism
of two decades. The motoring ladies with their straw-hats, their
wide-winged veils of blue or grey, goggles, and dust-coats, were at
once absurd and enchanting. The fury of the farmer, shaking his
fist after one of these early cars, that now look to us like baby's
high chairs in motion, resembled the wrath of the fox-hunting
squires of the 'forties when they saw the down express thundering
towards Mugby Junction. One draws a notion from the papers of
that time of country roads swirling with white dust, and of chickens
and pigs scurrying in front of the puttering small juggernauts.
Toad, Esquire, of Toad Hall, in Kenneth Grahame's *The Wind in
the Willows* was the complete Road Hog. "Toad the terror,
the traffic queller, the Lord of the lone trail, before whom all
must give way or be smitten into nothingness and everlasting night."
The speed traps of the country police, the appearances of the
Automobile Association solicitor at rural courts, the sermons of
local magistrates, and the fear that deaths and injuries on the roads
might one day grow as heavy as those of a military campaign were
like the pieces of a new jig-saw puzzle which the British were trying
to make fit.

The roads of Britain pulsed with a life such as they had not known since the 'forties when the railways put the coaches out of business. The old coaching inns stirred after their long, long sleep. During the next half of our century the development of motor transport must have dizzied the Tonbridge magistrates if they survived to see it. Trucks and lorries loaded with freight rumbled ceaselessly across the roads of Britain, all day and all night. The motor manufacturer became a man of weight in the general affairs of the nation. He was of as much consequence as the railway kings had been in 1846. In America, Mr. Henry Ford had become the pioneer of mass production and high wages, and set new standards in industry. In Britain, Mr. W. R. Morris (later Lord Nuffield) was looked upon with respect as the embodiment of the enterprise of the age. The bus weaved its way through the farthest country lanes and across empty moors that the railways had left undisturbed. The week-end habit spread from Belgrave Square to the Old Kent Road. Fleets of motor coaches, smooth-running and fat-cushioned, carried crowds to the seaside and the hills. This was a formidable challenge to the railways ; their freight and passenger receipts suffered ; and the old-established transport system had to come to terms with the new. George Hudson could not foresee the age of petrol. There were mergers of rail and road interests—the old processes of fear, rivalry, then compromise and, finally, amalgamation repeated themselves. Now, today, we see the railways, the road interests and the shipping concerns turning their eyes to air transport.

Not surprisingly, the romantics of this period began to discover a poetic charm in the railways. The roads, they said, had become nightmarish. They were mere dismal motor tracks. As you raced along them, all that you could see, amid the intermissions of the dust clouds, were filling stations, bungaloid growths and the gross excema of ribbon developments. If you wanted to savour the stilled colourings of rural England you must travel in gliding serenity by train. The railway cuttings were starred with primroses in April, and the wild rose wreathed them in June. At half-forgotten halts where the train stopped in the drowsy sunshine of late spring afternoons, you could hear the fluting of blackbird and thrush. At local stops, the country folk would get in, and you could enjoy much tranquil local gossip of crops and parsons, and heifers ; of prize marrows or prize babies. What social pleasures of this order were possible to those robots who travelled by car, almost bumper to nameplate, as on a conveyor belt, down the Brighton Road ? All this would have flabbergasted Hudson and Paxton and Russell, the railway editor. The old cliché of the wheel turning full circle was much quoted when the newest planners proposed that motor traffic should be given tracks of its own as had been done with the steam engine more than a century ago. There were drawings of huge tunnels underground, drenched in light and revealing a never-stopping river of swift vehicles.

The crowning years of the motor age came with the 1939-45 war. Two nations, remarkable for their aptitude in mechanical contrivance, the British and Americans, united their resources on D-day in 1944 to break into Hitler's robber's castle with a mechanised power built up to a great strength. A century of inventiveness was brought to a flash-point. Across the plains of Europe fanned out never-ending processions of tanks and mechanical monsters of every shape, some of them exceedingly grotesque. In front of the bulldozers trotted the ghost of a man with a red flag. On the backs of the huge amphibians rode the astral figure of the Tonbridge Bench of fifty years ago.

In the early part of the twentieth century, Mr. Shaw and Mr. Wells had seen the motor mechanic as a new type, a god of the machine robed in overalls, streaked by oil and grease. The assumption was that he would be a rebel, a free spirit in revolt against the old ways. Britain reared two generations of young men (and not a few young women) in whom mechanical skill was like the growth of a third arm. War teaches many other things besides geography, and, under pressure of the national extremity, the schooling of our youth in mechanical transport crammed a decade in a year. From the many inventions and concentrated experiences of the war, we may fairly expect advances in transport comparable to those which excited our forbears a century ago. The world spins down the ringing grooves of change, and even faster than it did when Alfred Tennyson saw a train for the first time. That great world, however, is a good deal less confident of its destination than it was then. It is not so confident as Tennyson was in the steam age. It is not so confident as Kipling was in the petrol age.

CHAPTER V

NEWSPAPERS, POSTS AND CABLES

I

TAXES ON KNOWLEDGE

THE rising middle-classes were feeling the need of better means of communication to express their philosophy and to consolidate their power. More trains, faster ships, telegraphs, cables—and a Press that would be free to spread and multiply—that was Progress. The age had a faith in communication as part of the democratic process.

Newspapers were far too dear in 1846 to be bought by more than a small fraction of the population. In the first six months of its life the daily circulation of the *Daily News* was 4,000 copies. There were at that time fifteen London dailies with a total circulation of about 100,000. To-day the London newspapers have a circulation of more than 10,000,000. They have increased one hundredfold ; the population has increased threefold.

At fivepence a copy the *Daily News* undercut *The Times* by twopence, but, all the same, fivepence was beyond the reach of most families. In the money values of today it would represent more than tenpence.* The dearness of newspapers a hundred years ago was due to a treble tax. There was the Newspaper Tax of one penny on each copy. There was a tax of 1s. 6d. on advertisements. There was a paper duty of threepence a poundweight. Ten years earlier the stamp duty on each copy had been fourpence.

The advertisement tax was applied freakishly. For example, the Commissioners of Inland Revenue had a trick of presenting a bill to a newspaper for a favourable book review on the ground that to commend a book was to advertise it. It was weak reasoning. The Commissioners might have remembered that after Macaulay had damned the poems of the Rev. Robert Montgomery with such a rain of critical sulphur and brimstone as was never before seen, the circulation of the reverend gentleman's blank verses leapt up. Faint praise was taxable, but strong damns were free.

The Government's penny duty on newspapers was represented by a red stamp printed on the right-hand bottom corner of the front page. Each sheet had to be taken blank to Somerset House

---

* The writer has been unable to find an economist who will commit himself to saying how much more than tenpence.

to receive the stamp—and that irked as a visible badge of servitude. Authority did not like newspapers. It sought to confine the inflammable sheets to as few hands as possible. There was a natural rivalry between Press and Politician that had begun long ago with the first illicit reports of Parliamentary debates, and years of agitation were needed before these taxes on knowledge, as they were called, were rescinded. Charles Dickens was an active sharer in that agitation. He thought it absurd that speeches should be made about the glories of a Free Press at a time when the Press was too dear for most men to buy.

Authority said that power should be confined to the governors, that knowledge was too dangerous a weapon for the governed. Progress had been spinning at far too fast a pace down the white road of the century. We should soon be in the ditch. The middle-classes retorted, " But ours is now the power and the glory. The benevolent autocracy of the coronets and the country houses is passing. Our rule is the true democracy. Democracy is progress, and progress means the spread of knowledge."

There was a major political principle involved in this agitation for a cheap Press. Its advocates believed that the whole people must be the jurymen at the grand inquest of affairs. If they were given the facts, they could be trusted to reach the right verdict. But democracy had no meaning if knowledge remained the privilege of a few. If the jurors were to give a true verdict, they must hear all the evidence. The Liberalism of that age affirmed its faith in the good sense and reasonableness of the average man, but the average man could not exercise these qualities if he were blindfold. " Tell the people the whole truth and they will come to the right decisions," said the philosophic Liberal of 1846.

Readers of the *Daily News* on 1 June 1846, were considerably surprised to find that day's copy marked Number 1 all over again. After less than five month's existence, the newspaper decided to break with its brief past and make a fresh start. There was one startling change—the price was cut in half. It was a bold effort to break through the barriers of taxes and duties which Government had built between newspapers and the public. It was an effort, too, to solve the problem of making a Liberal newspaper a popular newspaper at a time when Liberalism was becoming the dominant philosophy of the nation. In the event, the daring venture did not succeed, but it made the *Daily News* a pioneer of the cheap press.

This decision to cut the paper's price to 2½d. was made by that forceful man Charles Wentworth Dilke whose name is familiar to the readers of John Keats' letters. In April of this year the pro-prietors of the *Daily News*, far from happy at their losses, entered into an agreement with Dilke and his son, Charles W. Dilke, Junior, making them managers of the paper for three years and giving them an option of taking up a fourth share.

The elder Dilke (grandfather of Sir Charles Dilke, M.P., the gifted politician of unfulfilled renown who lived on into our times) was a man of parts and a man of taste, with a flair for business, and strong political instincts. Dilke believed that if the high price of newspapers were cut the number of new readers would be so large that the cheaper press would be economically justified. The widening of this franchise must surely have a considerable political effect. In the early years of the nineteenth century, *The Times* had radically changed the relations between Press and Government by refusing Treasury subventions. The day on which a doleful agent of the Government reported, "They won't take our money," was marked by a white stone in the history of the Press. It was as great a gain for newspaper independence as the overthrow of the censorship. Dilke by cutting the price of newspapers sought to carry independence a stage further. To his mind it should not be a holy right of a few to be informed about what was happening in Parliament—about what was happening to the nation—about what was happening in the world. A limited franchise of information was as bad as the rotten boroughs.

On the front page of that new Number 1 of 1 June was displayed a vigorous manifesto entitled, "A Few Words to the Public," written by Dilke. It declared that "the newspaper in the intellectual life of the nineteenth century is the great agent of modern civilisation." More than a century before, it said, there were eighteen newspapers in London, published daily or three times a week, yet now in 1846, when the population of the city was three times as great there were but fifteen.

"In the single city of New York, more daily papers are published than in all England, Scotland and Ireland put together," wrote Dilke, "The circulation of papers in Paris exceeds that of London twentyfold. How is this? Of a fact so startling where lies the explanation? What is the cause? PRICE !" And PRICE ! PRICE ! PRICE ! Dilke thundered day after day.

The first result of Dilke's bold stroke was the rise of circulation from 4,000 to 22,000. The new manager thrust hard at *The Times*. The Thunderer scoffed back at the *Daily News* as "a twopenny-halfpenny paper"—the "Little Benjamin of the Press." But despite the more than fivefold rise in circulation, the *Daily News* could not hold its low price. Before long, it raised it to 3d. Printing House Square believed that the rival must inevitably be forced back to 5d. as the only conceivable economic price. Before this happened, the *Morning Chronicle*, once a formidable political three-master, but now in decline, made an effort to retrieve its fortunes by lowering its price from 5d. to 4d. The result was to quicken its decay. Another threepenny newspaper, the *London Telegraph* rose, flickered dimly, and expired within a few months. (The *Daily Telegraph* that we know to-day was founded in 1855.)

In this general rout the *Daily News* was driven back to its old prohibitive price of 5d. Its neighbour in Printing House Square primly said we told you so. " Interested as we may seem in the affair," *The Times* had said in July 1847, " we maintain that the public are themselves interested in keeping up the price of the London daily newspaper which after all, is the cheapest thing in the whole world ; for nothing else can be mentioned in which you get so much for your money." (*The History of The Times*, 1841-84.)

Ever resilient, the *Daily News* made one more vain effort to stabilise itself with a threepenny sale. It was not until the spring of 1868 that the paper, after the taxes on knowledge had been swept away, reduced its price to a penny. This time courage was rewarded and not only circulation but profits rose. The price remained stable until the early nineteen hundreds when the competition of an even cheaper press forced the *Daily News* to cut its price to a halfpenny. It remained at that level until 1918 when it came back to a penny again.

The struggles of these early days were costly. In his book, *The Newspaper Press*, published in 1871, James Grant estimated the losses of the first ten year's working of the *Daily News* at £200,000, four times the original capital.

Some doggerel on the *Daily News* to the tune of " The Ivy Green," appearing in the *London Journal* for 1848, expressed the pleasure of the opposition over these losses, and struck at Dickens' humanitarian interests :—

> Oh ! the *Daily News* began with a bang.
>   And was going to shut up *The Times*,
> And twaddled that murderers never should hang,
>   And printed " large sympathy " rhymes,
> But still the old gallows its reign enjoyed :
>   And still did " The People " refuse,
> To trust to the rhymes that their friends deployed
>   In the sheets of the *Daily News*.
> *What* large sums they have learned to lose
>   Who first embarked in the *Daily News !*

In September 1846, the proprietors of the newspaper added to their responsibilities by starting an evening paper called *The Express*.

It survived until 1869. A subsequent *Express*, which also perished, was " much devoted to religious information." The *Daily Express* of our times was founded in 1900. The mercurial spirit of Lord Beaverbrook may be said to provide a certain link with the two forerunners, for he combines strains of the Radical individualism of the 'forties with the Calvinism of the 'seventies.

II

BY GASLIGHT

Mechanical progress in the production of newspapers was rapid during the century. The swift improvement in machinery became in itself a constant pressure towards a cheaper press and a wider dissemination of knowledge.

The Dickens-Dilke newspaper was created nightly in a gaslit atmosphere, heavy with lead dust, loud with snorts of steam and the jingle of the horses that drew the paper vans. According to Grant, the morning newspapers during that period employed around fifty compositors. The salary of a head printer varied from 5 guineas to 7 guineas. " The regular wages which a compositor receives on a morning paper when paid by the week is £2 8s., but many of them earn on an average £3 a week by working over hours. Their hour for beginning work is 7 p.m. and most of them remain till four next morning. A few remain till half-past four, after which the paper must be ' made up' for press." From 5,000 to 6,000 copies per hour came off the machines, which were driven by steam. The machines of 1946 produce a quarter of a million an hour.

The machinery made by Thomas Middleton of Southwark for printing the paper in 1846 served for 22 years. To meet the greatly expanded circulation brought about in 1868 by reducing the price to a penny, the *Daily News* bought two " Eight Feeder " Hoe machines constructed on the rotary principle. These produced 7,500 copies an hour. With the Franco-German war in 1870, the circulation again leaped up. The *Daily News* bought Web Machine No. 1 of R. Hoe and Company in 1871 at a price of £875. In 1873 six of the " Walter " web presses, invented by John Walter of *The Times* were installed. These gave the paper an output of 100,000 copies an hour. Here, as with the railways, we see the machine regarded as a friendly genie—the light-bringer. The extension of the capacity of the presses was thought of as a moral triumph; as a fresh victory in man's struggle to subdue his environment and to increase the sum of happiness.

Grant presents this picture of Fleet Street compositors of the mid-Victorian times, " their rooms are always heated, owing to the gaslight in which all their work is done, which is not only unpleasant, but very injurious to health. In the summer season, the heat in composing rooms is almost intolerable, while the number of persons in each room adds very much to the unhealthiness. In the months of June, July and August, it is sad to see the compositors at work. They are often seen to be literally gasping for breath. The effect of breathing for some years the hot and vitiated atmosphere of the composing room tells, as might be expected, on the health, and often ultimately on the life. As a class, compositors on morning papers are not robust or healthy ; and comparatively few of them attain to an advanced age. . . ." A haze of lead dust hovered over everything, and lead-poisoning was the occupational disease of the craft. Today it is almost unknown.

" It is by far the most interesting sight of all in newspaper establishments to see thirty or forty, and in some cases fifty men in one room. . . . All actively employed in what they call ' lifting ' type. All are silent as if they were listening to a solemn sermon, or as if each one of the number were the only one in the room. While thus busy ' at case '—another compositors' phrase—not a word is heard, any more than if they were at a Quakers' meeting."

In this reconstruction of the newspaper office of a century ago, Grant speaks of another figure with a powerful claim to notice. " I allude to the party whose duty it is to wet down the paper. In order that our morning journals, or indeed any journal, may be properly printed, it is indispensable that the paper should be first drawn through water, in eight or ten sheets at a time, and then allowed to lie for two days under the power of a pressing machine, applied to it for the purpose of making what is termed the ' damping ' equal. No paper would be readable were it printed on dry paper. The man whose duty it is to prepare the paper by ' damping ' lives in a sort of subterranean region. He lives in a humid and dark atmosphere, except so far as the darkness is illuminated by gaslight. There he spends his time, never seeing the light of day, never hearing the sound of a human voice, nor cheered by the smile of a human countenance. Except that he is in the vaults, where the process of ' damping the paper ' is carried on, he might be regarded as a prisoner in some dark and dismal dungeon. Never was man more completely shut out from the world." Yet, declares the historian, the damper was usually the most cheerful of prisoners, full of high spirits in his humid dungeon. The damper's occupation has long since gone, thanks to mechanical advance, but compositors still damp their galley-proofs to secure a clear impress.

III

ROWLAND HILL

The campaigners for a cheap Press were allies of the campaigners for a cheap Post.

In June 1846, the *Daily News* records a public dinner in honour of one of its heroes, Rowland Hill, the father of the Penny Post which had now ceased to be an experiment and was fast becoming a tradition despite the unremitting struggle of the Post Office officials to ensure its failure. In a leading article celebrating Hill's achievements, the *Daily News* reminds its readers that the facilities of the penny post required a cheap Press to bring them into full play. " The newspaper is everybody's correspondent. The newspaper is the real society for the Diffusion of Useful Knowledge."

Rowland Hill has lasting honour as a breaker of barriers, as a remover of No Entry signs. He had imagination. He had a warm sympathy for the poor and for their desire to send letters to one another. Himself a child of hard times, Hill said : " I early saw the inconvenience of being poor "—a notable example of understatement. But, above all, he had the quality most needed in his enterprise, the endless patient persistence of the drip-drip-drip of the water drops that wear away Government granite. He was a persistent man, a very persistent man.

The Penny Post had been introduced in 1840, but the experiment trembled in the balance for some years. Such pundits as Colonel Maperley, the Secretary of the Post Office, who had resisted the change, did their best to thwart its operations, and were filled with a quiet joy when the first years of its workings showed a loss. So perish all meddlers, they said. But Hill persisted.

Until Rowland Hill's reform the service of the mails was too costly for working class people. A single-sheet letter weighing less than one ounce cost 4d. to send to Richmond, 9d. to Birmingham and 1s. 4½d. to Edinburgh. The charge was immediately doubled if there were any enclosures within the single sheet, such as a newspaper cutting, and a large staff was employed at St. Martin's-le-Grand to scrutinise each letter under a searching light. The delays caused by this scrutiny meant that it sometimes took a letter fifteen hours to travel from the City of London to the suburbs. There were no stamps and no envelopes in those days, and every letter was paid for by its recipient on delivery. The revenue from the mails was about £1,500,000 a year ; the cost of distributing them £500,000. With the expansion of trade, postal revenues steadily dropped.

Hill was much touched by the plight of humble people who could

LAYING THE ATLANTIC CABLE

Paying out the land end of the cable from the stern of the *Niagara* (1857).

not afford to communicate with their relations in distant parts of the country. Family ties were broken. A youth going from London to Manchester might be as lost to his mother as if he had been transported to Botany Bay. Many stratagems were resorted to in order to circumvent the Post Office. One oddity of the situation was that there was no charge for mailing a newspaper, as the Government Newspaper Stamp was held to cover postal costs, and so men and women would communicate with one another by the device of underlining the names of the eminent in the newspaper, according to a pre-arranged code. Thus, if a wife wanted to let her husband know that all was well at home she would underscore the name of Lord John Russell ; while a mark under the Duke of Wellington's name might indicate that father was out of work again. Another trick of the time was to send a letter to a distant correspondent, well knowing that payment on it would be refused— but a glance at the handwriting on the outside would be a signal from the sender assuring the—so to speak—non-receiving recipient that he was still alive. One imagines an Early Victorian romance in which the lovers are poor and separated, she in Camberwell, he in Liverpool. They exchange vows by exchanging old copies of newspapers. The language of flowers is substituted for the vocabulary of politicians. By this means a dull debate in the House on the Broad versus Narrow Railway Gauge is transformed into lyrical protestations of undying love !

There was much bootlegging of letters by the last surviving Sam Wellers, and a passenger going by coach to a provincial town would be burdened by correspondence to distribute on behalf of his neighbours. The Post Office spent considerable sums of money and detective skill in preventing evasions, but as there were something like forty different scales of postal rates for the country, large fish and little fish wriggled out of the net.

Rowland Hill in his first pamphlet on postal reform, demonstrated by simple arithmetic that the cost to the Post Office of delivering a letter did not merely vary by distances, and that no charge ought to be greater than that paid on the shortest haul—the inner London district where the cost was one penny. The Tite Barnacles were outraged. Here was a troublesome fellow who must be put down. The Postmaster-General denounced his reform with a vigour that would have been appropriate to the exposure of a forgery. As Mr. Meagles said, " He has been ingenious, and he has been trying to turn his ingenuity to his country's service. That makes him a public offender directly, sir."

Here we touch notes that repeat themselves over and over again throughout our century in a variety of settings. A man of uncommon

parts is fired by the need for a reform. Many thousands desire it ;
only one or two will act. The pioneer is first gently dissuaded—it
being assumed that he is a little unbalanced and needs a week at
Brighton to tone his nerves. Then, when he persists, it is patiently
explained to him how wrong-headed and ignorant a fellow he is,
and that what he wants cannot be done because it would lead to
the ruin of his country. Is he not foremost a patriot ? He still
persists. Very well. He shall be first ignored and then mocked.
He still persists. Then he is denounced by a Very Important Person
as a monster. The thunderbolt falls. But he is still there. Then,
suddenly, in almost an absent-minded way the reform comes about.
The pioneer is tendered a complementary banquet by his old
enemies at which they sing, " For he's a jolly good fellow," and
he receives a decoration in the next Honours List. At this dinner
to Rowland Hill, in 1846, he was given a cheque for £13,000 from
his admirers. In earlier times he might have been burned at the
stake or have had his head chopped off on Tower Hill.

There was never a better example of a reformer hammering on
the doors until the rusty bolts gave way, for Hill did not see the
inside of the Post Office until after his great reform had been adopted.
At the time Hill published his pamphlet the number of letters carried
yearly was 126,000,000. In the House of Commons, Hill's reforms
were opposed, among other reasons on the ground that they would
increase the number of letters to 470 million yearly and that the Post
Office would collapse under the weight. St. Martin's-le-Grand would
be lost forever to sight under a white avalanche. Nobody would
ever get any letters at all. As a matter of fact, the most frightening
estimates of the Tite Barnacles were far exceeded soon after the
introduction of the Penny Post. How does it stand now ? Each
year during the 1939-1945 war the G.P.O. handled 6,550 million
letters as well as 205 million parcels and more than 100 million
registered parcels and letters. In 1939, 7,990 million letters were
sent. " Neither snow, nor rain, nor heat, nor gloom of night
stays these couriers from the swift completion of their appointed
rounds." And these couriers have certainly increased their load.

Envelopes were not used until the 'forties. Until then letters
were a single folded sheet sealed by a wafer. Hill talks of " little
bags called envelopes," and such is the natural conservatism of
man that it took a long time before the public accepted so bizarre
a notion. Nor is it astonishing that the Post Office resisted such
a revolutionary idea as fixing adhesive stamps to letters. Hill
had invented a square of paper with a glutinous wash on its back
in the 'thirties. But the safety of England and the solvency of the
Post Office obviously depended on collecting the postal fee

on delivery. Heaven alone knew the wicked tricks the public would resort to if letters could be prepaid by stamps. High officials were confident that the population would spend its evening hours and its Sunday afternoons removing the cancellation marks. One can readily imagine the agitated meetings inside the Circumlocution Office over designs, inks and marking machines to frustrate the public's knavish tricks. "Always suspect the worst of the people you govern," was the Tite Barnacles' axiom. The first stamps were printed in black with an obliteration mark in red, and the brick-reds that are familiar to all those who preserve bundles of Victorian letters in their attics came in with the beginning of 1841. Franking, which enabled Members of Parliament to send their own letters—and letters of their friends—without payment, went out in 1840. Its revival has been lately suggested to relieve M.P.s who find it hard to make ends meet.

IV

CABLES

There was another form of communication in which the newspapers and the mercantile classes were deeply interested—the " submarine telegraph."

An announcement to the readers in the first issue of the *Daily News* records that " at the hour of going to press our express from Paris has not arrived. The delay has in all possibility arisen from the stormy weather in the Channel or from the accident that occurred on Monday night on the South Eastern Railway."

In 1846 experiments had been made in laying a submarine cable from one side of Portsmouth Harbour to the other, but the enthusiasts who then believed that the cable could be extended across the Straits of Dover were few. The Governments of Great Britain and France made no effort to link the two countries by cable but granted permission to private enterprise in the shape of a certain Mr. Briggs to make an attempt. The first cable was laid from Dover to Calais in 1850 and worked well until a French fisherman hauled it up under the impression that he had captured a sea-monster. The newspaper records that the fisherman cut a slice from the cable to take home to exhibit to his village as a wonder from the realm of mermaids. In 1851 another and better-protected cable was laid, and from then on messages flowed between London and Paris.

The linking of Britain and America was a far more formidable enterprise. For the first twenty years of its life the newspaper was dependent on the mails for its news from America. In its first numbers there is recorded the impatience with which the arrival of the cross-Atlantic ships was awaited at Liverpool. The letters from the American correspondent and the packets of New York newspapers were brought by chartered express trains from the North. Even with events so late in history as the Civil War and the assassination of President Lincoln, British newspapers were dependent for their intelligence on the sea mails.

The struggle to span the Atlantic involved the loss of more than half a million pounds and was achieved only through the exercise of unquenchable faith and unwearying patience. The Atlantic telegraph is a memorial to that fertile genius, Lord Kelvin, a man who threw off ideas like a St. Catherine's Wheel throwing off sparks, but it is also a memorial to the devotion of British engineers.

The first vain effort to lay the cable was in 1857. A second attempt was essayed in the June of the next year, but the anger of the Atlantic storms defeated it. In July 1858, the struggle was renewed. There was boundless enthusiasm when the British ship, the *Agamemnon*, and the American ship, the *Niagara*, employed in the cable-laying were united, the cable spliced, and this message passed, " Europe and America are united by telegraphic communi-cation. Glory to God in the Highest, On Earth peace, Goodwill towards Men." It took some 35 minutes to transmit.

Sceptical minds had inquired—suppose that after these immense exertions you do succeed in bridging the Atlantic, will you have anything to say that is worth saying ? This wondrous new device will materially help the spread of commerce. But will it convey any thoughts as remarkable as the vehicle itself ? How much better off will Britain and America be because this barrier of time and the sea is broken down ?

The optimists could point to this choice of the message of the Angels of the Nativity for the binding of the nations. Were there any more exalted words in prose or verse ? Or any stronger foundation for the American partnership ? No incident better illustrates the conviction of the Victorians that the age of progress would inevitably lead into the age of peace, that through invention and mechanical advances men would be emancipated from old fears and old cruelties. It was a faith that was to suffer many disillusions, but it gave a meaning and an exhilaration to hard lives. It sustained the engineer through repeated disappointments, and obscure and humble characters were sustained in the knowledge that they were part of one increasing purpose. For a little over a fortnight the Atlantic Telegraph of 1858 went on working—then there was a blank silence ; somewhere in the chasms of the sea the cable had been broken. For a long time afterwards men went on vainly tapping messages. The blankness of defeat . . . the tapping in the void.

That reverse was so crushing and so much money had been spent that it was seven years before another attempt was made. That magnificent monster, the *Great Eastern*—the pride of Brunel and Scott Russell—was used this time to pay out the cable. Two-thirds of the way across the cable snapped. Another blow ! In 1866 the engineers made one more effort. This time, on 30 June, it was successful. The broken line of 1865 was also fished out of the sea and put into service. That story of the laying of the cable, as recorded in Dr. W. H. Russell's book, drawn from the archives of Cable and Wireless, is a tribute to the masculine virtues and the powerful faith of the Victorians. When it came to action, they were men who had no doubts. Things would come right because they willed it so.

In 1858 the Queen had cabled President Buchanan a message of fervent hope that the invention would serve as a new link in Anglo-American relations. The Queen lived long enough to be aware of the miracle of wireless. In the Isle of Wight in 1898 she observed with interest some odd structures which a young Italian electrician, Marconi, put up to communicate with Bournemouth without benefit of wires or cables. She was able to keep in touch, too, with her son's progress on board his yacht.

Each fresh extension of the power of human communication was thought of as a triumph for the liberal spirit. Railways, steamships, cables, cheap newspapers, telephones and, finally, wireless—these were seen primarily as new instruments of civilisation. The competition of the trader had become the moral equivalent of war. If nation could speak to nation, words of peace would be spoken. The engineers and inventors of the nineteenth century had a philosophy of humanism. Wheatstone, for example, could hardly be expected to foresee that there would be an Ems telegram, or Marconi to guess in 1898 to what uses his compatriot Mussolini would put the radio a quarter of a century later. The mechanical advances of the nineteenth century had a Lamarckian quality. It almost seemed as if men, by willing it, achieved new eyes that could see farther, and ears with an infinitely greater reach of sound. But their will was not the will to power. The impulse was towards knowledge, and emancipation, and friendship.

CHAPTER VI

THE SOCIAL FABRIC

I

THE PYRAMID

RINGING iron. Streams of golden sovereigns rattling from the bank tellers' little shovels. Blinding white lakes of Sheffield steel.

One draws an impression of the metallic solidity of English life a century ago from reading these files of the *Daily News*. Indeed, there are moments when one comes to see some of the chief figures of this time as themselves cast in metal; and titles such as the Iron Duke or the Steel King seem to be weightier than mere metaphors. There are many potentates of the age of whom it is said—" he is made of money." The mighty banker is always called Midas, and one supposes that the paradox of hungry men in a land of plenty is due to his fatal gift of freezing the barns at a touch to chunks of solid gold.

Society then was a steep pyramid of iron and bronze. At its top, the Queen and the Prince Consort. Then, in descending steps, the aristocracy, who made up for loss of power by increase in pride —then the upward-pushing middle-class, who were to fix the colour of the age; a middle-class in which there were at least three distinct sub-divisions; then the farm population and the working men and women of the cities, ever multiplying under the forcing process of the industrial revolution; then, at the bottom, so low as to be barely visible, the submerged tenth.

One sees a considerable up-and-down traffic on the steps that lead to the Throne. Skilled workmen are constantly moving up into the lower middle-classes. Vigorous characters in one layer of the middle-class thrust their way into the layer above. The aristocracy, after swallowing hard and making a grimace or two, accepts new baronets and peers who began life in commerce. George Hudson, the Railway King, is able to say jovially to Prince Albert, " It's all 'umbug, your Royal 'Ighness." Old privileges are claimed by new castes. Tennyson describes it elegantly as freedom broadening down from precedent to precedent. It was a common defence of a bad employer that he was a self-made man. Were his workmen unhappy and ill-used? Then they should bestir themselves, and fight their way up the staircase to wealth as he had done. Equality of opportunity to grow rich must not be cramped by too many factory laws. Long before Darwin gave the age the theory of evolution, society had accepted the principle of the survival of the fittest.

At the time our panorama begins, Victoria was not yet thirty. She had reigned nine years and had been married six. The girlish head one sees when a coin from the late 'forties turns up was immensely busy with State papers, with ceremonial and with entertainments ; high-spirited ; adoring Albert, respecting Peel, commanding the Duke ; and not at all reluctant to take sides in public affairs. An editorial in an early issue of the *Daily News* says that her Majesty has made it known she would be happy to give her assent to the Repeal of the Corn Laws. Victoria had become a Free Trader.

The pictures (and the cartoons) of the Queen in this year show her as a slender young woman in the becoming fashions of the middle 'forties, the skirt full—the crinoline was yet to come—and the low-cut bodice displaying slim shoulders. The hair is parted in the middle and drawn with Greek simplicity to the back of the head ; and the caricaturists always crown her with a thin circlet of gold. The amusing monstrosities of Victorian fashions lay ahead. This was an age of restrained grace in women's dress.

" All this for a girl," the Turkish envoy had said, shaking his head at the Coronation splendours nine years before. There were many in Europe, and not a few in Britain, who thought it improbable that the girl would long hold her throne. England in the 'forties was like a volcano on the morning of eruption. Smoke curled over the crater ; the atmosphere was sultry ; there were tremors of the ground on which the mansions of the Nabobs were built. The people were hungry. To an intelligent foreign observer like Engels, their discontents must surely burst in revolution. On Chartist platforms it was not uncommon to abuse the Queen as a parasite. The first of several attempts on her life had been made in 1839, the second in 1841. The Prince Consort's very virtues made him unpopular with the classes and the masses. Republican sentiment was strong, and it found expression in motions in the House embarrassing to the Monarch—and far more embarrassing to Prince Albert.

The storm which had long been gathering over Europe broke in 1848. Revolution blazed in one capital after another. Crowns toppled. But, by one of those paradoxes which stud British history, the stablest throne in Europe in that year of the breaking of nations was Victoria's. The heart went out of the Chartist movement at the moment when by the logic of history it should have won its great triumph. The revolution which the nervous expected would start with the demonstration on Kennington Common on 10 April 1848, never happened. The Duke of Wellington had garrisoned the city as though for a siege. Among the special constables who paraded the streets was Prince Louis Napoleon, afterwards Napoleon the Third. But no blood was shed. The march to the House of Commons never took place—there was a deputation in a cab. The crowd and the emotions evaporated, though the admirable lesson of permitting the expression of grievances was not lost on the age. It was as though the political instinct of the British people had deliberately chosen to take the middle way between revolution and reaction. By this choice they were spared not only the shedding of the blood at the barricades, but the black repression which followed. In the after years Britain became the single hope of freedom-loving men everywhere on the Continent and gave sanctuary to exiles from half a dozen countries. Those were the days before passports and Alien Restrictions. Soho from the 'fifties onwards was filled with the hubbub of escaped revolutionaries, living ,like Marx, in the direst poverty, producing their plots and stratagems and dreaming their revenges in small fly-blown restaurants, with each group shadowed by agents of the secret police of their countries who had slipped across on the Channel packet.

At the time that Dickens was planning the *Daily News*, a significant revival of trade union aspirations was taking place. The Grand National Consolidated Trades Union of 1834, with its 500,000 members, had dwindled away after a few months. Its dissolution had been speeded by the sentence of transportation on those early heroes of Trade Unionism, the Men of Tolpuddle. In the decade of want and hunger that came after, the energies of working-men switched to political agitation, to the Corn Law Repeal movement and to Chartism. (It is interesting, by the way, to trace throughout our century the rhythm of alternating political and industrial action which marks the advance of Labour.) In 1845 and 1846 the pendulum swung back again from political agitation to industrial activities. All over Britain the small local trade clubs began to join with one another to form large unions, country-wide in scale, but kept to a craft basis. Trade Unionism was to suffer many rebuffs after this, but it had come to stay and, decade by decade, was woven into the social fabric.

In Dickens, Carlyle and Disraeli there were three writers of signal power to illuminate the struggles of men and women—and children—in those swamps of despair to which the Industrial Revolution had condemned them. Kingsley with *Alton Locke* (1849) and Mrs. Gaskell—the Mrs. Gaskell of *North and South*

(1855) rather than of *Cranford*—were soon to add their persuasive voices inviting an understanding among the middle classes of the wretched state to which so many of their fellow countrymen had been reduced by an unregulated commercialism. The " condition of the people question " was not to be escaped. It was Conservatism's new leader, Disraeli, who had drawn this Hogarth-like picture of the coal mines : " Yet these are to be, some are, the mothers of England ! . . . Naked to the waist, an iron chain fastened to a belt of leather runs between their legs clad in canvas trousers, while on hands and feet an English girl for twelve, sometimes for sixteen hours, a day, hauls and hurries tubs of coal up subterranean roads, dark, precipitous and plashy ; circumstances that seem to have escaped the attention of the Society for the Abolition of Negro Slavery. These worthy gentlemen, too, appear to have been singularly unconscious of the sufferings of the little trappers, which was remarkable, as many of them were in their own employ. See, too, these emerge from the bowels of the earth ! Infants of four and five years of age, many of them girls, pretty and still soft and timid ; entrusted with the fulfilment of responsible duties, and the nature of which entails on them the necessity of being the earliest to enter the mines and the latest to leave it. Their labour, indeed, is not severe, for that would be impossible, but it is passed in darkness and in solitude. They endure that punishment which philosophical philanthropy has invented for the direst criminals, and which those criminals deem more terrible than the death for which it is substituted." That was life at the bottom of the pyramid.

But it was because men of great talent had written in this way that it came about that in the early 'sixties when industrial troubles began to multiply and employers' organisations were formed to meet the challenge of the strengthening unions, there existed a body of middle-class opinion that at least understood the grievances of the working people. This was an influence tempering class bitterness and serving as a link between Disraeli's two nations. One or two isolated acts of labour violence at this time caused undue alarm among the well-to-do. The Law Courts decided that trade unions were associations " in restraint of trade." That phrase had an ugly ring for the commercial 'sixties. Trade was a sacred thing. But such men as A. J. Mundella, Thomas Hughes (*Tom Brown's Schooldays*), and, in particular, Frederic Harrison, were quick to interpose on behalf of the unions, and, instead of a harsh struggle over the right to combine convulsing the country, there came the relieving labour legislation of 1871 and 1874. (This legislation has been frequently quoted in the debates of 1946 over the Repeal of the Trade Disputes Act.) It was in 1874 that the first two Labour

M.P.s were elected, Alexander Macdonald and Thomas Burt—Burt who sat at Westminster for many years, and whom some members of the present House recall as a fragile old man, with great gentleness of manners and a look of the quietest order of saint.

The year 1874 was marked by a wave of optimism over the future of Labour. Trade was good. The threat to destroy the power of the unions had passed. The attitude of the leaders closely resembled that of the leaders of American Labour in modern times. Most of them believed that their ends could be best achieved through an interplay of the two major political parties. They asked chiefly of Government that it should protect their right to organise and to bring pressure upon the employers to redress demonstrable wrongs. They were ardent defenders of the classic conception of British liberty. What they demanded, and what they achieved, was the widening of that conception to include their own right to combine and to agitate for better conditions. Only a very few of them at that time thought of the State as an instrument for re-shaping England. Indeed, many working men and the philosophic Radicals who were their friends were as hostile to State controls as the Liberty League itself. On one side, the humanitarian tradition, to which Dickens had given the impetus of his genius, regarded the bureaucrats of the Circumlocution Office as their enemies. Dickens had embarked on a joyous crusade to rescue humanity from the Tite Barnacles as well as from the Gradgrinds. On the other side, those who drew their inspiration from John Stuart Mill *On Liberty* feared the hurt that might be done to the spirit of man by the too-powerful State. The English radical, through the nineteenth century, was a man in perpetual protest against authority, against the power that said, " you go there—you do this." His quarrel, first with the aristocrat and then with the plutocrat was that both were dictators. The English radical never accepted the Hegelian idea that happiness and fulfilment were found when the individual was caught up and merged in the glory of the State. The private conscience was strong in him, and, even if he were a secularist, he showed the marks of his Nonconformist ancestry, reaching back to Cromwell's times, and before—to John Nameless. It was that " dissidence of dissent " of which Matthew Arnold complained. The German heresy said in effect, " Through the State you shall realise the majesty of man." The English radical said with certain defiance, " In my flesh I shall see God." In these happy years of the early 'seventies, the trade union leaders were confident that the integrity of the individual would be respected, as human understanding grew between the classes, and they were sure of their ability to better their condition by using the powers which the community had conceded to be legitimately theirs. There was a cheerful feeling abroad that through an enlightened relationship between master and man, and through the steady practice of negotiation, even the weapon of the strike might become unnecessary. If one had to choose an allegorical figure to represent Labour in that period it would be that of a young artisan, who in his bearing and appearance showed much natural dignity and a strong sense of self-respect ; a thoughtful fellow, greatly concerned to educate himself in his few hours of leisure ; and, most likely, of deep religious instinct. In the 'thirties and 'forties the working men had combined to create the friendly societies, and that impulse of a man to help his neighbour in sickness, loss and death, remained with the Trade Unions. The influence of the co-operative societies was also strong. Labour was consciously alert and assertive, but steering away from direct participation in politics.

Then, when all seemed poised and stable, the change came. Around 1875 a trade depression set in. With hard times, Labour suffered. There were many strikes. These taxed the resources of the unions to the limits, and for the most part the result was defeat. The agricultural workers unions of Joseph Arch were broken. Funds were exhausted by strike pay. Within seven years the membership represented at the Trades Union Congress fell off by two-thirds.

Out of the discontents and disillusion of the working men came a new thrust in trade unionism. The idea of a Samurai of skilled labour was abandoned ; wide recruitments increased the membership of the unions ; and, once more, there was a shift of emphasis from industrial to political action. By sifting the records of the newspaper, one can fix upon this as the time when Socialism began its powerful challenge to the individualism of the older Radicals who had formed the aggressive Left. It would be too easy a simplification to describe this as a swing towards Marxism. In any typical day of London weather one is likely to walk through mist, cloud, rain, sudden shafts of sun, and strange effects of atmosphere in which the spire of St. Bride's seems at moments to pierce the sky, while the dome of St. Paul's completely disappears. The mental climate of our century is rather like that. In the period of change and conflict that began in the late 'seventies one might see in one group Christian Socialists and anti-Socialist secularists, Republicans who were unbending individualists, and men who held the Crown in mystical reverence but were eager to expropriate the manufacturer. That notable lack of logic which always puzzles and often misleads foreigners in their dealings with Britain marks the period. Large numbers became converted to a belief in State control over broad fields. But many were unconvertible.

One of the fascinating things about the period is the confusion of thinking and action, and the strenuous debates, that arose from the effort to satisfy the demands of social justice and, at the same time, to preserve individual liberty. The extremists on one side declared that if liberty stood in the way of human happiness, then liberty must be curbed. The extremists on the other side said that hard cases made bad law—that freedom was a divine principle and that to abridge it would be to invite the retribution of the gods. Between these two extremes, the men of the middle way strove to reconcile justice and liberty, fraternity and liberty, equality and liberty. The series of Victorian compromises still affect our modern life and behaviour. During that age, both Liberal and Conservative Governments carried through Acts of Parliament to restrict what a man might do with his own—particularly when that own consisted of the human beings he employed. Was that austere and devout Tory nobleman, Lord Shaftesbury, a Socialist in his constant crying out for Factory Acts ? Was that middle-class Liberal, Samuel Plimsoll, M.P., a Socialist in his agitation against coffin ships and the cold murder for profit of merchant seamen ?— an agitation in which he became so frantic, through frustration by the snide and crafty, that the knowing ones said poor Plimsoll was out of his wits. But today we have Factory Acts. And today we have a Plimsoll Line. Looking back over the century, among the qualities that made the strongest appeal are the disinterested passion of a Shaftesbury and a Plimsoll, and the transforming imagination of a Charles Dickens operating through politicians, the Press and public opinion. Decade by decade, the area of common agreement over State intervention grew steadily greater. Richard Cross, who was the Home Secretary in Disraeli's 1874-80 Ministry, was regarded with considerable suspicion by some of his colleagues on account of the social reform legislation which he put forward. Sir William Harcourt's announcement, " We are all Socialists now," made when he introduced the Death duties in the Budget of 1894 was a breezy exaggeration, but it showed the way the world was going. In the writings of John Morley one perceives the growing pressure of the social conscience ; there comes the time when he is not able to sleep easily at night for thinking of great wrongs being done to poor men.

In those years of transition from 1875 onwards it was never quite clear where Individualism left off and Socialism began—even under the same waistcoat. Many of the Liberals who brought about the party's revival in 1906 had gone to school with the Webbs, and Fabianism carried out its strategic retreats and slow marches within the bosoms of some who rose to be Cabinet Ministers ! They sat on the same benches with men who inherited the faith of the Anti-Corn Law League of 1846—men who believed that the prosperity which Free Trade had brought to Britain showed that the free play of economic forces assured the greatest happiness to the greatest number—men who suspected that Socialism was no more than the Toryism of their youth turned upside down, and that Karl Marx and Disraeli were brothers under the skin.

Even after those portents, the forming of the Labour Representation Committee and the election of Keir Hardie to the House of Commons in 1892, the habit persisted of thinking of the Labour Party as the left wing of the Liberal Party. The belief seemed supported by such a career as that of John Burns, the working-man M.P. who became President of the Local Government Board. That *beau sabreur* of letters, Cunninghame Graham, who had been sentenced to imprisonment with Burns for his part in the Trafalgar Square riots of 1887, became also a Liberal M.P. Henry George's *Progress and Poverty*, published in 1879, inspired a fervent group of single taxers among the Liberals.

In February, 1946, three men who were survivors from the 1906 Parliament were entertained at No. 10 Downing Street to celebrate the creation of the Parliamentary Labour Party forty years before. There were observers in 1906 who probably quoted Browning's, " I have seen four and twenty leaders of revolt." There is nothing harder to forecast than the rise of a new political party, but there is nothing more certain than that a new political party inherits the intellectual debates of its predecessors. If one attends political meetings or reads *Hansard* nowadays, it is not difficult to trace the various strands from the past that are woven into modern thought and speech. One detects on the platforms of the Left the influence of the idealism of John Ruskin, of the romantic ardours of William Morris—the scientific method and sweet reasonableness of the Webbs ; the return to Cobbett in the hearty Merry Englandism, and staunch patriotism of Robert Blatchford, Alexander M. Thompson and *The Clarion* school—flavours, too, of Henry George, and Edward Bellamy's *Looking Backward*, and *The Dream of John Ball*. One hears coming through the modern voices the protest of the old Radicals and Chartists, and the accents of the political Nonconformity of the old time. It may be that some of these strains sound at variance, that it is not easy to reconcile the Shelleyan hymns to liberty with the passion of the Webbs for a tidy State. But, then, the most interesting thing in politics is often not the struggle between parties as the attempt of all great parties to resolve the conflict inside themselves.

One peculiar phenomenon of English politics, the Liberal-Labour tradition, remained strong for many years. The Parliament of 1918 saw the last of the Liberal-Labour M.P.s, but the Liberal-Labour state of mind was always more strongly represented among Liberal journalists than among Members of Parliament. It was very much the mood of the newspaper. It was expressed with force in the writings of H. W. Massingham and in such a book as C. F. G. Masterman's *The Condition of England* (1909), which embodies many of the experiences that his association with the *Daily News* had brought him. The book includes sympathetic studies of life in drab streets and the grimness of unemployment—who can forget the scarecrow processions of the workless amid the wealth of Edwardian days?—and it also includes an account of the lower middle-class revolt against the Progressive party in the London County Council elections of 1907, which comes near to being an analysis of the whys and wherefores of Fascism made long before the word Fascist had come into use. But the figure of whom one always wants to know more in this book, as in Chesterton's *Autobiography* and other memoirs of those days, is Will Crooks, the embodiment of the virtues of the British working-man. So much of the inner conflict of the century is summed up in his comment that when men talked of an Empire on which the sun never set he was thinking of a slum courtyard where the sun never rises.

II

THE PRINCE AND THE PALACE

It is instructive to follow the fortunes of Victoria's Consort through the files. This prince summed up in himself the virtues of the German people in that gentler age before Bismarck and the Empire. Albert possessed most of the talents needed for success in this life except charm, a sense of fun, and a knowledge of when to stop. He was a pedant, said his enemies; he was self-righteous; he was a superior person; he was tactless.* These are faults that matter less to us than to the men of 1846. It is the unusual quality of his mind that interests us today. The devotion of Victoria to his memory, his canonisation as Albert the Good, the Memorial in Kensington Gardens, and the tributes of Tennyson (" thro' all this

---

* Sir John Robinson used to illustrate the lack of humour in the Prince Consort by the following story. After dinner at Balmoral tales were being told of the intelligence of dogs. Edwin Landseer thought it time to end the testimony by giving an account of a dog who was sent to fetch a hidden five-pound note and brought back five golden sovereigns. The Queen laughed. Everybody, indeed, laughed except the Prince Consort. After the guests had gone to bed the Prince's equerry came to Landseer's room and said, with a smile, " The Prince wished me to tell you, Sir Edwin, that the Queen does not believe the story of the dog bringing back the five sovereigns."

tract of years, wearing the white flower of a blameless life ") have made it hard for succeeding generations to conceive of Albert as a human being rather than an image in ivory and gold. Of all men of his times, Albert was most strongly seized with the ideal of that marriage of invention and the humanities, of mechanical progress and ethics, of science and the arts, which should ultimately bring peace and happiness to all the children of men. It was a noble ideal. He was confident that it would be achieved long before a century had passed. Now that we are setting out on the same quest all over again in 1946, Albert seems to us an even more congenial figure in his disappointments than in his successes.

The newspaper in the 'fifties shows the Prince as untiring in his benevolent activities. Mechanics' institutes, popular lectures, experiments in chemistry, industrial designs, schemes for improving working-men's dwellings, the health of the poor, the music of Mendelssohn and Schumann all found in him a patron and a propagandist. Was a new invention discovered? Was a fresh machine projected? Then the Prince Consort was among the first to be stirred by its possibilities. Letters must be written— journeys taken—committees formed. Was a tartan to be designed? Was Buckingham Palace to be reorganised on a business footing and the Queen's expenses cut down? Were the sanitary arrange- ments at Windsor Castle to be put right? Was Granville to be chided or Palmerston checkmated? Then Albert was the man to take on the ungrateful job. He seldom minded making himself unpopular. One suspects, at times, an austere joy in being misunderstood.

Suspicion of the Prince was never allayed in his adopted nation. During the months before the Crimea War, the newspaper attacks on him reached a climax of violence. The country was in a mood for war with Russia and was not to be fobbed off. All the men of peace were execrated, but Albert most of all as the man who had forced the resignation of Palmerston, the darling of the nation. The *Daily News* led off from the Liberal side with a salvo against the Prince's unconstitutional interferences in policy, and the big guns of the Tory Press joined the barrage. A wild rumour ran round the town that treason had been discovered by the Ministers and that Albert had been sent to the Tower as a Russian agent. It was his misfortune to be a foreigner cast for a role that was both exalted and invidious at a period when England was high flown with national pride and anti-foreign feelings.

But for an ill-used Prince, an unappreciative world sometimes provided compensations. The supreme one came on the half- showery, half-radiant May morning in 1851 when Victoria opened the Great Exhibition in Hyde Park. This was the summit of Albert's career. It was also one of the peaks, one of the highest peaks, of the Victorian age. That strange and lordly building, utterly unlike any other building in the old world or the new, which Douglas Jerrold in a flash from the skies, had named *The Crystal Palace*, represented the optimism of the age, its ambitions and its simple faith in the natural goodness of the machine. On that fresh May morning the sun was reflected from a million square feet of glass. Inside that glittering pavilion there were arrayed the inventions and artistic productions of the civilised world. To an age enraptured by railways, the achievements of the great British engineers, Stephenson and Brunel and the rest, stood out in pride ; the shining locomotives displayed in the Exhibition were idols for the world to worship.

As one opens the old files for May 1851, there rises up the roar of a multitude. Never before had so many people thronged the capital. All night long the crowds had assembled in the streets. They had poured into London from the provinces. The men and women of the new cities were here, the new cities of the North and Midlands. Manufacturers who had become millionaires in the upsurge of national prosperity sat in their carriages in West End streets, munching chicken and drinking champagne. County families who had come up from the green depths of Dorset or Wiltshire to attend the exhibition gazed with interest upon their conquerors, the new men of the new time who were to be the masters of England. Skilled artisans in their Sunday best, with oiled quiffs and gay cravats—the best workmen in the world— had brought their wives and children to see a more brilliant pageant than the Coronation. England had become the workshop of the world, and the men who sweated in that workshop, had come to London to see what the world thought of the workshop. Their faces beamed with honest pride and child-like wonder. The town was thronged, too, with foreigners, and for once, at least, the heart of the British was genially disposed towards foreigners, that formidable heart being caught up by the mood of universal brotherhood and peace in which the Great Exhibition had been conceived. There were men here from Paris, Rome, Berlin, Madrid, St. Petersburg, Geneva, New York, Boston, Philadelphia. The Stars and Stripes were flying in friendly salutation from the U.S. frigate *St. Lawrence*. And Thackeray hailed—

> *Our brethren cross the Atlantic tides*
> *Loading the gallant decks which once*
> *Roared a defiance to our guns,*
> *With peaceful store.* ——
> *Symbol of peace, their vessel rides !*

THE TICHBORNE TRIAL

This is a contemporary drawing of the last scene in the Tichborne Trial.
The claimant, Arthur Orton, is seen shaking hands with his counsel, Dr.
Kenealy, Q.C.

There were be-diamonded turbans from the East—silken-vestured Chinamen—Indian potentates and Indian merchants. Victoria was " queen of innumerable realms," and all the Colonies were here. The ends of the earth had gathered in London that day to exhibit their peaceful arts and inventions in friendly emulation.

A vast hum of excited voices seems to rise from the faded pages, with the rustle and slurred rhythms of uncountable crowds, doing nothing but wandering about—staring—marvelling. From the first glimmer of wet dawn on that May morning these crowds are on the move, streaming across the bridges, turning towards Westminster to admire Barry's new Houses of Parliament, the most eye-filling building that the new age had yet created, with Pugin's decorations still freshly glowing. The crowds pour through the squares of Belgravia and Kensington. Everywhere bells are pealing jubilantly and thousands of flags are flying. Colonel Sibthorp's prediction that this May morning would see the excesses of the French Revolution re-enacted, with the riff-raff of London joining hands with the scum of Europe in pillaging the mansions of Kensington, is not borne out. These enormous crowds are very orderly and civilised. They have come to gape at the wonders, themselves being the greatest wonder. Hardly a geranium is brushed from a Wimpole Street window-box. The crowds exhibit that self-discipline which is familiar to those who have mingled in large London throngs on ceremonial days ; as though the crowds said to themselves that the more there were of them the quieter they must be.

At last they spy through the trees the first glitter of the palace of crystal which houses the Great Exhibition—and above the sparkling glass a storm of flags, the flags of every country in the world fluttering in the morning sun. Many in the crowds find it unbelievable that so frail, and airy, and dream-like a thing can exist at all. They catch their breath as though fearing it might dissolve while they watch.

There is an Oriental legend of an enchanter who, by playing a tune, conjures up a palace of diamonds and sapphires, with dancing fountains in its courtyards. Amid the carved mahogany and roast-beef heaviness of 1851, amid all the puddings, portliness and red faces, the first sight of the Palace seemed as ethereal as that sorcerer's mirage. Its fragile traceries, appearing among the fresh green of the Park elms, fascinated the crowds. Thackeray's May-Day Ode written for *The Times* on the opening of the Exhibition describes how—

D

> *A blazing arch of lucid glass*
> *Leaps like a fountain from the grass*
> *To meet the sun,*

and that conveys the impression of lightness and grace, a delicacy of dancing flame and leaping waters, which the Crystal Palace made on thousands and thousands of visitors to Hyde Park.

Nothing, also, tells one more about the popular emotions of that day than the effect they had upon the author of *Vanity Fair*, commonly accounted in his age the master cynic. He, indeed, was so moved by the spectacle of " Gaul and German, Russ and Turk, each with his native handiwork " that he wrote—

> *I felt a thrill of love and awe,*
> *To mark the different garb of each,*
> *The changing tongue, the various speech*
>   *Together blent ;*
> *A thrill, methinks, like His who saw*
> " *All people dwelling upon earth*
> *Praising our God with solemn mirth*
>   *And one consent.*"

If that wordly-wise observer of the shams of society could be so carried away by the emotions of the opening day, how would less sophisticated hearts respond ? We may guess from the notes which the Queen committed to her diary that evening. She wrote, " The tremendous cheers, the joy expressed in every face, the immensity of the building, the mixture of palms, flowers, trees, statues, fountains, the organ (with 200 instruments and 600 voices, which sounded like nothing), and my beloved husband the author of this ' Peace Festival,' which united the industry of all nations of the earth,—all this was moving indeed, and it was and is a day to live for ever. God bless my dearest Albert, God bless my dearest country, which has shown itself so great today ! "

The Queen's direct and uncomplicated emotion was shared by most of her people. In that springtime of Victorian promise the nation believed, as she believed, that it had risen to its truest greatness by offering the world its leadership in the arts of peace. From this noble example each country would surely come quickly to see that its happiness was bound up with its neighbours' happiness —that each would prosper through the other's well-being—that wars fought with cannon, or wars fought with tariffs, were schoolroom follies that grown men would put aside.

With the boundless increase in the productive powers of the world made possible by the new machines—with science as the fairy godmother of mankind, turning pumpkins into coaches, dead leaves into gold, and granting her god-child all the wishes of its heart, then the rule of everlasting peace and the reign of plenty were within human grasp. That was the meaning of the Exhibition. How wise, how luminous, how eminently reasonable! said everybody.

It was a great moment in our century. A wave of immense hopefulness swept over the country, a generous impulse towards fraternity. How fair a prospect stretched out before the people of Britain—and, indeed, before the human race!

One is tempted to linger over this day because on it, more than on any other day in the nineteenth century, the nation was buoyed up by a splendid hope for the future, not only for its own future but for the future of civilisation. It is true enough that the expansion of trade and the making of money were in their minds as well as altruism. But despite all that was cheap, and money-grubbing— even foolish—in the affair, at its heart there was for that shining moment a vision of what might be made of life. This was a genuine affirmation of faith in the power of men and good will to use the mechanical advances of the century for the well-being of earth's hungry millions.

If we look forward to another Great Exhibition—this time in 1951—it is not so simply from a desire to imitate the material achievements of those early Victorians as to rekindle that particular hope.

In the 'fifties the light soon faded within " the bright arcade " of the Crystal Palace.* Within little more than three years, the drums of war were beating. The troopships were setting out for the Crimea. Albert tumbled from his brief popularity.

And Tennyson was writing—

No more shall commerce be all in all, and Peace
Pipe on her pastoral hillock a languid note.

And,

For the peace that I deemed no peace, is over and done,
And now by the side of the Black and the Baltic deep,
And deathful-grinning mouths of the fortress, flames
The blood-red blossom of war with a heart of fire.

Something had gone very wrong. The Palace stood, but the dream had perished.

* In 1852, the Crystal Palace was removed to Sydenham, in South London, and opened there in 1854.

III

WEATHER NOTE

The fear that haunted many good people that the Crystal Palace would be destroyed by a rainstorm was not so wildly unreasonable as it now looks.

For many of the Londoners who scrutinised the skies so anxiously on that May morning remembered the extraordinary storm which burst over the city almost five years before. As this storm falls within our centenary sweep—it happened on 1 August 1846,—and on the principle that weather, like love and food, is a subject of timeless interest, this digression into the rain may be forgiven.

It was in the afternoon of that day that black clouds broke in hail. The storm lasted more than three hours. The hailstones were of a monstrous size and did great damage to the city's glass. At the Houses of Parliament 7,000 panes were shattered ; at Scotland Yard 300 ; at St. James's Theatre, 800 ; at Burford's Panorama, 10,000. On the south side of the river, there were miles of streets in which scarcely a single pane of glass was left. Hundreds of skylights were smashed, and the furnishings of many a poor home were spoiled by the inrushing waters.

At Buckingham Palace, the glass squares in the roof of the picture gallery were destroyed and streams of water cascaded down. In many of the royal apartments the flood stood ankle deep.

Theatres were swamped so badly that performances were cancelled. At Clerkenwell some decrepit tenements collapsed under the weight of water, while at the Duke of Buccleuch's great mansion at Ditton two thousand panes were out.

So far as one can trace, it was not until the Germans let their bombers loose on London in the summer of 1940 that the streets of this city presented so sorry a picture of broken windows. On that August afternoon of 1846 London was filled with that noise of glass on the pavements which became so familiar to us in 1940.

The end of the Palace came by fire not water. It was a sorry business on that November night in 1936 to stand on a roof and watch the flames eating up Paxton's dream of iron and glass. One reflected on what that building had meant to our forbears and of the pride and the hopes which had been attached to it on the May morning of its opening. Nor could one forget the place it had held in the affections of generations of Londoners. One thought of the music ; the series of concerts which August Manns, the most intelligent of German bandmasters, conducted there from 1855 to 1901 ; Sims Reeve, Charles Santley ; the balloon ascents ; the firework nights ; the packed trains on bank holidays. It was like watching the burning of a Victorian Valhalla where the gods of our fathers sat in a solemn circle waiting the end. The destruction of the Palace naturally created a great stir, but it was soon forgotten in the confusion of emotions created by the first reports of a constitutional crisis over the King's proposed marriage. On 11 December 1936, Edward VIII, the great-grandson of Victoria and Albert, abdicated. That was the real end of the Victorian tradition.

IV

HIGH LIFE

Disraeli's idea of uniting by an aristocratic renaissance the two nations into which England was divided a hundred years ago was a pet subject of ridicule to Jerrold and the young lions of the *Daily News* and *Punch.*

The trouble was that the nobility of the time did not always fill the romantic role for which Disraeli's imagination had cast it. There were complaints that in the early decades of the nineteenth century the hauteur of rank, fashion and quality was greater than it had been in the eighteenth century. Tradespeople, it was said, were treated as untouchables—and among the older families there was no discrimination between Wholesale and Retail ! Even professional men were made to feel their inferior station, and the story was told of a Countess who, when sick, would converse with her doctor only through the lady's maid, referring to herself, like the Queen, in the third person. " Tell him her ladyship has these symptoms . . ."

There was uneasiness rather than social assurance behind this top-loftiness. The landed aristocracy was on the defensive against the up-and-coming middle-classes.

This attitude is lighted up in that scene at Chesney Wold when Sir Leicester Dedlock hears that the son of his old housekeeper, Mrs. Rouncewell, has been asked to stand for Parliament.

" ' And it is a remarkable example of the confusion into which the present age has fallen ; of the obliteration of landmarks, the opening of floodgates, and the uprooting of distinctions,' says Sir Leicester with stately gloom, ' that I have been informed by Mr. Tulkinghorn, that Mrs. Rouncewell's son has been invited to go into Parliament.'

" Miss Volumnia utters a little sharp scream.

" ' Yes, indeed,' repeats Sir Leicester. ' Into Parliament.'

" ' I never heard of such a thing ! Good gracious, what is the man ? ' exclaimed Volumnia.

" ' He is called, I believe—an—Ironmaster,' says Sir Leicester slowly, and with gravity and doubt, as not being sure that he is called a Lead-mistress ; or that the right word may be some other word expressive of some other relationship to some other metal.

" Volumnia utters another little scream."

It is not surprising that such pretensions were a favourite target of the paper Dickens started and staffed. The resistance of the great landlords to the Repeal of the Corn Laws brought the Dukeries under such a rattle of fire as they were not to experience again until Mr. Lloyd George enfiladed them from Limehouse.

In those days the territorial magnates made and unmade M.P.s. They behaved like Sir Leicester, of whom it was recorded, " two other little seats that belong to him he treats as retail orders of less importance, merely sending down the men, and signifying to the tradespeople, ' You will have the goodness to make these materials into two members of Parliament and to send them home when done.' " The Duke of Richmond, incensed at the action of his brother, Lord Arthur Lennox in voting for Repeal, forced him to resign his seat for Chichester, and replaced him by the Duke's younger son, described in a contemporary newspaper as " a young sprig of nobility about as well adapted to be a teacher of the Chinese language as to be a legislator."

The Duke of Newcastle brought about the defeat of his own heir, Lord Lincoln in South Nottinghamshire as a punishment for supporting Peel and also forced Gladstone to withdraw from the representation of Newark. The Queen exhibited anxiety that a seat should be found for Gladstone, writing vigorously to Peel on the subject. It was not a quest which she would have undertaken with much enthusiasm a few years later. Similarly, the Duke of Buckingham kept out Mr. Fremantle, a former Chief Secretary for Ireland. Meanwhile the Duke of Norfolk gave the cartoonists a theme by earnestly recommending the virtues of curry powder to a hungry people.

After these demonstrations, the journalists on the Repeal side longed for a chance to humble the pride of the aristocracy. That chance was provided by a breach of promise suit brought in February 1846, by a tradesman's daughter, Miss Mary Eliza Smith against the young Earl Ferrers. This case amused the town and furnished columns of lively copy to the newspapers. It came to a sudden end when the Attorney-General, appearing for Lord Ferrers, showed that the love letters had been forged, and the Solicitor-General, appearing for Miss Smith, threw in his hand.

But during the hearings the young Earl and his friends had been covered in ridicule. The *Daily News* pounced. One day in February 1846, in the middle of the great Parliamentary struggle over the Corn Laws, the paper devoted its first leading article—not a word less than two thousand words long—to the Ferrers suit. " We feel that a fierce, malignant democracy will send forth a vulgar chuckle in contempt and derision of nobility," said the leader-writer, who, by all internal evidence was Douglas Jerrold. He made great play with the testimony of the Reverend Mr. Arden, who had been tutor to the earl, for his evidence admitted the world to the follies of high life. Lord Ferrers and his circle had been fond of dressing up in harlequinade clothes and wandering the countryside. The Reverend Mr. Arden under cross-examination admitted, " I have myself been disguised many a time, I have taken my shirt off and put it outside my coat ; and a handkerchief over my head. I believe I have sallied out in this disguise at night."

The clergyman agreed that at times when he had been resting on the sofa the young Earl had painted moustaches on his face. Then came the naive confession which travestied the feudal relationship of the parson to the peer. " In his dining room," said Arden, " I suppose he might do what he liked with me, and he did." The parson had been expected to get drunk, too, and loyally drunk he got.

" A Jack Pudding in orders," was the leader-writer's description of Mr. Arden. " A pulpit mummer, half-sot, half-zany." But the paper despaired of the Bishop unfrocking the reverend masquerader. It was gloomily sure that soon he would be holding services again, preaching the virtues of thrift and toil to the village folk. So there was Jerrold off again on his favourite sport of harrying the Bishops.

During the trial, it was shown that this nobleman who was little more than a boy, had held mock court in the family drawing room, arraying himself in a scarlet coat like a judge, and putting on his grandfather's wig. The household servants brought before him a man who had been caught stealing cranberries on the estate, and, after a rollicking trial, the criminal was sentenced to be " taken downstairs and there dosed with beer." The *Daily News* commented, " There is a happy blending of humour and mercy in this sentence that we most heartily recommend to the consideration of noble magistrates called to adjudicate upon paltry cases in the Game Laws."

But gradually the hostility of the landed aristocracy to the wealthy middle classes melted. Tolerance shaded into acceptance, and acceptance into the genial glow of discovered fellow-interests. Money seemed to be a powerful lubricant. Ancient titles and new fortunes were not for long found to be irreconcilable. The social successes of Merdle epitomised the reconciliation. Mr. Merdle was a very rich, very commonplace man who " oozed sluggishly and muddily " at his own parties, but whom Society delighted to honour. He was a company promoter " in everything good, from banking to building " (Merdle was modelled on John Sadleir, M.P., the fraudulent financier whose suicide saved him from criminal prosecution). To Merdle's dinners came " magnates from the Court and magnates from the City, magnates from the Commons and magnates from the Lords, magnates from the Bench and magnates from the Bar, Bishop magnates, Treasury magnates, Horse Guards magnates, Admiralty magnates—all the magnates that keep us going, and sometimes trip us up."

" Admiralty said Mr. Merdle was a wonderful man. Treasury said he was a new power in the country and would be able to buy up the House of Commons. Bishop said he was glad to think this wealth flowed into the coffers of a gentleman who was always disposed to maintain the best interests of Society."

The climax of the social comedy is that highly symbolic scene in Merdle's drawing room after dinner when Lord Decimus, the patrician in politics, strikes his bargain with Merdle, the boor in commerce ; and a day or two later it is announced that Merdle's witless stepson is appointed one of the Lords of the Circumlocution Office.

The coalition of old rank and new wealth was at last complete.

V

THE POWER OF A LIE

It was in 1846 that a youth of seventeen named Roger Charles Tichborne went to Stonyhurst. That was a very small item of news in a crowded year. But out of it was to come a most considerable stir—certainly the strangest story of high life that the newspaper printed in its century. The Tichbornes were an old, proud Hampshire family ; Roger Tichborne was heir to the baronetcy and to great estates. His mother, who had no love for English ways, had done her best to turn him into a French boy. She was a handsome woman and a headstrong woman. Her son took after her in looks, while her system of education was perfectly designed to make him a misfit at Stonyhurst and in the Dragoons. In 1853 this unhappy young man of great possessions threw up his Army career and set out to visit Latin America. The next year he was lost at sea ; the ship on which he sailed from Rio being sunk with all hands. Roger Tichborne's death was presumed ; the title and property passed to his brother. But his mother would not believe that he was dead. He had been picked up ; he was a castaway ; he had lost his memory ; he was hiding his hurt spirit in some far corner of the earth and she would surely find him. There were a score of explanations, and any explanation was more likely than that he could be dead. Out of that pathetic refusal of Lady Tichborne to accept the loss of her son sprang this most singular imposture of the century, a hoax of giant size that agitated the public mind for many years.

Lady Tichborne advertised for her son in newspapers in remote parts of the world. Eleven years after Roger Tichborne's disappearance word came from the other side of the globe that a butcher named Tom Castro had been found at Wagga Wagga in Queensland who, it was said, bore a strong likeness to the lost heir. All that follows from this seems to have been written by Mrs. Henry Wood and Miss Braddon in collaboration. It is understandable that long brooding had brought Lady Tichborne to such a pitch that for her the illusion was ever after bound to be stronger than the reality. What is more remarkable is the credulity exhibited by men and women who were under no such emotional compulsion. A man in Sydney who had known Roger Tichborne's father recognised Castro as the lost heir " because he looked so like his father." Less disinterested evidence of identity came from a Negro servant in the same city who had once been in the employ of the Tichborne family, and now attached himself to the Claimant. Lady Tichborne, happy that her faith had at last brought a sign from heaven, sent out money to bring Castro to England. The credulous and the crooked who now swarmed around him, both expecting to share his new fortunes, joined together to press the young butcher to go home to assume his heritage. During the voyage, the Negro instructed him in the part he was to play, and fitted him out with sufficient information about the family to enable him to engage in a plausible patter. The first meeting with Lady Tichborne took place in Paris. In former years her son's resemblance to her had been remarked upon ; he had been a lean and graceful youth with a clear-cut profile. The man who now addressed her as his mother was a mountain of unwieldy flesh, with a pendulous paunch, and a pudding of a face. Adoring France, Lady Tichborne had taught her son French from the cradle, and he had been mocked by his comrades at school because he spoke his own tongue with so strong an accent. But the Claimant could not speak a word of the French language. His speech was that of an illiterate Cockney. His letters and his manners showed a lack of education. He had no recollection of important happenings in his childhood, and he had a habit of suddenly remembering things that had never happened. Yet Lady

Tichborne recognised him as her child. She ascribed his changed appearance and his lapses of speech and of memory to the hard life he had led after his shipwreck. His sufferings apparently had even changed his hair from black to brown !

The will to believe was too powerful for the daylight facts. Not only the obsessed mother, but a number of other persons behaved from now on like characters in Pirandello's play—*Right You Are If You Think You Are*. One experiences in reading the reports of the Tichborne case, an uneasy feeling of the power of a lie to confound the obvious and make the commonplace stand on its head. It produces the same queasiness that parts of *Our Mutual Friend* induce. The earth seems to move up and down beneath one like a ship's deck. One sober and honest person after another succumbs to the hallucination. Respectable citizens begin to doubt facts that are as familiar to them as their own front doors ; the real and the visionary become hopelessly mixed. Unimaginative men ruin themselves over a dream.

There was a chorus of villagers to cheer the Claimant on his return to the home of his ancestors. The oldest retainers had no doubt of the identity of the young master. The family solicitor of the Tichbornes, a Tulkinghorn sort of fellow ; officers who had served with the heir in the Dragoons ; and local families who had known the heir since childhood were sure that this moving mountain of flesh was in truth Roger Tichborne. They did their innocent best to consummate the fraud by supplying the Claimant with intimate details of Roger Tichborne's brief history. These he greedily lapped up and stored in his hold-all mind. By this means the imposture was sustained for five years. The appearance of the long-missing heir to an old title and grand estates was an event certain to excite the imagination of the wider public. The narrative of Roger Tichborne's return delighted the readers of novelettes ; an abounding branch of Victorian literature. They had always hoped that this particular dream would come true. That it had come true showed that the world was not such a bad place after all, and that the happiest of all happy endings, wealth and a title, was part of the natural order. There grew up a vested interest of thwarted romanticism in the case. The circles of credulity widened, and the Claimant attracted from all parts of society adherents who kept faithful to him to the end. When, after Lady Tichborne's death, the impostor was driven to bring an action against the trustees of the estates, the public bought bonds to pay his legal costs. He had taken to high living with relish, growing ever fatter, and had run heavily into debt on the strength of his great expectations. During this action, which stretched over many weary weeks the fraud was exposed, but not with ease. It was shown that the Claimant's real name was Arthur Orton ; that he was the son of a butcher at Wapping ; and had gone to sea as a youth, jumping his ship in South America. He had taken the name Castro from a family with whom he had lived in those days. It was shown that he had once come home from Queensland to inquire after his relatives at Wapping.

In more senses than one, Arthur Orton cut a remarkable figure in the witness box. One sees him in the sketches of that time like an enormous fat spider spinning his web of falsehood ; a creature with a strong power of animal magnetism. It is one of the puzzles of this altogether bewildering case that Orton, a man of mean intelligence, should have proved so skilful a dissembler. He came near outwitting some of the sharpest wits of the Law. It was touch and go to the end of the long hearings. There were not a few who thought that if that gifted advocate, Sir John Duke Coleridge, had not stretched all his powers in his last speech to the jury—it was a speech that lasted three weeks—the verdict might well have gone to the Claimant. Then the Lie would have entered its full heritage and Arthur Orton would have been master of Tichborne Park. During the trial, more than a hundred witnesses swore that Orton was the rightful heir ; few of them were confederates ; for the most part they were honourable men and women ; they had been caught up from every walk of life into that great web of deceit. Orton himself exhibited the greatest aplomb.

Every now and then life throws up a liar of genius, a man who, as is often the way with genius, is dull in everything except his one natural aptitude. Such an artist was Arthur Orton, the most gifted and distinguished liar of the whole Victorian age. Heavy, boorish, with no tastes except the most elementary ones, with no conversation, slow-witted and uneducated, he yet contrived an impersonation drawn from a far different social world, and sustained it unfalteringly for weeks in the blaze of a public trial. He acted this role with such native power that he imposed on many persons far more intelligent than himself and nearly defeated the Law. This, the observer concludes, is what is meant by mother wit.

After his unsuccessful action against the trustees, Orton was charged with perjury. This trial lasted for 188 days and the Claimant repeated his astonishing performance. Cockburn was the judge ; the redoubtable Henry Hawkins the prosecutor. There was an element of the childish in Orton's composition that went together with that infernal cleverness,—stuck in his head like the toad's jewel—for in the dock he would amuse himself for hours by cutting out paper figures, donkeys, rabbits and little men.

The power of the living lie to affect men's minds, as though it were some kind of drug, was shown in its most marked form by the extraordinary conduct of his counsel, Dr. Edward Kenealy, Q.C. Kenealy, who had been an undistinguished barrister, employed in the humdrum business of the criminal courts, became a man possessed. He defended his client with such violence as to destroy his own career. After Orton was convicted and sentenced to fourteen years' imprisonment, Dr. Kenealy started a weekly paper to continue the fight for Orton's freedom. He was certain that a great injustice had been done, and that Orton was the true heir. Kenealy presented a striking example of a man with a persecution complex generated on another man's account. The intemperateness of his attacks on the judges was such that he was disbarred and disbenched, but he enlisted much sympathy among the public, particularly among the poor. In some wildly illogical way it was felt that Orton's condemnation was a social injustice. Had he been a gentleman, asked the poor, would he have been denied his inheritance ? The considerable army of the disinherited felt that the Claimant's wrongs were their wrongs. The under-dog sometimes picks strange heroes whose choice does more credit to his heart than his head. It was of a piece with the irrationality and confusion of values which Orton spread about him that he commanded so strong an attachment among the poor.

The Victorians being what they were, it needed only the injection of religious prejudice to raise the agitation to fever-point. That element was soon supplied. The Tichbornes were a prominent Catholic family, and so the rumour was spread about that the Jesuits had plotted to keep the rightful heir out of his own and were the instruments of his destruction. The power of Kenealy's frantic propaganda may be judged by the fact that in 1875 he won a by-election at Stoke on the issue of Orton's wrongs. The agitation reached its crest when Kenealy in the House of Commons moved for a Royal Commission on the Tichborne claim. It was denied, but so threatening was the mood of the Claimant's supporters that the Government feared " No Popery " riots, and soldiers were held in readiness for disorder. But after that day the agitation ebbed, and when Orton came out of prison, a shadow of his former bulk, he was received with indifference. His strange adventure helps to round out the sketch of an interesting age. It is a story that the mind lingers upon because under one light it appears a hideous parody of Victorian pretentions, and, under another, a pathetic example of those illusions which the poor share with the rich.

VI

TOLERANCE

Intolerance played its part in the Tichborne case. During the stretch of the century Catholics, Jews, Dissenters and Rationalists have had in turn to look to the help of liberal-minded men and women for relief from humiliating disabilities.

A hundred years ago a Jew could not sit in the House of Commons without forswearing his faith. The Government which Russell formed in the summer of 1846 went to the country next year. The City of London in those days was a Liberal redoubt. Among the four members of Parliament it chose at the General Election of 1847 there was, in addition to the illustrious Lord John himself Baron Lionel de Rothschild, head of the English branch of that family and leader of his community. In *Coningsby* and *Tancred* you may find his portrait painted with Disraeli's opulence of brushwork under the title of Sidonia, a figure of more than mortal size, draped in the robes of mystery and power. " Something Sidonian, modern, brilliant, strange," comes echoing in the memory.

But it is possibly more in the fashion of today to recall George Arliss, and that moment when the screen Disraeli turned to a banker for the money to buy the Khedive's Suez Canal Shares. It was Lionel de Rothschild who supplied the funds. What it meant to be a great banker in those times! In his Olympian way, Rothschild financed the Irish famine loan, raised sixteen million pounds to assist the Government in paying the costs of the Crimean War (wars were cheaper in those times) and was largely instrumental in funding the U.S. National debt. (No banker or combination of bankers could take on that task nowadays.) Although Rothschild exercised this great power in the world, he could not, on his election in 1847, take his seat without also taking the oath on " the true faith of a Christian," that being the solemn absurdity which the Law demanded. In the new Parliament Russell brought in a Bill to relieve Jews from this disability. It was carried by a large majority, with Disraeli and Gladstone supporting Russell. Then the House of Lords threw the Bill out. Four times did the City of London elect Lionel de Rothschild to a seat that he could not take without apostasy. The Lords yielded at last to the pressure of public opinion, but not until nine years had gone by, and many an unworthy argument adduced to deny an elementary civil right.

Long years before, O'Connell had pressed Catholic disabilities to an issue, but during the middle Victorian period the prejudice against Catholics remained strong, and it was never hard to blow

it to a flame. The cry of " No Popery " ran through the land when
the Roman sees were re-established in 1850. We are now familiar
enough with the title Archbishop of Westminster, but less than a
century ago it excited many excellent citizens to a frenzy. There
is nothing in the newspapers of that time which strikes us as more
alien to the spirit of the present than the coarseness of the attacks
on Wiseman and Manning. One draws from this a sense of honest
folk losing their heads. The agitation against the Catholic titles
exhausted itself by its own violence, and the Church of Rome was
soon to win a new toleration from the educated classes through the
charm in persuasive advocacy of Newman's *Apologia pro Vita sua*.
But fear and suspicion was never far below the surface. One finds
H. W. Nevinson—a distinguished name in the records of the newspaper—writing in 1930 in his *Rough Islanders*, " The underlying
Protestantism of the English, especially regarding the doctrinal
mystery of Transubstantiation, is often revealed, as by the rejection
of the Revised Prayer Book in the House of Commons (1928) and
by the widespread protestation against the celebration of High Mass
upon a football ground in June 1930. Or, to take an earlier
instance : in 1909 the Romanists proposed to carry the Host in
procession through the streets round their great cathedral in
Westminster. As leader-writer on the *Daily News*, I supported the
proposal in the name of religious toleration, though at the last
moment Mr. Asquith forbade the procession for fear of riot. But
for some days following, the Editor's table was heaped with letters
of righteous indignation, denouncing that article, ' obviously
emanating from a Popish pen ' as one ' Constant Reader ' expressed
it."

If the House of Lords failed to distinguish itself over Rothschild
and the Jews in 1847, the House of Commons certainly was not at
its best in dealing with Charles Bradlaugh and atheism in 1880.
In reading in the newspaper the Parliamentary debates on that
issue one begins to glimpse the central truth about toleration, that
in abandoning it one loses other values as well—self-respect and
natural dignity, a regard for truth and a dislike of cruelty. The
worst thing about intolerance would seem to be the harm it does
to the intolerant. It is like one of those drugs which creates a sense
of pleasure, but which sensible men never flirt with because they
know the final price is far too high. The efforts of the House of
Commons to exclude the member for Northampton produced a
singular deterioration in the House itself. That comes out strongly
in the reports which Gladstone as Prime Minister wrote to the
Queen during the debates, " With the renewal of the discussion
the temper of the House does not improve, both excitement and

suspicion appearing to prevail in different quarters." Then, in that early morning hour, when, by a majority of 45, it was resolved that Bradlaugh should be permitted neither to affirm nor to take the oath, even though he was prepared to conform, the House was beside itself with nervous excitement. The Speaker was compelled by the uproar to wait some minutes before declaring the division figures. The Prime Minister, sitting with quiet composure, wrote to the Queen amid the clamour, " It was an ecstatic transport, and exceeded anything which Mr. Gladstone remembers to have witnessed. He read in it only a witness to the dangers of the course on which the House has entered, and to its unfitness for the office which it has rashly chosen to assume."

The struggle between the rebel and the institution touched the depths of indignity when Bradlaugh was removed from the House by physical force. In reading John Morley's *Gladstone*, however, that chapter is redeemed by the account of the parallel struggle that was going on inside the mind of the Prime Minister. It was in 1883 that Gladstone, after much travail of conscience, introduced the Affirmation Bill. That decision stands for a change in the century as well as a change in Gladstone. Morley wrote, " It marks in a definite way how far Mr. Gladstone's mind—perhaps not by nature or instinct particularly tolerant—had travelled along one of the grand highroads of human progress." Gladstone, the devout High Churchman, whose largest political support came from the Nonconformists, had " started from the opposite pole to that great civil principle of which he now displayed a grasp invincible." The speech in which Gladstone extended the concept of religious liberty to include the atheist from Northampton was among the noblest speeches of his long life. What happened? The Bill was thrown out. Morley, on this theme, is magnificent. " All these impressions of sublime feeling and strong reasoning were soon effaced by honest bigotry, by narrow and selfish calculation, by flat cowardice. The relieving bill was cast out by a majority of three. The Catholics in the main voted against it, and many Nonconformists, hereditary champions of all the rights of private judgment, either voted against it or did not vote at all. So soon in these affairs, as the world has long ago found out, do bodies of men forget in a day of power the maxims that they held sacred and inviolable in days when they were weak." So soon in these affairs! There is a warning bell in these words.

The end of the narrative makes one understand why it is that some acute foreign observers find it hard to discriminate between the beauties of English compromise and the flatness of English anti-climax. Bradlaugh was kept out of the 1880 Parliament. In the 1885 Parliament he was allowed to take the oath and his seat without hindrance. In 1888 he carried an affirmation Bill of his own in a House in which Conservative Churchmen were dominant. As he lay dying in 1891, the House passed a resolution expunging the intolerant record of ten years before. Bradlaugh was then too far spent to be aware of this reparation. A few days later, when he was dead, Gladstone, recalling the struggle of the 'eighties, asked, " Does anybody who hears me believe that that controversy, so prosecuted and so abandoned, was beneficial to the Christian religion ? "

It is presumably easy enough for cabbages to be tolerant. It is less easy for those who, like the Victorians, felt passionately on matters of faith and were very sure of what they knew. The growth of toleration was not a gentle, inevitable process like the growth of an oak tree. Its triumphs were wrested from many a hot encounter, and were won not least of all in the conflicts of men with their own deepest instincts, sometimes seen not as a struggle between good and bad, but between two sets of virtues. The character of the modern Englishman owes a great deal to those struggles.

CHAPTER VII

MIDDLE-CLASS TRIUMPH

I

7D. IN THE £

ONE of the grievances shared by the old rich and the new rich in 1846 was income tax at 7d. in the £. It was cruelly high, they felt. But worse than its burden was the distasteful principle of the Government's prying into the private affairs of the citizen. The Victorians felt that there was no relationship more intimate and hushed than that which existed between a man and his money.

The Income Tax which Pitt had invented to finance the Napoleonic Wars had been abolished in 1815 amid such cheering in the House of Commons as has not been evoked since. But Peel was forced to revive the odious device in 1842. The Whigs were staunch for liberty, but had been poor at book-keeping while in office, and the budget deficit for the four previous years had averaged £1,500,000. Now, in 1842, the pundits were gravely perturbed by a Treasury deficit of £2,350,000. That was about a sixth part of what Britain spent every day during the peak of the 1939-45 war. The Budget of April 1945, provided for an annual expenditure of £5,565,000,000 with a deficit of £3,265,000,000. It fits into these reflections to recall that Lord Randolph Churchill sixty years ago resigned the Chancellorship because he recoiled from a budget of £90,000,000.

7d. in the £ on all incomes over £150! Within six years that austere financier, Gladstone, was to promise the steady year-by-year tapering of the income tax to its extinction. The Crimea War thwarted his plans, and the fair hope of Britain free of income tax was never attained. The men and women of Peel's time would not have found any of the mechanical wonders of our age too hard to credit, not even the atomic bomb, but they would have found it incredible that this tax could rise to 10s. in the £—and England still survive. For the Victorian Liberal, " peace, retrenchment and reform," were the words of sovereign power. One can dip into the leading articles in the *Daily News* for decade after decade and find the gospel of public economy preached. Modern ideas of deficit spending and a Budget of capital expenditure would have been incomprehensible to Gladstone or Goschen.

Despite the gloom that a sevenpenny tax cast upon their spirits the middle classes managed to live very well indeed; as comfortably as any class in any time or place. All the fruit in the orchard was theirs. They had become the bankers of the world. They had become the bridge-builders, the dock-builders, the railroad-builders of the world. Having opened up new frontiers in their own country, they prepared with inexhaustible enthusiasm to open up the frontiers of the whole globe. Britain was piling up those foreign assets which, with a " fanatical single-mindedness," she sacrificed to the winning of the 1939-45 war. The treasure of the Victorians was amassed with speed ; it was expended by their great grandchildren at a far greater speed.

They had a vast capacity for concentrated hard work. The driving energy of the American business man is often attributed to the stimulus of the climate of his country ; there must have been some powerful infusion of ozone in the Victorian atmosphere to produce these feats of labour. Their energies went roaring up the chimney. A man with the hundred and one interests of a Paxton would dash from one end of the country to the other with board meetings in this city, negotiations in that, inspections here, fresh enterprises to start somewhere else—up at five on winter mornings, long waits in the rain at Mugby Junction, missing meals, seldom spending a solid night in an easy bed. The age vibrated with a rush of wheels. No generation had a stronger sense that the clock was its conscience. They would finance the world with their loans, clothe the world in their cotton goods and their wools, make machines to subdue the jungle, and instruct the world in the lore of the peaceful arts. They placed at the disposal of the rest of mankind unrivalled services—their combination of experience and probity in finance—their merchant shipping that touched all ports and rode all seas—their insurances (Mr. Podsnap, be it recalled, was in marine insurance, and one may be certain that no matter how monumental an ass he may have been at the dinner table he was compact of sagacity in the office).

Their exports doubled and trebled themselves in twenty years ; and not the least of their exports were brains and brawn. There was not a corner of the planet, however rocky or sandy, in which their engineers, prospectors, administrators, scientists, workmen, soldiers and missionaries did not turn up. Some of their sturdiest stock went to the farmlands of the Middle West and Far West, to the mines of Pennsylvania, to the mills and factories of Massachusetts, helping to build up the great industrial empire of America. The population of the island leapt up from decade to decade—but on top of this, ten million emigrants went out from England,

Scotland and Wales. What vitality ! The Victorians felt that they had many excellent reasons to be proud.

Consider their pride as made manifest in the thronged and almost bursting square mile of the City of London, from whose counting houses and dingy offices the spider gossamers of the money power radiated out around the planet ; in the thickets of masts of London River floating in an eternal sulky opalescence, and in all the rowdy markets and bulging warehouses that lined its shores.

Consider their pride as shown by those mansions in Belgravia and Bayswater which were as roomy, if not as elegant, as the palaces of the merchant dukes of Venice and Genoa—houses built for patriarchs of commerce to rear families of ten and twelve and to command platoons of servants. In the years of the bombing of London not a few of these great houses were shattered, so that standing in the front door one could see the moonlight pouring through the high roof. Some, of course, were quite flattened out. One recalls an old lady on the Bayswater Road, on a morning after a raid, saying, " I am glad that Queen Victoria did not live to see this. She would have been very angry indeed."

II

PROTESTS

Middle-class manners and middle-class morals were becoming all-dominant, enforced by middle-class power and wealth.

But survivals of certain bad old customs lingered, the protesting voices of the humane growing louder meanwhile.

During July 1846, the *Daily News* recorded the anger aroused by the death of a soldier after a severe flogging in Heston Barracks, Hounslow. The military at first refused to permit the civil authorities to investigate the death, but the magistrates and parish officers forced an inquest. The soldier, Frederick John White, a private in the Seventh Hussars, had been sentenced by court-martial to 150 lashes for striking his sergeant across the chest with a poker. One of those details which light up the past, and make it seem at once more gruesome and more mild than one had imagined, was brought out in the evidence. It was explained that in military floggings the severity of the punishment was usually mitigated by employing boy trumpeters, too young to have developed strong arm muscles, to wield the lash. But White had been scourged by two sturdy farriers. After a long hearing, the jury found that the soldier had died from " the mortal effects of a severe and cruel flogging," and that the court-martial was authorised by law to pass " the said severe and cruel sentence." Then this strong rider was added to the verdict, " The jury cannot refrain from expressing their horror and disgust at the existence of any law amongst the statutes or regulations of the realm which permits the revolting punishment of flogging to be inflicted upon British soldiers, and, at the same time, the jury implore every man in this kingdom to join hand and heart in forwarding petitions to the Legislature praying in the most urgent terms for the abolition of every law, order and regulation which permits the disgraceful practice of flogging to remain one moment longer a slur upon the humanity and fair name of the people of this country."

There was an outburst against flogging in the Press, and there was a debate in the Commons which is interesting for the air of puzzled reasonableness of military M.P.s, alarmed lest so necessary a discipline—as they said—should be overthrown by a sentimental gust. In the Lords, the Duke of Wellington announced an ameliora- tion of the code of military punishment, but it was not until 1881 that flogging was ended. The *Daily News* recalled that the Duke had said, " British soldiers are entirely taken from the lowest orders of society." The public agitation over the fate of Private White started a movement to improve the condition of the soldier which persisted through the century.

Duelling was dying out, killed as much by ridicule as by law. In July 1846, the *Daily News* reports that a young Army officer, Lieutenant Hawkey, was tried for the wilful murder of James Alexander Seton by shooting him in a duel. Seton had forced his attentions on Mrs. Hawkey. In her husband's presence at a public ball, he had invited her to dance with him. The Lieutenant, flaring up, called him a blackguard and a scoundrel. Seton challenged him. In the duel, Seton was wounded, but he died from an operation on a tumour which had formed in the wound. Hawkey was acquitted, amid loud huzzas, and was restored to his commission. The newspaper in a scornful leading article on the case suggested that it was the outcome of a drunken brawl.

The decline in duelling was in large part due to the contempt felt by the middle classes for what they held to be a patrician privilege. If a plebeian murdered his enemy he was hanged, but if one duke shot another duke on the field of honour he was a hero of the drawing-rooms. That was unfair discrimination, said the middle-classes. They preferred, too, that in politics the duel of debate should be metaphorical and not literal. They considered that the celebrated duel between the Duke of Wellington and Lord

Winchelsea in Battersea Fields in 1819 over—of all peaceful subjects
—the establishment of King's College in the Strand had been an
absurdity.   When in 1845 the Radical Mr. Roebuck, M.P. for
Sheffield, declined to accept a challenge from a fellow-member
and induced the Speaker to treat it as a breach of privilege, gentlemen of the old school felt that the age of chivalry was at an end
and the age of bounders had begun.

III

PRISON SHADOWS

It was in 1846 that the Fleet Prison was torn down and there was
a public auction of its relics.   The memorial Hall in Farringdon
Street now rears its prim grey tower on the site of this London
Bastille which, at the time of its destruction, was close upon seven
centuries old.   It threw a shadow from the barbaric past upon the
cheerful stir of London in the 'forties ;   its memories were of man's
inhumanity to man.   Victims of the religious persecutions of Tudor
and Stuart times had been imprisoned in the Fleet.   It was here
that Prynne's ears were cut off and his nostrils slit in punishment
for his Puritan outcry against actresses.   After 1641, the prison was
kept for debtors and those who fell into contempt of Court.   Many
men and women suffered torment of body and mind in that place
during the centuries, but the most celebrated prisoner of the Fleet
was not a mortal at all, but an immortal myth—Pickwick.   During
the eighteenth century, debtors had been loaded with irons, and
were often tortured by corrupt gaolers.   These grosser forms of
cruelty were no longer practised in the nineteenth century, but
bankrupt men were doomed to a gradual decay and degeneration.
It was a harsh irony that a debtor had to provide money in order
to live in prison at all.

The interest of the age in its prisoners was tepid.   In one of the
early issues of the *Daily News* there is an account of a meeting to
honour the memory of Elizabeth Fry and to advance her principles.
She had died in 1845.   Lord Morpeth was in the chair ;   the
audience was small.   One imagines that to the bustling, full-blooded
world outside, these people who met in small upper rooms to spread
the teachings of Howard, Samuel Romilly and Elizabeth Fry
appeared freakish characters.   There had been reports enough in
the eighteenth and early nineteenth centuries on the corruptions
and cruelties of prisons.   There had been speeches enough in the
House of Commons ;   pamphlets enough.   Yet it needed the prison
chapters in *Pickwick* to set a spark to dull imaginations.   Those pages

gained in force from their setting; their shadows were all the sterner by contrast with the high spirits of the book. For two centuries debtors had rotted away in the Fleet. But there were many men of sensibility who never gave a thought to it until they read the account of Pickwick's melancholy stroll through the prison and of the death of the Chancery debtor.

It would seem to be not the least among the services rendered to his generation by a great writer that he can open the eyes of the blind when other means fail. He has the power to awaken pity and compassion in an insensitive age, and to teach the lesson of fraternity as though it were being taught for the first time.

The 'forties were a period of harsh sentences, of transportation and of the galleys. The last shipload of convicts was transported to Australia in 1867. There were many men of that time, not by any means hard and revengeful characters, who defended these customs. Useful citizens, inspired by high moral principles, often did so. Society must be protected, they said, and Law vindicated. Then, too, there was the pride which the age took in its own toughness. It was one of the pioneer periods in our history, and pioneers traditionally rejoice in their hardness of fibre. Macaulay, for example, attacked Dickens and other opponents of capital punishment for a lack of virility. The Man of Sensibility, who had been the last creation of the eighteenth century, was now out of fashion. It was the achievement of the great writers of the middle and late Victorian years to quicken the dulled sensibilities again.

Ever since *Great Expectations* was published there has been much acute critical debate as to what deeper meanings Dickens intended by making Abel Magwitch, the convict, the pivot of the story. Some have seen it as the writer's sharpest thrust against the conventions and complacencies of his time. To those who look at the fable under this light, Dickens appears to be taking a sadistic joy in demonstrating to the powerful, the rich and the proud that their power, wealth and pride derive from the murkiest depths of society. There is another theory that *Great Expectations* is a surgical operation upon snobbery far more drastic than any performed by the author of *The Book of Snobs*. Nothing shall be spared the snob. He shall taste the last bitterness in the glass. To this upstart Pip, it shall be driven home that his pretensions and fine manners owe everything to the favour of a wretch from the underworld.

Now all this may well have been part of Dickens' design. But in recalling *Great Expectations*, after putting the book aside for some time, it is not these things that one remembers best, but rather the pathetic reaching out of Abel Magwitch after affection. Magwitch is not an ogre crawling up from the depths, but a human being deprived of friendship and the civilities of life ; a man longing for a home. He comes forward holding out his treasure, wistfully hoping that no matter how much blood and dirt there is on that gold, it will buy compassion and love. Magwitch's great expectations are centred upon his chosen heir. In that sense, they are the highest and most touching expectations in the book. That these hopes were cherished in the shadow of death added to their poignancy. Magwitch had escaped from transportation, and, if he were caught, he would be surely hanged. That was how the Law stood in those days.

A recurring complaint made against Dickens by contemporary critics was that he showed too great a partiality for low life and that he treated the dregs of society as though they, too, were human characters. Severe moralists thought this dangerous. It could only result, they feared, in throwing a radiance over the criminal that would be bad for weak minds. But, as often happened with Dickens, he was a better judge of morals than some of their professional guardians. If it was a sermon they demanded, there could be no more sombre sermon on the folly of vice than that which presented Abel Magwitch in his mortal Hell, reaching out after a happiness to be for ever denied him. From what one remembers of Magwitch, one may be reasonably sure that if he could have escaped from his past and from the shadow of the noose, the chances were that he would have become a citizen of high respectability, have worn a beaver hat and gone to church. He might perhaps have become a little too conventional and strait-laced—but only the outcast can appreciate the attractions offered by a prospect of dull, settled conventionality. At the heart of this security would have been his pride in the social graces and worldly success of the son so mysteriously adopted. Yet all this was unattainable. Not even in that powerful section of the *Comédie Humaine*—"The End of Evil Courses" was the old text that the wages of sin is death better illustrated. (If, by the way, the reader is interested in the treatment of a parallel theme by a French genius, he can spend an hour or two in comparing Balzac's criminal Trompe-le-Mort with Dickens' criminal Magwitch, and also in comparing Trompe-le-Mort's relationship to Eugene Rastignac with Magwitch's relationship to Pip.) It is true that by investing his criminal with the pathos of lost hopes, Dickens contrived to make him a sympathetic character. But, in doing so, he also punished him by giving him the capacity to punish himself. The power to suffer ; the weight of the irrevocable ; the understanding of the true nature of happiness achieved only when it is too late to attain happiness itself—these are terrible endowments. But they are, at least the endowments of a human being.

IV

LIVING TO EAT

It was an early grievance of the *London Journal* that

The Daily News *never publishes wants*
Of footmen, or nurses, or cooks,
Nor many announcements of ships or of sales,
But only the Whitefriars books.

In retort to such gibes, the Liberal Press affected to pretend that
the *Morning Post* was written by footmen for butlers to read. Jeames
was represented as the embodiment of snobbery. We have now
moved into a world in which domestic help is so rare that the
powdered coachmen, footmen and the small boy " tigers " who
move across the pages of Victorian books and newspapers seem
fabulous creatures. The species has become almost extinct.

There was plentiful cheap labour for the home as for the factory
in the 'forties. Although modest establishments were equipped with
three or four servants, and twenty was not unusual in a rich merchant's house, the supply of domestics was greater than the demand.
Life below stairs, despite fatiguing hours and poor wages, was often
preferable to life on the farms, or in the mines, mills and workshops.
In a good house it could be a well-lighted and well-fed existence,
if an airless one. Illiteracy prevented many a young man from
becoming Mr. Guppy, the clerk, and he became instead Jeames
Yellowplush, the footman, displaying his silk-stockinged calves
and aping the aristocratic disdain of his master. The large
establishments of servants in the barn-like mansions of the wealthy
middle-class enjoyed the warmth of a community life. There was
a well-defined hierarchy topped by butler and housekeeper ; it was
a world in itself, with all the pleasures of gossip, intrigue and
scandals about the illustrious ; and an identity with the interests
of the family. As Mr. Tulkinghorn observed, a strong interest in
the fashionable great was a virtue in which few Englishmen were
deficient.

In the novels of the period one comes across butlers as overwhelming as bishops—there is the fearsome " Analytical Chemist "
of a butler whom the Veneerings kept to petrify their guests,
housekeepers as haughty as duchesses, august coachmen, buc-
caneering footmen, flouncing ladies' maids, and saucy Buttonses.
Of the Chief Butler in Mr. Merdle's princely establishment in
Harley Street it was said that his severity with his employers and
their visitors was terrific, and he never permitted himself to be

THE REFORM CLUB BANQUET TO IBRAHIM PASHA
July 1846.

approached with the slightest liberty. " He was a hard man, and would never bate an ounce of plate or a bottle of wine. He would not allow a dinner to be given unless it was up to his mark. He set forth the table for his own dignity. If the guests chose to partake of what was served, he saw no objection ; but it was served for the maintenance of his rank. As he stood by the sideboard he seemed to announce, ' I have accepted office to look at this which is now before me, and to look at nothing less than this '."

There were complaints that male servants grew too fat from high feeding. *Punch* has a John Leech drawing of a cherub of a footman so plump that he is bursting his livery—plush and silk stretched and strained over his unrationed rotundities. He seems to be weeping slow tears of lard as he tells the coachman, " Here's the marchioness bin and giv me notice because I don't match Joseph, an' I must go, unless I can get my fat down in a week." This was at a time when the Irish correspondents of the *Daily News* were describing the cabins of the peasantry as filled with scarecrows of skin and bones.

Yet though the living may have been high, the accommodation below stairs was often as cramped as in the forecastle of a ship. In the wealthiest establishments magnificent butlers retired to truckle beds in dingy basements, and portly footmen were crammed away at night in cubby holes as though they were rag dolls. Even a Belgravia mansion found it hard to accommodate more than twenty-two servants in comfort.

It was not in these wealthy houses that the harshest side of domestic service was to be marked, though an existence divided between cavernous basements and windy attics with five flights of stairs intervening, such as you may see in Bayswater, is not alluring to modern eyes. The darkest tyranny was practised in those suburban homes where shabby gentility struggled to imitate affluence, and one—or perhaps two—maid-servants were kept moving like mice on a treadmill all day long, making fires, cooking meals, washing, scrubbing, conjuring with loaded trays or full scuttles up the un-ending stairs, answering the bells, tending the ever-multiplying babies. These, and their sisters employed in the boarding-houses that abounded in early Victorian London—(" Commercial Boarding House. M. Todgers ")—might well have been eyeless in Gaza at the mill with slaves for all the fun they had.

The dungeon in which that most renowned of all slaveys, the Marchioness, was condemned to live out her dreary days, stood for many such dungeons : " It was a very dark miserable place, very low and very damp : the walls disfigured by a thousand rents and blotches. The water was trickling out of a leaky butt, and a most wretched cat was licking up the drops with the sickly eagerness of starvation. The grate, which was a wide one, was wound and screwed up tight, so as to hold no more than a little thin sandwich of fire. Everything was locked up ; the coal-cellar, the candle-box, the salt-box, the meat-safe, were all padlocked. There was nothing that a beetle could have lunched upon."

In this sphere of life, as in most others in that bygone world, the descent down the income scale is abrupt. On the top there is a well-upholstered comfort ; at the bottom there is a raw lack of most things that makes existence endurable. It was certainly not an inhumane age. Thanks largely to the genius of Dickens, its sensibility to injustice and pain was far greater than that of the Georgians, but in this sensibility there were large, yawning gaps ; abysms almost. The unhappy *slaveys* or *skivvies* of early Victorian gentility were a standard joke, like mothers-in-law or seaside landladies. The comic papers, the stage and the novelist were to make sport of them for some decades to come. Perhaps if the fun had not been so riotous, the crisis of domestic help in the nineteen-forties might not have been so severe.

The Early Victorian middle-classes took a solemn joy in giving large dinner parties. It was their supreme social expression— the flourish of the peacock tail. For the Smiths it was the easiest way to catch up with the Vere de Veres. One of the most enchanting of all Thackeray's shorter stories, *A Little Dinner at Timmins*, anatomises this snobbery of food, drink, and tuft-hunting. There falls unexpectedly into the lap of a young barrister a handsome brief in the railway litigation then so lucrative to lawyers. Mrs. Timmins makes this an excuse for giving a great dinner party to which she invites all the dull eminences and illustrious gargoyles she can reach, the local M.P. and his wife, the fusty Earl and frowsy Countess, the stylish young man from the Foreign Office, who is invited because " he might give some news of the Spanish squabble." Relatives are snubbed. Old friends are cut. Mr. and Mrs. Timmins experience agonies in preparing for the dinner. Meanwhile the barrister hides from his wife the sad news that the railroad companies have settled out of Court, and so his fifteen guineas a day refresher has ended. To the miseries of social climbing and the tortures of the snob are added the physical terrors of squeezing too large a party into too small a house. The modest kitchen staff mutinies at the importation of a French chef, an over-bearing fellow, who puts in requisitions for endless saucepans and appliances. The chef is dismissed, and finally—a revealing social touch !—the whole meal is ordered from a caterer's. It was about this time that the aristocracy had discovered the virtues of the caterer, as opposed to the domestic kitchen, and many a noble banquet henceforth was brought discreetly home in plain vans. Mrs. Timmins achieved her dinner, but at what a cost. Timmins was ruined, and it would take years to repair the domestic havoc. " Why, in fact, did the Timminses give that party at all ? " asked Thackeray. It was a question that might have been asked a hundred times every night in London.

In describing the arrival of the guests, Thackeray notes " a little crowd of blackguard boys and children who were formed round the door and gave ironical cheers to the folks as they stepped out of their vehicles." At every evening party in those days a chorus of ragamuffins gathered outside the house to hoot and jeer, to mock the arrogant and to ape the waddle of the portly. These Street Arabs assembled like a flock of starlings wherever there was company, chaffering and cheeping—then flew off again down the street to the next door where the flys and broughams were stopping. Their impudence was boundless, and they had no respect for ribbons and stars. The guttersnipe was as familiar a character in the pageant of Victorian London as the cabman. It was without doubt a healthy experience for the mandarins, for the Earl and Countess of Bungay and Mr. Topham Sawyer, M.P., to be subjected to this stream of free and uninhibited criticism when poised on the doorstep for their important entry. It reminded them that they were only mortal, and that there was a point of view—an upshot glance from the gutter—from which their solemnity and pomp looked exquisitely absurd.

From *A Little Dinner at Timmins* to Anstey's *The Man from Blankley's* at the end of the Victorian age, this theme of the heavily ceremonial dinner party runs through the annals of the middle-classes. The dinners of 1846 called for stronger stomachs than we in 1946, conditioned by rationing, could conceivably furnish. In February of this year one of the great classics of cookery was published, Francatelli's *Modern Cook*. Charles Francatelli had been chief cook and maitre d'hotel to the Queen. He dedicated his masterpiece to the Earl of Errol, Chamberlain of the Household, in the manner of a poet laying his sonnets at the feet of his noble patron. This inscription has a double interest—it reveals two characteristics of the age—its reverence for an earl and its solemnity over food. Francatelli wrote :

"My Lord,
    " The honour conferred on me in being permitted to dedicate the following pages to your Lordship presents an opportunity, of which I gladly avail myself, to express publicly my grateful

acknowledgments for the liberal encouragements and uniform kindness I have ever experienced, since I had the good fortune to come under your Lordship's notice."

Francatelli's book, which was a best-seller for many years, is filled with such feasts as stun the brain while they make the mouth water.   What pageants of food move across these tables !   What glittering processions shine like mirages above our post-war rations. Joys unattainable to us today are but the outriders of these majestic cavalcades that moved across our ancestors' sideboards.   One plunges into this testament of gormandising and picks by chance a menu appropriate to a simple and quiet domestic dinner party for twenty guests in the month of February.   Here it is, a strange relic disinterred from the sands of a lost civilisation :—

FIRST COURSE.

Purée of pheasant.   (2 Soups)   Brunoise soup.
(2 Fishes)
Crimped soles, Dutch sauce.   Fillets of turbot, à la Parisiénne.
(2 Removes)
Turkey à la Périgueux.   Braized roll of beef, à la D'Orléans.

Marrow Patties.

---

8 Entrèes :
Potato border, garnished with scallops of Larks.
Fillets of fowls à l'ècarlate, with Supreme sauce.
Turban of ox-palates, au gratin.   Fillets of widgeons, à la Gasçonne.
Sweetbreads larded, à la Monarquée.
Calf's ears, à la Tortue.
Mutton cutlets, à la Duchesses.
Quenelles of partridge, à l'Allemande.

SECOND COURSE.

Hares.   (2 Roasts)   Black game.
Small fondus in cases.   (2 Removes)   Polish Baba
Sultana of spun sugar. (2 Flanks) Meringue, à la Parisiénne.

---

8 Entremets :
Truffles, à la Piémontaise.   Variegated jelly, à la Victoria.
Crayfish, à la Poulette.   Bavarian coffee cream.
Seakale with white sauce.   Apricot nougats.
Brussels sprouts with Maitre d'hotel sauce.   Mirlitons.

Let us turn from this middle-class fare to a dinner given by the Queen in the month of August, the French being anglicised—

HER MAJESTY'S DINNER
(Under the control of C. Francatelli)

Soups
Clear soup with Quenels. Cream of Ptarmigan.
Cream of Lettuce.

Fish
Braised stuffed Pike. Eels and tartar sauce.
Turbot and lobster sauce.

Seasoned dishes
Roast best end of Venison. Pigeon pie.

Entrees
Roast Spring Chicken with cauliflower.
Stuffed Breast of Lamb. Stewed Chicken, with cucumbers.
Sausages of Chicken. Braised breast of Veal.
Oyster pies.

Roast
Leverets. Turkeys.
Wheatears.

Spicy Dishes (Appetisers)
Waffles. Lemon pudding.

Cold Dishes
Slice of salmon and mayonnaise sauce. Russian salad.
Macaroni au gratin. Poached eggs in jelly.
Globe artichokes. French bean salad.
Cinnamon blancmange. Puffed pastry with apple.
Fruit flan. Almond biscuits. Peaches and rice.

Sideboard
Roast beef. Roast mutton.
Hashed venison.
Clear soup and rice. Chicken soup.
Greengage tart.

Francatelli's epitaph should be Vanbrugh's :

> " *Lie heavy on him earth for he*
> *Laid many a heavy load on thee !* "

As for wines, the finest champagne is advertised in our paper this year at sixty shillings a dozen.

The mystery remains—how did they manage such meals ? Perhaps it was a Darwinian test, with only the fittest surviving to become the fattest. It is not astonishing that a world which dined so well was a world of early ripeness and plethoric middle age. Yet in that same world of inescapable portliness the cherished ideal was the fragile nymph with the hour-glass figure.

Later in the century, meals became less overwhelming. The Edwardians, in their turn, tended to grossness ; but in the past thirty years the British people have grown ever more abstemious. Taste, custom and fashion provided a training for those austerities of diet that were to be enforced by the war. The Victorians would have been as shocked as the Tudors by the limitations of a 1946 ration book.

For those Babylonian meals the setting and appurtenances were appropriately ornate. The arts of the silversmith and goldsmith were lavished on the construction of épergnes that looked like the Taj Mahal ; on fruit dishes and soup tureens rich with arabesques.

The Great Exhibition, however high its ethical purposes, had a lowering effect on public taste. It cast the Evil Eye upon Victorian artistry. The youthful William Morris staggered back in horror at the aesthetic standards which he found inside the Crystal Palace. Dickens wrote of it as " terrible duffery."

Decoration and design during this period are, for the most part, wounding to modern eyes. As prosperity increased, taste degenerated. There was too much of everything in the Victorian domestic interiors. Too much carved mahogany and ormolu ; too much red, green, yellow and purple plush, and too much patterned velvet ; too much piling on of gilt ; too many laced antimacassars, ribbons and bows. The colours of fabrics clashed like cymbals, for dyes were harsh ; and ornamentation trailed writhing, curling, twisting serpent-like over everything. The eyes ache in trying to take in those crowded, over-stuffed rooms with heavy grotesqueries of furniture that are too coarse to possess the charm of the bizarre ; the endless bijouterie and bric-à-brac, the loaded whatnots, the mirrors framed in plush and then limned over with birds and flowers, the overmantels encrusted with sea-shells ; the pom-poms, tassels and fringes, the wealth of mother-of-pearl, the jars of pot-pourri, the vases filled with bulrushes and peacocks' feathers, the bulbous glass cases enshrining flowers made of wax, or made of dyed feathers or fish-bones. Seldom was so much ingenuity so widely misplaced. One recoils before such an apparation as a marble nymph with a gilt clock-face stuck in her stomach !

V

WHAT WENT WRONG?

Acres of canvas were covered by the Royal Academicians of the Victorian age. When they come into the sales rooms nowadays, these once-admired pictures that brought high prices in the 'seventies and 'eighties, are sold for contemptuous sums. Never has a whole period of art been consigned so ruthlessly to the dustcart by the inheritors.

In 1846 Ruskin, writing on the subject of the exhibition of cartoons to decorate the new Houses of Parliament, declared, " Whatever is to be truly great and affecting must have on it the strong stamp of the native land. Not a law this, but a necessity, from the intense hold on their country of the affections of all truly great men. All classicality, all middle-aged patent reviving, is utterly vain and absurd ; if we are now to do anything great, good, awful, religious, it must be got out of our little island, and out of these very times, railroads and all ; if a British painter, I say this in serious earnestness, cannot make historical characters out of the British House of Peers, he cannot paint history ; and if he cannot make a Madonna of a British girl of the nineteenth century, he cannot paint at all " (*Modern Painters*, Volume 2).

It was in 1846 that John Everett Millais exhibited for the first time at the Royal Academy. He was then a youth of seventeen. His picture, " Pizarro seizing the Inca of Peru," had little to distinguish it, except a double measure of competence, from the trite conventionalities of the canvases that cumbered the walls of the exhibition. English painting at that period was as uninspired as the English theatre. It bore the same relation to Art as the plays of Sheridan Knowles to poetry. The output of canvases on historical subjects, with a continuity of stilted figures gesticulating amid velvet hangings was staggering. The young Millais was born with as fine a talent as any artist of his time, and the principle of life was too strong in him to accept the deadness of reiterated platitudes in paint. At the age of nineteen Millais rebelled. With his friend Holman Hunt, he resolved to break away from the pictorial conventions of the day and create a style of his own. The Pre-Raphaelite movement was born. This brotherhood was concerned with but " one idea, to present on canvas what they saw in nature."

It is remarkable that the average Englishman, no matter what his standards in art, is liable to grow more angry and abusive over painting than over any other subject except morals. It is curious that a people who are not greatly interested in aesthetic problems should wax so hot over issues that they regard as essentially trivial, while they preserve such admirable composure in discussing the future of the Empire, or the adverse balance of trade, or the relation of man to the State. Millais' change of style was received with as much violence of protest as Picasso was to provoke a century afterwards. (It was not overlooked that it was Holman Hunt's daughter who made public protest against Picasso in 1946.) Millais' turning aside from the theatrical scene-painting tradition of his time to present characters with expressions and attitudes studied from life was denounced as a blasphemy. The art critics of the day darted such epithets as " loathsome " and " revolting " at Millais for daring to paint flowers, leaves and grass with a minute and loving particularity. It is odd that a change in the manner of seeing a tree or a brick wall should excite such a moral rage, and be condemned in terms usually reserved by judges for their more sordid cases. Even Charles Dickens, of all men, was shocked by Millais, though he sensibly reversed his judgment not long after. The artist's worst offence was that he painted the boy Christ in the carpenter's shop as an appealingly human figure who had run a nail into his hand.

The pre-Raphaelites were at least fortified by the passionate eloquence of Ruskin (he who in later years was to accuse Whistler of flinging a pot of paint in the face of the public). Their protest against the flat and spiritless art of the times attracted the sympathies of men and women of imagination. But the promise of the rebellion was never fulfilled. When its victory seemed assured, Millais compromised with the forces of convention. He never painted the Madonna of the nineteenth century, although Ruskin discerned in him the talent to do so. The anger with which he turned on Millais was the measure of Ruskin's disappointment. Millais became the most fashionable painter of his age. The youth of infinite promise who had exhibited in the Academy of 1846 died just fifty years after, President of the Royal Academy. He had made a handsome fortune ; and the conventional critics of the 'nineties invoked his name to damn a new generation of rebels. If Millais had died in his early twenties, he would have become a force as well as a legend. The shipwreck of his considerable talent might stand for many such losses in that age.

But is it true to think of Millais as a Bosinney who made an unconditional surrender to the Forsytes ? It is probably fairer to say that, like many other artists and writers of his time, he discovered the Forsyte in himself. It would look at first glance like the complete conquest of commercialism, the triumph of a business man's civilisation. The artist in that age, unless he was such an uncommonly original character as juts up like a rock above the waves, was inevitably submerged by the dominant philosophy of material progress. A popular painter such as Leighton, for instance, enjoyed the same kind of worldly success as an eminent banker or politician. Leighton was as notable a figure in society as Lord Dufferin ; hostesses pursued him ; in that great age of dinner parties, he cultivated conversation as one of the fine arts ; he was expected to produce polished speeches to order ; his gifts as a linguist and natural diplomatist were much drawn upon ; and he knew that by the easy exercise of his brush he could make as elegant an income as a stock-broker. Leighton's peerage was inevitable. He would probably have made an admirable Cabinet Minister. One half expects to find in the Government lists of the 'nineties—" Chancellor of the Duchy of Lancaster . . . The Rt. Hon. Lord Leighton." With all this, it is not surprising that the lonely flame of inspiration was smothered by velvet and ermine. To be just, however, there was something more than the attraction of either the Gilded Calf or the fatted calf to bring about the capitulation of such a man as Leighton or a man of much greater potentialities, Millais. There was the assurance of a stable and settled order that is always inviting to a man who longs for success and a good life. There was a strong high wall built round the garden to keep out rough winds and thieves. Never was there any hint of disintegration ; of a society that was growing over-ripe. On the contrary, nearly everybody was optimistic. The orthodox had good digestions, and even the sceptics were cheerful. It needed a genius of the depth and integrity of Thomas Hardy to stand out against the persuasions of the age that all was right with the world. It is easier to resist tyranny than the pressure of a comfortable society that believes in itself and is eager to share its pleasures with you.

In the year of Millais' death and Leighton's death, there died also William Morris (1834-96). It is interesting to see how this remarkable man had sought in his turn to resolve the dilemma of the artist in the Victorian age. Morris (son of a partner in a firm of City bill brokers from whom he inherited a considerable fortune) was a man of prodigal genius—he had resources of intellectual and spiritual energy so vast that he could have been cut up to make a score of famous late Victorians. He was a talented painter whose

E

few paintings still give pleasure. He was a poet who, in *The Defence of Guenevere*, wrote some of the finest lyrics of the century. He was a prose-writer of distinction, and for a good part of his life he ran a successful business. He was a teacher—and he was a politician. Above all, he exerted an unrivalled influence over taste in church decoration, house decoration, painted glass, the weaving of carpets and tapestry, wall-paper designs, furniture and the art of dyeing ; while he crowned his career with the setting up of the Kelmscott Press, his last gift to his age being the noble Kelmscott Chaucer. No man was ever more traduced by his own pen than Morris when he described himself as the idle singer of an empty day. He was a movement rather than a man. His fertility of invention was unending. And never did he seek a lodging in an ivory tower. From his youth up he believed that art could not be divorced from life. He grew increasingly to perceive that it was entwined with economics, politics and the issues of good and evil. Until he was close on fifty, Morris was an active Liberal ; indeed, he held office as treasurer of the National Liberal League ; and he entered with a Gladstonian passion into the Eastern Question. But discontent at the slow advance of Victorian Liberalism towards social reform, and anger over coercion in Ireland, turned him into a Socialist. Morris reached the conclusion that art could not flourish in a world of grime and injustice. His belief that humanity had taken the wrong turning after the Middle Ages was intensified by what he saw in the slums of London and Manchester. For him, the Industrial Revolution was the parent of moral and physical squalor. So he declared his own personal war upon it. In 1883 Morris joined the Social Democratic Federation, and when the split came between the gradualists and the men who wanted " socialism in our time " he became the chosen head of the Socialist League formed by the seceders. He threw all his abundant energies and considerable means into the cause, writing his stirring *Chants for Socialists* for his working-men friends to sing ; editing the *Commonweal*, turning out pamphlets and speaking with fervour at street corners in most of the big cities. There is little doubt that at this time Morris believed the revolution to be imminent, that the golden age of the working man and the artist could be achieved by one final tug, as though, somehow, it were like pulling the levers of the transformation scene at Drury Lane. Disillusion came with events. The General Election of 1886 showed that England was so far from being ripe for a Shelleyan revolution that it rejected the cautious Liberalism of Gladstone and plumped for an order of Conservatism that was more conservative than Disraeli's, the Conservatism of Lord Salisbury. The Trafalgar Square riots of 1887 may have represented a magnificent protest, but they were not the barricades. It was the Chartists on Kennington Common all over again. As the vision of revolutionary change in Queen Victoria's time receded, Morris did the only thing that was in his nature to do. It was not in him to conform ; it was not in him to escape into cynicism ; it was not in him to fall into a dejected silence. He went back to writing ; he wrote with a kind of fierce copiousness. And he wrote as two men. One of those men was the chronicler of an infinitely far-off and legendary past, peopled by heroes and demi-gods. It was this poet who produced such romances as *The Wood beyond the World* and the sagas of the North. The second man in Morris fixed his dreams upon a fabulous future ; he saw a country beyond the blue distances of the farthest hills where men were kind and noble and disinterested ; and out of those imaginings came *News from Nowhere.* Half of Morris retreated into the past and the other half leapt forward out of sight. What Swinburne said of him may be true, that he drew his knowledge of life from books. (That, incidentally, is a fine example of a pot calling the kettle black, for Swinburne was the most bookish of all England's first-rank poets.) But Morris did save himself, and he showed a way of salvation to his age by his sense of absolute values. Through his work, and through his life, until the day of his death he affirmed that the word of beauty has the sanction of eternity, that to destroy beauty is that sin which is not to be forgiven. He was not a good politician, for a good politician, even when he is the best kind of idealist, will make allowances for men's weaknesses. But Morris was a good poet and a good artist, and he saw life as a pure flame. One such man would be sufficient to save a city from destruction.

VI

THE MARCH OF THE GIANTS

But if painting, like music and the theatre, seemed caught in a hopeless dilemma, the writers were gloriously free. That was a golden age of English literature. In the twenty years from 1846 to 1866 the ardent reader had to get up early in the morning to find what new and exciting thing had appeared. There is no better evidence of the vitality of this age than its books. Tennyson's first long poem *The Princess* came in 1847 ; *In Memoriam* in 1850 ; and *Maud* (bitterly criticised in its day, but put by modern critics in the first rank of Tennyson's achievements) came out in 1855. Browning was represented in 1846 by *A Soul's Tragedy.* His *Christmas Eve and Easter Day* came in 1850 ; *Men and Women* in 1855 and

Dramatis Personae in 1864. Arnold's first volume of poetry, *The Strayed Reveller and other Poems*, was published in 1849. From then on until the twenty years ended in a thunder clap with Swinburne's *Atalanta in Calydon* and the first volume of *Poems and Ballads*, English poetry disclosed one exciting new talent after another. 1858 brought William Morris' *The Defence of Guenevere* and 1862 Christina Rossetti's *Goblin Market*.

Proud, too, was the estate of the English novel in those years when Thackeray was at his peak and Dickens in his great middle period, when the Brontës and George Eliot were new discoveries. George Borrow's *Lavengro* appeared in 1851 and *The Romany Rye* in 1857. In 1859 the public was presented with Meredith's *The Ordeal of Richard Feverel*, while *Evan Harrington* followed the next year. Anthony Trollope published his first novel in 1847 and *The Warden*, the first of the Barsetshire saga, appeared in 1855. Mrs. Gaskell's *Cranford* ran as a serial in Dickens' *Household Words* from 1851 to 1853, and in that latter year appeared Charles Reade's *It is Never Too Late to Mend*. 1861 was the year of both *Silas Marner* and *The Cloister and the Hearth*. Charles Kingsley's *Westward Ho!* was brought out in 1855 ; and the first, and still among the best, novels of criminal detection, Wilkie Collins' *The Woman in White* imported a new shudder to 1860. So one can stretch out the catalogue almost endlessly.

The first and second volumes of Macaulay's *History of England* were published in 1848 (the year of Mill's *Principles of Political Economy*) and the third and fourth volumes in 1855. That was a mind and a style to sweep readers off their feet. The new books of 1859 included (as well as *Richard Feverel*) *Adam Bede*, Mill *On Liberty*, *A Tale of Two Cities* and *The Origin of Species*. It was a dazzling if disconnected group—so dazzling that one small book put out in 1859, a year of European crisis, passed almost entirely without notice. This was Edward Fitzgerald's version of the *Rubaiyat of Omar Khayyám*, published anonymously. Its remainder copies soon found their way into the twopenny box. That was the lame start in life of the book which became so popular later in the century that its fame almost merits a chapter on its own. The combination of seductive music and fashionable fatalism made Fitzgerald's *Omar* in the end an even better seller than Tupper's *Proverbial Philosophy* has been. In the 1910-14 period—and later—the bookseller's and stationer's shops were filled with gift copies of *Omar* of all sizes— *Omar* tear-off calendars abounded—and there was a swarm of burlesques, the Golfer's *Omar*, the Motorist's *Omar*, the Fisherman's *Omar*. Fitzgerald, the supercilious and shrinking artist, ran neck to neck with Ella Wheeler Wilcox and Laurence Hope, the lady who

wrote the *Indian Love Lyrics*. It was almost as though Robert
Browning's curse on Fitzgerald for his brutal jibe at Mrs. Browning's
death (" spitting with lips once sanctified by hers ") had pursued
him after his death.

There is a piquancy in some of the conjunctions of these twenty
years. In 1866, for example, the constant reader found both *The
Dream of Gerontius* and C. S. Calverley's *Fly Leaves* on his table.

The immense labours of Carlyle's *Frederick the Great*, which appear
to us now in our revulsion from German heroes the most wasted
of labours, were unfolded between 1858 and 1865. Ruskin, speculating on the true nature of wealth, was causing considerable
indignation at this time to the well-to-do. The serial publication
of *Munera Pulveris* in *Fraser's Magazine* in 1863 was suspended by
the outcry of the readers. It was a dangerous thing in the 'sixties
to rate the value of a flower higher than that of a railway share.
Newman's *Apologia* came in 1864.

Those were exciting years for the growing up of a young reader.
The mighty ones themselves were young in those days. Great
figures that now seem to have turned into stone gods were then
hot-blooded, striving and uncertain. The masters were then the
rebels. They were maligned, misunderstood, gossiped about,
scandalised, and each of them at one time or another got a bad
Press. It is a good exercise for the imagination to recall that there
was once a day when " Now sleeps the crimson petal, now the
white " was read for the first time ; and when " Where the quiet-
coloured end of evening smiles " was new. And so once was,
" Lovely are the curves of the white owl sweeping. . . ." There
was a day when people did not know what would happen in the
next chapter of *The Newcomes* or *Little Dorrit*. One's respect increases
for the generation which could provide a sympathetic audience
and ultimate fame for so many new talents ; so diverse in their
qualities ; several of them not being easy to grasp at first acquain-
tance. The literature of that age is a house of many mansions.
The splendour has lost its freshness nowadays. But what must it
have been like to discover its various designs and colours for the
first time ? What a great age—one says—to produce and encourage
such talent. But then one recalls, from the records of the time, that
the taste of our great-grandfathers was not always impeccable. The
second-rate was often preferred to the first-rate. The ineffable
Martin Tupper was for years a far more popular poet than Tennyson. His *Proverbial Philosophy* ran into scores of editions. As late as
1869 Browning was writing at the beginning of *The Ring and the
Book*, " Well, British Public, ye who like me not," and at the end
of it, "So, British Public, who may like me yet (Marry and amen !)."

One recalls, too, the deep emotions of Christina Rossetti on learning that Jean Ingelow—she who wrote *The High Tide on the Coast of Lincolnshire 1571*—had achieved eighteen editions ! There was always a Harrison Ainsworth to rival Dickens, and always a G. P. R. Reynolds to be more successful than Thackeray.

But the influence of noble talents is indirect as well as direct. The civilising force of a literature spreads through society by a hundred obscure channels. We have no means of computing, we can only guess how the attitude to life of the modern Englishman has been affected through that widening of sensibility and enriching of the imagination which we owe to the great Victorian writers.

CHAPTER VIII

THE CENTURY AMUSES ITSELF

I

ART AND TOM THUMB

A LONG account appears in the *Daily News* in June 1846, of an inquest on a celebrated character of that age, Benjamin Robert Haydon, the painter. Haydon was found lying in a pool of blood in front of the last picture on which he had been working— " a colossal painting of Alfred the Great and the first British Jury." He had shot himself and slashed his throat. This was the sorry end of great pride, fine ideals, many tantrums, a noble character, and a mistaken vocation. Haydon had more than once seen Shelley plain ; he knew what porridge John Keats ate, and had borrowed cash from him ; some fragments of Haydon's character had gone into the drawing of Harold Skimpole. Peel, in the middle of the Corn Law debate, had hurried money to relieve the immediate necessities of Haydon's last days. To generous minds among his contemporaries he was always " Poor Haydon," the artist whose reach exceeded his grasp. He sought to elevate his countrymen through the contemplation of the heroic and the august. The public displayed a diminishing willingness to be elevated. Even the noblest patrons did not possess wall spaces wide enough to hang his prodigious canvases. " Christ entering Jerusalem," " The Banishment of Aristides," " The Judgment of Solomon," " Pharaoh dismissing Moses at the Dead of Night after the Passover " were characteristic Haydon subjects. For years he had exhibited these painted acres to the public : in the 'twenties, thousands had come to marvel ; in the 'forties there were few. Taste had changed. Dickens, writing from Lausanne, thought " the account of the inquest one of the most affecting pieces of fact I have ever heard," but reflected that poor Haydon could not help being a very bad painter, and that his picture of Nero fiddling while Rome burned (shown in his last exhibition) was truly marvellous in its badness.

Modern critics also take a low view of Haydon's paintings, but (they say), how he could write ! The cognoscenti like to quote his sumptuous description of the coronation of George the Fourth, more picturesque than any of his pictures . . ." Something rustles, and a being buried in satin, feathers and diamonds rolls gracefully into his seat. The room rises with a sort of feathered, silken thunder."

Haydon was cut to the quick this year by the refusal of the Royal Commission to place one of his gigantic paintings in the new House of Commons. But the final mortification which brought him to suicide was the spectacle of the crowd surging past the door of his gallery in the Egyptian Hall, Piccadilly to another room to see General Tom Thumb, the American dwarf. This entry from Haydon's diary, read at the inquest, shows how bitter was that draught : " Receipts £1.3.6d. An advertisement of a finer description could not have been written to catch the public ; but not a shilling more was added to the receipts. They rush by thousands to see Tom Thumb. They push—they fight—they scream—they faint—they cry, ' Help ' and ' Murder.' They see my bills and caravans but do not read them ; their eyes are on them, but their sense is gone. It is an insanity—a *rabies furor*— a dream—of which I could not have believed Englishmen could be guilty." In one week 133 persons saw Haydon's pictures, while 12,000 attended Tom Thumb's levée.

That rushing of the thousands to see Tom Thumb reminds us how limited were the amusements of the public a century ago. London fought to see the dwarf at the Egyptian Hall during the day (the entrance charge being one shilling) and went wild with delight at his appearance at the Lyceum Theatre at night. A burlesque on the fairy tale theme of " Hop o' my Thumb " was written to display his nimble tinyness. His outwitting of the ogre was accomplished amid gales of enthusiasm. The *Annual Register* for 1846 records—" The knowing look, the readiness of manner, the air with which he entered upon a stratagem, and the quick movement of his little legs when he ran across the stage after the accomplishment of his plan, produced an effect altogether uncommon and irresistibly ludicrous. The little actor was highly applauded, and at the conclusion was nearly smothered in bouquets showered down upon him from fair hands, who had no recognition for poor Haydon." To the last, poor Haydon !

The public of the 'forties was enchanted by contrasts in size. In turning over the pages of the *Daily News* for June 1846, one discovers a profound sensation advertised in these terms :—

WONDERS !   WONDERS !   WONDERS !
NOW EXHIBITING, EGYPTIAN HALL, PICCADILLY.
GIANT   OX   AND   DWARF   COW
WELLINGTON, the great Devon Ox, weighing 1,200 lbs.
more than the Mammoth Horse.
AND Tom Thumb's Fairy Cow.

The theatre was at a low ebb. Dickens in his notice of Macready in the role of Benedick reflects scornfully on the " nobility and gentry . . . who seldom enter a theatre unless it be a foreign one ; or who, when they repair to an English temple of drama, would seem to be attracted thither solely by an amiable desire to purify by their presence a scene of vice and indecorum." In the Puritan revival of the 'forties, the prejudice against the playhouse was powerful. The middle-classes did not like " the strong smell of orange peel and lamp-oil, with an undercurrent of sawdust."

Until 1843, two theatres—Covent Garden and Drury Lane— enjoyed the monopoly of the legitimate drama. This right, granted under Royal Patent, created an indefensible form of privilege. It was circumvented as the prohibitive postal rates had been circumvented. The monopoly power did not extend to representations with music ; so a manager could defy the patent-holders by strumming a few notes of music at the opening of each act of *Hamlet*. Or what did it matter that *Othello* technically became an operetta or burletta if the glorious poetry was set free from officialdom's fetters ?

When Vincent Crummles sought a new vehicle for his company, he drew a French play from his drawer, and besought young Nickleby to make an adaptation, with parts and scenes grafted upon it to display the peculiar talents of his players—a dance being provided, of course, for the Infant Phenomenon, that little girl in the dirty white frock who had been " kept up late every night and put upon an unlimited allowance of gin and water to prevent her growing tall." There were managers more illustrious than Mr. Crummles who renewed the drama by similar cheap blood transfusions. Mediocrity stole, too, from talent nearer at home. During those early weeks of 1846 no fewer than four adaptations of Dickens' *The Cricket on the Hearth* were being staged simultaneously. The theatrical advertisements in the newspaper made sour reading for the editor ; the state of copyright was such at this time that Dickens drew not a penny in royalties from these performances. These pirates, in looting the treasures of his genius, defaced and dislustred them ; the adaptations were usually mean travesties, in which his humour became burlesque, and his narrative power reduced to terms of the *Police Gazette*.

Macready was leader of the theatrical profession at this time, an actor of high and cultivated intellect—brains supplying the lack of those assets of voice and presence which nature had denied him— an actor lacking the earlier incandescence of Edmund Kean or the later magic of Irving, but with an instinct for the thing finely done. Dickens honoured him. Browning wrote for him. When John

Forster was editor of the *Daily News*, he attended Macready's first nights and wrote the notices, considering these occasions as important as a big Parliamentary debate. Among Macready's leading ladies was Helen Faucit, who had a capacity for expressing a stilled beauty, and had the wit to know her own limitations. But Macready's attempts to persuade the public to accept intelligence on the boards were so many candles blown out by the great gusty monster, Vincent Crummles. He was an actor born out of his rightful age ; his setting often possessed a ghastly inappropriateness ; and of all the things that shouldn't have happened to him the worst came on his farewell visit to New York in 1849. On his appearance at the Astor Opera House, a riot provoked by the intrigues of his rival Forrest ended in 22 persons being shot dead by the soldiers who were called out to subdue the disturbance.

Through the twilight period of the British stage, certain other lights were constant. A name that means a great deal to the intelligent youth of 1946 meant a great deal to the intelligent youth of 1846 —Sadler's Wells. It was in 1844 that Samuel Phelps, who had been a member of Macready's company, began his eighteen years' sojourn at the Wells. During that period, with Mrs. Warner as his leading lady, Phelps produced thirty-one of Shakespeare's plays, purifying them from the accretions of those eighteenth-century improvers who thought they knew Shakespeare's business better than he did. Phelps was a dedicated spirit—his call was to preach the gospel according to William Shakespeare. His chief concern was that the words of the Master should be heard and remembered, and so he put audibility first among the theatrical virtues. His prime command to his company was—" Be heard. Be understood in the back row of the gallery." If one is to believe the critics, audibility is not first among the virtues of the modern stage. Phelps, the single-minded priest, in his modest temple at Islington, formed the taste of innumerable members of the Victorian middle and working classes, and preserved the steady brightness of the true tradition in a period when Sheridan Knowles was accounted a great dramatic poet.

Charles Kean's management of the Princess's Theatre, which began in 1850, represented another influence towards the refining of theatrical values. An Infant Phenomenon of a very different order from Miss Crummles made her first appearance at Kean's Theatre on 28 April 1856 : eight-year-old Ellen Terry played the boy Mamilius in *A Winter's Tale*. Nor is it inappropriate to recall that in the July of this year George Bernard Shaw was born in Dublin.

During the 'forties the London theatre saw the classic grandeur

of Rachel; in the 'fifties came Ristori, with her command of
passion and compassion; in the 'sixties the tea-cup comedies of
Tom Robertson brought a fresh note of naturalness into the fustian
and paper flowers of the Crummles Theatre. It was a promise of
spring, but it was to turn out to be a cold and tardy spring. For
years, French adaptations, juicy melodrama and spring-heeled
farces, crackling with excruciating puns, were to hold the stage.

Was there ever a more delightful absurdity than the old melodrama: its villains skulking in the likeness of the night, shiny
with hair-oil, biting their words like mongrels worrying a bone,
or laughing like fiends; its angelic leading ladies; its high-minded,
if wooden, young men; its aged parents, who always looked as
old as Methuselah; its precocious babes who were all infant
phenomenons? It was as highly moral an art form as the
tract. Its cardinal principle was that in Act Five Virtue should
always rise Triumphant and Vice Grovel in the Dust. No melodrama was ever written in which Wickedness stood erect as the last
curtain fell. That would have been as improbable as a sermon by
the Dean of St. Paul's in favour of Sin. The audiences could
watch the agitations of Innocence with composure, well knowing
that the mortgage on the old homestead would not be foreclosed;
and they could hiss the villain untroubled by any metaphysical
doubts as to society's responsibility for his being a villain. Black
was pitch, and white was a radiance, and there was no trifling
with the neutrality of grey.

There was a sense in which these old melodramas were a debased
order of Miracle Play. They were always on the side of the angels,
exuberantly and lushly so. They made Virtue, positively exciting,
tear-drawing and cheer-provoking; a trick which has since been
lost by more subtle forms of art. These folk dramas had an influence
on conduct and on political behaviour. Palmerston, for example,
could often translate foreign politics into terms of the Surrey-side
melodrama such as the simplest voter could comprehend. Audiences
who had seen the hero saved in the very second of his direst peril
by Badger of the Blues, sir, unfurling the Union Jack, and making a
resounding patriotic speech—the curtain falling on everybody
singing *God Save the Queen*—could quite understand what Palmerston
was up to when he sent the Fleet to Athens. It would be rather
more difficult for Mr. Ernest Bevin to get the same uncomplicated
response from audiences that had sat through an Ibsen or Tchekov
festival.

The melodrama was still flourishing in the London suburbs
thirty-five years ago, and survived in the provinces to a much later
date. The last of the great school of melodramatists whom this

writer remembers was George R. Sims, equally renowned for *The Lights o' London*, the Mustard and Cress column of witticisms in the *Referee*, and his testimonial to a hair-restorer. (Bret Harte's first stories were read with admiration by Charles Dickens in his last days. But when Harte first came to England the celebrity he most wished to meet was Sims.) Sims was moved by a social purpose in his melodramas. Like writers of greater distinction, he longed to redeem the squalor of London, and in 1920, at his journey's end. he wrote a series of articles for the *Daily News* to show how remarkable had been the improvements in the condition of the people in his working life. He had the social optimism of the Victorians, believing Progress to be irresistible. This recorder remembers Sims saying in his hoarse, genial voice, that seemed to distil seventy years of Cockney wisdom, " My boy, there are two professions left which suffer from the curse of casual labour, the noble profession of the docker and the equally noble profession of the writer." It was not until the last war that the curse of casualism was lifted from the dock labourer. The writer must still endure it.

If he moves forward half a century from 1846, the traveller is slightly stunned by the tropical profusion of talent in the theatre. The Lyceum had come to mean not that famous American warrior, General Tom Thumb and his twinkling legs, but Irving and Ellen Terry—she whose smile irradiates the recollection of all who ever caught a glimpse of her. About Irving, there was much dispute. To many he was the saviour of the stage ; he had purified and exalted it : he made it one with the high arts of poetry and religion. Mr. Shaw contrived with diabolical skill to present him as a more magnificent Vincent Crummles, a reactionary and slightly preposterous character, the enemy of the new ideas. There were others on whom, for different reasons, Irving's wizardry did not work. This writer recalls his father saying, " Irving! A stilted and pompous actor, with a voice like a peacock, who sawed the air with his arms. Irving ! Oh, very artificial." One suspects that Ellen Terry's charm was so attaching—in so great part seeming to be transformed always into a personal relationship—that even if it had been Garrick or Kean that were her stage partner he would not have been good enough for her in her idolaters' eyes. To one born too late to take a part in those party politics of the late Victorian stage all that remains is the memory of Ellen Terry in her last years ; of watching her give readings of her old Shakespearean parts. Her memory had always been treacherous. Now her sight was impaired, and she was fortified by horn-rimmed spectacles, and by a script written in enormous characters, the volume being as large as a conductor's score of *Siegfried*. But sure and safe above the batterings of Time glowed the essential quality, as though in her old age she were still Shelley's high-born maiden in a palace tower soothing her love-laden soul in secret hour " with music sweet as love that overflows her bower." It was quite obvious then how right Millais had been to paint her as a Lady Macbeth who looked very like the Ophelia he had painted in his youth. If there was anything in the Victorian fancy that great pictures acquired a certain glory from the genera-tions who had worshipped them, then it seemed even more probable that one was seeing reflected back from her the radiance of a jealous homage. Her look conveyed a dependence upon affection that was spirited and gay—never languishing ; an assurance that affection would always be forthcoming ; that, in this regard at least, life would not let her down. ·

The dispute over the merits of acting in one generation or another can never be settled, but in seeing Ellen Terry for the last time—with Charles Wyndham's profile bent towards her from an upper box, a head of rarified refinement stamped on a silver coin—one could at least understand that in the days before the cinema and radio there must have been an intense concentration on artistic pleasures. Those pleasures were not diffused, they were a crystal-lising of experience ; and people found them as dear and intimate as those snatches of poetry, learned in boyhood, which a man keeps to himself to the end of his days. A younger generation might come to snigger at the appearance of Sarah Bernhardt as Marguerite Gauthier on the screen and ask, " What did *they* ever see in her ? " The magic was not communicable through a new medium. It was not to be spread as thin as that. It depended on an immediate relationship between the artist and the audience, and upon a multitude of stored memories, past recognitions, overtones and associations. Nor is the peculiar value of this order of artistic experience, in which the Victorian age was rich, to be explained by any economic or social theory. It was something shared by well-to-do men and very poor men ; by the Philistine as well as the artist. It was not affected by the materialism of the age, nor by the revolt against that materialism. It was like the queer flight of butterflies across the Channel on that July day in 1846—a manifestation of the wayward and unpredictable nature of beauty, not subject to the laws of moral and political sciences.

The experience was sometimes all the more precious because it was purchased at the cost of a violent struggle with the conventions or with religious prohibitions. For those brought up among the stricter sects, the stage was lighted by the glare of damnation. Much less than a century ago it was regarded in many families as an act of impious rebellion for a young man or girl to go to the theatre. One can recall many a confession by an old lady of the fearful warnings of perdition which she had defied to steal her first visit to the play. It is one of the virtues of the Puritan tradition that it heightens the appreciation of the arts by investing them with a perilous sorcery. Those who had to snatch their reading of the great novels and poetry of the Victorian age furtively, and those who saw Irving and Terry under the shadow of a preacher's doom were likely to care more passionately for such arts than the dilettantes of Pall Mall.

Fortunate was the theatre-goer of 1896 who in a season could see the Kendals, Charles Wyndham, John Hare, Forbes Robertson, Mrs. Pat Campbell—and a whole diversity of Terrys.* There were the regal women—Evelyn Millard, Lily Hanbury, Winifred Emery. There were the well-graced actors, George Alexander, William Terriss, Lewis Waller, Martin Harvey.

It was a spirited theatre. A theatre that had Shaw hammering at its doors could not fall into a doze. The furious row between the Ibsenites and the anti-Ibsenites set the air moving in dusty rooms where nothing much had happened in a century. Ideas of change were breaking into the theatre as they were breaking into the rest of life. And adroit craftsmen like Arthur Pinero and Henry Arthur Jones were skilful enough in their adaptations of the new ideas to make Society feel a comfortable sense of Painless Progress.

But it is worth noting that it took the theatre fifty years to catch up with those ideas of Progress which were animating most of life's other spheres in 1846.

II

FULLY CHORAL

What of music in 1846 ?

A notice by the *Daily News* music critic of the Seventh Concert of the Philharmonic Society on Monday, 15 June, startles a little by touching a grievance that one had thought belonged peculiarly to our times—that the Beethoven symphonies are played too often. The modern listener who writes to the B.B.C. complaining that the *Fifth* or the *Eroica* is becoming as hackneyed as *Rule Britannia* and asking " Where is the new music ? " had his counterpart then. The music critic—it was Hogarth, Dickens'

* The Bancrofts had retired from management in 1885 with a fortune of £180,000. That suggests what the patronage of the middle-classes meant to prudent artists in those times.

father-in-law—writes " The concert last night began with a
symphony by Onslow, a composer who, in some branches of his
art, has gained a European reputation. But the composition of a
great orchestral symphony is an attempt to bend the bow of
Ulysses—an attempt in which only the very strongest can hope to
succeed. Beethoven's gigantic symphonies have absolutely crushed
this species of composition ; every new production is measured by
his standard and found miserably wanting. The Philharmonic
Society are blamed for constantly repeating the symphonies of
Beethoven and his two predecessors, Haydn and Mozart, but it is
no wonder they do so when they find that almost every symphony
of later date which they bring forward is (and deservedly) coldly
received." The critic describes the composition of the now-forgotten
Onslow as masterly, but " it has not that majestic simplicity, that
unity of design, those ravishing strains and overpowering masses
of harmony which Beethoven has taught us to expect in a great
orchestral work."

Of living composers of this period the most popular was
Mendelssohn. The feminine graces and constant felicities of his
music captivated the Victorians. To them this was the true
Germany—a fountain sparkling in the sun. At any moment the
arrogant French might land us in war ; what but sweetness and
light could come from the land of this gentle spirit ? All that
was plumply sentimental in the age warmed to Teuton romanticism ;
the castles of the Rhine were bathed in an orange mist ; the Lorelei
charmed country vicarages, and was regarded as almost an evangelical siren ; the ballads of Von Uhland and the dreamy blue
haze of Jean Paul's mysticism ; Gothic arches, Protestantism,
philosophy and the remembered sorrows of young Werther combined to create a genial glow among the cultivated. Everything
that was harsh, prickly and explosive was associated with the
French. The age felt that it owed a debt of gratitude to the German
race for the sublimity of Beethoven as for the grandeur of Goethe.

Mendelssohn, goading himself to a finish, completed *Elijah*
in this summer of 1846 and came to Birmingham to conduct its
first performance. The descriptions of the scenes in the Town Hall
on that morning of 26 August 1846, attest the musical enthusiasm
of the city. That a sudden burst of sunshine should flood the hall
as soon as Mendelssohn entered was read as a sign of Heaven's
favour. The audience, the orchestra and the great chorus rose
to cheer him. The demonstration was renewed at the end of the
first part, and then, at the conclusion the crowd surged round the
artists' room and caressed the composer, and the final picture is of
Mendelssohn pressing hand after hand in an affectionate frenzy,

tears streaming down his cheeks.   The exuberance of Birmingham on that hot August morning, writes one chronicler, was almost grotesque.

Mendelssohn's last visit to England was in 1847 when the Queen and Prince Albert attended the Exeter Hall performances of *Elijah*.   It was on this occasion that the Prince scribbled a note in his programme hailing Mendelssohn as a second Elijah, faithful to the worship of the true art, though encircled by the idolators of Baal.   (It was not quite clear at whom the Prince was jabbing.)

The composer's British admirers were pained to learn that he suffered a disagreeable experience on his way back to Berlin from this visit.   He was intercepted by the German police, and subjected to a humiliating inquisition, being forced to write out a long account of himself.   This arose from their confusing him with another Dr. Mendelssohn, a supposed revolutionary.   The Police State was being born.   Ninety years after his London and Birmingham triumphs, Mendelssohn's music was proscribed by the Germans. A note from Prince Albert on that subject would have been worth reading.

Oratorio commanded the passionate attachment of the Victorians; the Handel Festivals at Crystal Palace lay just a few years ahead. One of the most characteristic folk expressions of the middle-classes was provided by the *Messiah*.   Eighteenth-century Handel became a representative genius of nineteenth-century England.   Handel's abounding vital juices, his glorious flow, his optimism, his copious invention were congenial to the spirit of the age.   The soaring choruses became affirmations of belief in Progress.   Even a confession of sin such as *All We Like Sheep Have Gone Astray* was chanted rollickingly to one of the most cheerful melodies ever written.   And the *Hallelujah* chorus!   When the Crystal Palace organ and orchestra announced that triumphant theme—when the white-skirted and blue-sashed tiers of sopranos and contraltos, the dark cliffs of tenors and basses, emitted their blasts of choric ecstasy—when the audience rose like an army to its feet and swelled with their voices the cataract of sound—and the victorious shouts rose higher and louder in a frock-coated rapture—then, indeed, the Victorians knew that God was in his heaven and all was right with the world.   Matthew Arnold might write of the melancholy, long-withdrawing roar of the tide of faith from the beaches of *his* world, but for middle-class England—particularly suburban and provincial England—the Handel Festivals were like the morning stars singing together and the sons of God shouting for joy in the beginning of things.   But there was nothing shoddy in that emotion.   It had its springs in the best qualities of a virile

SOUTH TRANSEPT, THE GREAT EXHIBITION
From an engraving by H. Bibby, from a daguerreotype by Mayall.

age. One remembers, too, that so fastidious a patrician as Arthur James Balfour, the defender of philosophic doubt, had as high a regard for Handel as for Beethoven.

Germany was the dominant musical influence during a good part of the century. From the days when Sterndale Bennett produced his gentle, watery reflections of Mendelssohn to the days when that eminent musical critic Mr. George Bernard Shaw (Corno di Bassetto of the *Star*) brought forth *The Perfect Wagnerite* the supremacy was absolute. In delving among the records of the century one comes upon what appears to be a central opinion among cultivated men and women that Purcell had musical genius, and Edward Elgar had musical genius, but that between them lay a waste of sand. There were one or two men of unfulfilled promise, such as Hugo Henry Pierson, who had a deeper understanding than Gounod of what Goethe had in mind when he wrote *Faust*, but Pierson, born in Cambridge, found his spiritual and physical home in Germany. The memoirs of Dame Ethel Smyth, a gallant fighter on two fronts, feminism and music, showed how powerful was the gravitational pull of Germany. And a voice comes out of the past saying, " Arthur Sullivan—there was a melancholy business ! What talents he had, and to what a use he put them ! He might have been Purcell's heir, but he chose to become the heir of Offenbach. He might have written symphonies like *The Unfinished* and operas like *Fidelio*, but he sold out to success, and squandered his genius in writing trivial lilts and ditties to tickle the ears of the fat firstnighters at the Savoy." The curious thing is that this was said by people who had witnessed Sullivan's unhappy efforts to write in the grand manner, who had seen the fate of his ambitious opera *Ivanhoe*. The pride of the age demanded that its artists should produce noble and solemn works for the greater glory of that age in future times. So came the pressure on Tennyson to write *The Idyls of the King* rather than a handful of lyrics. So came the pressure on a natural portrait-painter like G. F. Watts to torture and waste himself on cloudy allegories. Napoleon in exile was asked why his Empire failed to produce works of literary genius. " It was all the fault of that Minister of the Interior," said the Emperor angrily. " I was always speaking to him about it, but he did nothing." The Victorians looked for coronation arches from their artists, as they expected victories from their soldiers. If they had been as wise as the Chinese, they would have been content in the thought that the briefest lyrics of Tennyson and the gayest tunes of Sullivan would be remembered gratefully by a later age. Posterity usually values small legacies. It prefers the bequest of a ring or a brooch to a white elephant.

It is a long road from *The Bohemian Girl* and *Maritana* to *Peter Grimes*. There is an amusing record to be written one day of the place of opera in the life of Britain during the past hundred years, but this unskilled hand will certainly not attempt it. The British always felt a little chagrined that they never produced a Verdi, a Bizet or a Wagner, though when one says the British in this context one means a small minority, for there are many good citizens with a liking for tunefulness who have always been well content with *The Lily of Killarney*. This writer once owned a collection of clippings from the *Daily News* which recorded the efforts made through the years to produce the great national opera, after that gifted Irishman, Sullivan, decided he could not achieve it for us. Some of the names of these lost ships are now too dim for record, but there will be not a few readers to recall the valiant endeavours of Joseph Holbrooke and Lord Howard de Walden—*The Children of Don* and the rest—before the first world war. And Ethel Smyth's *The Wreckers* which had passion. And Charles Villiers Stanford's *The Critic*, which had wit. There was Gustav Holst's ill-titled *The Perfect Fool* and Vaughan Williams' *Hugh the Drover*, full of that flavour of the grass roots of England which is a distinguishing mark of this noble composer. There was the Goossens and Arnold Bennett collaboration in *Judith*. . . . One had almost forgotten Delius and *A Village Romeo and Juliet*, which Beecham used to interpret with fine sensitiveness to its composer's spirit.

To write an opera is a desperate hazard. A book, however indifferent, will survive with the tenacity of a cat. Long after its author has forgotten even to be ashamed of it, it pops up in a sixpenny box in the Charing Cross Road. It remains in terrible permanence on the shelves of too faithful friends, and is dug out by a visitor attracted and deluded by its title. But unless an opera can secure election as a permanent member of that extraordinary club, of which *Carmen* and *Rosenkavalier*, *Don Giovanni* and *The Ring* are the incompatible members, it is as forgotten as last year's snows. For the past fifty years both the British and Americans have been striving to secure admission to this club. It is a queer club where cads of genius get in and gentlemen of talent are blackballed.

In 1846 they were preparing to convert Covent Garden permanently into an opera house. At Her Majesty's Theatre the Italians ruled without challenge. A number of the finest singers of a golden age, including Mario, accounted the most melting of tenors, were in London that season. To one brought up to think of Mario as the flawless artist, it is a trifle disconcerting to read the contemporary criticisms in the *Daily News*—that on some nights he is in no voice at all, or that he is at last showing a sense of understanding his roles instead of being merely the mechanical warbler of dulcet notes, like Hans Anderson's clockwork nightingale.

Rossini, Donizetti and Bellini were the admired masters. Soon London barrel-organs (with monkey in jacket and pill-box hat) would be playing Verdi's gayest tunes. The century of Covent Garden stretches out to the war-time silence, and to the revival of old glories this spring. Many have been the shifts in taste and fashion. During that period Meyerbeer, for example, blazed like a star, then went out. He who was once thought of as a genius is now not thought of at all. So far as one can discover, John Galsworthy was the last man of our times to feel about Meyerbeer what old Jolyon Forsyte felt. It is amusing to read some early criticisms of Verdi that present him as a harsh and violent revolutionary—then the middle criticisms of him as a tinkling music-box, all vulgar prettiness—then the appraisal of his true and singular greatness—the understanding of the beauty and power of *Otello* and *Falstaff*. It is amusing, too, to thumb the old Wagner criticisms, in which the disputations are as violent as those of the religious pamphleteers of the seventeenth century, with the public making up its own mind, and accepting the New Music for the very good reason that it found it enjoyable.

But the general assumption that a composer of genius has a hard fight to win recognition from dull, conventional minds is not confirmed by a study of the files. For example, in one of the early issues of the *Daily News* George Hogarth contributes a long and sympathetic article on the first performance of an adaptation of Verdi's *Nabucodnosor* (Nebuchadnezzar) called *Nino*. This seems to have been a clumsy version of the opera, heavily censored by the Biblical prejudices of the time. In reading this notice one recognises Hogarth as a sensitive and understanding critic striving hard through the fog of a bad adaptation to discover the composer's mind and intentions. The opera, he decided, was certainly Verdi's *chef d'œuvre*. " It displays a maturity of genius which we have not found either in *Lombardi* or *Ernani*. He is finding an independent style of his own. Till we heard it, we had not formed a very exalted estimate of Verdi's genius. But now, when we consider that he is still young, and, we trust, entering upon a long career, there is hardly anything too great to be expected of him." That was clear sight for 1846. It was indeed a long career. *Falstaff*, the most splendid fruit of that genius, came nearly fifty years afterwards (1893). Verdi lived until 1901.

To come to a more modest level of music, one notes in the newspaper of 1846 the appearance of the Hutchinson Family, announced as "a family of vocalists from the United States." Composed of three brothers and one sister, they sang before a "numerous and fashionable audience" at the Hanover Square Rooms on 10 February. The critic considered that they sang better without instrumental accompaniment. They were the forerunners of many generations of American singers—chanters of spirituals, of Stephen Foster's ballads, of rag-time, of jazz, down to the crooners and "hot" vocalists of to-day. The music critic of the *Daily News* recorded that the Hutchinsons sang a new piece called *Excelsior* written by a Mr. Longfellow, "of a somewhat wild and mystical cast, but in a lofty vein of poetry."

> *The shades of night were falling fast*
> *As through an Alpine village passed*
> *A youth, who bore 'mid snow and ice*
> *A banner with the strange device*
> *Excelsior !*

One supposes that this was the first time that the banner with the strange device was flourished before a London audience. It was to become a favourite showpiece of the Victorians—lisped by young reciters—sung by pale curates in drawing-rooms—roared by glee clubs, fining their roar at last to a ghostly whisper at the words, "Lifeless but beautiful he lay." Dickens was delighted by the Hutchinson family. He wrote to Lady Blessington, "They must never go back to their own country without your having heard them sing Hood's *Bridge of Sighs*."

United States influence in our entertainments was already marked. During that season of a century ago, in addition to the Hutchinson family and the dwarf, General Tom Thumb, a much more remarkable American, Charlotte Cushman was presenting a female *Romeo* to London and carrying audiences before her with the impetuous virility of her performances. The contemporary critic wrote, "In her bursts of anger, of despair, we altogether lost sight of the woman ; every feminine characteristic was entirely thrown aside in her powerful interpretation of the role. Her singular resemblance at the same time to Mr. Macready must have struck everybody in the house, even to his attitudes and inflections of the voice." Miss Cushman's sister played Juliet ; her performance was thought to be ordinary. Charlotte had genius.

For a spell, ballet became as greatly admired as it is today. The peak of the old romantic ballet had been touched the year before in the celebrated *pas de quartre* danced at Her Majesty's Theatre by four superb *ballerine*—Marie Taglioni, Carlotta Grisi, Fanny Cerrito and Lucille Grahn. The balletomanes of the

Victorian age were to speak of that forever afterwards as the supreme revelation of grace—an enchantment that flowered once on the air, and never could pass from their brooding fancy. The passion for the dance affected Christmas pantomime. Joey, the clown, was an old dog who had perforce to learn new tricks. Beside thieving and grimacing, he must now pirouette. The stage swarmed with coryphées in the Transformation Scenes of *Aladdin* and *The Forty Thieves*.

As early as 1846 the coloured minstrels were singing their ditties in London and the provinces. The Ethiopian Singers were at the Horns, Kennington !

Then there was the Panorama ! That made the mouths of the unsophisticated open wide.   Full-blooded spectacles, in lush colourings, with startling scenic tricks—eruptions of Mount Vesuvius harrowing the young by blinding rivers of white-hot lava, and villages devoured—the earthquake at Lisbon, the one that made Voltaire think so hard about the nature of Providence, with collapses of palaces and churches, and the bells dementedly ringing in the falling steeples. The Panorama was the nearest equivalent to the cinema that 1846 possessed.

Conjurers and magicians exhibited automata—mechanical men like Maelzel's chess-player. Some of these images would speak a few words—primitive ancestors of the gramophone. It was not until the end of the nineteenth century that Edison produced the talking machine. Happy are those old enough to remember the early gramophones, the vast wreathed horns, the winding up of the box, the metallic announcer piercing the blurred roar with those syllables of wonder, " ED-ISON BELL RECORD "—rur-rur-rur. And then the never-to-be eclipsed joy of hearing a soprano voice like a carving knife singing Tosti's *Good-bye*.   Since then, the instrument has developed in power and delicacy beyond any dreams of 1900. Before the days of the gramophone, the art of the singer and instrumentalists was a fugitive beauty. The song died on the air. Now the voice and artistry of the singer are saved from the tomb. Here, then, is one machine that has added greatly to the sum of human pleasure, and that not even the men of Erewhon would wish to destroy.

III

BALLOONS

A popular form of amusement of which no trace now survives was provided by Vauxhall Gardens, Cremorne Gardens and the Surrey Zoological Gardens.   These pleasure grounds were laid out in

Italian groves and twisting paths, broad walks and shadowy grottoes—there were classical statues and glimpses of the tarnished and malodorous Thames. The admission charge was a shilling. Here concerts were given and meals served in the open air ; there were firework displays, dancing and balloon ascents. The trees were hung with fairy lights. " The brilliancy of the stars rivalled the brilliancy of the lamps displayed in countless numbers," recorded the happy *Daily News* reporter who attended the reopening of Vauxhall Gardens on the cloudless first of June in '46. But the lights were never quite bright enough to reassure the moralists of the time. There was more than a suspicion of queer goings-on among the Italian groves. The forerunners of the London Morality Council were much exercised over Cremorne Gardens on the river front at Chelsea. Those whom the *Daily News* reporter described as " the more precise people who inhabit the locality of Chelsea " were starting an agitation which would eventually close the gardens. In their last phase they became too disreputable for the most tolerant live-and-let-live philosopher to defend.

" In the early part of this opening night at Cremorne, Mr. Green, accompanied by his brother, ascended in his balloon, which took a westerly direction." That was, at least, a harmless enough sport. The thread which links us most closely to the Cremorne Gardens of a century ago is air travel. Those early Victorians who had subdued the land with their railroads and the sea with their steamships were reaching out after the command of the sky. Aeronautics enchanted them. They foresaw that some day men would fly to America and the Antipodes. The Spencers, that great dynasty of balloonists, were lords of the future.

The balloons drifting over London on a fine afternoon were accounted a pretty sight. Pear-shaped, or, rather, inverted pears, of varying colours, sometimes green as a tree that had slipped its roots and had decided to float lazily out of the world—sometimes red as a sail—their names, *Victoria* or *Dauntless* or such-like, spelled out in a glitter of gold—they caught the sun and air with grace. Swimming in those transparent afternoons, high above all dust, above the clatter of wheels, swimming with such ease and liberty of motion, they set the mind dreaming of new and delightful forms of Progress. This was a rarifying upon the mechanical, the last refinement of an age of science. Was there any premonition of evil in the airy height ? No lines of Tennyson's came to be more often quoted than those from " Locksley Hall " :—

> *When I dipt into the future far as human eye could see*
> *Saw the vision of the world, and all the wonder that would be*

Saw the heavens fill with commerce, argosies of magic sails,
Pilots of the purple twilight, dropping down with costly bales :

Heard the heavens fill with shouting, and there rained a ghastly dew,
From the nations' airy navies grappling in the central blue.

The reports of the balloon ascents from Cremorne in that summer a century ago make pleasant reading. " The *Albion* balloon in which Mr. Green, the aeronaut, ascended, crossed over the Thames on this side of Putney Bridge when, after returning, it proceeded towards Uxbridge and, about 8 o'clock, having been an hour in the air, descended at Denham Park (Bucks) ". . . . On 30 June the balloon *Nassau* rose from Cremorne, went east and passed over Buckingham Palace where its passengers drank the health of her Majesty and Ibrahim Pasha (the Egyptian potentate then visiting London), in a bumper of champagne. *God Save the Queen* was sung by Mr. Van Buren, the company in the balloon joining in the chorus. The *Nassau* went on to Ongar, Essex, where it " descended in a cornfield belonging to Mr. Kynaston, a farmer, by whom they were most hospitably entertained."

IV

VARIETY

In 1846 the music-hall, which was to blaze with vitality in the late Victorian age, was in a puling infancy. Its cradle was the public house, as the cradle of the theatre had been the church. Since the days of the Georgians, rake-helly night haunts, such as the Cave of Harmony depicted in *Pendennis*, had provided singers for their patrons. The taverns raised the tone of this informal entertainment. We may see the rudiments of variety in those pages of *Bleak House* which describes the Harmonic Meetings held twice a week in the Sol's Arms, a public house off Chancery Lane where—a typical arrangement of the age—the inquest on the wretched Hawdon was held. " The chair is filled by a professional celebrity, faced by Little Swills, the comic vocalist who hopes (according to the bill in the window) that his friends will rally round him and support first-rate talent. . . . In the zenith of the evening, Little Swills says, " Gentlemen, if you'll permit me, I'll attempt a short description of a scene of real life that came off here today." Is much applauded and encouraged ; goes out of the room as Swills ; comes in as the Coroner (not the least in the world like him) : describes the Inquest, with recreative intervals of pianoforte accompaniment to the refrain—with his (the Coroner's) tippy tol li doll, tippy tol lo doll, tippy tol li doll, dee ! " There are many men still spry who remember the institution of the Chairman—and· the comics and serio-comics called upon, in turn, to perform in an atmosphere indigo with pipe fumes—the choruses roared out in bibulous gusto, with the heels of beer tankards hammering time on the tables.

Some of the " saloon theatres," or garden theatres developed by the public houses, ventured on elaborate and ingenious entertainments. The *Yorkshire Stingo*, which still stands between Marylebone and Paddington, was a tavern that set a high standard. The legitimate theatres grew jealous of this new form of entertainment, and instigated prosecutions for infringements of the law of 1844 governing theatrical performances. The contest went on for years, and judges pondered metaphysical definitions of what constitutes a stage representation. Ballet slipped through the net by describing itself as a divertissement ! Apparently any number of coryphées could dance on the tip of that needle. John Hollingshead, who, among other things, was a critic for the *Daily News* in Victorian times, has described how Charles Morton's *Canterbury* in Lambeth Marsh (one of the most renowned of London music-halls) produced Gounod's *Faust* for the first time in England. Not daring to present it with scenery and costume for fear of being suppressed under the Stage Play Act, the *Canterbury* presented the singers standing in a row on the platform wearing their every-day clothes. As a result of these unoperatic performances, the ear-tickling tunes of *Faust* were being whistled by the butcher's boys of South London before the opera reached Covent Garden.

By slow attrition the struggle was won—as the theatres themselves had won their struggle against the patent monopoly—and the mighty age of the music-hall unfolded quickly. Red-faced Little Swills, with his tippy tol li doll, was the forerunner of singers of such variegated talents as the Great MacDermott (*We don't want to fight but by Jingo if we do*), Dan Leno, James Fawn (*If you want to know the time, ask a policeman*), Marie Lloyd, Little Tich, Albert Chevalier (*My Old Dutch*), Eugene Stratton (*The Lily of Laguna*), Charles Coborn (*The Man who broke the bank at Monte Carlo*), Vesta Tilley (*Jolly Good Luck to the Girl that Loves a Soldier*), George Robey, Harry Lauder (*A wee deoch an' doris*), George Formby, Senior (*Standing at the Corner of the Street*) and, beyond them, a gallery whose names would fill more than one page. This sunburst of talent in late Victorian and Edwardian times was one of the unpredictable aspects of our century. It was another aspect of the great vitality of the period, a vitality which thrust out in so many diverse directions.

They were stamped by no single die, these singers. They were as various as the trades and characters of Demos itself. Some of them rode off thunderingly on a rich-blooded vulgarity, but many of the others developed a fine-spun artistry that was certainly not outmatched on the legitimate stage. Their songs, and the characters they created, were often acid on steel—biting social criticisms, from which one could learn a great deal about the tyrannies as well as the pleasures of the century. An artist like Albert Chevalier, who lived well into our period, re-created a way of life now lost to us—the flamboyance, the defeats, and the chivalry of the costermonger's existence ; and the vision of an Old Kent Road, at once more flaring and more endearing than the impersonal tram route we know today. A singer like the elder George Formby contrived amid his wry wit to convey a sense of the damp forlornness of mean streets as penetrating as that of another George—the melancholy Gissing. Marie Lloyd was a burning-glass of Cockney vitality, helping one to understand how the breed of Victorian Cockneys kept alive and cheerful in conditions that depress the modern reader of Charles Booth and Walter Besant.

Above all, there was one quality common to them—gusto. Their candle burned at both ends, and sometimes in the middle as well, but it was a torch while it blazed. They spent themselves in their performances, often going by cab from music hall to music hall, night after night repeating their exhausting routine. Their songs and pantomime were a distilling of experience, but at what a sacrifice were those precious drops squeezed out of the brain. It is a pity that the noble and expressive title of pro. has gone out of style. For these men and women were professionals in the same way that Dickens was a professional writer, or that Liddon was a professional preacher, or the great Victorian engineers were professional bridge builders. Their England had the deadly seriousness of the professional, but also the tremendous exuberance which is possible to a man who has so complete a command of his medium that it has become an extension of himself. These virtuosi could get a pæan out of a tin whistle.

Clowns of genius like Leno and Little Tich were essences of that happy lunacy which runs through the century and was common to all classes. To the middle classes Lear's *Book of Nonsense* and Lewis Carroll's *Alice in Wonderland* were roads of escape from the pomps and plumes, cares and tight lips of life. To the man in Queer Street a whoop of the pure lunar ecstasy like Miss Lottie Collins' *Ta-ra-ra-boom-de-ay* offered a similar relief. The Victorians had to snap the spell of their own solemnity from time to time. One likes to recall that picture of the king falcon of politics, Gladstone, linking hands with his wife and dancing gaily round the domestic hearthrug singing, "A ragamuffin husband and a rantipoling wife." But there is in Edward Lear, besides the escape into fantasy, a quality that can best be described by that homely phrase, laughing on the other side of one's face. One feels that the old men of the Limericks who do such outrageous things as waltzing with blue-bottles and living in kettles are really frightened of being crushed by the weight of the Albert Memorial, the dignity of the Queen and the dread authority of the Bishops. It is the quality of a small boy with too many bombazined aunts that is also manifest in some of the best music-hall comedians of the age.

The early Victorians had to devise most of their own entertainment, without mechanical aids or the mass production of fun. Compared with their descendants of 1946, the men and women of 1846 were ill-served with amusements and recreations. No films, no radio, no music halls, no organised sport. But the working people, and a great part of the middle-class, toiled such long hours they had little time or inclination for organised amusements. Sunday was a day of silent gloom. Sabbatarianism was all-powerful in the 'forties and 'fifties ; and it needed many eloquent speeches and many loyal petitions before museums and picture galleries could be opened on a Sunday or before bands were allowed to play in the parks. The humane Shaftesbury was the most implacable Sabbatarian of the age, and he influenced his jaunty father-in-law, Palmerston, in this direction. But sheer exhaustion as much as Puritan sentiment, made the Victorian Sabbath, crepe-hung, muted, shrouded—a day that crept by with nodding plumes ; Arthur Clennam's Sunday at home in *Little Dorrit* with the throb of the church bells in the empty city streets, expressing its melancholy.

V

FILMS

The century has brought great gains in leisure for the working millions and, with it, an immense provision of mass entertainment. It has all happened so fast that one loses count of the changes. Progress was a Santa Claus that with each succeeding Christmas brought the children more and more toys.

It was around 1890 that the continuous celluloid film was devised. The first living pictures were exhibited in London in 1896. On 20 February of that year the Lumiére brothers showed a series of one-minute films in the Polytechnic in Regent Street, and on the same day Robert Paul was showing his " animatograph " at the Finsbury Technical College. The first " cinema theatre " in the Capital was the Daily Bioscope in Bishopsgate, which opened on 6 May 1906. Out of that early Bioscope—with its flickering grey scenes over which an eternal rain was falling—with men and women strutting like mechanical dolls—and box-shaped automobiles tearing at insane speeds—developed a prodigious industry of entertainment. Regarded at first as an extension of the travel panorama that showed us Vesuvius spouting, the film slowly widened its scope. It reached out to farce and behold there were the Keystone comedies, displaying the cosmic glories of fat men glissading on banana skins, and of direct hits by custard pies. It discovered anew the endless charms of the female form—and lo ! the Mack Sennett bathing beauties were on parade. It groped after those effects which the theatre achieved through strong situations and the grapplings of powerful personalities. And Drammer arrived. The puppets of the old melodrama were rigged out in new clothes and made to move twice as fast. The mortgaged farmhouse was shifted bodily from Loamshire to the Dakotas. Inspector Manly of the Yard changed his shirt and became the Sheriff of Dead Man's Gulch. But Virtue remained Triumphant.

The fatal woman of the French and British drama was re-incarnated in the Vamp of the films. Sirens like Miss Theda Bara—the curl of their long gowns making them look like mermaids—brought delicious flutterings of vicarious adventure to the primmer suburbs.

One watches the unfolding of this large cabbage rose of the films through the old files. Towards the close of the first Great War there is a recognition in the newspapers that the new medium has produced a comic artist of genius, Charlie Chaplin, recognisably in the tradition of the great music-hall drolls. The little man with the peaked face, the sorrowing eyes, the pursued look, the blob of a moustache, the accordion pants, the cane, the deplorable boots, and the cat-like clutch on life, never relaxed through all disasters, becomes the first character of the films to be taken up enthusiastically by the intelligentsia. *Shoulder Arms* in 1918 turned a toy into an art form—at least, that was the fashionable view. With the dazzling advent of Chaplin, the cognoscenti began to treat the pictures with the respect they had long conceded the stage. Critics of immense erudition wrote of the social significance of Chaplin, talked of him in relation to the Italian *commedia del arte*, in relation to Till Eulenspiegel's Merry Pranks, talked of Dickens and Sam Weller, talked of Shakespeare and poor Yorick, talked of Grimaldi and the eternal sadness of the clown. Meanwhile the small urchins in poor streets were chanting to the barrel-organ tune of " Red Wings."

The moon shines bright on Charlie Chaplin.
His boots are crackin'
For want of blackin'
And his little baggy trousers they need mendin'
Before we send him
To the Dardenelles.

This was one of the few occasions in history in which the babes and the aesthetes trolled the same chorus.

It was in the middle of the war, too, that the forerunner of *Desert Victory* and of most war documentaries appeared—a picture of the Battle of the Somme that was a sharp-edged piece of photography, not sparing the murk and misery of that bloody engagement, and piercing through the gentle inanities of much then visible on the screen. It was a furnace-blast in a house of shadows.

Before the first German war ended, the films had become one of the chief forms of mental escape to hundreds of thousands of our people. They were a relief from the crowding sorrows of those times ; for the casualty lists of the war had woefully saddened the nation. Their gentle witchcraft lifted people out of themselves and supplied the beguiling illusion of a happier existence around the corner. An *ingénue* in pig-tails named Mary Pickford became an embodiment of artless girlhood. That emanation of innocence which, in Little Nell and Little Dorrit, had captivated the early Victorians would always melt the British public. And there was Douglas Fairbanks, all gallantry and cool bravado, turning the romantic trick as neatly as Lewis Waller had done. When Miss Pickford and Mr. Fairbanks came to London after the war the crowds poured out as though for a Coronation. The uncrowned royalties appeared on a balcony to receive the homage of a loyal multitude.

There was an engaging simpleness of soul about the adolescence of the films. Kind hearts were at a premium ; simple faith a commercial proposition. The supercilious looked down their noses when Mr. D. W. Griffith's *Birth of a Nation* was offered as an epic ; but the Gish sisters were all sweetness and light ; and Mr. Griffith was an evangelist, devising his huge frescoes as propaganda for peace and universal brotherhood. Love would conquer all ! . . . The films borrowed from the newspapers the device of the serial. *The Exploits of Elaine*, with Miss Pearl White left in the jaws of death at the end of each instalment and triumphantly wriggling out of those jaws at the start of each new one, kept the threepennies and sixpennies in a state of insupportable suspense week after week. Virtue went on Triumphing.

In 1928 there came that considerable change, the talkies.

The youngest generation of film-goers can have little conception of the prejudice against sound pictures which animated many of the silent votaries. Although the films were so young a form of entertainment, they had already created their own order of Trappists to whom speech was a sacrilege. Articles headed, " Can the Talkies Last ? " were published and quidnuncs usually answered—No. The artistry of the silent film, they said, could never be overthrown by canned music and vocal stridencies. Mr. Al Jolson's audible sobs in *The Jazz Singer* did not convert the sceptical, though they played havoc with the heart-strings of the unsophisticated. But the new invention was not to be resisted. Then there followed an agitated speculation among the fans as to how their silent gods and goddesses would meet the voice test. Many shirked it, remained silent, and so became forgotten. The effect of a Botticelli face and liquid eyes could be quite destroyed by a call-note like a tin-opener. Professors of phonetics, elocution masters and voice producers swarmed into Hollywood. Galatea was seen to be wooing Pygmalion. A few of the darlings of the silent days took the Great Divide with ease and grace. A sporting interest attached itself to the change. On that night when the most mysterious of the enchantresses was at last heard, as well as seen, and the cry " Garbo Speaks ! " went up, there was a disposition among her fans to breathe relief as when the horse has taken the water-jump.

In 1846, young men and women found a standard of manners in novels or the theatre. In 1946, considerable sections of Britain's youth draw their ideas about social conduct from the films. Styles of wearing the hair, ways of speech, standards of good looks, and methods of love-making have been greatly influenced by the screen. The film is drawn into the solemn studies of the anthropologist because of the effect it has had upon folk ways and because of the new idols of beauty and youth which it has set up. It has become a subject for the economist, not only because it is a considerable industry, but because it has widened social needs. The problem set by the old song, " How are you going to keep them down on the farm ? " has been increased by those unsettling shadows. The talking film and broadcasting have between them narrowed the gap between the accent and vocabulary of the several classes. In Thackeray's sketches, *The Heavies* (August 1846) one finds the elegant military dandy remarking, " Our wedgment is awdrd abwawd." Captain Ragg cries, " See that dem Mulligan dwiwve by, with that dem high-stepping haws?" Compare this with Mrs. Gamp's " ' Mrs. Harris,' I says, ' leave the bottle on the chimley-piece, and don't ask me to take none, but let me put my lips to it when I am so dispoged.'" Or, with Jo saying, "Thank 'ee. It's wery, wery kind of you, sir, and it makes me more cumfbler nor I was afore." Whether it is a good thing or a bad that varieties of dialect and brogue should be evened into uniformity is outside the scope of this inquiry.

VI

BROADCASTING

" Why can't they leave things alone ? " pleaded men of conservative habit.   But apparently this rash age would not leave anything alone.   It was not long after the end of World War No. 1 that rumours began to reach us from America of extraordinary developments in the use of radio.   Up till then, it had been thought of as the Puck of communications, putting a girdle round the world in less than forty seconds ; telegraphy without wires.   It was the white magic of life-saving, too, identified to the emotions by S.O.S. For twenty years the papers had carried stories of ships on fire or ships in distress whose passengers and crew had been saved through its agency.

But now—said reports from the other side of the Atlantic— Marconi's discovery was sprouting out in ways far removed from commercial traffic and the austerities of the General Post Office. In some strange way that we did not comprehend, it was being used to transmit popular entertainment—songs, and bands, and people talking.   To the traditionalists this was very disturbing. It was like hearing that bank directors were dancing in Lombard Street or that the Institute of Chartered Accountants had wreathed vine leaves in its collective hair.

On 14 November 1922, the British Broadcasting Company began a daily service of wireless programmes, with the call sign of the London Station 2LO.   (Their first broadcast had taken place on 3 November.)   The dominant figure of the company was a Presbyterian Scots engineer of beetling height and sombre personality, John Reith.   Although he was the master of this new sorcery, Reith was a recognisable inheritor of the Victorian virtues—a crag of moral purpose.   The listeners in those first days of wireless clamped headphones to their ears and patiently explored the crystal with the cat's-whisker until they lighted on the sensitive spot.   When at last they caught, coming from the other end of the tunnel a military band playing, "Land of Hope and Glory," this, they said, with a swell of emotion, is Progress Again.

These times have whirled us so giddily on their merry-go-round that we forget how limited broadcasting was in its scope twenty-four years ago. The masters of the new invention moved with considerable caution, anxious not to alienate the newspapers on one side nor the theatrical interests on the other. The total programme time for a week in December that year was 33½ hours. There were 23¼ hours of music in the month ; news represented 3 hours ; the Children's Hour 5¼ hours ; talks (including topical and educational discourses and broadcasts to schools) three-quarters of an hour a week ; and religion one hour a week. There was no dance music then—that came in March 1923. There was no variety —that was introduced with the Veterans of Variety in January 1923. The first dramatic performance broadcast was the quarrel scene from *Julius Caesar* February 1923, and the first operetta was heard in January 1924. In 1922 the B.B.C. orchestra was composed of eight players, with a microphone perched in front of each of them.

The social historians of this age will take note of the effect of the B.B.C. on the public mind and in the shaping of popular taste. Like other inventions of our century, wireless was an equalising force ; it brought more and more people into a community of interest. When our story began in 1846, the numbers of those who were well acquainted with what was happening in Britain and the world outside was limited. The lowering of the price of newspapers, the extension of mechanical transport, the penny post, the telegraph and the Education Act of 1870 in their several ways helped to thrust forward the frontiers of understanding. The problem of the century was always to bring closer the We who are governed and the mysterious They who govern us. The first time that the Cenotaph Service was broadcast a considerable part of the nation was able to take part in that rite of the nation's dead. So with other public occasions.

Early in its existence the B.B.C. began broadcasting opera from Covent Garden and concerts from the Queen's Hall. If one had been a music-loving cotton operative in Oldham or miner in Durham in 1846, one's chances of hearing Mario sing in *Lucia* would have been one in a billion. But from 1922 onwards, families in Lancashire mill towns or in Cotswold farmhouses alike could hear the most accomplished singers in Europe. Behind the audience under the roof at Covent Garden stretched an unseen audience of millions. There were few people now so isolated or so poor that they could not share the great orchestras with the cultured well-to-do. Musical appreciation is like the incidence of red hair ; it is a quality that zig-zags freakishly through all ranks ; broadcasting gave countless persons a chance to discover in themselves a joy in the best.

The effect on the general level of taste will be proved in the future, but there are signs that Britain today is a more musical nation than at any time since the Tudors. Up to Dr. Johnson's age, a writer of talent starved if he could not find a patron. Then a book-buying public was created, and literature became independent of the favours of a cultivated aristocracy. For many years, music in Britain has been dependent on the wealthy patron. With taxes what they are, Maecenas dwindles. As happened with literature long ago, a new audience has been called into being to redress the balance. What will it do with its power?

In 1925 the *Daily News* invited its readers to help it equip hospital wards with wireless sets. Nearly £90,000 was raised and 15,781 beds in 122 hospitals equipped. For many years letters were to flow into the office attesting the happiness which these sets had brought to the sick. To those in pain it was a healing ministration; and it relieved the tedium of convalescence. The Wireless for Hospitals plan owed much to the humane imagination of the late Hugh Jones, editor at that time. The Wireless Fund for Lighthouses and for the Blind were among several extensions of this benevolent activity.

It was on 1 January 1927, that the British Broadcasting Company became the British Broadcasting Corporation. From Reith to Haley is a short span—yet the sapling of Savoy Hill has become a tall tree with many branches. There were around half-a-million licence-holders in 1923; there are ten and a quarter million to-day.

The B.B.C. rendered services of signal value to the national cause during the war. Through those years when our fortunes were low, the B.B.C. was the voice of Britain reaching into the blackest corners of the prison house of Europe. The foreign broadcasts carried hope to the enslaved. Britain fought on; Britain would win; Britain with her Allies would break open the door and set the captives free. . . .

Our century is like a serpent with its tail in its mouth. Recalling the advance of broadcasting in the past 25 years one's thoughts turn back again to Faraday lecturing at the Royal Institution in 1846. Sir William Bragg, the physicist, speaking in 1927, said that there were two fundamental elements of wireless apparatus that were peculiarly Faraday's creation, the induction coil and the condenser, while Faraday had laid down the principles of the radio valve, though he never lived to see one. The owner of a wireless set when he tuned in his apparatus by turning knobs demonstrated laws that Faraday spent years of patient labour in elaborating. Clark Maxwell's ideas of electric waves in the ether, said Bragg, were derived from listening to an impromptu discourse by Faraday at the Royal Institution when he poured out thoughts that were still half-shaped in his prophetic mind.

THE EGYPTIAN HALL, PICCADILLY

CHAPTER IX

THE CRY OF THE CHILDREN

AMONG the faded newspapers of the past there are few things that touch the heart more than the records of children in the police courts. As one plods through the grey squalor of the Early Victorian court reports, there constantly recurs the image of the abandoned child, Poor Jos eternally being moved on. One's eye is caught by this typical paragraph from the police reports in the opening days of the *Daily News* of 1846 :—

" Melancholy Case

" A ragged half-starved looking boy, 12 years of age, named Piper, was charged with stealing a pint pot. On the previous day the prisoner went into a beershop in the Hackney-road, and called for half-a-pint of beer, which he drank, and walked off with the pot. He was, however, arrested soon after with the article on his person. The wretched appearance and simple look of the boy excited the curiosity and compassion of the magistrate. His aunt and sister, poor but decent-looking persons, stated that the prisoner had long been the victim of his father's dissipation, the father leading a life of idleness and vice. The poor child admitted that he had long been in the habit of stealing pots from public-houses and beer-shops—his father waiting outside to receive them. Their home was quite desolate, and the woman with whom his father had been cohabiting now lay there a corpse. The poor child, with tears in his eyes, added that he had been obliged to comply with his father's commands, otherwise he would have been severely beaten. He had no desire to pursue such a wicked course of life, but, on the contrary, eagerly wished to be rescued from it. The aunt and sister joined with the unfortunate youth in beseeching the magistrate to rescue him from his disgraceful position, and at all events to keep him from his father. The magistrate discharged the poor boy, and gave orders for the apprehension of the father."

Children turned into thieves at an early age or boys cast adrift on the muddy waters of London life are familiar figures in these pages. They are presented as ragged starvelings and hungry tatterdemalions. One notices that the magistrates invariably show compassion or express indignation at their condition, but the sad procession drags its way across the pages, and the implied assumption is that the victims—no matter how many there are—are subjects for private benevolence rather than for public action.

The classes—as we have seen—were greatly isolated from one another, and, even in the small compact London of that period, it was easy enough for a rich business man to go daily all his life from his office in the City to his comfortable home at Camberwell without ever having a glimmering of how the mass of Londoners lived. Dickens' apostrophe to society on the death of Jo sought to fix a general responsibility as well as to unseal the sympathies ; and such words, written by the favourite novelist of the middle-classes, could not help stirring a conscience even in the complacent. "Dead, your Majesty. Dead, my lords and gentlemen. Dead, Right Reverends and Wrong Reverends of every order. Dead, men and women, born with heavenly compassion in your hearts, and, dying thus around us every day."

Yet this was a period when a child lucky enough to be born into a comfortable home might enjoy not merely good food and a warm bed, but the tenderest solicitude for its spirit's happiness. 1846 was the birth year of two artists who may be said to symbolise the exquisite refinements of this affection—Kate Greenaway and Randolph Caldecott. If all that one knew of the treatment of children in Victorian times was derived from their graceful illustrations, one would say that this was an age which worshipped the child with sensitive discrimination and delicacy of apprehension. No fume is here from the black spells brewed in the school to which Jane Eyre went, or in Dotheboys Hall. There were two worlds for the child, the world peopled by the blithe fantasies of Edward Lear and *Alice in Wonderland*, of Hans Andersen and Mrs. Ewing, and that of Quilp and Fagin ; of the dripping mine where the whip was used, and the city slum where physical distress and moral evil were part of the one nightmare.

Here follows another report from the file of 1846 which describes a child being bought and sold like a puppy:—

" *Extraordinary Occurrence*

" The neighbourhood of Farringdon Street has been thrown into a state of considerable excitement from a rumour, which gained credence in every quarter, that a young woman of the name of Taylor had sold her illegitimate child, a little boy of the tender age of 3 years, under circumstances as singular and romantic, as they evince a total want of that feeling of human nature which in general distinguishes a mother's love and attachment of her own offspring. From enquiries made under circumstances of no ordinary difficulty, we believe the following is a tolerably accurate narrative of the facts :—It appears that Thursday last a lady, dressed in the first style of fashion, and bearing all the outward indications of the highest respectability drove into Farringdon Street in her carriage. The lady introduced herself to a relation of the young woman, Taylor, and on finding that Taylor had a male child of the age stated, she desired to see it, and for that purpose returned to and waited in her carriage. The mother instantly set out to fetch her daughter and child from their domicile in Chandos Street, and on their return together the child, a smart, intelligent, prepossessing little fellow, was exhibited to the lady who at once made overtures for his purchase. The unnatural mother of the child consented to the sale, and received the earnest of half a sovereign. The carriage drove off with the lady and her newly acquired purchase but returned again in a brief space of time and showed the unconscious boy denuded of his dirty rags with which his limbs were encased but now superbly clad in new clothes, hat and feathers of the most tasteful and expensive kind. They again drove off, the lady promising to renew her visit on Monday next, and then to pay any sum from £2 to £5 they might require. The grandfather of the child is loud in his denunciations of his daughter's conduct and is determined to trace the matter to the bottom."

The century represents a steady struggle towards the full emancipation of the child ; the rescue of the innocent from the dungeons of Bluebeard's Castle. No one would pretend that this world of 1946 is the best of all conceivable worlds for a child to be born into, but the changes in a century are heartening none the less. There are many men alive to-day who as children of seven and eight worked long hours in the cotton mills. One of these is Mr. J. R. Clynes who sat in the House of Commons until the last election (1945) and had honourably filled high offices of State. Mr. Clynes' autobiography is a testimony to the transformation in the people's condition shown in his lifetime and a confession of faith in the democratic method under which such changes can be wrought without that bloody revolution which Engels and Marx conceived inevitable in the 'forties.

With the Industrial Revolution, there came the most rapid expansion of population this country has known. The population was 10 million in 1801, 14 million in 1821, 20 million in 1851 26 million in 1871 and 36 million in 1901. It more than trebled itself in a century. When England became the workshop of the world and the mine-owners, mill-owners and factory-owners were clamouring for more and more hands, child-labour, like woman-labour was a prized commodity. Or, perhaps, it would be more apt to describe it as a wasted commodity. The men of a century ago were zealous for public economy, but they were prodigal beyond measure of the country's natural riches. Among these resources of the nation the most precious were its children. They were the offspring of as sturdy a stock as earth could show ; they were the inheritors of a grand tradition of craftsmanship and of diverse skills ; they were born with hope, loyalty, fortitude and industry in their blood. To put it no higher, it was odd such shrewd men of business should waste so rare an asset.

The report of the Commission on the employment of children in the coal mines, issued in 1842, shocked even the self-complacent. It was a chronicle of almost unrelieved darkness. Tiny infants, sometimes no more than five or six years old, or even younger, were thrust down the pits. Little creatures who had but lately learned to walk and talk were put on guard at the ventilating doors in the mines, imprisoned in darkness for many hours at a stretch. Boys and girls of tender years, half-naked, often running on all fours like animals, took the part of pit ponies in drawing trucks through the narrow subterranean corridors. They were treated with less care than animals. Often they were beaten and maltreated. Fever, dirt and ill-usage carried many of them off to merciful extinction. But the children of the poor were in plentiful supply. There was always a multitude of new little victims crowding on the heels of their brothers and sisters. " Infanticide is practised as extensively and as legally in England as it is on the banks of the Ganges, a circumstance which apparently has not yet engaged the attention of the Society for the Propagation of the Gospel in Foreign Parts. . . . There are infants that will defy even starvation and poison, unnatural mothers and demon nurses." It was not a Chartist who wrote that. It was not a Radical. It was Benjamin Disraeli.

The debates in the House and in the Press during the period make sad reading, for it is always sad to see men of integrity so bemused by economic doctrine that they become blind to moral evils. One feels that the Victorian design of tragedy was a good man struggling with a theory.

The revulsion of feeling caused by the report on conditions in coal-mines stopped the employment of children underground, but the fight over child labour in mills and factories was a stiff one. The opposition included men of high principle who genuinely believed that it was wrong for Government to interfere with the happy rhythm of supply and demand and that the expanding commerce of Britain's glorious era of Free Trade would be wrecked if young children were not put to work. One reads solemn adjurations by the economists to the humanitarians to repent of their mad propaganda before they brought ruin on their country. About the same time similar arguments were being used in the United States to sustain slavery.

Elizabeth Barrett Browning in *The Cry of the Children* expressed
the strained bitterness of sensitive men and women :—

> For all day, we drag our burden tiring
>   Through the coal-dark, underground—
> Or, all day, we drive the wheels of iron
>   In the factories ; round and round.
> " For, oh," say the children, " we are weary
>   And we cannot run or leap
> If we cared for any meadows, it were merely
>   To drop down in them and sleep."
> For all day, the wheels are droning, turning—
>   The wind comes in our faces—
> Till our hearts turn—our head, with pulses burning,
>   And the walls turn in their places.

That was an age of orators, and of orations lasting sometimes
five hours, but over the chasm of time into which much glittering
rhetoric has vanished, the voice of Shaftesbury describing a begrimed
scrap of humanity beaten to a pulp by a slave-master in the coal
mines, reaches us with the timeless appeal of pity and divine rage.

It is extraordinary to watch the moral and intellectual contortions
of good men and kindly men in their effort to justify the conditions
of child labour. They were in this dilemma, that having adopted
with enthusiasm the religion of Continuous Progress they could not
admit that their god had enormous clay feet. To a man who had
come away from the Great Exhibition exalted by the glory of
mechanical advances and filled with the mystical ardours of commerce, the suggestion that the shining white god, Progress had some
of the attributes of Moloch sounded like blasphemy. So one got the
queer paradox of the defenders of child serfdom working up a
genuine moral indignation of their own. The Benthamite spell lay
heavy upon them. The theory of the Larger Good and the Wider
Freedom was invoked to justify the exploitation of the helpless. The
significant thing is that the first cracks in the gigantic orthodoxy of
mechanical Progress were brought about by the children, by the
feeblest and least regarded creatures of that age. There was no
philosophy that could long endure such criticism as that expressed in
Mark Rutherford's Deliverance :—"As we walked over the Drury Lane
gratings of the cellars a most foul stench came up, and one in
particular I remember to this day. A man half-dressed pushed open
a broken window beneath us, just as we passed by, and then issued
such a blast of corruption, made up of gases bred by filth, air
breathed and rebreathed a hundred times, charged with odours of
unnamable personal uncleanness and disease, that I staggered to

the gutter with a qualm which I could scarcely conquer. At the doors of the houses stood grimy women with their arms folded and their hair disordered. Grimier boys and girls had tied a rope to broken railings, and were swinging on it. The common door to a score of lodgings stood ever open, and the children swarmed up and down the stairs carrying with them patches of mud every time they came in from the street."

Successive acts regulating the employment of children did much to end a curse, but not everything. Infants continued to be ill-used in places beyond the reach of factory inspectors. In small trades the abuses continued for a long time. The chimney-sweep's boy, about whom Blake wrote one of his most affecting poems, was a too-familiar sight in London and provincial towns long after 1846. These children were chosen for their smallness; they were sent up the chimneys naked; many suffered burns, others were suffocated or were trapped in the twists and turns of the chimney passages, while a great number died from hideous skin diseases caused by soot irritation. Flues and chimneys were often intricate, but one of the wickedest things ever done in that period was the falsifying of drawings to persuade the House of Lords Committee that chimneys could not be swept except by thrusting little children up them as no brushes could be constructed to curve round the labyrinthine windings from fireplace to roof.

There was a wide callousness about children and a lust to make money which stifled the natural instincts and was beyond the reach of any Act of Parliament Shaftesbury could devise. Men and women who had been brutalised by evil conditions lacked the protective tenderness to their young which is common to apes and tigers.

The first part of our century was concerned with making sure that children should be treated at least as well as domestic animals. The National Society for the Prevention of Cruelty to Children (founded in 1884) bespoke a growing consciousness that our treasured personal liberty did not include the right to maltreat the young. Then, again, such a man as Dr. Barnardo showed an uncanny gift for taking waifs and converting them into useful citizens. Working as a doctor during the cholera epidemic which swept the East End in 1865, Barnardo was saddened by the spectacle of numberless abandoned children on the streets. There was no place for these homeless urchins except the thieves' kitchens. Barnardo contributed to the general betterment of our times by proving by countless examples that a good environment would redeem the worst heredity. No child is beyond redemption, said Barnardo. He helped to break down a gloomy belief in the predestination of the poor that made all change on their behalf appear hopeless, if not, indeed, impious.

It might have been thought that the enlightened self-interest which made the Victorians such enthusiasts for invention and scientific progress would have made them also as earnest advocates of popular education as were their contemporary Germans, Frenchmen, Scandinavians and Americans. Eager as they were to extend Britain's leadership in the world, they must surely have regarded a well-educated community as a prime asset. Not so. For many years education was looked upon as an adornment of life rather than a necessity—a silk hat and a rose in the buttonhole. In the 'forties and 'fifties, most wealthy merchants shied at sending their sons to a university. That was all very well for the gilded lilies of the aristocracy, but toilers and spinners in these roaring times had to begin early. A boy designed by his father to inherit a great commercial enterprise would be sent to the counting house at fourteen. As for the children of the poor, the sooner they were put to work the better for them, and for the country. The census of 1851 showed that of four million children between the ages of 5 and 15, two millions were on no school list of any kind, while the majority of the other two millions had the poorest scraps of education thrown to them.

Fifty years ago when Margaret McMillan (for long a contributor to the *Daily News*) undertook her pilgrimage on behalf of the children in Yorkshire and Lancashire many of the operatives were still sceptical and suspicious of education. They had started young in the mill and were proud of it. It was good for the soul to be introduced early to the practical business of earning a living. Half-time was a training in character as well as an economic advantage. They could not comprehend this Scotswoman's romantic belief that the most wretched baby born in the slums was a king in his own right and that he was the inheritor of the treasures of the centuries.

Dickens had no philosophic theories about education. He had no philosophic theories about utilitarianism. When he thought about education, his brain lighted up with a series of vivid images and tableaux. In his letter on the first Ragged Schools which appeared in the *Daily News* on 4 February 1846, he draws this sketch of the class he saw : " Huddled together on a bench about the room, and shown out by some flaring candles stuck against the walls, were a crowd of boys varying from mere infants to young men : sellers of fruit, herbs, lucifer-matches, flints ; sleepers under the dry arches of bridges ; young thieves and beggars—with nothing natural to youth about them ; with nothing frank, ingenious

or pleasant in their faces ; low-browed, vicious, cunning, wicked ;
abandoned of all help but this ; speeding downward to destruction ;
and UNUTTERABLY IGNORANT." (The capitals were
Dickens'.)

Abandoned of all help but this !—that was the key ; there was a
desperate clinging on his part as well as theirs to this one hope of
redemption. If in the rank-smelling slum these child outcasts,
too villainous and dirty to find a place in any charity school,
could achieve but the faintest glimmering of the dignity of man
and the beauty of the world, then not for them but for their children,
not for today but for tomorrow—and perhaps the morrow might be a
hundred years ahead—there was a chance. He saw ignorance as a
disease, as a creeping infection that was the root of a host of sick-
nesses. He saw ignorance as the great crime which spawned
criminals. Nothing haunted him more in his recollection of prisons
than the sight of full-grown felons being taught to write, struggling
with a painful clumsiness to form the letters of the alphabet,
reddening as they had never reddened over their crimes, in the
attempt to shape babyish A's and O's.

Dickens wrote of the Ragged Schools as an effort " to suggest
to Society that its duty to this wretched throng, foredoomed to
crime and punishment, rightfully begins at some distance from the
police office, and that the careless maintenance from year to year
in this, the capital city of the world, of a vast hopeless nursery of
ignorance, misery and vice ; a breeding place of hulks and jails ;
is horrible to contemplate."

The country had to wait until 1870 for W. E. Forster's Act. There
were men of mark and men of learning who dreaded the consequences of compulsory education, even of this elementary order,
far more than they dreaded the almost contemporary invention of
dynamite. Education meant teaching Caliban how to name the
bigger light and how the less ; it meant teaching Caliban the
language in which to curse his master.

The effort to " widen the skirts of light " in education has never
been an easy one. The struggle to give more people a chance
to read and to write and to know what the world was about, was
of a piece with the struggle to give more people a chance to vote,
to communicate with one another through a cheap postage, to be
informed through newspapers that they could afford to buy, to
take their share in the life of the community. These extensions
of human faculty were always resisted by those who honestly believed
that the people were happiest when they knew least and exhibited
no curiosity about the bigger or the lesser light. The conflict of
philosophies was joined over Forster's Act ; over Balfour's Act

of 1902 which angered the Nonconformists ; over Birrell's Bill in 1906 which foundered in the House of Lords ; over the Fisher Act of 1918. The leading article on the great Act of 1870 regretted that the scope of the measure was not wider. It lamented, too, that bitterness between the sects which was to cloud counsel for many a year.

During the whole period, efforts to safeguard the body as well as the mind of the child were intertwined. There was the legislation of 1906 which provided for the school feeding of ill-nourished children—recognising that mites with empty stomachs were not likely to obtain much profit from instruction—and there was Herbert Samuel's Children Act of 1908 which codified and extended many benevolent ideas. The furnishing of medical inspection for boys and girls, and the steady development of school sport during these past decades have helped to raise the physical standards. Infant clinics, and the development of such enterprises as those Miss McMillan and her sister originated years ago have spared many lives and saved much suffering.

For a modern pessimist there are few exercises more cheering than to compare the group photographs of classes in poor neighbourhoods today with those taken forty years ago. Of all visible tokens these enable one to say, " Things may not grow perfect, but some get better." How stunted and white-faced those boys of the past look, with their rubber collars, long black stockings, and cropped hair, the fringe being cut low on the forehead. There doesn't seem much glow on those faces, much gleam in those eyes, but an air of mute acceptance that this is not going to be a very good world. One speculates as to how a teacher would be able to strike a spark from them, or convey to those little chaps the glories of man's estate and man's future. Contemporary pictures from these same schools furnish a gallery of happier and rounder faces, of keener eyes and robuster bodies. Here (one says) is material with which a teacher could work. Here is promise. During the war, the condition of numbers of the bomb-exiled children shocked the country houses that took them in. Such a book as *Our Towns* makes dreary reading, suggesting that Disraeli's Two Nations are still unfused. But when one looks again at streets one knew as a boy, a confidence in a different order of Progress from Gradgrind's and Bounderby's comes back. *

One of the significant changes of the century is the way in which the community has turned to education as their doubts about mechanical Progress have increased. There was a time when, at the

* It is in the perspective of these decades that one can best appreciate the inspiration of Baden-Powell in founding the Boy Scouts.

peak of the Victorian triumph, the popular philosophers delightedly hailed the universe as one prodigious machine, men being neat little machines wound up to go for three score years and ten. All that those little machines needed was the correct fuel and lubricating oil. But the clockwork universe left to itself had a trick of producing not only more clockwork machines, but supernatural horrors, more terrifying than anything in the old demonology. Pure mechanism attained its height with the doodlebug, the rocket and jet-propulsion. Determinism culminated in the splitting of the atom.

This, said Victorian survivors, was not at all what the Prince Consort had in mind on that May morning when the Great Exhibition was opened. The truth of one of the major guesses of Dickens was perceived—that Thomas Gradgrind might turn out to be a worse villain than Fagin or Wackford Squeers. " Now, what I want is, Facts. Teach these boys and girls nothing but Facts. Facts alone are wanted in life. Plant nothing else, and root out everything else. You can only form the minds of reasoning animals upon Facts : nothing else will ever be of any service to them. This is the principle on which I bring up my own children, and this is the principle on which I bring up these children. Stick to Facts, sir."

The accumulation of facts unrelated to any philosophy of existence was seen to lead to universal anarchy instead of universal prosperity. A vision of the Artful Dodger with a tea-caddy packed with atomic energy alarmed the closing years of the century. Gradgrind was seen to be handing out little bombs wrapped in cellophane to the village schoolchildren instead of Christmas oranges.

It was in the years between the wars that H. G. Wells wrote, " Human history becomes more and more a race between education and catastrophe." What has happened since has reduced Wells to a black nihilism, in comparison with which Schopenhauer was sunny, and has sharpened the sense of urgency in less pessimistic minds. The century which opened with the sacrifice of the babes to the Moloch of the machine ended with the command—" Educate the babes or perish."

CHAPTER X

TOWARDS HEALTH

I

THE DANCE OF DEATH

AFTER dipping into the files of the middle 'forties one is left astonished at the toughness of our ancestors. Why, for example, didn't our great grandfathers in London, and other big cities, perish by the hundreds of thousands in such a hot summer as 1846? The sanitary conditions were lamentable. Every circumstance predisposing to plague was present. In 1846 there were still 200,000 undrained cesspools in London. There was still no sewage-pipe connection between most of the houses and the main drains. The Thames was a sink. The stench from the river was vile, and at certain times of the tide M.P.'s could not use those Committee Rooms of the House of Commons which faced it. Even the Serpentine was so befouled by the poisons draining into it from the Westbourne stream that it breathed death on citizens taking the air in Hyde Park.

The congested city burial grounds were strewn with skulls and bones—and half-buried corpses, among which drunken grave-diggers buffooned a horrible dance of death. They were vulnerable ghouls, many of them catching the infections of the graveyards and swiftly joining their victims. In the dark of night the body-snatchers flitted about. Contemporary descriptions of these Golgothas, as Dr. George W. Walker called the burial grounds, are no reading for a queasy stomach. They are Jacobean rather than Victorian. The dance of the diggers in the graveyard is very like a scene from John Webster. The excellent Dr. Walker was tireless in pamphlet-eering and speaking against these scandals, but the odd thing is that it was necessary for him to raise such a commotion on the grounds of the menace to public health before any remedy was tried. One would have thought that the dangers of these rat-thronged bone-yards would have frightened every mother of a family within a five miles radius to enforce action.

The death of the proud and magnificent Lady Dedlock at the gate of one of these foul places is—like so much else in Dickens—symbolical of the double world of the Victorians. "The gate was closed. Beyond it, was a burial ground—a dreadful spot in which the night was very slowly stirring, but where I could dimly

see heaps of dishonoured graves and stones, hemmed in by filthy
houses, with a few dull lights in their windows, and on whose walls
a thick humidity broke out like a disease.   On the step at the gate,
drenched in the fearful wet of such a place, which oozed and splashed
down everywhere, I saw, with a cry of pity and horror, a woman
lying."

Sensitive spirits turned from the ugliness of that time to dream
upon a fairer past.   In the prologue to *The Earthly Paradise* William
Morris besought his readers :—

> *Forget six counties overhung with smoke,*
> *Forget the snorting steam and piston stroke,*
> *Forget the spreading of the hideous town ;*
> *Think rather of the pack-horse on the down,*
> *And dream of London, small and white and clean,*
> *The clear Thames bordered by its gardens green.*

The patient earth could absorb the city's pollutions during the
centuries when London was relatively a small place, the houses
interspersed with fields and gardens, when meadows lay between
Westminster and Temple Bar and when Kensington was remote
from Whitehall, and Streatham was a spa.   But with the swift
growth of the city, with hundreds of thousands of human beings
huddling into the new slums, London was in peril of poisoning itself.
In *Bleak House* there are sketches in indigo ink of such haunts.
A slum like Tom-All-Alone's, which existed not far from where the
News Chronicle office now stands, was " a villainous street, undrained,
unventilated, deep in black mud and corrupt water—though the
roads are dry elsewhere—and reeking with such smells and sights
that he who has lived in London all his life can scarce believe his
senses."

Our forbears did not show themselves at their best in tackling
bad sanitation.   The Podsnap attitude of not speaking of things
which might bring a blush to the cheeks of the young person
was widely approved.   Drains and sewers were subjects which
Podsnap swept behind him with scythe-like movements of his
majestic arm.   While the middle-classes dismissed the subject as
unsuitable for polite conversation, the aristocracy thought that
people who bothered about it were amusing frumps and fidgets.
The drains were regarded as useful barometers ; if the smell was
particularly poignant then it meant that we were in for a spell of
hot weather.   As late as 1871 the Prince of Wales (Edward VII)
contracted typhoid through the bad drains of a Yorkshire mansion
where he had been staying.   It was not easy to stir up a public
opinion to goad sleepy local authorities.   In the newspapers,

references to the dangers were tucked away at the bottom of columns. Turning the pages of the file, one has a hazy impression of an odd indignant doctor or two suggesting, during the hot weather, methods of flushing to abate the nuisance, but of no large sections of people getting worked up about it, no orators thundering as they had thundered over the Corn Laws or Slavery.

The death rate was high. It says much for the natural vigour of our forefathers that it was not far higher. From 1838 to 1840, the average mortality rate in London was 37.38 a thousand, and in some of the slum districts, 60 per thousand. Vile diseases flourished. In these poorest parts of the town the open sewer crawled down the street, choked with filth. Hillocks of decaying rubbish were left uncleared. Flies swarmed, carrying fever to the wretched children in the tenements. Drinking water was contaminated, and typhoid and cholera were never far away. There had been one cholera epidemic in 1832 in which over 5,000 Londoners died ; another epidemic in 1849 was to cause 14,000 deaths. The drawing-rooms of Belgravia might affect a patrician disdain, but plague had no respect for Debrett. " Tom has his revenge. Even the winds are his messengers, and they serve him in these hours of darkness. There is not a drop of Tom's corrupted blood but propagates infection and contagion." As in *The Masque of the Red Death*, pestilence joined the revels, the unbidden guest whom no silk curtains could shut out.

The housing of the people is a subject of universal concern in 1946. All parties in the State are pledged to make their utmost exertions in this cause. It provides some of the most spirited debates in the Commons, and in the public opinion polls it runs far ahead of all other subjects in interest. A hundred years ago, however, there were not many to care what happened to Tom-All-Alone's. A report of the first meeting of the National Association for Improving the Dwellings of the Industrious Classes appears in the *Daily News* during March 1846. The object of this Association was to erect houses for the working-classes combining in their construction improvements in drainage and ventilation, a proper supply of water " and such other advances as can render their sanitary condition as complete as practicable." The Association had been formed, it was said, in consequence of the evidence produced before the Parliamentary Committee appointed to inquire into the health of towns—" which evidence disclosed a state of circumstances connected with the domestic habits and dwellings of the poorer classes of the metropolis and other densely populated districts fearful to contemplate and urgently calling for a remedy." The reporter observed that " there was a highly respectable though not a very numerous, attendance at the meeting." It was not a subject, like Repeal, which would draw audiences of thousands. It was not a fashionable scandal.

Some of the speeches, read a hundred years later, give Gustave Doré glimpses of the London of that day. Lord Morpeth, the Whig M.P., asked his audience if it had " ever tracked the swarm of human life, of decrepit age, of blighted manhood and of stunted infancy into the steaming and reeking receptacles of filth and fever, and every kind of loathsomeness, into which they are but too often stuffed and crammed—and this, too, within a stone's throw of your own most luxurious dwellings, in the near neighbourhood of the gaudiest theatres, of the halls of legislators and of the shrines of religion."

Another Whig M.P., Lord Ebrington, spoke of visiting the streets at the back " of the magnificent dwellings in Regent Street, those streets in which what I may call the aristocracy of the working-classes are living—and I remember the foetid and oppressive smells of every sort of animal and vegetable decomposition—or the *closeness*, if possible still more offensive, proceeding from the repeated respiration of the same polluted atmosphere."

There were many street improvements taking place in London at this time. In 1845, for example, Trafalgar Square had been cleared of nests of tumbledown houses. The trouble was that whenever such rookeries were broken up, no other homes were provided for the dispossessed, and they swarmed into the already overcrowded slums in other parts of the town. William MacCullagh Torrens contributed much vigorous writing on the subject of the neglected condition of workman's housing to early numbers of the *Daily News*. Torrens (1813–94) was a fortunate man: as an M.P. he was able to carry into effect the reforms he had advocated as a journalist. He was a pioneer in housing and, through his exertions, the Artizans' Dwellings Bill was passed. It was in 1846 that Torrens' book, *The Industrial History of Free Nations* was published. Incidentally, it was Torrens who made the celebrated diagnosis of Ireland in 1867—" It contains only two classes, Fenians and flunkeys."

The effort to remedy the sorry conditions of public health was a weary one. London's plethora of overlapping authorities—each jealous of the other, each thwarting the other, each vying with the other in narrow stupidity—tangled and tripped up the reformers in yards on yards of red tape. There were no fewer than seven separate Boards of Commissioners of Sewers exercising authority in London at this time. It was not until 1848 that it became compulsory for houses to be equipped with water-closets and for the drains to be connected with the main sewers. It was my Lord Cholera that in the end brought about the establishment of the Metropolitan Board of Works in 1855 as the central authority exercising power over the medley of squabbling local authorities. In 1850 the unholy spectacle of the burial grounds was ended by the Board of Health being made a Burial Board for the metropolis and power being given to the Privy Council to close the city graveyards. The city workers of today know many of them as pleasant oases amid steel and ferro-concrete where crocus and daffodil grow in the spring, and the sparrows peck and twitter in the sunshine, and lovers meet, and junior clerks eat their luncheon sandwiches.

II
ANAESTHETICS

What cheers the spirits most of all in traversing this century is to mark the successive conquests over death, disease, dirt, pain, and wretchedness. Not all the centuries before it, lumped together, did as much as these hundred years to diminish the sum of physical suffering. It is not pleasant to contemplate what internal operations and amputations were like in the days before anaesthetics. Especially on a child. Or the deaths in hospitals from gangrene and septic poisoning. Or the suffering that was endured by innumerable women as a result of the midwifery of which Sairey Gamp was an ornament.

Our disillusionment with Science and Mechanical Progress has inclined us to be contemptuous of the facile optimism of the Victorians, of their faith that things get better if men will it so. But that optimism has at least been vindicated in medicine, surgery and public health. Those were men and women of exalted character as well as professional skill who freed their fellows from pain and saved children from untimely death. Across the years —rising from the trivia and mustiness of old newspapers— comes the voice of Pasteur speaking at the inauguration of the Pasteur Institute (1888) : " Two opposing laws seem to me now in contest. The one, a law of blood and death, opening out each day new modes of destruction, forces nations to be always ready for the battle. The other, a law of peace, work and health, whose only aim is to deliver man from the calamities which beset him. The one seeks violent conquests, the other the relief of mankind. The one places a single life above all victories, the other sacrifices hundreds of thousands of lives to the ambition of a single individual. The law of which we are the instruments strives even through the carnage to cure the wounds due to the law of war. Treatment by our antiseptic methods may preserve the lives of thousands of soldiers. Which of these two laws will prevail, God only knows. But of this we may be sure, that science, in obeying the law of humanity, will always labour to enlarge the frontiers of life." As we move, uncertain of our bearings, into the atomic age, these words of Pasteur go with us.

That century enlarged the frontiers of life. There are major conquests over pain, sickness and misery still to be won ; to those who are enlisted in today's army of human liberation the pioneers of the past century send signals of encouragement. Their experience shows us that despite the close-ranked opposition of apathy, cupidity, prejudice, selfishness, pathological fear of any change, and downright honest stupidity, high mountains can be laid low by a minority of resolute men and women who know what they want and never falter in their struggle to achieve it.

One discovers over and again in these researches into old files how much that touches us nearly today we can trace back to 1846. It was towards the end of that year that a piece of news reached the paper that now looks to us in retrospect of greater import to the bulk of human beings in our century than most of those large affairs of State which claimed major attention. The American despatches—this, remember, was before the Atlantic cable—recorded that a dentist in Boston, a Dr. Morton, had achieved remarkable results in the previous September by employing sulphuric ether to produce general anaesthesia and the gas had been used with unfailing success in a number of graver surgical operations than the drawing of teeth. A contemporary account reads quaintly, " It is a mode of rendering patients insensible to the pain of surgical operations, by the inhalation of the vapour of the strongest sulphuric ether. They are thrown into a state nearly resembling that of complete intoxication from ardent spirits, or of narcotism from opium. This state continues but a few minutes—five to ten—but during it the patient is insensible to pain. A leg has been amputated, a breast extirpated, teeth drawn, without the slightest suffering . . . The effect is not exactly the same on all. In some the insensibility is entire and the patient is aware of nothing which is going on ; in others, a certain degree of the power of perception remains, the patient knows what the operator is doing, perceives him, for example, take hold of a tooth and draw it out, feels the grating of the instrument, but still has no pain. There are no subsequent ill effects to detract from the value of this practice, none even so great as those which follow a common dose of opium."

Within two days of the results of Morton's discovery reaching this side of the Atlantic the first tooth extraction under the gas took

WHEN HOLIDAYS BY TRAIN WERE NEW
A Musical Souvenir.

place in London.   Within another two days, Liston, the surgeon, had used ether in amputating a man's leg in University College Hospital.   There should be a centenary celebration of this victory over pain.   The new treatment was swiftly and widely adopted ; Sir James Simpson, the obstetric surgeon, applied it to child-birth.   Next year, Simpson discovered the anaesthetic properties of chloroform.   This readiness to accept the new thing warms the heart until one discovers that 46 years earlier the great Humphry Davy (of the miner's Davy lamp) had found out, and tested on himself, the power of nitrous oxide gas to relieve pain, and recommended that it should be employed in surgical operations. Eighteen years later, the many-sided genius of Faraday demonstrated that sulphuric ether possessed the same pain-destroying qualities.   It is saddening and maddening to reflect that if the discoveries of Davy and Faraday had been applied in surgery earlier a world of suffering would have been avoided.

Simpson, despite his authority and prestige, was strongly opposed by a considerable section of his profession.   In Bertrand Russell's words, " It required, for example, more evidence to persuade them that anaesthetics may be used in childbirth than it would have required to persuade them of the opposite."

In the century that has gone by since 1846, men, women and children beyond counting have been spared the tortures of the old surgery.   A widened sensibility—an increasing awareness of other people's pain was manifest during the age.   The average man was a more humane being, a more sensitive organism, at the end of it than he had been at the beginning.

III

THE LAW OF HUMANITY

Surgery before anaesthetics.   Hospitals before Lister.   Nurses before Florence Nightingale.   Let us think on the past, and give praise to those who enlarged the frontiers of life.

Lister was a student of 19 at University College, London, when anaesthetics came into use.   The deadening of pain had removed one gruesome terror from the hospitals but others suddenly multiplied.   The number of patients who died from gangrene after operations, even simple ones, became shockingly high.   In some institutions septic poisoning raged like the plague.   The coming of ether and chloroform enabled surgeons to perform complicated operations which would have been unthinkable under the old conditions when everything depended on speed and a swift release for the writhing, conscious victim, but, by a bitter irony, this boon led to a higher death-rate. The sick now avoided the hospitals for a new reason. They were macabre places—with the surgeons in their stained operating coats, the unsterilised instruments and the neglect of the simplest precautions against infection. The hospitals had become in the terrified eyes of the poor the antechambers of the mortuary. It was to this evil of sepsis that Lister, with his capacity for taking endless pains, addressed himself. His first antiseptic experiment (1865) was the painting of compound fractures with carbolic acid. Pasteur's theory of germs came as a lamp on Lister's path, and there is no better example of the operation of Pasteur's law of humanity than the interplay of ideas between Frenchman and Briton. While prancing politocos and seedy generals were making bad blood between the French and British these men of healing were giving unselfishly to each other's achievement, hugging no secrets, patenting no rights. Lister, by applying the results of Pasteur's researches in fermentation to surgery, brought about one of the benevolent revolutions of our time.

Then one imagines the meeting of the two . . . Lister humbly confessing that he owed everything to Pasteur, and Pasteur embracing Lister as one of the benefactors of mankind. How mean much of the diplomacy of that day looks by comparison !

The end of Mrs. Gamp was brought about by the daughter of a Derbyshire country gentleman who had no taste for social pleasures but had a vocation for nursing the sick. In the year our story opens, Florence Nightingale, then 26, was deeply committed to her long apprenticeship. She trained herself as though possessed by a prophetic vision of Scutari. Aware of the failings of her country in hospital management, she spent years working in better-equipped institutions abroad. In 1854 came the day for which this dedicated woman had prepared herself. Britain was angered by stories pouring home about the condition of the wounded and sick soldiers in the Crimea. It was of a piece with the mismanagement of the campaign that there had not been the barest provisions made for the care of the wounded. Grisly tales reached London of affairs at the large hospital at Scutari. The wounded were dying by hundreds. Out of bad sanitary arrangements sprang fever and pestilence. The death rate in the hospitals rose to 42 per cent.

Authority in a panic turned to Florence Nightingale. With a staff of 37 nurses, she went to the Crimea, arriving in time to receive the wounded from the charge at Balaclava. Florence Nightingale in the Crimea transcended the vetoes of flesh and blood. She was everywhere at once—twenty-four hours a day—

present in operating rooms—arranging the reception of new batches of wounded—consoling, inspiriting, giving orders. She caught the fever that burned through the sick wards, but that enemy did not subdue her.

Despite Lytton Strachey, most of us still know Florence Nightingale through the pictures of the Lady of the Lamp, but these sentimentalise a woman who was anything but a sentimentalist. She never suffered fools, and she had a horror of dirt. One sees her, brisk and brusque as the Victorian housekeeper outraged by the romanticism of the male that has suddenly turned the home into a senseless mess. She loathed waste ; and waste of life was the worst of sins. Her *Notes on Nursing*—which are the burial service read over Mrs. Gamp—and her reports on hospital management carried common sense to that peak where it looked like genius.

The emancipation of the race from pain and sickness is one of the best hopes bequeathed us by the Victorians. This goes on, come fair or foul in politics. Recent advances in surgery have mended bodies and saved lives that would have been lost in Lister's time. X-rays have provided an eye to penetrate the deepest-rooted troubles. Radium—discovered by the Curies—has been an invaluable ally against one of the worst of the remaining ills of man. In late years M. and B., the sulphanilamides, and penicillin have been added to the well-stocked armoury.

Turning over the pages of the *Daily News* in its jubilee year, 1896, one lights upon reports of inquests on those who had died from hydrophobia. That was a death horrible to think about. A mad dog at large in a village frightened the inhabitants more than the zooming of a V.1 did in 1944. Pasteur's last gift was the cure of the mad dog's bite. He had been unsure of his discovery. It was a tremendous moment when, after many self-searchings, he put his faith to the test and administered for the first time his treatment to that young American boy infected with rabies who had been sent to him as a last desperate recourse. The treatment took ! One more of the blind fears had been conquered . . . " One must go on working," said Pasteur on his death-bed. There will always be work to do.

One traces through that age the development of a theme of priceless worth to the children of men—the fraternal association of the healers. That was an ideal not corroded by fear and disillusion, as faith in scientific invention became corroded. In the quest for the unifying principle, which is man's deepest need, here, at least, seemed one part of the answer. This was a universal activity which linked men together through their own most unselfish instincts.

CHAPTER XI

IN WAR AND PEACE

I

WAR CORRESPONDENT

IN 1870, two years after it had become a penny paper, the *Daily News* enjoyed a spell of sudden and startling success. In one week, its daily sales rose from 50,000 to 150,000. This was in large part due to Archibald Forbes' messages from the Franco-German war front. Forbes, a professional soldier—he had served in the Royal Dragoons—was the discovery of that decade.

From the Crimea War until 1870, William Henry Russell, of *The Times*, was the prince, as he had been the pioneer, of Victorian war correspondents. Russell belonged to the age before the telegraph. His despatches from the Crimea which brought down the Aberdeen Government (and were among the finest services any journalist has rendered his countrymen) were letters collected by courier. He had time to reflect upon the course of an action, to see it in the round, and to impose an historian's judgment on the management of masses.

Forbes, the new man in the field, was a creature of the electric telegraph. In the Franco-Prussian war, he did not always wait for the end of a battle to report it. Sometimes he did not even wait for its beginning. He dealt in anticipations. Attaching himself to the Crown Prince of Saxony, he won that commander's confidence and was made privy to the secrets of Prussian strategy. Hence he was often able to telegraph to his newspaper a forecast of an action, rather in the manner of a reporter who secures a politican's speech beforehand and wires it with the warning " Hold till released." The Crown Prince did not share the usual military passion for concealment.

In the 'forties the Victorian public had become aware of a new kind of romantic figure on the stage of affairs. The war correspondent contrived to unite the power of sword and pen. He communicated to homekeeping readers the harsh excitements of a campaign in wild parts of the world and the courage of anonymous and inarticulate men. He was often drawn by a chivalrous attachment to share the hardships and to make known the virtues of small peoples struggling against despotism. Or he was a man who had found the dull comforts of city life intolerable, and had broken through the net to follow Garibaldi. During the gilded age of the

Victorians the war correspondent represented the adventurous protest. Forbes making his celebrated ride—120 miles in 15 hours through perilous country—to bring the news of how the day had gone at Ulundi, and G. A. Henty going with Wolseley through the swamp and bad lands to Kumasi infected with a romantic restlessness the City clerks coming up to Liverpool Street or Cannon Street in the suburban trains. Among the *Daily News* war correspondents of this period was Edmond O'Donovan, the Irishman, who loathed a comfortable life at home, feeling, he said, like a Red Indian in patent leather shoes. He found his greatest happiness in the wildness of Merv, the roof of the world, and he was killed in the massacre of Hicks' expeditionary force in the Sudan. And there was Muller, the young American, who entered Metz with the Germans, sent a brilliant dispatch giving the first news to the world of Marshal Bazaine's surrender, then was never heard from again, being, it is supposed, shot and buried in a nameless trench.

The opening passages of Forbes' recollections of his service with the paper give the authentic note of romance over the hill : " Well do I remember that September morning of 1870 when, for the first time, I climbed the rickety staircase of the old *Daily News* office, and stood in the manager's room before the quiet-mannered man who surveyed me steadily through his spectacles as he listened silently to the nervously uttered proposition which I ventured to put before him. Robinson wasted no words. ' I want you to start for Metz tonight,' was his extremely succinct reply to my broken and stammering utterances. My heart rose to my mouth. For now, after disappointment on disappointment, the great chance had come at last, with all the prestige of a great paper whose war correspondence was already the talk of the town—with all the scope for making a name, if, indeed, the capacity to do so did haply abide in me. Two days later I was on the foreposts on the east side of Metz, my welcome a shell from Fort St. Julien which burst in front of me in the street of the village of Flanville."

The mild-mannered man quizzing Forbes through his spectacles was Sir John Robinson, who had been appointed manager of the *Daily News* in 1868 and retained that post until 1901. Robinson's first contribution to the newspaper, made in February 1846, was an account of a meeting of Wiltshire farm labourers to protest against the Corn Laws, the occasion which prompted Dickens' *Hymn of the Wiltshire Labourers*.

It was due to Robinson's skill in direction that the reporting of the Franco-Prussian war reached so high a standard. He chose a strong team of correspondents and encouraged them to use the telegraph not only to relay brief facts but long descriptive accounts.

The Franco-Prussian war was an early example of *blitzkrieg*, as the Prussian attacks on Austria and Denmark had been. Robinson's arrangements were more than justified by the headlong rush of events and by the interest which the overthrow of the Second Empre excited. Forbes' despatches and those of his colleagues creatied a stir in Britain and were copied throughout the world. With the verve of the new direction, the newspaper speedily became successful. Robinson's masterful and zealous administration bridged the period from the Franco-German to the Boer War.

One of the newspaper's owners in 1870 was Henry Labouchere* —"Labby" M.P.—whom Queen Victoria was later to look upon with shocked eyes as though the Lincoln Imp itself had popped up in Parliament. Born to wealth, he had equipped himself for a career in the diplomatic service by spending some months with a travelling circus and then by living with a Chippewa Indian tribe. Labouchere was in Paris throughout the Siege, and his letters to the paper, brought out by balloon post, were racy with his candour and Gallic irreverence.Labouchere did not trust Jules Favre's offer, made with a subtle smile, to give the newspaper correspondent's despatches a priority balloon, for he suspected that censorship was the price of priority. So he committed his letters to the ordinary balloon post, addressing them to that engaging actress, Henrietta Hodson who, then playing at the Queen's Theatre, London, afterwards became Mrs. Labouchere. Labouchere's *Diary of a Besieged Resident in Paris* gave that other side of war for which there is little room in most history books. The mordant and unsentimental note of the man, which scandalised the Podsnaps, comes out in such passages as these : "The sufferings from want of food have been a good deal exaggerated. Horse-flesh, particularly the flesh of cab horses, is not particularly toothsome, but it is as nourishing as ox-flesh. The same may be said of cats, dogs and rats ; the last, in a ragout, are just as good as rabbit ; rather better, indeed, it struck me. There was, too, an unlimited store of wine. The bread was bad, but a soup made of this bread soaked in wine was staying . . .

" Everyone in Paris became a strategist. He had a plan like Trochu. He breathed war, and he made it his mission to discuss and criticise the military events. I confess that I never could make head or tail of the strategy of a combat, and if I had described it in detail I should have had to evolve the strategy from my moral consciousness. I thought, therefore, that it would be more interesting to the readers of the *Daily News* to give them an idea of what was going on, from the standpoint of an inhabitant of a

---

* The other chief proprietors at this time were Samuel Morley and Henry Oppenheim, the financier.

place besieged who knew little of war. On the whole, I think that the inhabitants thoroughly enjoyed themselves. They were convinced that the eyes of the world were on them ; all work had ceased ; almost everyone wore a uniform. The regiments of the National Guard marched to the ramparts, spent twenty-four hours there without incurring any great risk, and then marched home again with a band and half-a-dozen vivandiéres preceding them, glowing with their patriotic achievement and under the admiring eyes of their fellow-citizens . . . It is true that a portion of the town was under fire towards the close of the siege, but the bombs were few and far between, and most of them, for some unexplained reason, did not burst. The chance of being injured by them was therefore infinitesimal . . . Life to the great part of mankind is monotonous, a siege is a novelty, and affords a great deal of pleasurable excitement. Moreover there is a certain degree of coziness in being separated from the rest of the world, which leads to general friendliness." The coziness soon vanished in the fires of the Commune, and in the bloody repression of the Commune. Forbes, mauled by the mob, finally made his way out of Paris, while it was still burning, by the simple device of scribbling Queen Victoria's name on one envelope and the name of the Foreign Secretary, Lord Granville on another, and flourishing them in the faces of all guards. Forbes was the one passenger on the night mail-boat from France, he reached the *Daily News* office at six in the morning, and by eight an edition of the newspaper containing his account of Paris in flames was on the streets. Robinson, when he came in at ten o'clock found him asleep with his head on the Post Office Directory.

There were not many in 1870 who divined any menace to Britain in the proclamation of the German Empire at Versailles. A considerable part of middle-class opinion doubtless agreed with Queen Victoria's Court Preacher at Balmoral that the defeat of France was a just punishment for her sins. The decadence of our neighbour was a grand theme for English moralists, and the explanations of the collapse of 1870 are uncannily like the explanations of the collapse of 1940. History may not be repetitive ; the moralist nearly always is. The ambitions of Napoleon the Third had long troubled the British ; while the tinsel gauds of the Tuilleries were contrasted unfavourably with the solid mahogany vertues of the British Court. The evangelical sentiment of the country was much drawn to the new German Empire as a Protestant power. The middle-classes could never make up their minds whether an atheist Frenchman or a Catholic Frenchman was the more dangerous.

II

BY JINGO!

In 1878 a passionate feeling against Russia seized the country. The Great MacDermott gave raucous expression to it in the ditty that he sang night after night at the London Pavilion :—

> *We don't want to fight, but, by Jingo, if we do,*
> *We've got the ships, we've got the men, we've got the money, too.*
> *We've fought the Bear before,*
> *And while we're Britons true,*
> *The Russians shall NOT have Constantinople.*

Imagine that NOT coming out as a roar, heavily accented by a great stamping of feet and pounding of fists.

The Empress Jingo was a legendary ruler of Japan who is said to have invaded Korea seventeen hundred years ago. Nobody can be sure whether it was she, or a Persian saint named Jingo, who gave the song-writer—G. W. Hunt—his inspiration, or whether he invented the name in the intoxication of the moment. But he had given the language a word that was felt to have the ring of perfect inevitability. It was a word that politics had been waiting for. It was a new word for a new mood. Tennyson, ever the sensitive barometer, produced his ultra-patriotic verses, *Hands All Round*, soon after, and they were parodied as *Drinks All Round* in lines that began :—

> *A health to Jingo first, and then*
> *A health to shell, a health to shot !*
> *The man who hates not other men*
> *I deem no perfect patriot.*

It was hinted that this parody which wounded the Laureate was written by Andrew Lang, for years one of the *Daily News* leader writers. Lang was a natural Conservative who wrote leading articles for a Liberal newspaper. He was balanced by those writers for the *Morning Post* who remained staunch Liberals. Some of his most engaging writings for the paper were collected in a volume happily entitled *Lost Leaders*. But the interesting thing about Lang's Conservatism was that it belonged to so ancient a tradition that it was affronted by the raucous imperialism of his day. To him that savoured of Whiggery at its worst and so, without cynicism, the oldest of Tories was able to write the most passionate Liberal leaders.

" By Jingo ! " bawled the crowds in the streets, in the pubs, in the clubs. They tramped down Whitehall singing, " The Russians shall NOT have Constantinople." Crying " By Jingo " a mob smashed Gladstone's windows. For Gladstone was against any show of war.

In the end, the House of Commons voted a £6 million credit, the Fleet was sent to the Dardenelles, the Russians climbed down, the Congress of Berlin was arranged. The fever was over. But the word stayed. And the fever returned.

It was the late 'nineties that seemed almost wholly dedicated to the Empress Jingo. The country had travelled far from the amiable universalism of 1851. The Great Exhibition celebrated the peaceful arts of the whole civilised world ; but the Diamond Jubilee (1897) was resplendent with the pride of an Empire. Progress in 1851 had been seen as an enormous railway train by which all humanity might be carried to the Earthly Paradise. Progress in 1897 was made up of saloon coaches for first-class passengers only, and there was no room for the lesser breeds without the Law. Characters so diverse as the Prince Consort, Peel, Gladstone and Cobden had once seen Commerce as the gentle hand maiden of Peace. Now Commerce was as martial as Boadicea in her chariot. In his parody of Tennyson, Lang—if Lang it was— had written :

> To all the Companies that long
> To rob, as folk robbed years ago !
> To all that wield the double thong
> From Queensland round to Borneo !
> To all that, under Indian skies
> Call Aryan man a blasted nigger ;
> To all rapacious enterprise ;
> To rigour everywhere, and vigour
> Drinks all round !

There were not a few old-fashioned Conservatives as well as Liberals who felt that those reproaches could be even better addressed to the 'nineties. There was a combination of a shrill imperialism with a passion for speculation. In the 'forties, the money-making instincts had been concentrated upon railways and the extension of our own interior frontier. Now it was fixed upon the Empire. The Rand millionaires were admired as Hudson and Sadlier had been admired fifty years before. To an earlier genera-tion, the mystery of Africa had been illuminated by the moral grandeur of Livingstone. Now it was the backdrop to Barney Barnato, a very different kind of hero who ended his feverish days by leaping from a ship at sea. The imperialism of the 'nineties represented the philosophy of mechanical Progress debased into the grammer of mechanical Force.

Men were the abstracts of the times. What had happened to Joseph Chamberlain was such a change as had affected many lesser characters. Once he had been the republican Mayor of Birmingham. Then he had been chief among the austere Radicals in Parliament. Once upon a time he had caused offence to the Queen and alarm to the rich by describing Reform as the ransom which Society must pay for its security. Now, Colonial Secretary in Lord Salisbury's Government, he was the bright star of the imperialists, " Jove's planet over Africa."

Then, too, what had happened to Swinburne was a chronicle of the times. He who had been the sun-crowned rebel of the 'sixties and 'seventies, the laureate of freedom, flinging his Greek fire at kings and priests, and praising, with all his glorious excess of praise, Mazzini, Kossuth, and Victor Hugo, was now writing patriotic pieces that won the applause of the Primrose League. It was generally thought, though, that the dazzling Kipling with his piston rhythms, his jagged raciness, his soldier's slang, and his small-boy's delight in guns and engines, expressed the spirit of the age far more effectively than the older poet who once had written, *When the hounds of spring are on winter's traces.* Then there was the imperial chant of the gifted Henley, for whom life went on broken wing—*England, my England, what shall I do for you?—What is there I would not do?*

The pounding of the drums, the shrilling of the fifes rose in crescendo to the war—to the days when the troopships sailed for South Africa and the subjugation of the Boer farmers ; the troopships that sailed with the bands playing, *Goodbye, Dolly, I must leave you,* and *Two Little Girls in Blue.*

Hilaire Belloc's *Verses to a Lord who in the House of Lords said that those who opposed the South African Adventure confused soldiers with money-grabbers* revealed a Muse unafraid to challenge Kipling's.

> " *Where those three hundred fought with Beit*
> *And fair young Wernher died ?* "

repeated the Opposition glad of this young voice.

The sardonic voice went on chanting :

> " *The little mound where Eckstein stood*
> *And gallant Albu fell*
> *And Oppenheim, half blind with blood*
> *Went fording through the rising flood—*
> *My Lord, we know them well.*"

It was amid the strange fevers of these times that the modern history of the *Daily News* began. The political Opposition was rent by the issues of the war. Under the editorship of E. T. Cook, the *Daily News* had become attached to the Liberal Imperialists, the section of the party which, including Asquith, Grey and Haldane, supported the war. Of the London dailies, two alone opposed the Government, the *Daily Chronicle* and the *Morning Leader*. Then, half-way through the war, the *Daily Chronicle* was captured by the Liberal Imperialists, and its editor, H. W. Massingham, resigned.* This was a blow to that considerable mass of opinion in the country who had followed Campbell-Bannerman in opposition to the war.

Among the most intrepid opponents of the war was the young member for Carnarvon Boroughs, David Lloyd George. He displayed his courage by penetrating the fortress city of Joseph Chamberlain when the war was at its peak. A mob outside Birmingham Town Hall cried for his blood, and he had to be smuggled to safety dressed up as a policeman in concertina trousers, sleeves draping his knuckles, and a helmet perched on his wild hair. Lloyd George was anxious that the Liberals opposing the war should find a voice in the Press, for it was becoming increasingly hard for them to win a hearing on the platform. Their best hope seemed to lie in securing the *Daily News*. Its support of the Government and the Boer War had alienated many readers, Sir John Robinson, whose sympathies were with the Boers had resigned, and it was losing money heavily. Its owners (Lloyd George found) were willing to part with it.

In his " Life of George Cadbury," Mr. A. G. Gardiner recounts the story. " Among those whom he, Lloyd George, approached was George Cadbury, who was known to be very strongly against the policy of the Government. His opposition was based not merely on his religious convictions in regard to war in the abstract, but also on his belief that the motives behind this war were wrong. He took the view that it was a mine-owner's war waged for financial interests, and that the public passion was being exploited in the cause of higher dividends and cheap labour. He was convinced that the future of South Africa depended upon Briton and Boer becoming united in a common patriotism."

Up to this time, George Cadbury had confined himself to those business interests centred at Bournville, which had been created and developed by himself and his brother, and to manifold social, religious and educational activities which were dear to his heart.

* Through all this, however, the tradition of the independent war correspondent was sustained. The Boer War messages of A. G. Hales had the vigorous quality of Forbes. E. T. Smith, the last of the war correspondents of the old school, was shut up in Ladysmith.

He had always avoided publicity and had resisted pressure to stand as a candidate for Parliament. It was a break with the habits of a lifetime to be concerned with the direction of a national newspaper, but the issues of the war had touched him so nearly that when he found his support was indispensable, he advanced enough money to secure the *Daily News* for the cause he believed in.   George Cadbury had no thought at that time that he would be other than a member of a syndicate which would sustain the paper, but fresh money troubles soon gathered.   The management of the South African war was as ill-contrived in its early stages as the Crimea had been, and the ingenious tactics of the Boer Generals made it infinitely protracted.   The supporters of the war vented their disappointment on the Opposition on the somewhat capricious grounds that without their encouragement the Boers would capitulate. The *Daily News*, as the chief newspaper of the Opposition, was boycotted by adver-tisers.   Its situation steadily worsened until the day came when George Cadbury was faced with the choice of assuming single responsibility for the paper or seeing it pass again into the hands of the Liberal Imperialists.   He took up the burden.

The mood of the country changed rapidly with the ending of the war.   The self-confident imperialism of the 'nineties was followed by disenchantment, and self-questionings.

Kipling twanged his lyre in a minor key and produced :—

Let us admit it freely, as a business people should,
We have had no end of a lesson, it will do us no end of good.

He smote the lyre again :—

We have had a jolly good lesson, and it serves us jolly well right.

These were not, perhaps, Kipling's most flashing phrases, but, all the same, they were expressive.   Mafeking Night, with its wild dances and the flaring bonfires in the streets, was the last festival of the Empress Jingo.

Queen Victoria died before the war came to an end.   One looks at the newspapers for January 1901, heavily edged in black.   She had reigned for sixty-four years.   She had passed with the century. The overwhelming mass of the readers had no memory of a time when Victoria was not their Queen.   She had fulfilled in a unique degree the symbolic function of the monarchy.   The Queen had given her name to an age unequalled in its pride and splendour ; in its expansion and amassing of riches ; and in the combined quality and quantity of the illustrious men and women who adorned it.   There is an interminable argument among the his-torians as to whether history is a science or an art.   The quidnuncs may be left to settle that during the next hundred years. For us small fry, gambolling with all the blissful freedom of pariah puppies outside the academic palisades, there remains an undeniable aesthetic pleasure in the spectacle of the Queen's reign. Like a fine play or novel, it has an artistic consistency and unity of its own. One well-used title after another seems to fit it perfectly—*Milestones*, or *The Forsyte Saga*, or *Great Expectations*, or *The Way of all Flesh*. But one is left dissatisfied with each excellent title. For the subject is so much more than any of them, or all of them. That work of art, the Victorian age, is like one of those modern orchestral scores in which half-a-dozen themes or more make an appearance, are interwoven, are played against one another, are turned upside down ; take wings with the first violins, or are blared out on the brass, or are savagely chucked down among the double basses ; they change their shapes and appear to get lost forever, then turn up again with the thundering assurance of the full orchestra in C major. Through the eleborate Victorian counterpoint, one traces the fortunes of such themes as faith in inevitable progress ; belief in the benevolence of science ; an acceptance of the evolutionary character of our political institutions with freedom slowly broadening down from precedent to precedent ; the reaching out towards unity and the search for free communication between man and his neighbour ; the effort to extend the conception of liberty ; together, of course, with such brassy motives as the urge to power and the love of hard cash. With all its complexity and its diffusion, the symphony had majesty of form. The music that was to come after was shapeless as well as harsh.

After the reading of many biographies, one is still left uncertain as to how ordinary or how extraordinary a human being Victoria really was. The Queen on whom so strong a light poured down for so great a length of time remains in large part an enigma. But the Queen as a symbolic figure is clear cut on a golden coin. Her death in that cheerless January of a new century appeared to many of her subjects like a shifting of their earth's foundations. The age and the woman had become so identified that it was inconceivable the one could continue without the other. The sense of security, and of complacent acceptance of the values of the Gilded Age, began at once to weaken.

The new century, whose dawn was so cold, turned back to some of the themes that had been sounded in 1846. There was a quickening of interest in the condition of the people. The University and Public Schools Settlement movement brought young men of the upper classes into touch with the life of mean streets and often inspired them to go into politics to remedy injustices which had

shocked them. Toynbee Hall had become a nursery of talent for a
new generation of Civil Servants and politicians. It was there that
the young William Beveridge prepared his first study of *Unemployment*, and there that a great contribution to Charles Booth's monumental *The Life and Labour of the People of London* was made. Streams
of influence as diverse as the Salvation Army and the Fabians,
as the Christian Socialists and the plays of Mr. Shaw, all
contributed to a more sensitive awareness of social problems.
In the year that he resigned from the staff of the *Daily
News* (1899) Richard Whiteing produced *No. 5 John Street*, a novel
that had a marked effect in the ten years following its publication.
No. 5 John Street presented life in a tenement in the year of the
Queen's Diamond Jubilee, that year of fanfares and pageantry.
The contrast between imperial pride and domestic squalor was
forcefully made in Whiteing's pages. His factory girl, dying of
consumption, his anarchist and his old Chartist were brought
forward as figures more worthy of the contemplation of the age
than the Rand millionaires. Such books as Arthur Morrison's *Tales
of Mean Streets* and *A Child of the Jago*, and George Gissing's novels
of " drab realism " made a new generation of middle-class readers
conscious of the lives of the poor, as the novels of Dickens, Disraeli,
Kingsley, and Mrs. Gaskell had done half a century before.

The 1906 General Election showed how sharp a turn the country
had taken from the mood of the 'nineties, and it showed, too, how
powerful remained the Free Trade sentiment of the people, for
the final ruin of the Conservatives was effected by the schism in
their Party over the Tariff issue which Mr. Chamberlain had
raised. Free Trade was the clinching issue ; but the election was
not simply a defensive fight ; it represented the forward thrust of
a new spirit. Mr. Balfour's Government was overwhelmed, the
Liberals were installed with a majority of 356, and the
new Labour Party captured 39 seats. This was sixty years
after Peel had given place to Russell. In the years between
there had been a steady change in the spirit of British
Liberalism. The aristocratic Whigs who dominated Russell's
Cabinet of 1846 were concerned to preserve the traditional
liberties of the subject, to sustain the authority of Parliament against
the Crown, and to show benevolence to liberal movements in
despotic kingdoms abroad. (When Lord John was her Prime
Minister, Queen Victoria said she wished he could sometimes
talk to her of something other than himself and the Glorious
Revolution of 1688.) The Whigs of 1846 would have found Lloyd
George as prickly a porcupine as Feargus O'Connor of the Chartists.
They had little concern with economic freedoms, and it took much

prodding to interest them in bad housing, bad drains, factory conditions, and the plight of small children in the mills.

With the 1906 Parliament the process that had begun when Gladstone joined hands with Bright to create the new Liberalism of the 'seventies had become triumphant. One might say, too, that the process begun when Charles Dickens wrote *Oliver Twist* had attained a new, though not a final stage, in its evolution. It was in the finest tradition of Whig statesmanship that South Africa should be granted self-government. The wounds of the war were healed thereby and Britain won the friendship of two leaders whose help was to prove beyond price in later years—Botha and Smuts. But other measures that were far outside the conceptions of Whiggery were to engage the new Parliament. There was the Trade Disputes Act which freed the Unions from the fetters laid upon them by the Taff Vale judgment. Under that judgment heavy damages could be imposed upon a Trade Union for any acts committed by its agents whether it had approved them or not. There were Old Age Pensions, the Miners' Eight Hours Act, the Children Act of 1908, the Trade Boards Act which dealt with the evils of the sweat shops, and the Small Holdings Act. Unemployment Insurance and Health Insurance were to follow.

This forward thrust of social reforms was deeply appealing to George Cadbury. The newspaper which he had saved from shipwreck during the frenzied days of the Boer War became a spokesman, and, indeed, a pace-setter for the resurgent Radicalism of 1906-14. Three members of the staff became members of the new House, C. F. G. Masterman, P. W. Wilson, and Chiozza Money, and a fourth, Vaughan Nash, became private secretary to the Prime Minister, Sir Henry Campbell-Bannerman.

George Cadbury had been one of the founders of the National Old Age Pension League. He, together with his eldest son, Edward, and Charles Booth (of *Life and Labour of the People in London*) furnished the large proportion of the funds which enabled the League to awaken public opinion to the distresses of the aged poor. Edward Cadbury's name is recorded on the tablet in Browning Hall, London which commemorates the passing of the Old Age Pensions Act in 1908. That Act involved a principle which today is common form to all parties, but was angrily disputed forty years ago—the responsibility of the community for the succour of its weakest members. Or it might be more precise to say that it was a revival in a different form of the principle of the protection of the weak which Shaftesbury had so nobly vindicated in the Factory Acts. There were two lines of argument advanced against this humane reform. One sprang from a queer kind of Calvinism. It was held that if a man was predestined to be poor and wretched, then poor and wretched he must remain, and it was not for the State to interfere with the balance of nature. It was certainly wrong to use taxes levied on the prosperous to feed the unfortunate. The care of the helpless should be the concern of private benevolence and the individual conscience. What was the right function of the State? To provide for the defence of the community against external enemies and internal criminals, and to hold the ring for the free play of economic forces. The second line of criticism was a newer one—it declared that such humane enactments, while seeming fair and just on a short view, must in the long run lead to an impairing of individual freedom. We were on our way to the Servile State, said these critics. It was seriously contended that if a few shillings a week were given to old men and women to help them retain their independence and self-respect, then somehow the traditional liberties of our people were in danger. Those who had never shown much zeal for freedom when it was threatened by the strong, now argued its metaphysics against the weak with all the energy of Mill. What greater menace could there be to a free people than that a city charwoman or a farm labourer's widow, grown too old to work, should be corrupted by a State pension of 5s. a week? In this connection one cannot help recalling E. V. Lucas saying, " I have heard all the great orators of my time—and have blushed for them." The Old Age Pensions Act was the beginning of Britain's New Deal. It was the forerunner of many enactments, brought forward by Governments of varying political complexion, all based on the community's acknowledgment of its obligation to those members least able to help themselves. With the years, the debate shifted from the principle itself to the question of the limits of the application of the principle. One has seen an identical process of political evolution take place in the United States, a quarter of a century later. The frontiers of State benevolence as well as of State control are likely to be a major concern of our democracy for some years ahead. It seems obvious, now looking back over the century, that the modern demand for social security and the redress of social injustices would be the certain outcome of these labouring years. The beginnings are apparent enough in those agitations of the 'forties described in the early pages of this book; in the speeches of Shaftesbury; in the novels of Mrs. Gaskell and Henry Kingsley, not to speak of greater names. In this regard, as in others, one sees the design of the century rounded out, the figure in the carpet made complete. Some called it the extension of liberty into the economic realm; others decried it as the negation of liberty. Might it not be fairer to call it a part of the movement towards fraternity?

GARIBALDI'S VISIT TO LONDON : April 1864

Arrival at Charing Cross.

One of the contributions the *Daily News* made to the revival of the social consciousness was the Sweated Industries Exhibition, held at Queen's Hall in 1906, for which George Cadbury cheerfully found the money. This demonstration of the evils of sweat shops led to the passing of the Trade Boards Act which fixed minimum scales of pay in industries where the wage rates were inhumanly low. Board of Trade figures in 1906 showed that 50 per cent. of the women in industry aged 18 years and over earned less than ten shillings a week, and in two or three trades alone did they receive an average of fifteen shillings a week, the lowest amount on which it was then considered a woman worker living by herself could exist. In the tailoring trade the average wage of women workers was thirteen shillings for a 58-hour week, while 25 per cent. received less than ten shillings each for a full week.

The catalogue of this exhibition is a melancholy chronicle of the exploiting of the poor and friendless. Here is an artificial flower maker described as a clever woman and magnificent worker : " For fifty years she had made artificial flowers, and for skill and indomitable perseverance she has no superior. She can neither read nor write. Her rates of pay are for making violets 7d. a gross, geraniums 7d. a gross, buttercups 3d. a gross, roses 1/3d. to 3/6d. a gross. Her average working day is 14 hours and her average earnings 10/- weekly. Her husband is also a flower-maker, but is nearly blind and quite an invalid. Until recently they occupied an underground room, for which 4/6d. weekly was paid. To support herself and her husband without parish relief, or philanthropic aid, she has often worked fourteen, and even sixteen, hours daily ; her only respite has been to carry her finished flowers to the factory, and bring back other materials. On her way home, sometimes she will purchase a little black silk and some black bristles, and, when other work fails, these she will make into black tulips, or ' ragged roses ' and other symbols of bereavement and sorrow, and the half-blind husband will rise from his bed, wander into the streets, and dispose of them at a mourning warehouse for 3½d. per complete spray."

The sum of one penny was paid for carding 384 hooks, and one person, working eighteen hours a day, could earn about 5/- a week at this employment. The average weekly reward for matchbox making at 12 hours a day was less than 5/-. The rates paid for tennis ball sewing was 4½d. to 6d. a dozen. Babies' bonnets were made for 2/- a dozen, ties at 4½d. to 5d. a dozen, pinafores at 2/- a dozen, shirts at less than a penny an hour. The laborious work of chain-making eleven hours a day produced an average wage of 6/- to 8/- a week . . . There are many pages of such records.

G

This was happening less than forty years ago. It was still true, as true as it had been in Victorian times, that men and women of generous and kindly disposition were unaware of what life was like in the third-floor backs. Neither the Factory Acts nor the activities of the Trade Unions were able to protect these unorganised workers, who, hidden away like lepers in cellars or in East End tenements, toiled all day long for a few pence. Here was the old trouble of the insulation of groups in urban life. When the city grew so big as to be impersonal, it became possible for whole sections of the people to sink into the depths without their fellows knowing it. London during the nineteenth century had engulfed a number of small towns and villages, and in doing so had destroyed that sense of relationships which exists in small communities. In that soulless immensity, the idea of the brotherhood of man had become a rhetorical ornament of no living meaning, a gilded phrase to inscribe upon a banner or to round out a by-election speech, but having no reference to Tom, Dick and Harry who might be im- mured in the cellars beneath the hurrying feet of the home-going crowds. It was the honourable task of journalism to rescue fraternity from the clammy fogs of abstraction, and to say, " here is a man with a name, a face, a body and a soul who claims your help and for whom you are in some part responsible : will you answer— 'Am I my brother's keeper ?' "

The great editor identified with this period of social reform was A. G. Gardiner.* By the warmth and supple eloquence of his writing, he inspired more than one generation, and widened the sensibilities of classic Liberalism. His portrait galleries of the illustrious of that age, republished as *Prophets, Priests and Kings, Pillars of Society* and *The War Lords*, have long outlasted their period, as Hazlitt's *Spirit of the Age* has outlasted its time. The impermances of politics became fixed in the bright colours of his portrait painting. His staff included such signal talents as H. W. Nevinson, R. A. Scott-James, E. C. Bentley (of *Trent's Last Case* and the *Clerihews*), H. M. Tomlinson (*Gallions Reach* and *London River*), William Archer (Ibsen's first English translator), H. N. Brailsford, H. Wilson Harris, J. Stuart Hodgson, afterwards editor, and S. K. Ratcliffe who was to become one of the best-liked British lecturers who ever toured America.

Gardiner was a political journalist of unquenchable fervour. But he also possessed a sensitive affection for the arts : music, painting, poetry, the theatre, and the indigenous English art of cricket. In his youth he would have liked to follow one of his heroes, William Hazlitt, in becoming a painter. For the art of writing, his passion

* A. G. Gardiner died 12th March, 1946.

was unbounded. Under his inspiration the newspaper gained notable literary repute. He gave Gilbert Chesterton his head, and that was like giving a comet its head; a dazzling incandescence swept across the paper, trailing a vaporous tail a million miles long that seemed to enfold everything in Creation. When one opens the files of those years the book page draws one's eye away from the dusty political skirmishes. One feels almost as one felt about the generation of the 'forties—how lucky they were! Many fine talents were then in their prime ; books were events. Happy the reviewer who could square his shoulders to tackle *Mr. Polly* or *The Man of Property* or *The Old Wives' Tale*. Good subjects were in excess. A man could ponder whether he should write a piece about the cruel brilliance of Kipling, or the humanism of Galsworthy, or the robust realism of Bennett's *Clayhanger*. Or there were the patterned coils of that glittering serpent of wickedness, George Moore to fascinate and repel the Puritan conscience, the last and most brilliantly marked of the snakes that St. Patrick had expelled from Ireland. Or there was W. H. Hudson's Rima, and all the soft enchantments of Hudson's reveries. Enthusiasm for the writers of the time was of a piece with the intoxication of the discovery of new forms of music, such Russians as Moussorgsky and Borodin for example, and of new ideas in art—Post-Impressionism, in particular. The anthologies of *Georgian Poetry* which began in 1912 excited almost as great a stir as the first appearance of the Russian Ballet. John Masefield's *The Everlasting Mercy*, and *The Widow in the Bye-Street* and *The Daffodil Fields* enjoyed such a success that it almost looked for an hour as if narrative poetry might rival the novel. The young ardently believed that this neurotic period, drifting towards Civil War, was about to produce an artistic renaissance. One day would bring the exquisite dilemmas—for reader as well as writer—of Henry James' last period, the sensitive snail's horn thrust forth and then disappearing amid a glorious tangle of leaf and flowers ; the next day would produce Joseph Conrad's symphonic orchestration of the themes of fortitude, honour, loyalty. It was not until 1914 that *Chance* made Conrad for the first time a popular writer. Nobody precisely knew why (for *Chance* was not the best of Conrad) but suddenly the wind veered to fill his sails. It had been in 1894, just twenty years earlier, that a Polish sailor named Korzeniowski left the sea to dedicate himself to the extraordinary enterprise of becoming an English novelist.

Hardy had abandoned the novel before the new century opened, but his vigorous old age flowered in a second April of poetry. "And did you once see Shelley plain ? " This writer recalls

Gardiner mentioning casually to him in after years of Hardy writing in gentle remonstrance at being labelled pessimist, not in hurt dignity as an alderman writes to an editor complaining that he has been called a councillor, but as a Catholic might write who has been inadvertently described as the Imam of a mosque by some writer who could see no difference between one great religion and another. Nothing could be more wounding to Hardy than Chesterton's jape about the village atheist brooding over the village idiot.

Some element of that peculiar sense of reverence for a great writer that the Victorians exhibited persisted until the first World War. There had been a day when Andrew Lang, turning in the direction of Tennyson's home, genuflected slightly, and said in a hushed voice, " That is where the Master lives." The obeisances were not quite so profound in Edwardian and Georgian times. But even such an irreverent Puck as Max Beerbohm displayed— and displayed in his parody most of all—a respect for the genius of Henry James that was like the respect of an earnest young priest for a great Cardinal. Such devotion to the author of *The Portrait of a Lady* made H. G. Wells, with his joke about a hippopotamus picking up a pea, appear like a Cockney urchin cocking a snook at the Lord Chancellor. Arnold Bennett, coming to town in Wakes Weeks clothes and with all the truculent, " I want to be shown " manner of the cousin from the Five Towns, wrote of a glimpse of Swinburne on Putney Hill as a tourist from Stoke overwhelmed by the first sight of the dome of Saint Paul's. " By the heavens, it was a noble sight. I have not seen a nobler. Now, I knew by hearsay every crease in his trousers, but nobody had told me that his face was a vision that would never fade from my memory."

The writers were not unwilling to sustain the hierophantic role. The appearances of William Butler Yeats in London were like the pastoral visitations of a bishop. All these great men were indeed apt to behave like bishops. Shaw was a witty, clear-eyed and disruptive bishop, like that Bishop of Autun who served so many masters. Wells was a thundering and cheerful evangelical bishop who had obviously been a boxing curate in youth. Kipling was a missionary bishop of an intolerant orthodoxy, sending home a collection of fascinating snapshots of exotic scenes which were much prized even by those who hated his theology. In their divergent ways, they were all bishops of a Church Militant, assuming by right a prominent hand in public affairs ; they were given a high place at the banquets of life, they flourished their lawn sleeves among the peers of England, they engaged in a delightful punditry on official occasions, and were nearly all up to their necks in high politics. It was said that if the resistance of the Diehards had forced the creation of the 400 new peers, even so shy a faun as J. M. Barrie would have been rigged out in ermine.

The splendid fact was that books were not limited to the bookish. Poetry was not confined to some tiny community smaller than the Shakers or the Duck River Baptists. A big novel would make as much noise as a scientific invention. There was nothing over-precious or cliquish about this cultivation of literature. It greatly extended the area of human pleasure ; it widened the limits of existence itself ; it enhanced the pure excitement of living in a transitional age. The period between the Boer War and August 1914, had a vigour and glow of the inner life, as well as a violence in politics, that was lacking in the grey shapelessness of the years between the two world wars. The political struggles of those days are dim and confused memories—the Lords' Veto, Home Rule, the Welsh Church Bill, the Marconi Affair—but the books still stand upon the shelves, or the best of them do. There are many who remember with a particular gratitude the literary pages of the *Daily News* in those years. For in them was reflected the grace and vitality of a highly civilised period. The distinguished link with that tradition, the pledge of its continuity in these times, is Robert Lynd, accomplished critic and most graceful of essayists.

A newspaper in which Chesterton was letting off his chinese crackers and showers of golden rain, and whose leaders were written by Charles Masterman, could not lack exhilaration . . . One catches glimpses of the brilliant recruit to Liberalism, Winston Churchill, beaming with self-confidence, appearing in the office to touch up a Masterman leader. He wrote one which ended with the Disraelian inquiry—" Where is the statesman to be found who is adequate to the times ? " The world is not likely to forget how that precise question was answered three decades later. Mr. H. J. Gregory, the Head Printer of the paper recalls Mr. Churchill, puffing a cigarette, *not* a cigar, entering the composing-room and squaring his shoulders at the desk to write.

Those were days of a cheerful humanism, as distinct from a bleak humanitarianism. Mr. Churchill, while at the Home Office, saw John Galsworthy's play, *Justice*, and was moved to end the cruel system of solitary confinement. There was a general confidence that this new conception of Progress was irresistible, that in Mr. Churchill's phrase " Humanity was swinging bravely along the grand high road."

But as one reform after another was carried by that Parliament, the forces opposed to social change rallied. It was a time when Henry Chaplin, who had run through two splendid fortunes and was drawing a State pension of £2,000 a year, could declare amid

hearty cheers, not in the least ironical, that Old Age Pensions of
5/- a week would sap the vitality of the country by discouraging
thrift in the poor.* It was a time, too, when measures of ameliora-
tion that a modern Conservative would reject as faint-hearted
came to be attacked in phrases borrowed from Burke on the
French Revolution. There was a genuine alarm among the men of
property. Lloyd George's budget of 1909 was seen to be " the
end of all things," and with the challenge to the veto power of the
House of Lords the country found itself in the sharpest constitutional
crisis since the Reform Bill. The newspaper and its proprietor
were much abused for their advocacy of reform. Mr. Gardiner
quotes George Cadbury as saying with good humour, not with any
bitterness, at this time, " If I spent my money on deer forests and
personal splendour, I should be a very good fellow, and have a
very good time, but because I spend it in ways that I think will
help to drive misery and wrong out of the world, I am a humbug,
and a hypocrite. Well, it's always been so, and always will be so."

Newspaper finance remained an intractable problem. In
February 1904, the price of the *Daily News* had been cut to a
halfpenny, and while this brought a considerable increase of circulation it failed to balance the budget. The fate of that fine
Liberal paper, the *Tribune* which lost around £500,000 in its two
years of life (1906-08) discouraged thoughts of the *Daily News*
returning to a penny. So the alternative stroke of simultaneous
publication in London and Manchester was tried, and the circulation rose to close upon 400,000 daily. The losses continued.

Writing of this period, Mr. Gardiner relates, " The struggle had
now become the dominating concern of George Cadbury's life.
He had entered into it unwillingly, and it had brought him nothing
but financial loss and personal abuse. He became the target for
the attacks of all who hated the new social policy pursued by the
Liberal Government . . . That policy had been advocated and
made possible largely by the influence of the *Daily News,* and its
opponents struck at George Cadbury as the most effective way of
attacking his paper. But the more he was slandered, the more he
became convinced that it was his duty to continue the struggle . . .
So far from retreating from the journalistic field he, in 1910,
advanced still farther into it."

The proprietors of the *Morning Leader* and the *Star,* two newspapers
with a sterling Radical tradition, were anxious to dispose of them
and, to save them from falling into Conservative hands, George

* It was of Chaplin that the first Duke of Westminster observed that all the
crowned heads of Europe should give him £100,000 a year to show them how to
spend their money.

Cadbury agreed with members of the Rowntree family to buy them out. The *Daily News* and the *Morning Leader* were fused in 1912.

With this fusion, which promised a more prosperous spell than the paper had enjoyed since the South African War, George Cadbury gave up command to younger members of his family. In 1907 he brought in his third son, Henry Tylor Cadbury, " who had been engaged in farming, but who gave up that career at the request of his father, and with his friend, Bertram Crosfield, who later married his sister Eleanor, undertook the task of management, under a board of directors, of which his eldest brother, Edward Cadbury, subsequently became chairman." (Mr. Edward Cadbury, a director of Daily News Limited, since 1902, was its chairman from 1911 to 1930. He summed up the Liberal philosophy of the newspaper in the words he used when the foundation stones of its new building were laid in 1926 by Lord Oxford and T. P. O'Connor, " The first and greatest of our political principles is that of human freedom, liberty of thought, liberty of speech, freedom for each to develop his or her personality to the highest possible degree.")

" In the Trust Deed which he caused to be drawn up for the transfer of his interest in the papers, the bulk of the shares were disposed of so as to provide that their policy should, as far as was humanly possible, be maintained on the lines which he approved, and that the profits that might accrue should be applied to certain specified purposes in which he was interested." A majority of the Ordinary Shares of the Daily News Limited, and thus the control of the papers and their policy, were handed over in 1912 to Trustees who are debarred from drawing any profit from their trusteeship.

In the letter which he sent to each of his sons who were trustees of the newspaper, George Cadbury wrote, " I want you to know that the money that I have invested in these papers would otherwise have been given to charities. I had a profound conviction that money spent on charities was of infinitely less value than money spent in trying to arouse my fellow countrymen to the necessity for measures to ameliorate the condition of the poor, forsaken and downtrodden masses which can be done most effectively by a great newspaper. This will no doubt make you feel some responsibility as to how dividends from these shares, if there be any, should be spent, though they will be absolutely your own to spend as you like."

" If you champion the cause of the poor who cannot do anything to recompense you, you must expect savage attacks from those whose interests may be affected. I have been bitterly attacked in Society papers, also on the other hand by anarchists who desire a violent revolution, and who know that progressive legislation will make this impossible." (*The Life of George Cadbury*.)

Mr. Henry Cadbury bore active responsibility in the Bouverie Street office continuously for 23 years during many periods of fierce competition, and violent political change. He retired from London for health reasons after the amalgamation of the newspaper with the *Daily Chronicle* in 1930, but has remained on the Board of Daily News Limited, greatly esteemed by a staff to whom his leadership through troublous decades is an ineffaceable memory. The direction of a Liberal newspaper in those years of storm and transition when a new world was being born was a task that called for constant courage and resource.

The years between the end of the Boer War and 4 August 1914, were years of threats and harsh politics. The skies seemed never clear of thunder clouds. Indeed, clouds was a constant word in the newspaper contents bills of that period. Clouds in the Balkans, gathered, dispersed, gathered again, until that fatal day when the posters reported a cloud over Serajevo that never dispersed. Clouds over the coal mines, clouds over the railways, clouds over the dockers. There were always clouds over Ireland, rolling so low that no one could see the road ahead. Out of the murk one hears the jingle, " Ulster will fight and Ulster will be right." There was the *donner und blitzen* of old Wotan moving west from Germany ; and another tag of the times comes back, " We want eight and we won't wait." The wanted eight were dreadnoughts.

The sense of impending doom shadows the newspapers of these years. In May 1910, in the middle of the constitutional crisis, Mr. Asquith, the Prime Minister, went on a visit of inspection to Gibraltar. Aboard the yacht *Enchantress*, he received by wireless news of the death of King Edward VII. Many years later, as Lord Oxford, he wrote, " I went up on deck, and I remember well that the first sight that met my eyes in the twilight before dawn was Halley's comet blazing in the sky. It was the only time, I believe, that any of us saw it in our voyage. I felt bewildered and indeed stunned. At a most anxious moment in the fortunes of the State, we had lost, without warning or preparation, the Sovereign whose ripe experience, trained sagacity, equitable judgment, and unvarying consideration counted for so much. . . ."

The truce that followed King Edward's death did not long endure. In the Ulster Rebellion, the " complete Grammar of Anarchy " was compiled. At Blenheim in 1912, Mr. Bonar Law, the Leader of the Opposition, depicted Mr. Asquith's Government as " a Revolutionary Committee which had seized by fraud upon despotic power. In our opposition to them we shall not be guided by the

considerations, we shall not be restrained by the bonds which would
influence us in an ordinary political struggle. We shall use any
means, whatever means seem to us likely to be most effective." A
few months later a Liberal orator declared, " If the civil and
parliamentary systems under which we have dwelt so long, and
our fathers before us, are to be brought to the rude challenge of
force ; if the Government and Parliament of this great country
and greater Empire are to be exposed to menace and brutality ;
if all the loose, wanton and reckless chatter we have been forced to
listen to these many months is in the end to disclose a sinister and
revolutionary purpose ; then I can only say to you, ' Let us go
forward together and put these grave matters to the proof.' " The
cadences of the sentences and the ring of the words are not to be
mistaken. The orator was Mr. Churchill. He had been born in
Blenheim.

It is worth pausing at the year 1913 because that was the last
year of the old way of life. The culture of the Forsytes was flowering
for the last time. The great peony was nodding its head ; soon
a high wind would come to strip off its petals. This was the last
year of peace before that Thirty Years War which has left nothing
in the world as it was. In 1913 a glittering structure of beliefs and
customs, of arrangements and loyalties which the Victorians had
thought to be everlasting was about to dissolve.

CHAPTER XII

DRAGON'S TEETH

I

ORACLES

SO, then, to 1913. Let us see what happened to the hopes of 1846.

It was in this year that the German Emperor, Wilhelm II—Victoria's grandson—celebrated the twenty-fifth anniversary of his accession. In the long procession bearing tributes to that illustrious fraud, was a deputation from 54 Peace Societies in the United States led by Mr. Andrew Carnegie, the Scot, who made a fortune in American steel and spent a large part of it giving libraries to British towns. Presenting his illuminated address, Mr. Carnegie thanked the Kaiser " for twenty-five years of peace."

" I hope we shall enjoy twenty-five years more," said the Emperor winningly.

Mr. Carnegie was overcome. " You are the best ally we have," he said.

One pictures the Kaiser's face at that moment, glazed and stiff as a cardboard mask, and almost as false—with the twin spikes of his moustaches on sentry duty over the mouth.

It was in this same year that the Palace of Peace was opened at The Hague. There was a careful symbolism in its decorations—wrought iron from Germany, British stained-glass windows, marble from Italy—and a carpet given by the Sultan of Turkey. Mr. Carnegie was graciously permitted to pay the bills.

Next year the world plunged into the first German War. Grey, looking into the dusk from his room at the Foreign Office, uttered the phrase that has been quoted endlessly since, " The lights are going out all over Europe ; we shall not see them lit again in our lifetime." Now more than thirty years later the lamplighters are still struggling to relieve Europe's black-out. In 1919 an American general said, " This war has not come to an end with the Versailles Peace Conference, it will go on for another twenty years." He was a sound oracle.

It was in March, 1913, that a professor was inaugurated President of the United States. " This is not a day of triumph, but a day of dedication," said Woodrow Wilson at the close of his inaugural address. " Here muster not the forces of party, but the forces of humanity. Men's hearts wait upon us, men's lives hang in the balances, men's hopes call upon us to say what we will do. Who shall live up to the great trust ? Who dares fail to try ? "

No shadow of war lay over Wilson's mind in that hour any more than its shadow lay upon the world, but those words had a strange ring ; a meaning that was hidden to the orator. There was the rhythm of marching men in them. The end of the world—that world of granite assurances—was coming.

For the first time since Lincoln, the *Daily News* could hail the rise in America of a leader cast in the classic mould of Liberalism. The reforms of Wilson's first term were the New Deal of their time—he called them the New Freedom—and the response to him on this side of the Atlantic was akin to the welcome which Roosevelt was to evoke twenty and thirty years later. The cross-fertilisation of British and American political ideas was becoming marked.*

Looking into the files of the *Daily News* of the 'nineties, the reader may still be captivated by the sketches of Parliament written by H. W. Lucy who was for a short time editor of the paper, and lived on into our times to amuse readers as Toby M.P. of *Punch*, retiring in 1916. Amid the sands of dullness, strewn with the white bones of lost causes, these pieces invite the traveller like smiling oases. Lucy had a talent for investing a drab debate with charm, one of the rarest talents in the world. An impish humour crackled in his reports ; he concentrated the essences of odd characters ; he made the business of the House as lively as a novel. Harry Furniss' illustrations to Lucy's articles in the *Daily News* were thought to be a notable innovation in journalism, but there was really little need to illustrate a writer whose style was itself a series of rapid pen-and-ink sketches. The paradox of Lucy was that although he spent a long life in the gallery of the House of Commons, his greatest contribution was made to American politics. For he may be said to have created a President. In his youth, Lucy contributed his sketches of Parliament to the *Gentleman's Magazine*. These were read by Woodrow Wilson, then an undergraduate at Princeton, and stirred immortal longings in him. Politics !—there was the dream of action to pull a student away from his books ; there was the power to move masses of men, and to mould the world nearer to the heart's desire. It was Lucy's writings that fired Wilson with the resolve to become a politician; he modelled himself upon the master orators of the British Parliament ; and sharpened his wits and his tongue in the constant practise of debate. The late Wendell Wilkie once told the writer

* The admiration which the President's ideals evoked is shown in Mr. Gardiner's character sketch of him, and in the admirable *President Wilson, His Problems and His Policy*, written by Mr. H. Wilson Harris, then assistant editor of the *Daily News*, now editor of the *Spectator* and M.P. for Cambridge University.

of these pages that he held Wilson to be the greatest of American
Presidents because he was never afraid to march far ahead of the
procession—because he was willing to dare all in the exercise of
conscious leadership.   Through his studies, Wilson was steeped in
House of Commons tradition, and, when he became President, he
sought to bend the rigid American Constitution—the system of
checks and balances—in the direction of Parliamentary government.   He addressed Congress in person ; he would like to have
transplanted Question Time from Westminster to the Capitol.
Above all, he sought to assert in Washington that powerful leadership of a compact majority which had fascinated him in watching
Gladstone and Disraeli through the telescope provided by Henry
Lucy.   But the American Constitution is designed to thwart any
concentration of authority.   So in the end it came about that a
man who by nature was a great Prime Minister became a frustrated
President.

Wilson bestrides the pages of the newspaper from this year until
the Greek tragedy of his downfall.   As the war with Germany
lengthened and losses mounted grievously, as the submarine grip
tightened, the eyes of Britain turned ever more anxiously to America.
What would she do ? A maladroit phrase of the President's, spoken
on a railroad platform, " too proud to fight," exasperated the
British, while the chilly precision with which the President enun-
ciated the doctrine of the freedom of the seas at a time when they
were fighting for their lives seemed to them inhuman.   There were
gloomy days when it sometimes looked even conceivable that the
U.S. would declare war on Britain.   Wilson's re-election in 1916
on the ground that " he kept us out of war," and choirs of American
mothers singing, " I didn't raise my boy to be a soldier," made
succour from the United States appear even more remote.   Then
came the unrestricted U-boat warfare; " sink at sight"; Wilson's
wrath; and his declaration of war.

The authority of the President was boundless on that day—
8 January 1918—when he gave the Fourteen Points to the world.
It was an assumption of moral leadership such as had not been seen
for half a century.   The Fourteen Points seemed to sum up the
noblest hopes of European Liberalism.   Illustrious ghosts were
stirring.   But this time it would not be the desperate struggle of
romantic rebels in mountain passes, or forays by moonlight, but an
act of universal liberation to be accomplished by powerful armies
and navies.

The enthusiasm for Wilson touched a new summit with his
sponsorship of the League of Nations.   This was the war to end wars.
Out of the wrecks of the past would rise the Parliament of the

world. The Rule of Peace would be assured at last, " consciousness the Will informing till it fashions all things fair." Men felt within themselves a resurgence of those brave Victorian hopes which made 1851 so radiant a year. That blest pair of sirens, Progress and Peace, were to be restored to their joint dominion. The faith of our fathers has been justified at last, men said.

It all ended in the disenchantment of Versailles and in the repudiation of Wilson by the Senate of the United States. The pictures of Lloyd George, Wilson and Clemenceau, in the grey gloves, around the Peace Table, come back to one like an allegorical grouping of Cynicism, Pedantry and Despair. There comes back, too, the picture of Senator Lodge taking his terrible revenge upon his rival.

Disillusion swept the world. The Land of Promise turned out to be the Waste Land and mankind set out with heavy hearts to trudge through the new wilderness. Economic distress was soon to be added to political woes. But Wilson's dream did not perish with Wilson. The Assistant Secretary of the Navy in the Adminis- tration he formed in 1913 was a promising young Democrat from New York, Franklin D. Roosevelt. President Roosevelt lived long enough to see the San Francisco Conference lay the foundations of a world order such as his old leader had conceived. In his blackest hour of defeat, after he was struck down by paralysis, Wilson never lost faith that his countrymen would one day vindicate him.

Two other names on the pages of 1913 catch one's eye. On 16th January, Raymond Poincaré, the square-fisted Lorrainer, was elected President of the French Republic. In far-off China the first Republican Parliament was meeting. Yuan Shi Kai became the provisional president of China and cheered the new Republic with the promise that it would last ten thousand years.

II

FLIGHT

The conquest of the air was advanced one stage further in 1913. Blériot had flown the Channel in 1909 and in so doing had shown that Britain had ceased to be the inviolable island. But few persons took the implication seriously, any more than they felt concerned over Rutherford's researches into the atom that were taking place at the same time. It was said that Blériot's flight pointed to an amusing but expensive form of competition with the Channel steamers, and there were wise comforters to assure us that the air- plane would never possess any military value greater than that of

observer balloons. Pégoud in 1913 showed the British that a man in
one of these clumsy machines could dart, skim and wheel like a
swallow, or tumble in the air like a pigeon without crashing. "Loop-
ing-the-loop " entered the English phrase book. Those spirals, and
somersaults, and breath-taking swoops over Brooklands opened
the minds of some thoughtful watchers to the possibilities of the
future. If within nine years of the first stuttering flight at Kitty
Hawk, a plane could cavort like this, being as responsive to its rider
as a horse, what might it not do in another nine years ? Suppose
the aviator (that was what they called him then) took with him
some brick-bats to drop on people's heads ? Why, if he were as
adroit as Pégoud, he could single out a town, a street, even a
house. Brhh !—that was like one of the wild scientific romances
which this fellow Wells had been writing for the *Strand Magazine*.
The mass of men, smilingly sceptical then of danger, persisted in
regarding Pégoud as a kind of music-hall trick cyclist who had taken
to the clouds. It was appropriate that Mr. Harry Tate should
add *Flying* to his repertory of burlesques. There were old men
watching Pégoud's contortions in the clouds who recalled seeing,
when boys, the lazy drifting of the balloons over the housetops from
Cremorne Gardens. Each age had its craze. It was balloons then,
it was flying machines to-day, and nothing much came of it.

Fear would come only with the first bomb. . . . Dreadnoughts—
they were the things to bother about. Fortunately for us, said the
practical, we have a spirited First Lord of the Admiralty, Winston
Churchill, to see that Britain's Navy is in trim to meet the growing
German Menace. We want eight and we won't wait.

III

COURAGE

There are some happenings of the past which kindle the imaginations of today as instantly as on the morning when they first took
the front pages. Such was the account in the early days of 1913 of
what had happened to Captain Scott and his companions in their
ill-starred expedition to the South Pole. There was no vainglory in
Scott's farewell, but an invoking of that finest essence of patriotism
which is the inheritance of all men. Captain Oates, stumbling into
the blizzard to die that his companions might have a better chance
of life, would be an abiding inspiration. In Scott's diary after pages
of precise scientific recordings the reader came across such a
passage as this—" We are weak, writing is difficult, but for my own
sake I do not regret this journey which has shown that Englishmen
can endure hardship, help one another, and meet death with as

great a fortitude as ever in the past." That was a flash of pure light
in those intemperate times. Then again, Scott wrote, " We took
risks—we know we took them. Things have come out against us,
and therefore we have no cause for complaint, but bow to the will
of Providence, determined still to do our best to the last. . . .
Had we lived, I should have had a tale to tell of the hardihood,
endurance and courage of my companions which would have
stirred the heart of every Englishman." The tale was told. It will
always stir the hearts of Englishmen.

Garnet Wolseley died this year. This great soldier was commemorated while he lived by a monument more remarkable than
a statue of himself in gold. He had passed into the vernacular as a
synonym of trust. When the man in the street assured his neighbour
that " It's all Sir Garnet," he was expressing the ultimate reach of
security and confidence. Wolseley's death inevitably recalled his
march to the relief of Khartoum and the death of Gordon—Gordon
who had symbolised for the Victorians courage and moral grandeur.

Scott and Gordon !—it is by such examples that the spirit of
a people is renewed from generation to generation.

IV
THE WOMEN

With all our troubles, we seem a most equable and placid people
compared with our fathers and mothers in 1913. The violence of
the domestic scene in that year is something to marvel at. Turning
the pages of the newspaper is like going out in a gale. At any
moment a slate may fall off on one's head. Violent galloping and
gun-running in Ulster. Labour violence. Violence at the docks.
Violent storming in the House of Commons. The effect is
deafening. The age is certainly not dying peacefully.

Most remarkable of all is the violence of that band of resolute
women, the Militant Suffragettes. Day by day one reads of windows
smashed in the chief streets of London, of empty mansions burned
down, of acids poured into pillar boxes, of Ministers assaulted, of
the slashing of pictures in art galleries. . . . Home-made bombs
are placed in public buildings. One such bomb half-wrecks
Lloyd George's new villa at Walton Heath. £500,000 worth of
damage is done by arson and wrecking in this campaign. It was in
June of this year that Miss Emily Davison, a leading spirit in these
exploits, threw herself in front of the King's horse in the Derby and
was killed.

The newspaper photographs of that year must seem very odd to
the eyes of the young. They depict women in the ungainly long

skirts of the period, sleeves to the wrist, high collars, and ugly hats tilted downwards from a pile of hair, flourishing *Votes for Women* banners, grappling with portly policemen in a cloud of dust or being carted away like so many sacks of potatoes. What strikes one as most singular in these pictures is the contrast between the primness of the ladies' appearance and the ferocious things that are happening to them. Here (you would say) is a deaconness or the principal of a ladies' college who had fainted in the street. Not so ; she has been knocked down humiliatingly in a baton charge. That frail and sensitive poetess has undergone the indignities of forcible feeding several times.

The women who were the storm troopers of the Militants were mostly drawn from the middle classes, and there were not a few of noble birth in their ranks. In this revolt which filled the columns of 1913 with the crack of splintered glass and the smoke of burning houses there was a paying-off of a long score of injustices. For the women in the sweat-shops of the East End there was the hope that their wretched conditions might be improved if they could have a voice in the election of the M.P.s, but for the rich and gently nurtured women in the movement this was a rebellion against all the gods of Victorian domesticity. In particular it was a revolt against that Zeus of a mahogany and ormolu Heaven, the Victorian father. It was the rebellion of Georgiana against Podsnap. The bitterness of this civil war between parents and children found its most effective expression in literature in Samuel Butler's *The Way of All Flesh*, published in 1903, the year after Butler's death. It is worth recalling that it was Butler who, thirty years earlier had described the revolt of man against the machines.

Earlier centuries had valued the intelligence of woman, even if that discrimination was exercised between narrow limits, but one great weakness of the nineteenth century had been the popular illusion that woman was at one and the same time a naturally inferior being and a celestial being—a kind of half-witted angel. To the Victorians in romantic mood, she was so exquisite a spirit that she must be spared from the contamination of the world, while her understanding was so feeble that it was absurd to waste money in the attempt to improve it. Georgiana, the Podsnaps' daughter, " seemed to take occasional frosty peeps out of childhood into womanhood, and to shrink back again, overcome by her mother's head-dress and her father from head to foot—crushed by the mere deadweight of Podsnappery." Her early views of life were " principally derived from the reflections of it in her father's boots and in the rosewood and walnut tables of the dim drawing room." Driven round the Park at her mother's side in

HARRIET MARTINEAU

the custard-coloured phaeton, " she showed above the apron of
that vehicle like a dejected young person sitting up in bed to take a
startled look at things in general, and very strongly desiring to
get her head under the counterpane again."

Until the end of the 'forties there were few ways open to an
intelligent girl to get an education. At the time the story of our
newspaper began, the liberalising influences of the age were
beginning to make an impression in a neglected sphere. In 1848
Queen's College was founded ; Bedford College came in 1849 ; the
North London Collegiate School in 1850. John Stuart Mill's
book, *The Subjection of Women*, published in 1869, exerted a
smouldering power. Women's Rights began to be talked about ;
then agitated. The movement was first met by guffaws, next by
snorts from the army of paternal Podsnaps, finally by an exasperated
hostility. Women, they said, were unsexing themselves. By 1870
the Queen was writing in this strain, " The Queen is most anxious
to enlist every one who can speak or write to join in checking this
mad, wicked folly of Women's Rights with all its attendant horrors,
on which her poor feeble sex has been forgetting every sense of
womanly feeling and propriety. God created man and woman
different—then let them remain each in their own position. Woman
would become the most hateful, heartless and disgusting of human
beings were she allowed to unsex herself, and where would be the
protection which man was intended to give to the weaker sex ? "
Her Majesty added darkly that a certain lady of rank who supported
the cause ought to be whipped.

This heart-cry from the Queen reflected the general feelings of
Society. It was odd, however, to find this sketch of women as a
species of weak, straggling Virginia creeper drawn by a woman who
was one of the most powerful characters of her age. There was
nothing feeble in Victoria's relations with her family or with her
Ministers. She was a match for the most headstrong and dominating
men with whom she debated the conduct of public affairs. Neither
Palmerston nor Gladstone would have described her as a clinging
vine. To the general flowering of talents which marked her age—
the great age which bore a woman's name—women had made
notable contribution. Who could be more ruthlessly efficient than
Florence Nightingale. By comparison with her, poor Lord Raglan,
the commander in the field, had been feeble indeed. Where was
to be found a more powerful intellectual equipment than George
Eliot's ? In political journalism there was no more formidable
character than Harriet Martineau, for long the leader-writer of the
Daily News. Society itself was dominated by a group of noble
ladies of iron strength of mind and majestic presence. And those

women who against great opposition founded such institutions as
Cheltenham Ladies' College could never be reproached with
infirmity of purpose.

" He for God only, she for God in him," decided the Queen.
It may be left to the Freudians and Adlerites and Jungists to dissect
the psychological reasons for the Queen's immoderate anger. But
in the debates over the Franchise it is curious to see how Woman,
the political abstraction, was treated as something quite separate
from women—either public servants like Florence Nightingale or
the innumerable women who were wives, mothers, sisters.

Despite the Royal displeasure, the Women's Rights movement
went on growing in strength from decade to decade. It was a
many-sided struggle—to obtain educational advantages equal
to those enjoyed by men, to secure entry into the professions, to
protect the property rights of married women and to win a status
in the factory. But for years all was gathered up in the demand for
the franchise.

The justification pleaded by the Militants for their campaign
of violence was the endless disappointments and the maddening
frustrations of the Parliamentary process. Although the House of
Commons had voted in favour of granting the suffrage to women,
the two major parties were split, and so no Government Bill was
produced. The Women's Question would be suspended indefinitely
in the air.

The *Daily News*, while it had no liking for arson as an argument,
said that it was but simple justice in a democracy that women
should be enfranchised. Ministers were divided on the issue, Grey
and Lloyd George were in favour, Asquith was against and Lewis
Harcourt was so extreme in his opposition to it that, as Lord Hugh
Cecil sharply remarked, it was hard to believe he could have been
born of woman. There was a Woman's League Against the
Suffrage, headed by Mrs. Humphry Ward, whose novel of
religious doubt, *Robert Elsmere* had entranced Mr. Gladstone
in the 'eighties. The world has forgotten what violent tempers
were aroused in this fight, how much damage the militants caused,
and how roughly they were treated. The history of the day before
yesterday is the history that is least known. It may be that in a
century's time this remarkable passage in the history of our times
will attract more curiosity than it does today.

When the war came in August, 1914, the women's militancy
ceased. Those subjected to forcible feeding and to the provisions
of the " Cat and Mouse Act " were amnestied. In the end the
Vote was granted in 1918 as a recognition of the services which
women had rendered in the war. As often happens in our country

the decision was made for reasons other than the merits of the case.

The last word in the story was one of Time's small ironies. The first woman to be elected to the House of Commons was an Irish rebel, a Sinn Feiner, who was also a Polish countess—the Countess Markievicz. She never took her seat, her allegiance being to the Irish Republic, and so it fell out that the first woman to sit at Westminster was the fiery particle from Virginia, Viscountess Astor.

The emancipation of the sex has not produced those consequences that Queen Victoria feared. In a struggle for survival even fiercer than the 1914-18 war, the nation came to depend a great deal on the energy and devotion of its women. There were seven and a half million of them in the Services or in war work of one order or another. The prospect of hundreds of thousands of young women dressed in khaki and blue was outside the visions of Queen Victoria, but, a fearless woman herself, one may be sure she would have honoured the courage of the Service women and their sisters of the factories and Civil Defence who showed such coolness under the blitz.

CHAPTER XIII

THE RISE OF SPORT

I

CRICKET AND FOOTBALL

THERE is a contrast between Then and Now which catches the eye in going through the files of a century ago—how rare are the references to sport ! A few paragraphs are given to the chief race meetings of the year, the Derby and Ascot. At intervals in the summer a cricket match is recorded, but with no greater prominence than the Saturday afternoon score of a Boy's Club receives in a local paper. Where is football ? Where tennis ? And where, in the name of the Flaming Tinman, is boxing ?

The impression conveyed by these old newspapers is that the two principal pastimes of the middle-class Englishman in those days were work and politics. For the masses there was little enough leisure and few opportunities to use it healthfully. It was not to be marvelled at that men and women who laboured weary hours and slept in styes should turn for solace to that cheap and ever-ready brand of forgetfulness, gin at twopence a tot. The gin-shop was for many almost the sole road of escape from the encircling squalor of life. Among the social changes which have marked this century, none is more striking than the great development of public sports and the provision of outdoor recreation for ordinary people. These have contributed to the emancipation of the body and mind of millions. They have altered the spirit and the physique of our people.*

It has been said that nothing has done the fame of Dickens greater harm—especially with the young—than the illustrations of Cruikshank and Hablot K. Browne. They " put readers off," is the common complaint. Those ugly caricatures stand in the way of our really seeing the glorious creations. If only it had been left to the reader to imagine what Pecksniff or Mr. F.'s Aunt looked like ! To a modern taste, Browne's drawings too often resemble those freakish vegetables which gardeners sometimes exhibit, a potato that looks like an old man or a radish that looks like a witch. These grotesques are powerful enough to blur the living pages of the novels—and there are some critics who appear to write Dickens

* The railways and the development of sport were both instrumental in bringing city dwellers out of the small houses in the narrow streets. It is not out of place to mention at this point other ventilating influences. There was Ebenezer Howard's *Garden Cities of the Future* (1898) which was the inspiration of Welwyn and Letchworth, and there was the movement to remove manufactories from city smoke and grime initiated by Bournville and Port Sunlight.

down on the strength of having looked at the plates by "Phiz". But in the case of the illustrations to *Oliver Twist*, it may well be that Cruikshank, who was a much finer artist than Browne, fell short of the immortal stuff he was asked to illustrate because he was so intent upon the mortality around him. It must be remembered that Cruikshank was a propagandist first and an artist second, as one may see in that swarm of drawings, hundreds of them, which he put out to help the Temperance party. In most of the caricaturists of this period there is displayed a sheer physical ugliness which tends to become boring rather than shocking. It may well be that Cruikshank missed the timelessness of Bumble because he was so concerned with the timeliness of his illustrations as political cartoons. As a propagandist, he seized the chance to demonstrate pictorially what the Industrial Revolution had done to the men, women and infants impressed into the service of the machines. So he produced this gallery of fat ladies and human skeletons, of villains looking like earwigs and eccentric creatures looking like fungus, of children terrible as withered goblins. Even the country figures seem to have crept out of the cellars of the big cities with mould upon them. A century of healthier living has improved the physical appearance of the ordinary people out of all Cruikshankian recognition, and for this shall we not praise the parks and playing fields as well as the hospitals and sanitary engineers?

Most studies of the national character, produced in recent years, particularly those by foreign lands, have fastened on the love of sport as a prime quality of the British people. "Sport is the poetry of the English," writes a Frenchman, overlooking for the moment our not inconsiderable line of poets from Chaucer onwards. Erudite Germans have traced the influence of the playing fields in our public life and on our foreign policy. Sport, too, has been one of our chief exports. Seeing a French football team, or a Basque tennis champion, or an American golfer or the Moscow Dynamo Club, the British crowd good-humouredly reflects that these are all converts to the grand missionary religion which spread out from these little isles. We have come to think of the habits of mind and code of conduct derived from cricket and football as being as long-established as Magna Carta. Or we have a vague idea that it was King Alfred who originally exhorted the Danes to play the game. The truth is that so short a time as a century ago sport was an enjoyment of the few. Its extension to the millions, with all the changes in social habit that this has brought has taken place since the *Daily News* was born. Most of our games have ancient roots—tennis, they say, reaches back to the Persia of 2,400 years ago—but they had either been outlawed or forgotten in the first half of the nineteenth century. Bailey Junior, serving M. Todger's Commercial Boarding House in the 'forties, would have had as little hope of a Saturday afternoon in a playing field as of becoming Viceroy of India. In 1846 cricket was the only form of sport that had any considerable following, and it was still largely a countryman's tradition, a glory of the village greens, an inherent quality of that older England which the tide of industrialism was fast submerging.

The discrimination between Gentlemen and Players has afforded a subject for several generations of satirists of English manners. It is but fair to record on the other side that, throughout the eighteenth century, cricket had been one of the few influences bridging the gulf between the classes. Peers of the realm, squires and country gentlemen were lampooned for demeaning themselves by playing at cricket on commons and in forest clearings with persons of such low condition as butchers and farm boys. A cricket match was sometimes regarded as a more vulgar form of electioneering than the Duchess of Devonshire kissing the Westminster butcher to steal a vote for Charles James Fox.

This healthy tradition of the mingling of classes on the village green persisted into the Industrial Revolution and remained one of the correctives to that all-encompassing snobbery which marred the Victorian age. In George Meredith's gleaming comedy of early Victorian assumptions, *Evan Harrington*, the village cricket match of the men of Fallowfield against the men of Beckley provides an engaging picture of a fellowship between the classes. " Under the shadow of the downs they stand, beneath a glorious day, and before a gallant company. For there are ladies in carriages here, there are cavaliers ; good county names may be pointed out. The sons of first-rate families are in the two elevens, mingled with the yeomen and whoever can best do the business. Fallowfield and Beckley, without regard to rank, have drawn upon their muscle and science. One of the bold men of Beckley at the wickets is Nick Frim, son of the gamekeeper at Beckley Court ; the other is young Tom Copping, son of Squire Copping, of Dox Hall, in the parish of Beckley." There was the same easy equality in the match between Dingley Dell and All Muggleton. But such agreeable companionships did not extend to the labouring masses in the big cities.

We turn back again to our birth-year, 1846. It was in the August of that year that the first All-England Eleven took its bow in Sheffield, captained by the redoubtable William Clarke of Nottingham. One might regard this as one of the beginnings of organized sport which came to mean so much in the nineteenth century. The contemporary paintings of this Eleven are pleasant period pieces in which one remarks the tall hats of beaver, the white trousers, the coloured shirts and starched collars and cravats. Pads and gloves are not yet worn. The bats are unlike those of to-day—toy-like and frail, they seem, and almost shaped to the use of glorified rounders. At the match between Dingley Dell and Muggleton, it will be recalled, the players were in " straw hats, flannel jackets and white trousers—a costume in which they looked very much like amateur stone-masons." Pickwick was invited into the marquee by " one very stout gentleman, whose body and legs looked like half a gigantic roll of flannel, elevated on a couple of inflated pillow-cases." The cricket grounds in that period were rough and unkempt, sometimes needing a scythe before the wicket, with the ball getting lost in the long grass, and serious players complaining that they were not to be regarded as beaters at a shooting party.

A peep into the files during this period shows that the travels of these top-hatted cricketers around England was the best advertisement that the game had yet been given. Cricket reports were not considered to be news in those days, and it did not occur to clubs to invite the reporters to their matches until late in the 'sixties. So it comes about that in dipping into the bound copies of the *Daily News* for the 'forties and 'fifties one must not be surprised to find a name of power like Lillywhite peeping out from an obscure paragraph at the bottom of a column. With the railway system still fragmentary, the Eleven made many of their journeys by coach, in the Pickwick manner, penetrating into parts of the country where the game was still looked upon as a strange charade. It was the *picaresque* period in cricket. It became a signal honour for a local youth to be chosen to meet the Eleven, and their appearance—half-gipsy, jaunty, almost that of Vincent Crummles' company—excited emulation. Their tours led the way to those county matches which became a dominant sporting interest in the 'seventies. But it was not until gifted players were dissuaded from free-lancing for three or four counties in one season that county patriotism could assert itself, pure and entire.

The modern age of cricket—the cricket of the huge crowds at Lord's, of the blazing headlines, of the hourly communiques about the state of the pitch, of the posters, cartoons and the signed articles by professional players—was born after the visit to England of the first Australian team in 1878. On 27 May of that year the country was almost as deeply stirred by the rout of the M.C.C. as by the Great MacDermott's electrifying ditty, *We don't want to fight, but by Jingo if we do*. This was the first appearance at Lord's of that legendary hero Spofforth—who came to have the fascination of Old Nick himself—and it was on this day of fire and brimstone that, taking six wickets for four runs, he was christened the Demon Bowler. The arrival of the Australians in London had created a languid interest ; Lord's was half filled to see the start of the match. But their victory excited a greater curiosity about Australia itself than half a century of books and political orations. " Botany Bay," the Podsnaps had said, sweeping the thought behind them lest it bring a blush to the cheek of the young person. Now there was a clamour by fashionable hostesses to be told all about kangaroos, wallabies, blue gums and squatters. The cold shower of defeat stimulated English cricket, and at the first Test Match two years later England won, though the visitors so comported themselves as to show that they would be bold challengers in the future.

The return of the Australians in 1882 produced the most mulled-over game in all cricket. Australia won by seven runs, after it seemed impossible for Australia to win, and in the excitements of the last half-hour one spectator fell dead, another was caught biting chunks out of his umbrella handle and others collapsed as though hit on the head by a hammer. (The Muse of History asks America if anything so thrilling ever happened in baseball.) The daemonic Spofforth on this day of days took 14 wickets for 90 runs, and the small boys were flung into ecstasies of adoration for one who had so plainly sold his soul to the Devil. There is much about that match in the library of cricket. But when one turns up the next morning's issue of the *Daily News*, the report is sedately tucked away under the generic title, Sporting Intelligence, although a sub-head does concede, " Extraordinary Finish." The occasion is dignified by an editorial comment on the theme that " the fine caprice of cricket almost rivals the glorious uncertainty of the Law," and there is a complacent conclusion worthy of Uncle Joe Pumblechook, that the success of the Australians is, after all, a tribute to the proficiency of English cricket.

This was the reverse which created the legend of the Ashes. The *Sporting Times* commemorated the Australian triumph with this obituary notice :—

In Affectionate Remembrance
of
English Cricket
which died at the Oval
on
29th August, 1882
Deeply lamented by a large circle of Sorrowing
Friends and Acquaintances
R.I.P.

N.B.—The body will be cremated, and the Ashes taken to Australia.

The squib of that sporting journalist has become one of the myths of the race. The loss of these metaphorical Ashes aroused an enthusiasm for cricket equally strong in all classes. The race, said the stalwarts, is always at its best when it has had a knock to its pride. The game became the nation's passion in the 'eighties and 'nineties, and the great players of the period—Fry, Hirst, Jessop, Hayward, " Ranji," Jackson and the rest—were made much of. In a later age we have seen a like hero-worshipping of such figures as Hobbs and Hammond. The great characters of the game seem somehow to escape the penalty of an ephemeral fame. Such a figure as Sir Pelham Warner is held in a living regard for his endearing qualities of heart and mind in a way that must arouse the envy of many a politician. One crop after another of small boys treasured the pictures of their heroes and compiled endless tables of batting averages. Over the period, like Jove himself, looms the inexhaustible W. G. Grace, with his impending thundercloud of black beard, his tough longevity and his prodigious records. For decades this powerful personality was the very embodiment of the game, and as such he must rank as a considerable figure in the social history of our century.

The interplay of Australia and England has lasted now for nearly seventy years, and the Test Match is an institution whose vitality seems proof against the assaults of Time. Its resumption is one of the pleasures of peace to which multitudes look forward as a reward they have earned in the war. Test cricket is a mystery of English life which puzzles many foreigners who have assimilated almost every other English sport and custom as easily as swallowing oysters. Even a people who are as close to us in a hundred ways as the Americans are colour-blind to cricket. Save for the Dominions and the Colonies, the game has never been an exportable commodity, though where it has taken root it appears indestructible. In Van Cortlandt Park, New York, for example, it is pleasant to see—as this writer has often seen them—West Indian Negroes, who have been living in America for years, playing cricket week after week unseduced by baseball. The infidels scoff ; but for the faithful there can be no going back ! Watching them, one remembers that in the cricket chapter of " Pickwick," Alfred Jingle recalled with staccato gusto the match in the West Indies when the bat was in blisters, the ball scorched brown and the native fielders fainted by the half-dozen.

It will be the ultimate triumph for the British when on some far-off Saturday they induce the Kremlin Eleven to turn out against the White House Eleven for the Security Council Cup. It has been said that cricket is as hard to translate into another

language as the poetry of Shakespeare into the language of Racine ;
that its savour can be appreciated only by the British palate.
There is no other game which is written about by its votaries as
though it were of a part with music, painting and verse. And in
no other game are there so many candles burning before the niches
of past heroes. Francis Thompson's lament, " O, my Hornby and
my Barlow long ago " sounds that elegaic mood which possesses
the constant cricket-lover. The game is for ever entwined, too, with
the associations of its setting.   No matter how many desolate
summers have soaked the crease, no matter how often it has been
played against a drop-scene of gas-works and brick villas, the name
brings up the thought of dappled oaks and beeches, of green-and-
azure afternoons with the stretch of gleaming turf " where the
run-stealers flicker to and fro," of huge, snowy clouds floating
over the Downs, and a sense of pastoral content. Cricket is endeared
to the Englishman because it is identified with his country in its
fairest aspects, with all that is easing to the mind. Its associations
are remote from the roarings of the machine age, and the modern
Briton, returning from the wars, prizes it because he cannot conceive
of any diversion of man further removed from the making of the
atom bomb. There is in its cult a shy, sidelong acknowledgment
of beauty by buttoned-up characters who would blush to find
themselves admiring the landscapes of John Constable or the portraits of Gainsborough. But to prove the redness of the corpuscles
that run in the veins of cricket, it is not necessary to invoke the
more-than-American toughness of our Australian brothers, nor
to recall the undying enthusiasm of those counties which are all
compact of iron resolution and no-nonsense—Lancashire and
Yorkshire. It is when one sees the white-faced youngsters in the
slum parts of our big cities playing with all the single-minded
absorption of Hammond at the Oval on some bitten scrap of dusty
ground that one realises its enduring vitality. It is one of the few
institutions in our country which are equally honoured by the
patricians, the intellectuals and the working man. Even the jokes
that it sprouts help to sustain its empire.

What does the reporter of 1846 say about football ?   His account
makes quaint reading to-day :
" On Tuesday last, the ancient Shrovetide diversion of Foot-ball
was played most lustily at Kingston-upon-Thames; the inhabitants
of which good old town claim this pastime as a right obtained for
them by the valour of their ancestors. Kingston was one of the
strongholds of the Anglo-Saxons ; and tradition relates that the
Danes, in a predatory excursion, were stopped here by the firm

stand made against them by the townspeople, until assistance arrived from London, when the enemy was defeated ; and the Danish General being slain, his head was cut off, and kicked about the place in triumph. This happened on a Shrove Tuesday, whence the origin of the custom ; the foot-ball being regarded as the symbol of victory. Foot-ball was, however, played many centuries since, at other places besides Kingston, on Shrove Tuesday ; so that the above origin must be treated as a mere tradition, unless Kingston may have set the example. It has, for ages, been noted for its popular pageants, sports, and pastimes, as shown by the Church-wardens' and Chamberlain's accounts, containing entries of many payments, from money collected from the inhabitants, in support of these festivals. Among them are the KYNGHAM, or pageant of the Three Kings of Cologne ; Robin Hood ; and the May-game.

" Foot-ball was played at Kingston, on Tuesday last, by two clubs, one called the Thames-Street Club, the other the Townsend. They began at eleven o'clock in the morning, and kept up the ball till five o'clock in the evening. The rule is to kick the ball throughout the town ; and whichever club gets the ball nearest the meeting-place at five o'clock, wins the game. There are no stakes but the honour of victory ; and the parties dine together in the evening. The poorer classes play also, for money and beer, subscribed by the townsmen. The annual game is supported by some of the wealthiest inhabitants in and around Kingston ; and the majority of the Corporation are understood to be favourable to the maintenance of this old English pastime. When the ball is driven into the river, the sport is ' fast and furious ' : the antagonists dash into the stream, and wade about in the struggle. A few years since, when the Shrove tide was so high as to be above the arch of the bridge, one of the players leaped after the ball from the parapet into the river, and was carried by the force of the stream through the arch, but was providentially rescued on his reappearance on the opposite side."

With the general stimulus to outdoor games which came in the 'forties, football was slowly becoming something more than a traditional ritual, like burning the guy on November 5th. It was as far back as 1823 that a youth, seizing the ball in his hands and running with it, created the Rugby Union game. At the time that our particular curtain rises, Association Football was in a sorry muddle. A diversity of rules existed. Some clubs let the players use their hands ; and in the conduct of the game fair and foul were much confused. In 1848, a group of ex-public schoolboys met at Cambridge to draw up a set of rules, but small heed was paid to these amiable law-givers. More and more clubs sprung up in the 'fifties, and the confusion over rules multiplied. It was not until 1863 that a second conference took place from which those stern masters, the Football Association drew their authority. A code was agreed upon, ordaining that only feet should be used, and most of the clubs accepted this new authority. The idea of a Football Cup dates from 1871. It was in 1885 that professionalism was allowed. Then, through the 'eighties and onwards came the founding of those celebrated professional clubs whose fortunes have been followed with such fidelity by millions ever since. Merely to mention such names as Crystal Palace, Aston Villa, Blackburn Rovers, the Arsenal, Preston North End, Everton, Bolton Wanderers, Chelsea is to stir romantic enthusiasms and old loyalties. Such a name as Charles Buchan has been a magic name handed down from father to son. A number of the professional clubs that fill the headlines on the sports pages originated in Sunday schools, or other church activities. Boys kicking a ball in a field would start a club in the 'eighties, and it would grow into the professional organisation we know today with its fine ground, its expert management, its impressive balance-sheet, and the high transfer fees for players who seem as costly to acquire as Old Masters. Aston Villa, for example, was sponsored by a Wesleyan Chapel, Fulham and Everton grew out of a Sunday school, and Bolton Wanderers began as the Christ Church Football Club.

By the 'nineties the great Saturday afteroon crowds had become a familiar sight. For years before the war nearly a million saw Cup Matches each Saturday. There was a wealth of other professional and amateur matches, and wherever the traveller went in town or country he saw on every stretch of open ground the great game, caught at one stage or another of its development. It is computed in an unpublished survey of the London Passenger Transport Board that by the nineteen-thirties something like four per cent. of the total population of Great Britain spent their leisure hours on a Saturday afternoon watching football. Since the war, the revival of interest in the game has been swift, and within a week or two of V.J. day there were crowds of half a million at the matches. In two major wars the British soldier has found relaxation by playing the game almost in the cannon's mouth. He has carried football to the most outlandish quarters of the globe, has played it on the snow-fields, under brassy tropical skies and in clearings of the Burmese jungle. He comes home with a fresh affection for it.

Football has provided not a few bright colours to dull lives in back streets ; it has drawn upon a civic pride in following the fortunes of the home-town team ; it has supplied one of those communal interests which unite men in a world where there is much to divide them ; it has been the folk festival of ordinary people. If one pursues a tea-taster's methods in our files for the past thirty years, it is borne in upon one to how high a pitch the skill of football has been carried. It parallels the change in the theatres from the star system to the conception of a team directed by a producer. Football used to be dominated by the star forwards— the Beerbohm Trees and Lewis Wallers of the field—to whom the rest were largely a supporting caste. Nowadays in a good Cup match the tactics and interplay of the team are soldierly.

II
PEOPLE AT PLAY

The gentle charms of croquet exhale a fragrance, like those of dried rose leaves, in many a Victorian novel and in the magazine drawings of that period. It is a game that evokes a vision of Victorian elegance. It was perfectly adapted to the Du Maurier beauties, daughters of the gods divinely tall, but also divinely dark ; grave and spiritual ; as graceful on the lawns as silver beeches. Croquet, too, calls up the roses in the rectory garden ; pale young curates horribly embarrassed by their wild strokes ; and an infinity of placid *Punch* chuckles. It was by its tranquil nature well suited to the delicate stratagems of Victorian love-making and match-making. Survivors from that age report that croquet was responsible for more middle-class romances than any other social activity, not excepting the waltz, the polka and the quadrille.

It maintained its mild sway over the Victorian gardens until a more strenuous sport dispossessed it. In the 'seventies, the half forgotten game of tennis was suddenly revived by our grand-fathers—and more particularly our grandmothers—with an astonishing brio. The credit for its rebirth is usually given to a Major Walter Wingfield who in 1874 invented a portable court of hour-glass design. This was a construction of strangely shaped nets, named fearsomely *Sphairistike*—which sounds like an incan-tation in black magic. To cry Sphairistike at Wimbledon to-day would not raise a pantomime demon, but though the Major's invention has long since perished, he stirred an enthusiasm for the game which mounted with each decade.

As with football, there was at first a fine confusion over rules and many experiments similar to Wingfield's. There was no agreement about the height of the net, or the length of the court, or the ethics of service. In 1875 the senators of cricket, the M.C.C., turned their august gaze on the pastime and presented it with a code—rather, one fancies, in the manner of a judge of the High Court condescending while on vacation to adjudicate the Dunmow Flitch. But the judgment handed down from the Marylebone Bench did not please the followers of the revived game, and the search for a more acceptable code went on for some years.

In the next stage of its swift advance, lawn tennis owed much to the authority on whist, " Cavendish " (Henry Jones). It was he who introduced it to the All-England Croquet Club at Wimbledon. Never was a more ravenous cuckoo entertained in a more yielding nest. It was not long before the very name croquet vanished from the Club, and Wimbledon became synonymous with lawn tennis. The first championship was played there in 1877. The men and women of the late 'seventies and 'eighties became enraptured by the exhilarations of this new game.

To modern eyes accustomed to the fierce athletics of Wimbledon the variety of tennis played then might be disdainfully dismissed as pat ball. To a lady swathed in a cloud of skirts and humped by a bustle, the ballet-like leaps of modern tennis were not conceivable. The net was low, the attack genteel, and the exercise pleasant. It was commended by their physicians to chlorotic young women. But, as in other fields of sport, a sharper bite and a swifter tempo were brought into the game by converts from overseas. The championship tennis which was presented at Wimbledon in the years between the wars had a swift precision which was not foreseen when the Association was founded in 1886. In skimming through the files for the nineteen-twenties and 'thirties one sees how the game became more and more a vehicle for the picturesque personality. The tennis correspondents were able to provide the reading public with a gallery of figures who were as amusing to watch as the players on a stage. A century ago the human longing for favourites had to be satisfied chiefly with Royalty, statesmen and authors, who might stay the course for fifty years. But in the new age, popular idols changed so fast it was hard to keep pace with them. The champions of sport competed with the darlings of the screen for the affections of the public. The mannerisms of Mlle. Suzanne Lenglen during her long reign provided unending material and one read articles contrasting the styles of Miss Helen Wills and Miss Helen Jacobs, or Miss Dorothy Round and Miss Betty Nuthall which were as erudite and ingenious as a piece written in the 'forties to compare the acting of Rachel and Ristori.

Golf, which has also enjoyed a remarkable revival in the past fifty years, has created its own vivid characters who have enlivened the headlines and inspired the cartoonists. In the earlier part of the twentieth century the prowess of Braid, Vardon and Taylor gave publicity to a game which, before the 'eighties, was, like other games, thought of almost as a lost art. In the years between the wars the fortunes of a Tolley or a Bobby Jones were followed with a rapt attention by many thousands. The game produced its notable women champions, and the tussles between Miss Cecil Leitch and Miss Joyce Wethered were stern and spectacular.

Although the Royal Blackheath Club was formed three and a half centuries ago, as recently as fifty years ago a man carrying golf clubs would provoke stares and laughs on the London streets. The confusion of the general public over the purpose of the game was not lessened by the early golfers' custom of wearing red coats. They were likely to be met by cries of *Yoicks* and the onlookers felt cheated when horses did not appear. There were few golf courses in the London area forty years ago ; by 1939 there were at least 150 clubs, and it was believed that there were more than 100,000 regular players in and around London. The change from the days when golf was thought of as a half-barbaric, half-comical tribal custom of the Scots has been swift. A considerable industry has grown up around it, and in its service many fine courses have been laid out by seaside or in the depths of England. Golf has been one of the health-givers of our times ; it has led its devotees into pleasant places.

The spread of organised sport from the Universities and public schools to the elementary schools took place in the latter part of the period of our survey. This has been one of the equalitarian movements of our times. The sports ground became a meeting ground for men and women, boys and girls of separate classes and pursuits. Sport was found to provide a language of common acceptance, and to express in plain terms a code of conduct that could be put to the touch in large and little affairs. When Arnold of Rugby established that public school tradition which has been so greatly wrangled over ever since—exalted, abused, reverenced or derided—he set a mould that has been followed in fields far beyond his vision. A system of education whose chief aim was to produce an administrative class for an expanding Empire laid heavy weight upon the value of sport in the shaping of character. The argument ran that it was a self-discipline ; it subdued the ego to the restraints of a team ; it set loyalty in high regard ; it taught respect for an adversary and frowned upon a war dance over his fallen body ; it ruled out many smart and tricky devices. If the precepts of the team spirit and good form might sometimes become freezing to the artistic spirit—to the Grecian qualities in the English genius—they were congenial to the Roman strain in the race ; and it is a matter of history that they have long since been taken over by the elementary schools.

The playing fields movement and the development of public parks and recreation grounds have provided our people with a means for healthful recreation which would have been the privilege of the well-to-do a century ago. In our first chapter it was noted that in 1846 an Act was passed turning Battersea Fields into a Park. These fields, where the Duke of Wellington had fought his duel with Lord Winchelsea, had fallen into low repute, being a haunt of rogues and ruffians. They were converted into one of the fairest of all London parks, lining the water-front with their chestnuts and smooth lawns, and furnishing acres of sports grounds. This fine playground shows how wide is the sweep of open-air recreation to-day, for here you will see not only urchins at football or cricket, young men and girls at tennis, but grandfathers intent over bowls. The popularity of bowls—a game, that in bygone centuries was outlawed by the State, and cursed by the Church as leading souls to damnation—is ever growing. In 1903, 9,500 games were played in L.C.C. Parks while in 1926 50,000 were played, and the figure for 1939 was far higher still.

In the magazines of the 'forties, such as the *Illustrated London News*, there are engaging drawings of Henley Regatta. The first Oxford and Cambridge Boat Race took place in 1829 but it was many years before the contest of the Light and the Dark Blues was thought of as a national event. Rowing has greatly increased in favour in the last half-century. In the 'eighties there were about four clubs of any importance on the metropolitan reaches of the Thames. Before the war there were fifty on London River and on the Lea.

There are other pastimes drawing millions which were unknown less than a generation ago. There is dog-racing, the pursuit of the greyhounds after the mechanical hare. Before the war, more than 2,000,000 persons attended dog-racing meetings each month, over half of their attendances being represented by the London tracks.

The island race has discovered so many diverse means of amusing itself during the past century that it would seem unnecessary for serious-minded men to tease their brains to draw up reports on the use of leisure. If there is one thing that the British people have shown themselves adept at in the past fifty years it is in the filling of their idle hours with sports, pastimes and recreations. They have an immense natural talent for amusing themselves. It is doubtful if they will be at a loss in the bright days coming when, as the pundits promise, we shall work one hour a day, and atomic energy will supply our needs.

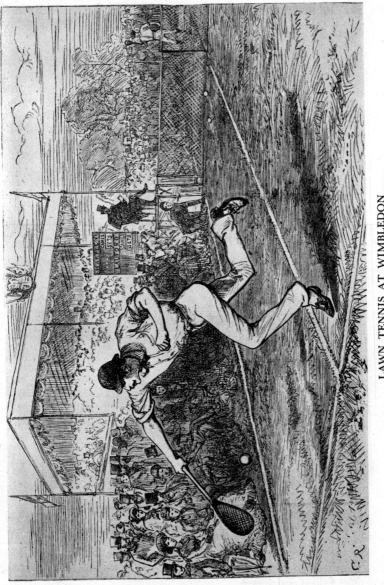

LAWN TENNIS AT WIMBLEDON
An early Champion.

Let candid friends abroad criticise the British for complacency, hypocrisy and general dullness ; it shall at least be accounted to virtue in them that they never show pique at being beaten at the games they have taught other countries to play. They communicate the pleasures of tennis to the world—fifteen nations were represented at Wimbledon before the war—and, lo, a Lenglen or a Tilden, or a Helen Wills lords it on the grounds where the British revived the game. Golf spreads from the British Isles to the United States— and a Bobby Jones comes across the Atlantic to claim their trophies. Their secret joy in cricket is carried to the uttermost ends of the Empire, and the Australians return to lick them at Lords or Old Trafford. They present football to the world—and rejoice when out of Moscow comes the Dynamo team to triumph on their fields. They accept this ordering of affairs with a philosophic grace.

After diving into the files to dredge the bones of old sporting controversies, one comes to believe that what the Englishman instinctively feels is this—" I play games to amuse myself—to keep fit—to enjoy a sense of well-being—to expend my stored-up energy— to forget the boredom of totting up accounts and making up ledgers—to enjoy the pleasant companionship which sport brings, and to be in the open air."

One of the best qualities of the Briton resides in setting the pleasure of the game above the yearning to collect medals. To concentrate on a sport from a sharp desire to win and to prove a superior training appears to the Briton irrational and beside the point—it brings into recreation the grim Monday-morning business of profit and loss, sink or swim, from which Saturday afternoon should be the bright reprieve. The Islanders contend, too, that they disperse their energies over so many sports—from table tennis to Rugby, from hockey and lacrosse to water-polo—that their muscles and science scorn to fine themselves down to one concentrated excellence. The graceful and unashamed amateurishness of the Dingley Dellers still prevails. While it endures, we may be certain that our people will still find a natural refreshment in their Wednesday and Saturday afternoons, and will not fall into too heavy a solemnity over losses or gains.

III

THE CORINTHIAN FANCY

There is one aspect of the sporting life of the century which demands a section on its own because it doesn't at all fit into the general panorama. During the early decades of our century, prizefighting was carried on almost as though it were a political

underground movement. Its promoters communicated a rendezvous to its patrons with all the mysteriousness of the scouts of a
secret society. Its champions were whisked about the country to
escape the police. It was a sport on the run.

Prize-fighting, which had died with ancient Rome, had been
revived in a full-blooded magnificence by the English aristocracy
in the eighteenth century. A nobleman would spend as many
guineas on a favourite pug as on a racehorse. Pugilism was protected
by a powerful aristocracy. Byron in *Don Juan* bears testimony
to the respect in which he held the champion, John Jackson—
" Gentleman Jackson "—from whom he took lessons. With the
rise of the middle-classes in the nineteenth century and the revival
of Puritanism, pugilism fell into disrepute. It had long been illegal,
but the law was intermittently enforced, and the fight manager,
like the landlord of Chesterton's *Flying Inn* would hurry his sign
from one green retreat to another.

To read accounts of some of the contests of early Victorian times
is to be reminded of America under Prohibition. There is the
same double-talk by legislators, and the same winking and nodding
by the police to show where their sympathies resided. A word in
the ear of the top-hatted Peeler outside Paddington, and he would
whisper the right train to catch, much as the New York policeman
in the nineteen-twenties was the best guide to the speak-easies on
his beat. The railway companies were forbidden by law to carry
passengers to a prize-fight, but somehow they always managed
to run trains for the Corinthian Fancy to the most out-of-the-way
corners of England. Lord Palmerston, the Prime Minister, made
little secret of his feelings and was the first in the House of Commons
to subscribe a testimonial guinea for Tom Sayers. On a famous
fighter abandoning the Ring and becoming a preacher, Palmerston
observed (quite seriously) that John Bright would have made as
grand a pugilist as Sayers if he had given his mind to it in his
youth.

In a captivating book about those times, *Pugilistica*, there
is a racy account of the difficulties which beset the ardent followers
of pugilism who wanted to see the match between Jem Mace and
Joe Goss in September 1863. " In the face of a vigilant and
hostile magistracy and police, managers necessarily adopted
unusual precautions to confine the knowledge of the time and place
to none but safe men. Accordingly, not only was the day kept
secret, but it was not until overnight that even the line of rail and
amount of fare were disclosed to intending 'excursionists.' When
the ' office ' (ticket office) was given to those who were prepared
to invest £2 2s. in cardboard, the rendezvous was stated to be the

Paddington terminus of the Great Western, and the time two o'clock a.m. of the morning of St. Partridge, 1 September 1863, and thither at that unreasonable and unseasonable hour did the sheep destined for the shearing eagerly repair."

Thieves and roughs always knew of one of these excursions, and they poured to the station for loot. In the dark of that September morning outside Paddington there was considerable disorder. Pockets were picked ; men were knocked down and robbed. At 4 a.m. the train steamed out, and the company believed, though they were not sure, that they were going to Wootton Bassett in Wiltshire. There was a stop at Didcot to pick up some Oxford University bloods. The Place set for the fight was five miles from Swindon. On the fresh greensward the fight between Mace and Goss had just begun, when a low cry of warning came from the sentinel. Immediately after, a band of Wiltshire policemen tumbled into the ring. The stripped fighters fled, their seconds tearing after them with their clothes.

The police showing no disposition to do anything more than take possession of the Ring, the fighters and their supporters piled back into the train, and the G.W.R. obligingly returned them to Paddington. The day was still young, and the referee, after cogitating his rule book, announced, "I shall order (as I am empowered by the Rules) the men to meet again this day at Fenchurch Street Station and go down to Purfleet. When there, we must be guided by circumstances." For circumstances one should doubtless read police.

The cabbies at Paddington Station whirled the company, by now a trifle jaded, to Fenchurch Street. As one of the cabmen said, " They were a-helping some of the right sort out of a fix." Another obliging railway company saw that the party reached Purfleet at 3.30 in the afternoon. There the suspicious activities of an " Essex calf " (a policeman) disturbed the pilgrims, and off they went again by ferry to Plumstead Marshes, murmuring at the extra ten shillings for water hire. On a lonely stretch of land at Plumstead the fight was at last resumed. It lasted 19 rounds, taking 1 hour 55 minutes and 30 seconds. Mace won.

That was not a long contest for those times. Many of the fights of these bare-knuckled champions stretched out to ninety or a hundred rounds. Such characters as Jim Belcher, Tom Cribb, Tom Sayers, the Benicia Boy, the Gas-Man, the Tipton Slasher and Bendigo must have been made of iron bones, game hearts, and more than mortal flesh. The match between Sayers and Heenan (the Benicia Boy from America) in 1860, created a public commotion by its ferociousness, and did much to lead to the final suppression of pugilism without gloves. The fight took place at Farnborough, was seen by 1,200 persons and lasted 2 hours and 20 minutes. The railway tracks through London were lined with Metropolitan Police armed with cutlasses. The contest ended indecisively. The Ring was broken at the 37th Round by the police and the crowd, and although the referee called an end, the fight was carried on by those two unquenchable giants for five more rounds amid a deafening confusion. At the end, Heenan, quite blinded, struck out like Samson at Sayers' seconds and then raced madly into the fields.

A general revulsion of public opinion made it impossible to resume the contest on some later day. A championship belt was awarded each fighter, and flowery pieces were written to the effect that Britain and America might be equally pleased with the valour of their competing sons. The American Press was at first greatly put out by the disputed decision. This was the first of many such exchanges of courtesies across the Atlantic.

That strange and violent world of the old pugilists has vanished, surviving only in certain spirited pages of William Hazlitt, of Thackeray (who commemorated the Sayers-Heenan match in both prose and verse) and of Conan Doyle. The bare-fisted prize fight sustained its own knock-out blow in the 'sixties with the establish-ment of the county constabulary throughout England. There was no field to which the Fancy might repair that was beyond the reach of the Law. The sport fell into its lowest repute. Then boxing with gloves was brought forward to take the place of prize-fighting. In 1866 John G. Chambers founded the Amateur Athletic Club, and the Marquis of Queensberry laid down that code of rules which made the Ring respectable, and brought it to a truce with the Law.

The language of some of the boxing writers of that period while not of the quality of Hazlitt or Thackeray, has a charm of its own. One lingers over it because it shows how salty our slang was a century ago, possessing a gay fantastication of language usually identified with Broadway. The phrase-book of the Fancy is as picturesque as anything in George Ade or Damon Runyon. The situations in prize-fighting tend to repeat themselves, and so the writers avoided monotony in description by their ingenuity in finding synonyms. Of two fighters hitting each other on nose and mouth it is said, " each got pepper on the nozzle and whistle." The prize-fighter's nose at various stages is described with such pleasing variations as these : " a smasher on the proboscis," " a tap on his nasal prominence," " a severe straightener on the snuff-box," " pinked him on the smeller," " he got home on the snuffer tray,

removing a piece of the japan," " he napped him on the sneezer,"
" a tap on the scent-box," " a crack on the olfactory projection."
Among circumlocutions for eye one discovers these : " his left
peeper," " his right ogle," " the spectacle beam." The mouth,
of course, becomes the kisser, and a blow on the kisser which draws
blood, " fills his potato trap with ruby." No pugilist had a face—
they were all furnished with mugs or dials—cheerful mugs or black
dials. The process of drawing blood produces many euphemisms ;
the " ruby streams," " drawing the claret " and " bringing the
carmine " are fairly familiar to-day ; but phrases such as " the
home-brewed appeared," " tapping his best October " (ale), " his
cork was drawn," and " there flowed more Lafitte of the premier
cru " bespeak a grisly inventiveness.

Hazlitt in his account of the first fight he saw, that between the
Gas-Man and Neate, records the battering the Gas-Man sustained,
until he came to look " not like an actual man, but a preternatural,
spectral appearance, or like one of the figures in Dante's Inferno "
. . . " It was not till the Gas-Man was so stunned in the seventeenth or eighteenth round, that his senses forsook him, and he
could not come to time, that the battle was declared over. Ye who
despise the Fancy, do something to shew as much pluck, or as
much self-possession as this before you assume a superiority which
you have never given a single proof of by any one action in the
whole course of your lives." That is an epitaph with which the
Fancy might well be content.

CHAPTER XIV

THE BALLET OF COSTUME

I

MRS. BLOOMER'S POLKA

ONE general theme of our story has been the emancipations which these hundred years have brought. The freeing of women from certain barbarisms of fashion is not the least notable of the social liberations. The girl of 1846 looks out from the family album, mercilessly tight-laced, glazed stiff by convention, and hedged about by prohibitions. That tight-lacing is a symbol of many restrictions. Staring from the cardboard frame at her great-granddaughter of 1946, she might wistfully say, " Angels alone that soar above enjoy such liberty."

The endeavours of many unrecorded rebels, many doctors, many matrons whose forthright sense prevailed over custom, together with the liberating influences of two great wars, have set women free from a despotism that held them in thrall a hundred years ago. Marching down the road with a cheerful swing go the young women of 1946 in jerseys and slacks of grey, black or skyblue. Never were figures less cribbed than these. Seeing them, one ought in all justice to say, " Mrs. Bloomer, how thou art vindicated." But the doom of Mrs. Bloomer—Mrs. Amelia Jenks Bloomer, to be exact—persists. Bloomer, alack, never was a name to be taken seriously. It was an easy mark for the jesters. Had the lady married a Cavendish, a Vanderbilt or a Smith, men and women might have accorded a respectful hearing to her words—for sensible words they were. As it was, ridicule that defeated her in her lifetime, has clouded the recollection of her in the pages of social history. She merits a niche as a reformer, but she survives as a confused kind of joke that nobody is quite sure about. Bloomers was first the nickname given to the courageous women who followed her example ; then it became attached to an ugly form of underwear ; and now it remains in the modern memory as an uncertain echo of Victorian music-hall humour.

Turning the pages of the *Daily News* for 1851* one finds this heart-cry from a misunderstood woman :

" To the Editor,

" Sir,—May I be allowed in your columns to ask why the

---

* This year had another significance for women. It was in 1851 that Isaac Meritt Singer displayed his first sewing machine in a Boston store.

British public is so horrified at the idea of women dressing in trousers seeing that they have for many years tolerated a number of men from the North of the Tweed wearing petticoats—and shockingly short petticoats too?

Yours,

AMELIA BLOOMER."

One may sympathise with Mrs. Bloomer wheeling in anger on her tormentors, but the retort was not well-timed. For it was in Finsbury of all places that a baying crowd had stopped her from speaking, and a jibe at the kilt lacked point among these Cockneys.

Mrs. Bloomer was born in New York City in 1818, edited a magazine in the U.S., and was one of the earliest advocates of women's suffrage. The right to wear comfortable clothes and the right to vote were bound together in her mind, and both were somehow caught up in her zeal to abolish Negro slavery and to prohibit the sale of liquor. It was in the 'fifties that Mrs. Bloomer came to Britain to persuade her sisters to break the bondage of corsets and tight-lacing. Although her name was later linked with any trouser-like garment worn by women, the original reform she proposed was the wearing of long, voluminous pantalettes under short skirts. This costume could by no wildness of fancy be described as licentious, and it certainly was not revolutionary. The guarded women of Turkey had been wearing something like it for centuries. It was, in truth, a conservative reaction in favour of health, comfort and ease. But the conventions of that age were so rock-bound that even a return to an old fashion could shock with the force of a new blasphemy.

The public insisted on considering her as an amusing monster. An impartial eye would probably conclude that while Mrs. Bloomer's ideas on dress reform were sound, the models she produced were ugly. If an elegant simplicity had been added to good sense, she might have had better success. There was a lack of guile in this lady. And there was rough justice in the popular instinct which made bloomer a slang synonym for a well-intentioned blunder.

When she could gain a hearing, Mrs. Bloomer declared that " the women of America found that they had one despot in the way, one that refused to be questioned either by morality, religion or law. That tyrant was known to the world by the name of fashion. That tyrant the women of America had determined to bring before the bar of public opinion on three special charges. First, that nature had been violated and life endangered ; second, that in consequence of its requirements a vast amount of money had been expended which might have been diverted to higher and holier purposes ; and third, that by encumbering women it incapacitated them from rendering services to society worthy of their high destiny." It was good rhetoric, and, despite the gusts of raucous laughter, it went ringing down the century.

One reads in the newspapers for this year that a number of London women supported Mrs. Bloomer in her campaign and faced the ridicule of audiences by standing at her side in the outrageous costumes. A ball was arranged at which the women pledged themselves to appear only in bloomers. The public curiosity was such that Madame Tussaud felt justified in adding a group of ladies in pantalettes to her waxworks. *Punch* wrote satirical verses. The medical papers defended the reformer. Scurrilous doggerel about her was hawked on the streets. That, at least, is a testimony to the virtuous commotion which Mrs. Bloomer caused.

Mrs. Bloomer's mission perished amid guffaws, but she had sown seeds of discontent that did not perish. Forty years afterwards, during the bicycle craze, the great arc of the cycle track in Battersea Park, curving past the lake and flower-beds to the chestnuts by the river bank, was filled with gliding and racing young women who, to the distress of their aunts, wore bloomers, indisputable bloomers.

II

DANCE OF THE SYLPHS

Apart from the warm glow which Mrs. Bloomer casts upon our century, the records of dress are largely records of humble servitude to a tyrant full of whims.

It is commonly said that fashions mirror history. There is an assumption that one can deduce the rise of Empires and the shock of revolution by turning the pages of albums of costumes. It is easy to identify the grave simplicity of the modes of 1846 with the revulsion of the young Queen from her wicked uncles ; to see reflected in them the resolve of Victoria and Albert to refine manners and improve morals. Nor is it difficult to regard the foam of frills that came flooding in from Paris in the late 'sixties as an expression of the light-headedness as well as the light-heartedness which marked the " gaslit tragedy " of the Second Empire. And one may detect in the ornate adornments of the 'eighties that craving for display which marks the upsurge of new riches. Many men who followed Samuel Smiles' precepts of self-help, who rose from poverty to make great fortunes in commerce, insisted on their wives and daughters scintillating like Bond Street show-cases. This display of captive and caparisoned womanhood declared to all the world how well their lords had done. It was an illustration of Veblen's theory of conspicuous spending. Part of Mr.

Merdle's ransom to Society was paid in the jewels with which he loaded Mrs. Merdle.

These aside, there does not seem to be any good social or political reason why tight-lacing should be fashion's worst cruelty in the 'forties, and then be brought in twice later in the century ; or why such a parasitic growth as the bustle should appear in the 'eighties ; vanish ; then come back like an evil dream in the 'nineties. Fashion sometimes rode by the side of history, but at other times galloped off across the fields on wild adventures of its own.

Looking at the drawings and photographs of 100 years ago— photography was already well established as an art, and Mr. Beard was advertising his " speaking camera likenesses " in the first issue of the *Daily News**—one remarks the sylph-like elegance of the girls. The reigning beauty is a creature as fragile as a Dresden shepherdess. A small head " sunning over with curls " is framed by a taking bonnet. Of all forms of head-wear, the bonnet was best framed to add piquancy to a smile and poignancy to a tear. In a score of forms—small as a handkerchief, or large as a cabbage ; a wreath of flowers or a wide umbrella of straw ; lost on the back of the head or swallowing a pretty face in its funnel, so adding to the hazards of Victorian kissing—it survived year after year. Gone now is the coal-scuttle and gone the poke-bonnet, but an observant eye may yet mark elderly women in the slums, who wear black bonnets trimmed with jet, built to a model such as the Queen favoured to the end of her reign.

The general taste that governed the fashions a century ago was admirable. There was a floating grace suggesting that women could dance like a wave of the sea if they chose. In the drawings of the time they all look like Taglioni and Fanny Ellsler, made of thistledown and starlight. Silk was the favourite stuff ; the colours were soft and tranquil. "Many dresses," said the fashionable guide for 1846, " are made in silks with a satin stripe or pattern. The favourite colours are deep blue, violet, china green or black. They are trimmed with bands and bows of velvet. For dinner dresses, rich damask silks in pink, white or blue are preferred. They are trimmed *a la* Louis XIV with flounces of lace."

Above all, the girls of this period had waists surpassingly slender, but who could guess what tortures brought into being this flower-

* The advertisement read: " Beard's Improved Photographic Portraits, so highly eulogised by all the leading journals, are taken daily from nine till six, at 34, Parliament-street, Westminster ; 85, King William-street, City, and the Royal Polytechnic Institution, Regent-street. ' The brilliancy and warmth of tone gained by the patentee's new method of colouring add materially to the excellence of the portrait. . . . The portrait stands out in bold relief, clear, round and life-like.' "

like grace ? Those Titania waists were attained only through a most ruthless tight-lacing. The bodices were laced at the back, and brawny maids from Devon farms were brought in to pull, tug and haul at the laces to constrict their mistresses to the shape of an hour glass. It was a Chinese torture, costing dear in health. Not a few of the sylphs died.

III

CRINOLINE WALTZ

The crinoline in the mid 'fifties came as a liberation. The flowering fullness of the new style made the waist *seem* smaller, and so women were spared the agony of being pressed to death by steel and whalebone. This graceful fashion prevailed for many years. Before it grew over-blown, it was most fitting to a Victorian heroine. It created the illusion that woman was an unearthly being, a wafted apparition of beauty who was exempt from the vulgar necessity of legs. The impression was much enhanced by the lighting of that early Victorian scene. Gas, which had excited alarm when it was first shown in London streets in the early years of the nineteenth century, had become widely used in the 'forties. In 1846 there were over 400,000 houses in London so lighted. Old playgoers insist that much of the witchery of Irving's productions at the Lyceum Theatre in the 'eighties was due to a gas lighting which spread a spell across the stage never to be rivalled by garish electricity.

So, too, in drawing rooms and ballrooms. Under the green enchantment of gaslight, beauty rising from the shimmering cloud of the crinoline and floating into the waltz brought a throb of romantic pleasure to young hearts. The realist might complain of false illusion ; saying, " women were never like that." But in an age that was an age of prose—despite its admirable poets—the crinoline at its best was a poetic thing. Jeremy Bentham would never have invented it, but Paxton might. Amid the grim functional shapes of the machine age, the locomotive, the steamship, the factory building, the derrick, the crane, and amid the too, too solid furnishings, here was a delightful extravagance, a setting free of the fancy. The manifold petticoats which had plumped out the full skirt of the 'forties were replaced at first by horsehair frames, then by steel hoops and air tubes. The full-blown silks endured for more than twelve years—roughly from 1854 to 1866—*

* The crinoline was worn, of course, long after 1866. There is always a considerable difference between the fashion plates of a period and the dresses that are seen in the street.

a long life for a mode, but in the end the machine age did defeat it. Active matrons came to hate it. It was one thing for a girl to glide like a cloud across a long drawing room, but it was a very different matter to regulate the conduct of these swaying pneumatic hoops in coaches, omnibuses and railway trains. The crinoline belonged to a more spacious age ; to mansions, terraces and parks rather than to Ludgate Circus or to the London, Chatham and Dover Line. Imagine, for example, a woman rigged out in full sail of silks and velvets like a China clipper attempting to negotiate that London street scene on which the curtain rises in the first chapter of *Bleak House* :—" Foot passengers, jostling one another's umbrellas, in a general infection of ill-temper, and losing their foothold at street corners where tens of thousand of other foot passengers have been slipping and sliding since the day broke (if this day ever broke) adding new deposits to the crust upon crust of mud, sticking at these points tenaciously to the pavement and accumulating at compound interest."

From time to time one comes across paragraphs in the newspaper about women being injured when the billows of the crinoline were caught by the wheels of traffic ; and there were old wives' tales of girls being whipped up by the wind like balloons and carried over cliffs.

IV

CAKEWALK

Ugliness came in when the crinoline went out. In 1866 dress became deflated in front, and acquired that fearsome hump, the bustle. Rows and rows of fringes began to decorate the skirts in front ; and rows upon rows of bows adorned it at the back. By the middle 'seventies, the dressmakers ordained that women should wear a projection at the back of some two feet or more from which loops of chocolate-box silk descended in a cascade over a smother of frantic frills, garnished with rosebuds. A fashionable beauty sometimes appeared like a many-tiered wedding cake that had been sliced downwards instead of across. Women who had drifted as gracefully as swans across the polished floors of the 'fifties now presented the appearance of a pastry cook's parade of confectionery. One half expects to see " Awarded the gold medal of the Paris Exposition " appended to them.

One might perhaps trace a link between the arabesques and curlicues of these dresses and the baroque politics of Disraeli's Prime Ministership. The Great Asian Mystery of Disraeli, his brand of romantic Imperialism, and such theatrical surprises as proclaiming the Queen Empress of India, set a tone to the age. The respectable went in search of the picturesque, as exemplified by the Dolly Varden vogue. Liberal ladies and Conservative ladies, brokers' wives and provincial Mayoresses appeared for a spell in undulating hats and flowered paniers that made them look like emigrés from the court of Marie Antoinette—which was about as far distant from their natural selves as any charade dress could be. By the end of the 'seventies, when the Asian Mystery was beginning to loose its magic, the style had reverted to honest plainness again, although the skirts retained an appendix called a spoon which looked somewhat like the trailing back feathers of a pheasant. This happy device ensured that every woman was her own carpet sweeper, and out of doors the train had to be held in the hand to prevent it collecting the grime of the streets. But the lines of dress were fairly austere, and at last allowed a recognisable resemblance to the human form to be disclosed. From time to time during the century the feminine shape makes coy emergences, like Diana from the rushes, then retreats again into the rustle of the bustle or a foam of chiffon.

V

PATIENCE QUADRILLES

After the intermission of simple straight lines, the zig-zag of fashion brought in huddle and muddle again. The dresses of the 'eighties are disfigured by cabbage-like bunchings which would sometimes use eighteen to twenty yards of material, making the daughter of the gods look like a bundle for the laundry hastily tied together with insufficient string. Even when in the later 'eighties fashion becomes amorphous, the fussiness of the ribbons and lace, of braid and fringe of bows and flounces, worries the eye. In 1885 that horror, the bustle came back again, but by this time the despotism of fashion had become less absolute, for in their diverse ways both the aesthetic (or *greenery-yallery*) movement and the development of sports brought a new freedom to women.

The girls of the high aesthetic line at whom Du Maurier smiled and Gilbert laughed seem now, in the pictures of the period, to turn the laugh against their satirists. For no matter how foolish it may have looked to walk down Piccadilly with a poppy or a lily in " your mediæval hand," or to decorate one's rooms with Japanese fans, peacock plumes and willow-pattern plates, the girl friends of Bunthorne could appear without remark to-day in Kensington High Street or on Ealing Broadway. For the dress of the feminine aesthetes was plain, simple and free to modern eyes and had delicate and discreet colourings. It is the conventional dress of the late 'eighties that would cause laughter in the streets today, and the progression of a bustle in the Strand would hold up the traffic as effectively as the breakdown of a bus.

In the 'nineties, which may have been gay but were undoubtedly ugly, came that distortion of dress, the leg-of-mutton sleeves worn with bell-shaped skirts. The records of the early days of the twentieth century are marked chiefly by a return of wasp waists and by a whorl of skirts that froth at the bottom with lace and tulle as though they were so many waves churning upon rocks. A woman of fashion with a seventeen-inch waist and a vast cartwheel hat had a perilously top-heavy look, and it was not clear how she could survive a high wind. To a modern eye the sufferings which this new generation of victims endured for the sake of an ethereal form were not justified by the picture that was left. These ladies, with their dislocated anatomies, appeared in the end to be suffering from malformation of the hips. Collars of lace or other fabrics sustained by whalebone, were worn as high as the stocks of Wellington's grenadiers and gave a rigid, choked appearance. There was also a habit affected at this time of adorning the shoulders and arms of dresses with fishlike fins of gauze.

Glancing at the fashion drawings which appear in the *Daily News* at the turn of the century, one observes that women had decided to become tall as young pine trees again. During all these years, indeed, the sex appeared able to elongate or shorten at will. Woman, like Alice in the underground hall, alternately ate the little cake which made her shoot up to the ceiling and drank from the little bottle which shut her up like a telescope. By taking thought, she could most certainly add a cubit to her stature. Beauty was wrought from within. The haunted and haunting ladies of Rossetti and Burne-Jones were declared to be outrageously untrue to flesh and blood when the canvases were first exhibited, but within a decade or so, Rossetti damozels were trailing their mysterious sorrows through Suburbia and puzzled business men in the provinces found themselves the fathers of Burne Jones sibyls with brooding eyes. The exquisite artistry of George du Maurier, whose women appeared improbably tall, patrician, and wrapped round in their own dreams, produced its own imitations in Bayswater and Belgravia.

One attitude is common to the 'seventies, 'eighties and 'nineties—homage to beauty. In those decades the fashionable fair cast a charm over all classes. Crowds would gather before the windows of West End photographers to gape at the profile of a beautiful

Duchess. When Lily Langtry first came to London, men and women in restaurants and hotel lobbies would stand on chairs to see her pass. The classic grace of Mary Anderson caused audiences to draw their breath when the curtain rose to reveal it, and the magic of her look was such that few cared to ask the disagreeable question whether she could act at all. With the twentieth century this adoration of public beauty slowly decayed. It is said that beauty, being rarer then, was the more greatly prized. It seems likely, too, that the fair women of that time fulfilled the popular demand that there should always be some fairy-tale characters in the world. From one generation to another the poor, the sick-at-heart and the down-at-heel have always cherished the fantasy of a race of radiant beings who are forever young, and beautiful, and live in the sun. To those who have many troubles the thought that there are some people who have no troubles at all seems in itself a consolation. For the disinherited can dream themselves into such happier existences.

The beauties of the Edwardian musical comedy stage fulfilled this destiny. It is doubtful if any film star of today ever appears such an embodiment of April, and all the young romance of the world, as did Miss Lily Elsie gliding into the *Merry Widow* waltz.

With 1910 there came another unpredictable twist in fashion. Women's dress returned then to an almost Grecian severity ; and the tight fit reached its extreme in the hobble skirt. Here was the philosophy of clothes running counter to the spirit of the age. For these were intemperate times, and the newspapers were filled with the immoderation of women. Fashion, as in despair, sought to impose a strait jacket upon her daughters and to fetter their knees. While the Suffragettes were planning a guerrilla warfare in which the capacity to run fast was essential, the dressmakers were producing skirts of such a tightness that well-dressed women at a garden party moved with stammering steps like competitors in a sack race. H. G. Wells' Ann Veronica, going to prison as a militant would have won Mrs. Bloomer's nod for her principles, but have drawn a sigh for her crippling clothes. The Suffragettes' chief contribution to the debate on what women should wear was to slash the Rokeby Venus in the National Gallery for not wearing anything. Like so many other English rebels, these ladies were Puritans.

In 1911 some belated disciples of Mrs. Bloomer appeared in a chaste variation of Turkish dress called the Harem Skirt. They were hooted and pelted on the streets. Some had to seek a refuge in shops from the anger of the crowd. No one seems to have interviewed the Sultan on the subject.

VI

FOXTROT

But the ghost of Mrs. Bloomer had not long to wait for vindication. After the 1914-18 war women appeared in short, tubular dresses. These were like the tunics of pages at a mediaeval court, and the short-cut hair that became the vogue at this time heightened the illusion of boyishness. It was as though the sex had risen in a mass-revolt against the frilled fripperies, laces, feathers and arch mysteries of the first years of the twentieth century. Mr. Shaw was probably as responsible as any man for the change of mood that brought the change of mode. Year after year, with unflagging wit, he had attacked the romantic illusion. He had riddled the " tushery " of the Victorian theatre, had turned conventions inside out, and exhibited woman as the pursuer and man as the pursued. Now his influence was manifest on a generation of girls that had been uprooted by the war. " Heaven help us women if you ever eat a steak," Mrs. Pat Campbell had said to Shaw at a stormy rehearsal ; but he wrought his revolution all the same on a vegetarian diet.

Edwardian beauties surviving into this post-war age observed with dismay the abandonment at one stroke of centuries of artifice. All the gaudy rhetoric and ingenious conceits of clothes were given up for the most matter-of-fact of styles. Herrick's " erring lace which here and there, enthrals the crimson stomacher," and the ribbons that flowed confusedly, and the " winning wave, deserving note, in the tempestuous petticoat " were scorned by these new Calvinists. To show their contempt for the standards of coy beguilement and kittenish charm that had prevailed fifteen years before, they sought to look as much like their young brothers in smocks as possible. The Edwardian dowager, focussing a shocked lorgnette, commented acidly that girls would be boys nowadays, and observed with a certain justice about the extremer styles that they were like the sheathed wings of grasshoppers. Venerable artists, recalling the sumptuous proportions of Etty's nudes and the more delicate roundness of Leighton's *Psyche* asked indignantly what had happened to curves, the prerogative of womanhood since before the Flood. Even the consumptive maidens of Rossetti and Burne-Jones had retained a rueful grace of femininity. Not at their last breath could anyone mistake them for pages at the court of King René. There were dark rumblings from eugenists on the theme of race suicide. But the young things of the 'twenties were unabashed and impenitent. Truth to tell, the mode was inelegant but it was honest ; it was also hygienic ; and the epithet, *functional*, which was then becoming popular, could fairly be applied. The waist was so free and uncorseted that at last no waist was apparent at all. Above all, the young woman of the period insisted that she would destroy for ever the myth that women were as legless as mermaids. In the crinoline age it had been assumed that woman was half a disembodied essence, wafted exquisitely to and fro on a silken cloud. The disclosure of an ankle scandalised. Charles Dickens fell in love with Ellen Ternan, the actress, on finding her melted in tears in her dressing room over the prospect of showing a few inches of leg on the stage, a dilemma rare in the modern drama. The revelation of black stockings out of a whirl of petticoats in the notorious *can-can* confirmed the sober Briton's worst fears about the French, and only too completely explained the collapse of the Second Empire. In view of the harshness of past prejudices, it was remarkable that the outcry was no louder when woman made the great decision to demonstrate that the Creator had endowed her with knees.

VII

HARLEQUINADE

In the Canterbury Pilgrimage of our century the male travellers appear in the drabbest hues. The sex as a whole had given up any pretence of being peacocks when knee-breeches and flowered waistcoats went out, but dandyism fought a rearguard action well into the 'forties. In that decade characters so dissimilar as Count D'Orsay,* Charles Dickens and Benjamin Disraeli were noted for the brilliance of their waistcoats and cravats. The young Disraeli must have looked like a Bird of Paradise. In the daytime he would walk out in green velvet trousers and a canary waistcoat ; and for evening wear he would choose a dress-coat of black velvet lined with white satin, a waistcoat blazing with flowers worked in gold thread, white gloves with an array of flashing rings on the outside, while he carried a cane of ivory inlaid with gold, from which dangled a tassel of black silk. One must add to this the effect of profuse ringlets of hair, dyed and varnished to a raven's-wing black. This was an afterglow of the Regency, of the age when the man of fashion anguished over his wardrobe and his figure as greatly as any

---

* In the issue of the *Daily News* of 9 March 1846, appears this advertisement : " Count D'Orsay Paletot [loose overcoat] distinguished from all others now in use by its gentlemanly appearance and elegant style. Produced under the Count's immediate direction by Grosjean, tailor to King Louis Philippe by special appointment. Lama paletot with silk sleeves, £2 2s. od. Ditto for winter wear, £3 3s. od. Quadrant, Regent-street." Elegance was not expensive a century ago.

THE MAN WITH THE RED FLAG

regnant beauty ; of the days of the *exquisites* when the Prince Regent burst into tears because Beau Brummell sneered at the cut of his coat ; and Byron starved and drank vinegar to preserve his waist.   By the time the mid-Victorian zenith had come, both Dickens and Disraeli were usually dressed as sombrely as any chairman of a railway company, in black frock coat, grey trousers and black cravat.   Gone were the hyacinthine locks tumbling on the collar.   Gone were the jewels and flashing colours.   But to the end of his days Disraeli pinned the celebrated false curl each morning to his forehead and Dickens' diamond studs and links sparkled into an age that thought them showy and vulgar.

In the word of today, the dandy was an exhibitionist.   The flirt of fine plumage was designed to startle a stupid world into acknowledgment of uncommon talents.   Sometimes there was a diabolical pride in the dandy's composition ; the dark, Byronic joy in being a damned soul.   He was the lonely rebel who struck his poses in the most elegant (and crowded) drawing-rooms ; he was the outcast who took good care always to mix his griefs with the best society.   With Disraeli, whose career now looks to be an impossible sequence of triumphs over a hopeless series of obstacles, the affectation of dandyism was a gamble that came off.   The glittering display shocked, repelled, irritated at first.   But he was sought after as a curiosity, and so, the outworks of society being breached, the hard intelligence and the witty tongue completed the conquest.   Disraeli bedecked himself to attract attention ; Dickens put on rainbow-coloured waistcoats to show that he had triumphantly arrived.   When he was a young reporter living in rooms off Holborn, he wore cropped hair and was as sober-suited as a crow.   It was in the first flush of his success with *Pickwick*, *Oliver Twist* and *Nicholas Nickleby* that the novelist imitated D'Orsay. " I am coming," said Disraeli.   " I am here," said Dickens.

The chronicles of men's wear during the century are without doubt a proper pride and joy to the learned editor of the *Tailor and Cutter*.   But to the innocent amateur dipping into the records of the past they are as dull and shapeless as the trousers of the Right Honourable W. E. Forster's statue in the Embankment gardens. No Mr. Bloomer appeared to defend man from the despotism of *his* fashions.   The change from pantaloons to trousers, the conquest of the beaver by the hideous stove-pipe hat, the evolution of the cravat into the tie form a tedious, sad history that points no moral and adorns no tale.   And who now remembers that in the restless nineteen-twenties there was an uproar over a voluminous garment called Oxford bags, said to have originated at Cambridge?

CHAPTER XV

AN AMERICAN SUMMARY

THERE was one part of the world in which the news that Charles Dickens was to start a daily newspaper was received with an angry buzz. To many Americans in 1846 he was the most disliked of Englishmen. Two of his books, *Martin Chuzzlewit* and *American Notes* had deeply wounded them. The bitter brilliance of the American chapters of *Chuzzlewit* had led to the novel being burned nightly on the stage of one of the New York theatres ; and to most of the Press of the United States Dickens was a monster of ingratitude. He had bitten the hands that had fêted him. Worse : he had also complained that some of the hands were dirty.

Two things are worth remarking in this early example of an Anglo-American brawl, because both have a bearing upon our current relationships.

The first is that if one looks at those pages in *Chuzzlewit* and *American Notes* which gave the strongest offence in the United States one finds that they bear a close resemblance to those pages in his other books which strongly offended many respectable Britons—mill-owners, factory managers, M.P.s, Chancery judges and workhouse masters. It was not American society in the 'forties that he was attacking, but cruelty and stupidity everywhere. Dickens had his fellow-man on his conscience, and he always remained on his conscience, if he travelled three miles or three thousand miles. If Dickens criticised the system of slavery, then flourishing with all the pride of an institution that never expected to die, he did so because he saw it as a more frightening extension of the system of industrial serfdom which had revolted him at home and which also seemed an enduring institution. Dickens and Abraham Lincoln approached the problem of slavery from opposite ends, but their conclusion was the same, that the slavery of black men or the slavery of white men was equally dangerous to all men, for slavery was not something that could, in the end, be confined to any one class or condition.

Dickens did not spare the American politician—but then he had never spared the British politician. He was the first, but not the last, to discover that there are Coodles, and Buffys, and Tite-Barnacles beside the Potomac as beside the Thames. If he did not hide what he thought of Jefferson Brick of the *New York Rowdy Journal,* he had certainly never hidden what he thought of Potts of the *Eatanswill Gazette.*

The particular bite in the acid that is perceptible in his American studies is that of a disillusioned lover. In the famous dialogue about the United States in *Lavengro*, it is truly said that many are critical of that country without ever having been there. But Dickens was not of that order. On his first visit he lost his patience with America because it fell short of his unreasonably high hopes of it. It was one more example in his life of Great Expectations turning into Bleak House. In the suppressed first chapter of *American Notes*, he drops a significant aside, " I went there expecting greater things than I found, and resolved as far as in me lay to do justice to the country, at the expense of any (in my view) mistaken or prejudiced statements that might have been made to its disparagement." Dickens went to America believing that he would find there the England of his dreams, a pure and noble fellowship of democrats. He was a man of genius escaping from his own creations. The shock was all the greater when he found the new scene peopled by the characters of his early novels, in different clothes and going under different names, but surprisingly unchanged in themselves.

In a self-revealing passage in *American Notes* he wrote, " The following dialogue I have held a hundred times : ' Is it not a very disgraceful circumstance that such a man as So and So should be acquiring a large property by the most infamous and odious means, and, notwithstanding all the crimes of which he has been guilty, should be tolerated and abetted by your Citizens ? He is a public nuisance, is he not ? '

' Yes, sir,'

' A convicted liar ? '

' Yes, sir.'

' He has been kicked, and cuffed and caned ? '

' Yes, sir.'

' And he is utterly dishonourable, debased, and profligate ?

' Yes, sir.'

' In the name of wonder then, what is his merit ? '

' Well, sir, he is a smart man.' "

There are many pages in these *American Notes* of the first editor of the *Daily News* which look forward to the disenchantments of his later novels. In the passage just quoted, there is also an anticipatory ring of Mark Twain, the old and bitter Mark Twain who was disillusioned by America's Gilded Age as Dickens had been by its Age of Bronze. One might almost suspect that Dickens had discovered *The Man who Corrupted Hadleyburg* before Mark Twain met him. Dickens found that " all kinds of deficient and impolitic usages " in the United States were " referred to the national love of trade." But if his eyes were opened, they were opened to the failings and falsities of the religion of Material Progress in Britain as well as in America. His first major novel after *Martin Chuzzlewit* was *Dombey and Son*, that sombre study of the worm at the heart of commercial pride ; the novel whose villain is Carker, the most sinister because he is the most efficient of all Dickens' villains ; Carker the toothy pioneer of the managerial revolution, who at the end is cut into a hundred bits by that symbol of devouring Progress, the railway locomotive. It is not unfair to say that through his unhappy first trip to America Dickens discovered much that was wrong with Victorian England.

We agreed that there was a second aspect of Dickens' celebrated dispute with Uncle Sam that had a bearing on current affairs. It is simply this, that the quarrel ended in each respecting the other more. The triumphs of Dickens' second visit to the United States have often been depicted. What is more important is that from 1846 until now Charles Dickens has served as a permanent British Ambassador to the American people. Whoever has represented us in the Washington Embassy, he has represented us in unnumbered homes. Nine of his novels have sold at least a million copies each in the United States, and five others half a million apiece. One discovered during the war that the bonds fabricated by the genius of Dickens were delicate as silk but tough as steel. To many who had never set foot in our land it had become as real a place as their native town. In the days of the blitz, they would speak angrily of Copperfield's old home, or Sam Weller's lodgings being destroyed, as if these were the houses in which members of their own families had lived. Who can say how great an influence such sympathetic magic exerts in finally determining the attitudes of peoples separated from one another by great distance and by cultural and economic divergences ?

It is not surprising, after such a beginning made by such an editor, that the relationship between Britain and America is a sub-ject to which the *Daily News* and latterly the *News Chronicle* has accorded a first importance. It is a variegated record, shot through with fine hopes and sorry disappointments, with powerful loyalties and old-rooted prejudices sometimes in conflict ; with the worst never happening and the best always falling a little short of expectations. There is, however, one element which is constant from 1846 onward—the resolve of our people never to permit war between the two countries. This was as steady a purpose in the early decades of the century when America was weak in man-power, and a debtor not a creditor nation, as in the latter decades when she grew to be the Colossus of the West. There was more than one occasion in those hundred years when war would have been easy enough ; tempers

were often hot ; provocations sharp. But the instinct of the two
peoples, as much as the skill of their leaders, always prevented the
fatal breach. The modern school of American historians have made
it clear that the basic assumption that Britain would not fight
the United States, was a fostering benefit to the growing Republic
throughout the nineteenth century. The Monroe Doctrine was,
in effect, underwritten by the British Navy. In that climate of
assured Atlantic peace, there took place the wondrous expansion of
the Republic, the winning of the West and the development of the
material resources of that thrice-favoured Continent.

Bismarck said towards the end of his life that a special Providence
watched over children, drunken men—and the United States.
In a retrospect of the past hundred years it does appear as if there
were a benevolent angel that had protected the Anglo-American
partnership from the consequences of folly, greed, ancestral prejudice and wilful wrong-headedness. In our beginning year,
1846, the signs were not good. Of all forgotten controversies none
now seems more dust-laden than the Oregon Boundary dispute
between Britain and the United States. But a hundred years ago
it was conducted with passion, and the enemies of England were
fondly hoping it would embroil her in war with the United States.
It is a little comical now to read a leading article in the *Daily News*
deprecating the warmth of the Boundary dispute, and commending
the lofty spirit of Senator Daniel Webster's " metaphysical speculation " that within a century's time Oregon would be neither British
nor American, but was destined to become a separate nation.
No one thought of danger on the Pacific side—of Japan as a potential
menace. She was then a shrouded hermit among nations.

" Fifty-four Forty or Fight," was the geographical cry of the war
party in the United States. In the *Daily News* of 5 March 1846,
there appeared a Letter to the Americans from that master of
English prose, Walter Savage Landor. " We come from the same
cradle ; we have been taught to speak by the same mother. . . .
Shall we fight, brothers as we are ? Shall we fight about a gravel-
pit and a brake ? Before you strike, listen and reflect. Do not
utterly repudiate arbitration. . . . O, my friends ! you have rejected
the imposing and fallacious forms of European governments ; will
you not also reject the vices and crimes on which their power has
risen, and obliterate the stains of blood and barbarism by which
they are polluted ? " The letter contains this prophetic reflection,
" There are, perhaps, born at this day in America some who will
live to see seventy millions on that continent who speak the language
of Milton and Shakespeare ; and, within a century after their
decease, in the same language may be given the watchword on the

Wall of China and in the passes of Himalaya." The watchword was given by American soldiers in China and India something less than a century after Landor wrote that letter.

London awaited with anxiety the coming of the mails from America recording the latest turns of the Oregon dispute, and one observes that the votes in the U.S. Senate were sometimes cast to catch the sea-bag. Peel in 1846 now signifies the abolition of the Corn Laws, but, seen in the grand vista of history, Peel's settlement of the Oregon dispute before he fell from power is as remarkable a service, and one whose results have lasted longer. In this negotiation he was forbearing and candid, conciliatory and prudent, and showed an understanding of the far-ranging necessity of the American connection. This great Minister would seem to deserve more honour on this account than he has yet been given.

One of the most honourable memories of the old *Daily News* is that it stood almost alone in the London Press in taking the side of Lincoln and the North in the American Civil War. The other London newspaper which declared for the North was the *Morning Star* which, a few years afterwards, was absorbed in the *Daily News*. The *Morning Star* had been founded by Cobden and Bright to advance that historic trinity of Victorian Liberalism, Peace, Retrenchment and Reform. Its last editor in 1869 was no less a man than John Morley.

In the provincial Press there were those who understood Lincoln and the mighty issues of the war—notably that great newspaper the *Manchester Guardian*—but the bulk of the London newspapers were vehemently against the Northern cause. In the stand it took, the *Daily News* of the 'sixties ran counter to the opinion of most educated persons in Britain, although working people, by a sure intuition, inclined to the Northern cause. Many distinguished Liberals of that time, including Gladstone, did not hide their sympathies with the South. To modern eyes this appears a singular aberration in the Victorian Liberal tradition. But there were reasons. In the first place, the slavery issue was held in suspense until the latter part of the war. To many British Whigs and Liberals the war aim of the North, the preservation of the Union, seemed an attempt to impose by force an unpopular Government upon a proud and chivalrous people. To men who had been brought up in the romantic tradition of the rights of minorities and who had encouraged revolt in Europe, the Southerners could quite well be presented as the victims of a tyranny. The cultural and economic ties between Britain and the Southern States were strong. It was the Cotton States that were true to Free Trade, the religion of middle-class England, while the industrial

North had fallen into " the damnable heresy " of Protection.

The relativity of idealism was never better shown than by the high-minded persistence with which many Liberals backed the wrong horse in the Civil War.

Among the conservative upper classes in Britain, there was also a warm sentiment of kinship with the Southern planter aristocracy. Those who detested the spread of democracy in Britain would rejoice to see it overthrown in America. The country gentlemen, of the Sir Leicester Dedlock model, who had been outraged by the domination of British life by the commercial classes, viewed the manufacturers of Massachusetts with even deeper disquiet than the manufacturers of Manchester. The books of Captain Basil Hall, Mrs. Trollope, and Dickens' own *Martin Chuzzlewit* had given polite society a fixed distaste for the Yankees. The cavaliers of Virginia and the gentlefolk of the Carolinas living elegant existences in their pillared mansions evoked a sympathy such as the French nobility enjoyed in Britain during the Revolution. It was widely felt that a gracious civilisation was in peril of being submerged by a stampede of Yahoos, of Jefferson Bricks and Elijah Pograms. It must be confessed, too, that the Southerners were much more adept in the arts of propaganda than the Northerners. Not until the course of the war was more than half run did Lincoln try to repair the damage done by the adroit presentation abroad of the Confederate case. Until the day of his assassination, Lincoln was grotesquely misdrawn by most of the chief organs of opinion in this country. He was depicted as a gorilla, a savage, a freak ; a kind of Caliban who had reached the White House by brute cunning. It is unbelievable to us now that the sublimity of mind, the New Testament tenderness, and the Old Testament visions of Lincoln could make so light an impress. The House of Commons and the Press resounded with reports of atrocities committed on the gallant Southerners by the barbarous men of the North. To illustrate the mood of many Britons of that period, take these lines from a speech in the Commons by Mr. Horsman, a Conservative member. (The *Daily News*, 25 April 1863.) " In the South there is no shackling of the Press, no suppression of the Law, no abridgment of the liberty of the citizen, but all classes have rallied as one man under a President (Jefferson Davis) who by the dignity and moderation of his counsels, by the high bearing of his army, and the devotion of his people, has given an elevation to the Southern cause which has won for it slowly, incredulously and reluctantly—now in the third year of the war—has won for it the irresistible, the universal and generous sympathies of the people of Europe. But when we turn to the North what a contrast is there exhibited ! Their military failures, great as they have been, sink into insignificance compared with the moral downfall they have exhibited. Their war has been against freedom and civilisation." As for the emancipation of the Negroes, Mr. Horsman asked, " What judgment can we in this Christian assembly put on it except to denounce it as one of the most atrocious crimes against the laws of civilisation and humanity that the world has ever seen ? . . . The free Republic has been metamorphosed into a military tyranny. The President is a more irresponsible despot than the Czar of Russia. Liberty of person, of motion, of speech, of writing and of thought are all annulled—the Press is coerced and gagged—the state prisons are filled with political offenders."

Until the last months of the war it was widely believed in Britain that the Confederacy could not be defeated, and there was great pressure put upon the British Government to intervene to force a settlement which would recognise the independence of the Secession States. Gladstone and Russell were both in favour of doing so, but the majority of the Cabinet prevailed against them and so there was narrowly avoided one of the major disasters of history. There were a number of sharp diplomatic incidents—such as the *Trent* case in which the Federals removed two Confederate agents from a British ship—but they were resolved in the end through the good sense of Washington and Whitehall. In contrast to the passionate Southern partisanship of the fashionable world was the attitude of the Lancashire mill workers who, although robbed of their livelihood by the Northern blockade of the cotton ports, stood staunch for Lincoln. There is nothing finer in the chronicles of Anglo-American relationship than the exchange of letters between the working men of Lancashire and the war-burdened President. The working people divined what Gladstone with his great gifts of mind and heart did not see, that there could be no argument in favour of slavery, or of a society based on slavery, that would or could stop short at the colour bar. If the elaborate economic, social and religious justifications advanced for enslaving the Negro were sustained, then inevitably they would be employed at some later stage to bind in fetters the poorer classes of white labour. If the institution of slavery was ratified by Southern arms, then helotry would spread beyond the Disunited States. It was an even larger issue than an American issue, it was a war to preserve the democratic future. Lincoln had said that a nation could not endure half-slave and half-free. Could a world endure half-slave and half-free? Wisdom, which was lacking to splendid intellects, was granted to untutored working men.

In its championship of a cause that was obnoxious to many

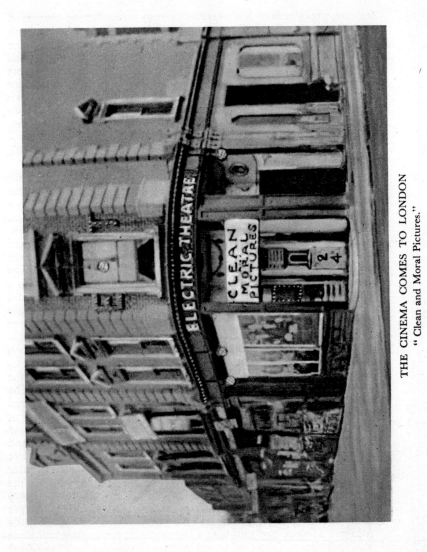

THE CINEMA COMES TO LONDON
" Clean and Moral Pictures."

eminent Liberals, including the paper's hero, Gladstone, the *Daily News* was powerfully briefed by its American correspondent E. L. Godkin, an Englishman who afterwards became a celebrated reform journalist in the United States—Godkin of the *Post* and the *Nation*—and by a leader-writer of uncommon parts, Harriet Martineau. So far as one can trace, Miss Martineau was the first woman to be regularly employed on the staff of a daily newspaper. She is usually credited with being the original of Dickens' Mrs. Jellyby, so completely engrossed in the welfare of far-away natives that she neglected her own home and family. Dickens did not like Miss Martineau. He had reason. He had attacked—with justice—conditions of labour in the factories, and she had defended the manufacturers in a pamphlet marked by the rasping insensitiveness to human values of the *laissez-faire* school. Her benevolence —like most people's benevolence—had its blind spots. But if Miss Martineau was wrong about serfdom at home, she was right about freedom in America. Enfeebled by poor health, tortured by pain, and cut off from the world by a wall of deafness, she yet contrived to perform prodigies of work and to build up a chain of acquaintances that girdled the world. She knew the United States intimately, both North and South, and had seen enough of the evils of chattel slavery to make her as strong an abolitionist as her friend Harriet Beecher Stowe. Harriet Martineau's editorials on the Civil War had the force of events. W. E. Forster said of her, " It was Harriet Martineau alone who kept English opinion about America on the right side through the Press." Both Miss Martineau and Godkin were undaunted in their faith that the North would win—and this at a time when the military quidnuncs in the Pall Mall Clubs were proving nightly over dinner, with the aid of strategic spoons, forks and pepper pots that Lincoln's Generals were hopelessly routed*.

After Lincoln's assassination, his British critics made generous amends for their misjudgments, and *Punch's* palinode was noble :

> *Yes, he had lived to shame me from my sneer,*
> *To lame my pencil, and confute my pen—*
> *To make me own this hind of princes peer,*
> *This rail-splitter a true-born king of men.*

Lincoln has been for so long a saint in the British calendar that we have forgotten how cruelly he was maligned in most of our prints while he lived. Unhappily, historical memories are longer

* Miss Martineau wrote her leading articles in the quiet of her home in the Lake District, more than 250 miles from London. She said that her natural sympathy with the policy of the newspaper was so strong that she had no need to visit its office. The conditions of leader-writing have changed in eighty years !

in the United States. There is a prodigious library of books on Lincoln, and few biographers are as magnanimous as he was in overlooking slights upon his name. The recollection that a large section of British society had taken the part of the South and had agitated for active intervention rankled for years. That ships for the Confederacy had been built and fitted out in British yards was remembered against us, and the claims for the depredations caused by the *Alabama* long served to bedevil relations. In the first glow of their victory over the South, some of the Northern newspapers cried out for a war with Britain. Those who today are surprised at anti-British feeling in the United States should remember that the Briton is often the over-painted villain of American historians.

The legacy of bitterness was discernible thirty years later in the trouble over the Venezuelan Boundary. A smouldering dispute between Venezuela and Britain about the frontier line of British Guiana suddenly crackled into a brisk fire when gold was found in both territories. President Cleveland sprang forward with a pounce that startled two Continents. The Monroe Doctrine was affirmed with the vigour of an angry landlord shaking his fist at a trespasser. " Today the United States is practically sovereign on this continent, and its fiat is law upon the subjects to which it confines its interposition," asserted Mr. Olney, the Secretary of State, in his Note to Britain. Those were big words. Long afterwards, Olney confessed that they were drawn so strong because America then " appeared so completely negligible a quantity " in English eyes. Strong words had to compensate for a weak Navy. That happened precisely fifty years ago. What comment is there but the oldest of bromides—how things have changed !

The pouncing diplomacy of President Cleveland and Mr. Olney created a ferment in the public mind, and the growls of the war dogs were audible. American opinion, like British opinion, was excitable in the closing years of the nineteenth century. With both, a feverish imperialism ran a parallel course.* With Britain, its climax was the Boer War. With America, it was the war with Spain. That special Providence which protects Anglo-American relationships employed on this occasion that fantastic character, the Emperor Wilhelm of Germany. With a maladroitness that was remarkable even for the Emperor, he sent President Krueger, the Boer, a telegram of congratulations after the Jameson Raid. The appearance of this eminent fisher in troubled waters powerfully reinforced the conviction of the British Government and the British

* There was a chaplain of Congress of this period who prayed that God might make America swift to avenge insults. Chaplains have become less militant with the years, and Congress more urbane.

people that a clash with America must be averted.   Once more the deep Atlantic currents making for conciliation manifested themselves.   In such times as these there are always men and women of good-will on both sides of the Atlantic who come into quiet action. It is a white conspiracy—an enlightened cabal—that persists from generation to generation.   In the Venezuela dispute, Salisbury reflected the mood of the people that a breach with America would be an absurdity as well as a sin.   An arbitration was arranged which satisfied both Britain and America.

The spirit of accommodation has survived such moments as that in 1911 when Champ Clark, the Democratic Speaker of the House of Representatives, speaking on the Reciprocity Bill with Canada said, " I am for it because I hope to see the day when the American flag will float over every square foot of the British North American possessions clear to the North Pole." It survived the dismal arguments over war debts in the nineteen-twenties when hoarse voices on one side cried, " Uncle Shylock " and hoarse voices on the other shouted " Welsher ! " It survived the wrangle over naval parity. (Who now, outside retired Admirals, even remembers it?) It will survive the current disputations over financial and economic policies.

The high enterprise of Anglo-American partnership has never been so easy as the old-fashioned shakers of hands across the seas fondly dreamed it. It demands qualities of imagination, forbearance, and an understanding of differences in culture, traditions and environment that are hard to expect of men and women brain-wearied with the day's work and the rearing of their families. Prejudices are easily stirred between peoples who live three thousand miles from one another, and we have always with us the busy traffickers in ill-will in the black markets of politics. But the records of the century behind us sustain the vision expressed in the peroration of Mr. Churchill's address to Congress on 26 December 1941, " Still I avow my hope and faith, sure and inviolate, that in the days to come the British and American peoples will for their own safety and for the good of all walk together, side by side, in majesty, in justice and in peace."

The exhilaration of the adventure lies not so much in the sense of the irresistible flow of events in one direction as in the sudden, warm radiance that comes often from thundery skies. Those who took any part, even the smallest, in the establishment of the system of Mutual Aid during the war or who saw how General Eisenhower welded into a unity men of the most diverse temperaments, can never feel too cynical about the chances of human beings working together in an unselfish fraternity. It happened once. It can happen again.

CHAPTER XVI

THE MIDDLE YEARS

I

FUSIONS

FLEET Street is full of phantoms. Many ghost-ships sail at night when the rotaries have ceased running. They range from the *Morning Chronicle*, whose finest reporter was Charles Dickens, to the *Morning Post*, which turned High Toryism into daily literature ; from Mudford's *Standard* to Greenwood's (and Stead's) *Pall Mall Gazette*. Among the lost ships none is more affectionately remembered by the middle-aged Londoner than the sea-green incorruptible, the *Westminster Gazette*. It was begun in 1893 by Sir George Newnes as a penny evening newspaper, and provided Liberal sanctuary for E. T. Cook and the staff of the *Pall Mall Gazette* who had resigned when the first Lord Astor acquired the paper for Conservatism. The choice of green paper was ingenious. It piqued the curiosity of the town, and if it provoked lampoons, so much the better for its fame. As one recalls it, the hue was nearer to the salty emerald of deep water than the green of hills and lawns. The yellow sheets on which Pulitzer's New York *World* was printed had given a generic title to the Press of shocks and sensations. Green was to be the tint of sweet reasonableness ; " annihilating all that's made to a green thought in a green shade." After Cook became editor of the *Daily News* in 1895, J. A. Spender was appointed in his place. For more than thirty years, Spender in the *Westminster* stood as the vindicator of Liberal idealism, expressing his judgments with sagacity and fineness of temper. There was embodied in Spender the grand age of Liberalism ; its enthronement of reason above the passions and prejudices of men ; its cultivation of tolerance towards even the intolerant ; its sense of the unique value of the individual ; and its belief that the unity of men could be achieved without destroying their diversity of talents. Small in circulation, the *Westminster* grew large in influence. To Spender's gifts of lucent exposition were linked the talents of his cartoonist and assistant-editor, F. C. Gould. Gould had a robustious humour, a zest for political sport, an infallible setter's nose for humbug, and a draughtsmanship that made innocents think at first he couldn't draw at all. He saw the majestic pundits of the early nineteen-hundreds as a child might see them—wooden and doll-like, with stiff, marionettish arms. The force of an imagination that ran counter to the rules of the Linley Sambourne or Bernard Partridge order of cartooning persists, and to come upon Gould's drawings today is to get a strong impression of the sawdustiness of Eminent Persons, or to feel that Alice—with whom he identified himself so often—was saying, " Who cares for you ? You're nothing but a pack of cards." It was in the *Westminster Gazette* that two brilliant wits made memorable appearances. Anthony Hope's *Dolly Dialogues*—which seem now as remote and delectable as cream meringues were printed in its columns. So, too, were the fireworks of that matchless maker of mischief, " Saki " (H. H. Munro).

Newnes sold the *Westminster* in 1908 to a Liberal group including the first Lord Cowdray. Not long after the 1914-1918 war, the paper changed from a London evening to a national daily, and from green paper to white. But the times were not propitious, and in 1928 the *Westminster Gazette* was absorbed by the *Daily News*, the paper being known for a time as the *Daily News and Westminster Gazette*.

Two years later a fusion between the *Daily News* and *Daily Chronicle* took place. The story of the *Chronicle* is a romantic one.

After the newspaper tax was repealed in 1855, cheap papers swarmed in London. Among them was the *Clerkenwell News*, a newspaper which served the interests of a part of London which was then, and still is, as mysterious to the fashionable in Belgrave Square as to the aesthetes in Bloomsbury. To most it is known, if at all, through the pages of Arnold Bennett's *Riceyman's Steps*, in which a harmony is wrought out of several shades of grey ; and cobwebs, shadows, meanness and human pain are transfigured by a brooding artistry. In the 'fifties and 'sixties the *Clerkenwell News* reflected a full-blooded, bustling lower middle-class and artisan life—largely in the wealth of small advertisements with which it was loaded. When Edward Lloyd bought it in 1877, he astonished Fleet Street by changing it overnight into a national newspaper— indeed, it was boldly presented as an " imperial morning newspaper." The *Daily Chronicle* was born. It leapt at once into the front rank of the London Press, being conducted with spirit and imagination, and the marks of its unusual origins long remained to give it a flavour of its own. It carried into Fleet Street a feature that has endured to this day, those small advertisements that revealed the wants, the hopes, and the working life of the honest burghers who crowded into London during the era of expanding trade. The social historian might learn a great deal about the by-ways of British life over the decades by a study of these wants. The *Daily Chronicle* maintained, also from its Clerkenwell beginnings, an advocacy of the rights of that sad political minority, the Victorian

Londoners. As these pages have shown, London in those times suffered from as feeble a form of government as any city has suffered, and we have seen, too, how slow was progress in the essentials of public health. A huddle of authorities—vestries and boards and commissions—disputed the prize for incompetence. The sprawling monster was hydra-headed, but most of its heads were witless. The *Daily Chronicle* shared, with the *Star*, the honours in that revival of pride in London which led to the creation of the Borough Councils, the elected School Board and the L.C.C. Civic politics came to possess glow and excitement for our fathers. The young Progressive party attracted some of the most distinguished talents of that age, and the first L.C.C. displayed almost as much eminence as the Forty Immortals of the French Academy. That *grand seigneur* of politics, Lord Rosebery, took the chair—and retained it during day-long sessions amid the dryest dust of necessary routine—finding for a time, at least, a distraction from that boredom with man and lassitude of ideals which blighted in the end his dazzling promise.

One of the first aldermen of that Council was Frederic Harrison. There was a remarkable man !—one whose life spanned a great part of the century, and who summed up in himself the development of men of progressive habit. He was born in the reign of William the Fourth and died in 1923, the year that saw the installation of the first Labour Government. This writer recalls talking with Harrison on his ninetieth birthday about the changes he had witnessed in his long life. In his extreme age Harrison still bore witness to the qualities that marked the eminent Victorians, an overflowing abundance of nervous energy and a universality of mind. One held one's breath as that venerable figure shot up and down the ladder placed against his towering library shelves to seek a quotation from Ruskin or check a reference to hours of labour in the 'forties. Harrison was the most renowned English disciple of August Comte, and Positivism, " the religion of man," remained his creed to his death. Jurist and historian, his vivid sympathy for the condition of the labouring masses, made him the champion of trades unionism in the 'sixties, and, more than any man, he may be called the father of its code of protecting laws. Harrison had solved for himself the problem of bridging the gulf between Disraeli's two nations and he was a happy man.

On the wider stage of affairs the *Daily Chronicle* developed into an advocate of a robust order of Liberalism. Under the editorship of A. E. Fletcher (1890-95) it swung to the support of Home Rule. This was at a time when the Liberal Party had lost in that cause both the gilded solidity of the old Whiggery, as represented by

Hartington, and the energy of the new manufacturing class as represented by Chamberlain. Fletcher's editorship mirrored the evolution of Gladstone's Liberalism in uniting a passion for Home Rule with a vigorous domestic radicalism, and a searching criticism of privilege. As the old falcon of politics grew older, he veered more and more Leftwards. The veteran who at 84 became Prime Minister for the fourth time would have appeared as almost the wildest of anarchists to the young Mr. Gladstone saluted by Macaulay in 1839 as " the rising hope of the stern and unbending Tories."

H. W. Massingham, who had been Fletcher's assistant, succeeded him, but his editorship came to shipwreck in 1899 through a sympathy with the Boers not shared by the proprietors. But he left a lasting mark on the newspaper by his cultivation of those literary columns which Fletcher had brought in. Massingham and Fletcher were journalists to whom literature and politics, literature and life were indivisible. Under their direction, the literary pages of the paper opened windows on the world of the imagination for numberless readers. The part that such newspapers as the *Daily Chronicle* and the *Daily News* played in forming the taste of men and women whose education at the Board Schools was ended at fourteen, or earlier, should not be forgotten among the shaping influences of the century. They served in part as a home university. There are names that keep their lustre into 1946 in the *Daily Chronicle's* literary roll ; among them, Lionel Johnson and Francis Thompson. The author of *The Hound of Heaven* is an ancestor to be proud of.

In foreign affairs the *Daily Chronicle* championed with gallantry the cause of small peoples tortured by the Turks. Those were the days when Dr. Parker at the City Temple was denouncing, with the thunderings of a vehement oratory, " Abdul the Damned on his accursed throne." In home politics, the *Daily Chronicle* was known for its sympathy with those sections of the working people who at that time were least privileged and found it hardest to secure a redress of injustices. Like the *Star* again—T. P. O'Connor's *Star*—it took the side of the London dockers during that strike in 1889 which is something not forgotten even today east of Aldgate. Associated with that struggle is the towering figure of Cardinal Manning, whose spiritual authority, thrown upon the side of the dockers, was of incalculable benefit to them. It was said of the old Cardinal as he moved about Dockland that he was

" *attired,*
in sudden brightness like a man inspired,"

and there are legends still told in the East End today of an unearthly radiance that hung about his head as he talked to the strikers. It is to the newspapers rather than to the books of this period that one must go for an understanding of its social ferment. One would have thought that the emergence of such a figure as Keir Hardie, with his gentle gravity, his Walt Whitman " adhesiveness," and his Puritan strength would impress the intellectuals as having some prophetic meaning. Instead, he was regarded as a music-hall diversion. " Don't Keir Hardie," was thought to be a very good joke, and this deeply earnest Scot who had a full sense of the tragic destiny of man was misrepresented as a comic anarchist in cap and muffler coming down to the House of Commons in a brake, with tooting horns and concertinas. It is an interesting footnote to the history of these times that the essential characteristic of Hardie, his deep respect for human dignity and for the domestic virtues, prompted him, when the Queen died, to compose what is one of the best because it is one of the most sincere tributes to her. He protested with vehemence against " the barbarous display of the blood-thirsty implements of war, amidst which the remains of a peace-loving woman will today be laid to rest." Then he wrote, " It is as the pattern wife and mother, the embodiment of the virtues upon which the middle-class matron bases her claim to be considered the prop and mainstay of the race, that Queen Victoria was known and respected. The pomps and ceremonies of her station do not seem to have had any charm for her, while her manner of dressing was plain, almost to dowdiness. The quiet retreat of Balmoral, far removed from the turmoil and intrigue of fashionable society, had for her a charm which few can appreciate. The pomp and panoply of martial life was as far removed from such a life as anything well could be." There is in that passage an echo of the key-note of the peaceful and bourgeois England of the late 'forties.

This Puritan attitude was shared by large sections of Society who found Hardie's Socialism abhorrent. One part of the Queen's strength lay in her fidelity to the Roundhead virtues while much of the popularity, as well as many of the embarrassments, of her son sprang from his revival of the Cavalier tradition. After the Prince Consort's death, the Queen withdrew for years into a privacy of grief. The emotion that overwhelmed, and for a time paralysed her, is revealed in the letter she sent Mrs. Lincoln after the President's assassination in 1865—" No one can better appreciate than I can, who am myself *utterly broken-hearted* by the loss of my own beloved husband, who was the *light* of my life, my stay—*my all*—what your suffering must be." As the years passed, her seclusion attracted sympathy for the woman, but diminished interest in the Queen.

The ceremonial role of Monarchy which has a considerable importance in the British scheme of things was neglected. The court of the Prince of Wales provided an escape from this preoccupation with mourning weeds. For the gay and light-of-heart it was an absolution. For the fashionable it supplied an excuse. For society it furnished a standard. The easing of manners was widely welcomed. Marlborough House brought elegance into the dowdy provincialism of the 'sixties. But the more Puritanical part of the nation preferred the austere code of Balmoral. Such a liberalising of custom as introducing the smoking of cigarettes at dinner (after the ladies had withdrawn, of course) might be overlooked, but the Marlborough House set, according to the gossips, went farther than that ! The Prince was unfairly attacked for his personal extravagance ; with the Queen in seclusion, he was forced to expend money in entertainment which should have been borne by the Palace. The paragraphs multiplied. The Prince of Wales was always on friendly terms with the Liberal leaders, and through their agency a meeting at dinner was arranged with the editor of the chief Liberal newspaper, Mr. Frank Hill. Hill, editor of the *Daily News* from 1870 to 1886, was celebrated for his biographical portraits ; he could be merciless in his drawing of a character. The Prince had an art of winning men which his father lacked. At this meeting, it is said, the Radical editor capitulated to his charm and candour.

For an explorer into the past, it is much harder to isolate the period of the 'nineties, to see it as a picture on the wall in which the figures are related to one another in a simple composition and the colours are in a harmony, than it is to isolate the more unified world of 1846. Here the lights are broken, the shadows in conflict, and half a dozen artists of different schools seem to have been at work on the confused canvas. In one corner there is a piece of the bravura battle-painting of imperialism, all flashing swords and foaming horses, red coats and cannon-smoke in the manner of Meissonier or Lady Butler. On the other side there is Civic Virtue, austere and starward-staring as represented by the new L.C.C., and the brawny raised arms of Labour, in the style of Ford Madox Brown ; while in the middle distance droop Aubrey Beardsley's languid daughters of the *Yellow Book* amid a plantation of the sunflowers of sin. Ernest Dowson, fluting low, " They are not long the days of wine and roses," and Kipling playing ditties of Empire on his mouth organ ; Richard Le Gallienne in quest of the Golden Girl, and Barney Barnato in quest of gold ; H. M. Hyndman, the Marxist, and Arthur Balfour, the philosophic doubter ; Shaw and Wilde, two Irish playwrights born in the same year ;

I

Lady Windermere's Fan and *Mrs. Warren's Profession* ; Fabians and Sherlock Holmes ; the Webbs—and Mrs. Annie Besant ; Yeats, clothed in the Celtic twilight, and John Burns, the pride of Battersea—what a party to find in the same parlour ! Susceptible youth had the choice of following the lead of either Cecil Rhodes or George Moore.

Despite the tired satyrs and raddled nymphs of the Decadents, it was also a hearty and strenuous age. The *Daily Chronicle* encouraged that aspect of it by the interest it took in adventure and exploration, being identified with Nansen's North Polar expedition and Conway's journey across Spitzbergen, as later it supported Shackleton's expeditions. The other side of this medal was the paper's public service in exposing the pretensions of adventurers, notably Louis de Rougemont, whose turtle-riding exploits in the tropics gained a hearing from the British Association, and the Polar claimant, Dr. Cook, who was neatly punctured by Philip Gibbs.

Liberalism, which had seemed an irresistible force in the mid-Victorian epoch, suffered a series of schisms from the time of the Home Rule split in 1886. The secession of the Liberal Unionists ; Gladstone's last campaign and his last defeat in the cause of Home Rule ; the Parnell Divorce with its effect on the English Nonconformist supporters of the Nationalist Party—there was never any end to the bedevilling of English politics by Ireland. It had the effect of denying Home Rule to England. Sorely-needed social reforms were suspended because of this eternal preoccupation. Mr. Hammond's recent book on Gladstone and Ireland suggests how much England might have been spared in treasure and well-being if the old leader's voice had been heard by his countrymen.

It was a ragged period for the Liberal journalist. Newspapers were constantly changing sides, financial supporters and powerful advertisers moved to and fro across the stage, while editors took part in an exhausting game of musical chairs. E. T. Cook held no fewer than four editorships in succession in ten years. During the breach over the Boer War—" the war to the knife and fork " at the National Liberal Club, so called because each side expressed its emotions by giving complimentary dinners to its heroes— the *Daily Chronicle* was captured by the Liberal Imperialists while the *Daily News* passed to the pro-Boer side, Cook moving as editor from the *News* to the *Chronicle*. His chair at the *Daily News* was then filled by that man of many talents, R. C. Lehmann—athlete, M.P., *Punch* humorist ; a wit of high principle ; an artist with a strong social conscience. After Lehmann's few months of editorship began the long reign of A. G. Gardiner.

The war over, the unity of the party was secured again, and there followed that shining Indian Summer of Liberalism which lasted from 1906 to 1914. During this period the *Daily Chronicle* was under the control of an editor of conspicuous ability, Sir Robert Donald (1904-18) and it became, like the *Daily News*, a spokesman for the spirit of radical reform that stamped the period. The paper was noted for the quality of its foreign correspondence. Among its writers none is remembered with kindlier feelings than Gibbs, whose *Street of Adventure*, recounting the loss of the *Tribune*, preserves the scent and savour of the Fleet Street of forty years ago. Because it is the chronicle of an honourable failure, that book has served as a more persuasive recruiting agent to journalism than most records of success.

The Liberal Party was once again grievously rent by the circumstances of the General Election of 1918. During the opposition of its two most eminent figures, the *Daily Chronicle* was on the side of Lloyd George while the *Daily News* took the part of Asquith.

The long shadow of Ireland still stretched over our politics. In the last phase, before the signing of the Treaty, the ancient grudge was at its bitterest. After the Easter Rebellion of 1916 what chance could there be for the old compromises? While the *Daily News* was publishing the vivid despatches of Hugh Martin about the Black and Tans, the *Daily Chronicle* was defending Mr. Lloyd George's Irish policy on the Lincolnian ground that the union must be preserved. In December 1919, Dublin Castle suppressed that long-established organ of constitutional nationalism, the *Freeman's Journal*. The *Daily News* promptly offered its editor two columns of its space a day to express his opinions. For three weeks the *Freeman's Journal* accepted that sanctuary, and then the military censorship was lifted. If a man of 1846 came back to earth in 1946 he would note with relief that at last the Irish problem has been lifted out of British politics. For good? he would ask.

In 1918 the *Daily Chronicle* was bought by Lloyd George and a group of his supporters, and Donald gave up the editorial chair, being succeeded by Mr. E. A. Perris, who had been News Editor. In 1927 the paper was taken over by Sir David Yule and Sir Thomas (now Lord) Catto, Lloyd George keeping a minority holding, while Lord Reading, who had been Viceroy of India, became for a brief spell its chairman. Subsequently the control of the newspaper passed to Mr. William Harrison of the Inveresk Paper Company.

As these pages do not pretend to do more than give some impressions of the changes of a century as shown in the looking-glass of a newspaper, this is not the place to dwell upon the financial problems which beset the *Daily Chronicle* in its last phase, or to

I*

present the details of the amalgamation with the *Daily News*, out of which the *News Chronicle* was born in 1930. It is sufficient to record that the direction of the paper has been in the hands of Sir Walter Layton, as chairman, with Mr. L. J. Cadbury as vice-chairman. Mr. Cadbury is chairman of the Daily News Limited, the parent company of the *News Chronicle* and the *Star*. Mr. Bertram F. Crosfield and Mr. Cyril A. Kew are joint managing directors. The editors of the *News Chronicle* have been, in succession, Mr. Tom Clarke, Mr. Aylmer Vallance, and Mr. Gerald Barry, who has occupied the editorial chair since 1936. The Manchester office of the newspaper has been directed for many years by Mr. W. H. Armitt.

II

GREY PANORAMA

The meeting of two streams in Liberal journalism came at the beginning of that dark, strange period in Britain's history whose breaking point was reached on 3 September 1939. In 1930 the economic storms were already upon us. The Stock Market collapse in the United States had brought down the glittering towers of American prosperity, long the envy of foreigners. As the ground shook from that fall, other mansions began to rock. Throughout 1930-31 the economic situation of Britain steadily worsened. The Labour Government, led by Ramsay MacDonald, found itself hemmed about by troubles. The number of out-of-works grew steadily, and great sums were borrowed to meet the deficit in the Unemployment Insurance Fund. Trade languished, revenues wilted, and there shone no speck of day at the other end of the tunnel. The full measure of Britain's predicament was brought home by the report of the May Committee on public economy in July 1931. This caused fright in the money markets, and withdrawals from the Bank of England began. A political crisis followed. The Labour Government was torn between the orthodox financiers and the inflationary school. A suspicion, harboured by a considerable part of the Labour Party, that Wall Street was leagued with British bankers to force cruel economies and to thwart Socialist policies increased the bitterness of the argument and made a compromise impossible. The political crisis was at length resolved by Mr. MacDonald resigning, and forming a National Government with Conservatives and Liberals. The bulk of the Labour Party, disavowing its leader, crossed into Opposition, and at the subsequent General Election was reduced to little more than fifty members.

The irony of the situation was that the National Government formed to retain England upon the gold standard, for fear of the consequences of departing from it, gave up the gold standard within a few weeks. England still stood. But the psychological shock for those old enough to have been steeped in Victorian habits of thought was considerable. To the traditionalists, the vanishing of the sovereign in the 1914-18 war had seemed like losing hold on one of life's grand assurances. The golden coins had been so comforting a symbol of the pride and certainty of the Victorian age. Podsnappery ridiculed and pitied foreign nations who did their business with trashy paper currency, and, glancing contemptuously at the designs on it, dismissed it as a William Morris wallpaper. His Majesty's head in gold was the proof of the position that Britain held in the world. The clink of those good solid coins in the pocket was a brave music of which the ear never tired. Although the sovereigns never came back, the restoration of Britain to the gold standard in 1925 was considered by the surviving Forsytes and Podsnaps to be the surest sign of a return to health after the enervating fevers of the war, and they approved the cartoons of the day which showed the £ triumphantly staring the $ in the eye. Now, in 1931, Britain was deliberately abandoning in peace-time the gold standard which the Victorians saw as the base of Britain's power. That was change indeed.

This was a point in their history at which many people stood silent a while to reflect upon the roughness of the road they had travelled since the war. Nothing seemed to have gone right. . . . May the writer be here allowed to break away from this impersonal record to recreate those emotions in terms of his own experience : " The films have a method of concentrating ten years of history in a series of flashes. One's memories are rather like that. I see the House of Commons that was elected at the end of the war, the House described by Stanley Baldwin as full of hard-faced men who looked as though they had done well out of the war, and called by another observer ' Bottomley's pit '. At the same time, I see the unveiling of the Cenotaph in Whitehall, and the crowd that remained in the street until after midnight to put flowers there, or to look at the flowers. The Cenotaph appeared white and new in the lamplight, and the griefs were fresh. It was a raw evening, and the flowers, as I remember them, were loaded with a heavy dew. This memorial stood as a token of the sharpest loss that Britain had sustained. The war had been a costly one, but most costly of all in robbing the country of a great part of its youth. The effects of that loss on the national life were to be felt for many a year. The tomb of the Unknown Dead in Westminster Abbey was an inspiration that came later. But nothing could ever touch the heart with regrets and forebodings like that first evening at the Cenotaph."

" There were many acrid jests current at that time about the war profiteers ; about the contrasts between the condition of the new rich and the new poor ; and about the flood of honours in which some murky reputations were bathed. The label, ' a city of dreadful knights ', was pinned upon more than one city. The poetry of Wilfred Owen and Siegfried Sassoon replaced in favour the poetry of Rupert Brooke. One of the literary influences of the time turned out to be the fashionable tailor, Dennis Bradley, who, in his advertisements had expounded, with many an epigram, his theory that the Young Men had been destroyed by the evil Old Men. From then on the cynical mood became more and more fashionable in letters. The stream of debunking books began. A French writer during the war contrasted the two generations of Englishmen, the Kipling hero and the Galsworthy hero. Now we were seeing the Aldous Huxley puppet replacing the Galsworthy gentleman.

" One recalls the return of the delegates to Versailles, the important, shiny cars streaming away from Victoria, and, in particular, one glimpses again, suddenly under the cross-rays of the lamps, the sombre, brooding face of Winston Churchill, at that time still perceptibly the young Churchill, with the look of a discontented young Caesar, enigmatic and pale. One had to wait for the publication of *The World Crisis* to obtain the clue to what Churchill was thinking in those days about the settlement of Europe. The return of the peace makers from Paris was not greeted with enthusiasm, for disillusion had already set in. The brief period of prosperity after the war was soon gone. The year 1921 was one of the most doleful in the century. There was a headlong fall in prices ; bankruptcies multiplied ; credit was frozen. It was, by the way, the year in which, with a singular appropriateness, Mr. Galsworthy brought the first part of the Forsyte Saga to an end with *To Let*. Timothy, who lived on the Bayswater Road, having rounded his century, had died in happy unawareness of the decay of the Forsyte values. Soames's reverie at the funeral reflected the shattered domes and broken pillars of the city of his pride. The glory of the age of property had passed. The gold changed to dust in the grasp of the possessive instinct. The stability and assurance of the Victorians had dissolved ; the future was bleak and uncertain. Whatever new age was coming, it would not be a Forsyte age. So these belated Victorians found themselves ' wandering between two worlds, one dead, the other powerless to

be born.' The unemployment figures shot upwards. One began
to be aware that gathering crowds and processions of the workless
were common to all the big cities that one went to. The demand
for relief put an almost insupportable strain upon the finances of
local authorities. . . . Side by side with the growing darkness of
the industrial future, there developed the cult of the hare-brained
in Society. It was the period of the Bright Young Things. Lord
Carnarvon's discoveries in the Valley of the Kings in 1922 seemed
like a reproach levelled across the centuries. The serene beauty of
Queen Nefertiti, risen from the tomb, made a debutante of the time
tearing through Piccadilly Circus on a treasure hunt, mop-haired
and crazy-eyed, look like a barbarian.

" I find myself jolting up and down in a bus travelling over
rough Highland roads far from the trampling of Antic Hay. My
companions are a group of London mayors—Labour mayors, their
party having carried a great number of the London boroughs.
They have come so far from Cockneydom in pursuit of the Prime
Minister. Mr. Lloyd George, not in good health, is resting at
Gairloch in these remote and untroubled wilds, ' in the Highlands,
in the quiet places, where the old men have rosy faces.' The
Mayors have pursued him to present the plight of the boroughs,
and to urge that unemployment is a national concern and that its
cost should be borne by the Government. The reluctant Prime
Minister hears them. Their spokesman is the Mayor of Hackney,
a young man named Herbert Morrison, whose distinguishing marks
are an unruly quiff of hair and a precocious skill in deploying his
arguments. ' It is not an easy thing to appease hungry men,' he
says, ' we have reached a point where passion and despair may get
the upper hand.' A disillusioned Lloyd George, who should have
retired in the hour of his glory, returns a sympathetic reply. In an
aside, he recalls how he had once lived on fifteen shillings a week ;
so he, at least, knew what it was like to be poor. After the deputation withdrew he said of its spokesman, 'That is a young man who
will go a long way in politics. Prime Minister one day ?—who
knows ? ' Then he fell to speaking of his own daring defiance of
Gladstone.

" There were other envoys in the Highlands in those autumn
days ; one afternoon I saw a car bring Mr. de Valera's two emis-
saries to Gairloch. So began those negotiations which, after painful
delays, suspensions, and threats of renewed war between Britian
and Ireland—the whole scene being haunted by that bogey word,
sovereignty—at last led to the creation of the Free State.

" Many discontents met together to bring about the end of the
Lloyd George government in 1922. That year was marked by a

resurgence of Conservatism, and, contradictorily, a strong leap
forward by the new force in politics, Labour. Liberalism was being
squeezed out between the two. One recalls the meeting at the
Carlton Club whose decision ended the Coalition, with a glimpse
of Lord Birkenhead going up the steps of the Club in the grand
manner of a French aristocrat ascending the scaffold, his hauteur
unmoved by the presence of a fierce young man shouting ' Judas '
at him, this being a reprisal for his support of the Irish settlement.
This was a mordant twist of history, for only nine years before
F. E. Smith had been the much admired Galloper of Ulster.
Austen Chamberlain, Balfour, Lord Curzon and he now found
themselves greatly abused for their acceptance of the Treaty.
A statesman who grows with the times is apt to leave his supporters behind. A statesman who sheds his illusions sheds his
friends as well.

" At that party meeting the Conservatives rediscovered an old
leader, Mr. Bonar Law, and found themselves a new one, Mr.
Baldwin. After seventeen years, there was a Conservative Prime
Minister at No. 10 Downing Street again. With Mr. Bonar Law,
we entered a period of comforting watchwords and reassuring
symbols. Mr. Law, who in his early years as Leader of the Opposition, had been renowned for the vehemence of his words, now came
into power on the quietest word of all—Tranquillity. Max Beerbohm had once represented him as the strenuous pounder on the
drum, with Arthur Balfour, the elegant violinist, standing by,
murmuring, ' What virtuosity ! How sure, how firm a touch !
What verve ! What brio ! What an instrument!' Now the resonant
drummer had become a charmer on the flute. The first photographs of the new Prime Minister at his desk in Downing Street
showed a face that expressed a resigned and gentle sadness, the
melancholic thoughtfulness of the Scot. It was widely known that
he had been a tempering and sagacious influence in the inner
counsels of the war, and this reputation, coupled with the dignified
moderation towards all men that marked his conduct as Prime
Minister, commended him to the distracted middle classes, who,
having suffered cruel losses in the war, seemed now to be faced
with ruin in the peace. Mr. Law's promise to break with the caprices
and extravagances of the Lloyd Georgian epoch, to end that taking
of hazards whose startling climax was the Chanak incident, was
welcomed by a tired people. It was a triumph of the plain over the
coloured. There was even, among older persons, a tendency to
believe that Tranquillity implied a revival of the Victorian virtues.

" Looking back, one reflects that while England was showing
this preference for the muted word and the quiet leader, the cult of

violent men and whirling words set in on the continent of Europe. In the year that Mr. Bonar Law was Prime Minister, the March on Rome took place. We were treated to the first pictures of the little bald dictator on the balcony, the chin jutting forward like a fender, the lips spouting arias in the grand operatic style. *Ritorna Vincitor* ! Hail the Sacred Ego ! We have buried the putrefying corpse of liberty, so let us dance on it. Pout the chest, swell the head ! . . . There was a tendency in cooler climates to smile at this as pure Southern exuberance, the appearance of *Tartarin of Tarascon* in politics : the quip about the bullfrog of the Pontine Marshes inflating himself was admiringly retailed. It was also pointed out that this operatic character had his uses, for he made the trains run on time. To those brought up in the tradition of George Hudson that was an admirable compensation. Meanwhile, the faces in the street were turned upwards to the balcony ; they stood for all the blind, almost obliterated faces that one sees in crowd photographs, the features melted into a grey blur. All over Europe there were these hordes of empty faces looking upwards for a light; of nameless men looking for a name. The image on the balcony was the projection of their needs ; it was created out of their impotence and jealousies, and out of their longing for power and importance.

" In the election of 1922 which gave Mr. Bonar Law a comfortable, though not an excessive majority, the Labour Party made considerable gains. It was the reinforced Left wing of that party which determined the choice of its leader in the House, Mr. Clynes being replaced by a man who had received much obloquy during the war, and was feared as a revolutionary, Mr. J. Ramsay MacDonald. Mr. Law's tranquil reign lasted but a few months. His health gave way, and he died soon after his resignation. Lord Curzon, the magnifico, was passed over—however disenchanted the age might be, it was not so homesick for the past that it would accept a Prime Minister in the Lords—and Mr. Stanley Baldwin entered No. 10. Once again, poor Lord Curzon ! He was not even compensated by the Dukedom, which so much human magnificence allied with so much intellectual energy appeared to make inevitable—if only to raise the sagging prestige of Dukes.

" So began a political rivalry and partnership which was to dominate the inter-war period ; for nine years Mr. Baldwin and Mr. MacDonald alternated in the seats of Gladstone and Disraeli, then they came to sit side by side. Mr. Baldwin came in with the full assurance of preserving Mr. Law's tradition of low-pulsed politics, of muted strings and blinds drawn against the dust and heat outside. Again one remembers the pictures that the knowledg-

able and misleading propagandists put forth ; in such trifles is to be
found the flavour of an age. There was Mr. Baldwin with his pipe.
As in later and more exciting years a certain great man's cigar
became a symbol of jaunty defiance, so Mr. Baldwin's pipe, puffed
placidly or sucked philosophically, was the symbol of the mood of
the 'twenties. It provided a pleasant narcotic ; it exhaled good will.
Then, too, there were the highly popular photographs that showed
Mr. Baldwin gazing in genial meditation on his pigs. It was a
curious deception which showed how dangerous the arts of publicity
may sometimes be. Mr. Baldwin was a cultivated man ; he was
related to talents so genuine and diverse as Rudyard Kipling and
Edward Burne Jones ; yet a myth was needed at that time, the
myth of a bucolic leader, a simple and honest Yorkshire-pudding
kind of man who made no pretensions to cleverness ; and Mr.
Baldwin's uncommon intelligence enabled him to give the public
what the publicity officer thought it wanted. Such a Minister
would have been ideally suited to a really tranquil age, such an age,
say, as that of George the Second.

"Mr. Baldwin's first term of office was brief. With unprofessional
candour, he went to the country for a mandate to levy protective
duties. He was beaten. One remembers that General Election as
the last on which the old Free Trade sentiment was the determining
power. It was the ghost of Cobden that overthrew Mr. Baldwin
on that first test. This was nearly eighty years after Repeal, but the
influence of the Anti-Corn Law League had not exhausted itself. I
remember that in the country districts there were still old men and
women who came forward on Opposition platforms to repeat their
parents' stories of the hungry 'forties, long heard in the cottages,
and to echo Lucy Simpkins's cry, ' If we be purtected, we be
starved.'

"For a newspaper which had been founded to support Repeal,
the issue had a classic simplicity . The country gave a loud ' No ' to
Protection, but it did not utter a clear ' Yes ' regarding an alternative to Mr. Baldwin. No party had a majority. Labour held
190 odd seats, the Liberals 150. What would happen ? Who
should rule ? There was much consternation among the well-to-do
at the prospect of Mr. Ramsay MacDonald, the outcast of the war,
forming His Majesty's Government. In some quarters the decision
of the Liberals to vote the Labour Party into office, if not into
power, was regarded with the fascinated horror excited by an act
of treachery. There comes back the image of a stricken Duchess,
blanched to the lips, saying of Mr. Asquith, ' I cannot think how
Herbert could do such a thing.' From the scrapbook of memory
there comes, too, another picture ; of a business man with cherubic

face and roly-poly figure, intended by his Maker to express an all-embracing joviality, quivering with rage at the sight of Mr. Mac-Donald. This happened, as I recall it, at the lunch of some business man's club ; one of those lunches designed in a fuzzy way to show each side that the other is composed of not such bad chaps after all. The little man was a pitiful sight, for it is not good to see a natural flow of the milk of human kindness so patently curdling before one's eyes. His friends at table had difficulty in holding him back when Mr. MacDonald was speaking, although the eminent revolutionary's voice was soothing and the words disarming. The little man seethed and bubbled ; he fizzed as though he had a head of steam in him ; his eyes glazed as he looked at that noble head ; and his apple cheeks deepened to purple. At last he gasped ' Traitor ' in a faint voice, the air came hissing out of him as out of a toy balloon, and after that he was still. I caught a glimpse of the same mercurial little man at a dinner given ten years later in honour of Mr. MacDonald, then leader of a national Government supported by a great Conservative majority. Once again he was beside himself, but this time he was caught up in an ecstasy o hero-worship. In politics, if only you live long enough, almost every villain becomes a hero, and every hero . . .

" That first Labour Government did not last long. But, despite its fugitive existence and undistinguished end, it represented historic change. Forces that had been growing in strength during the century were then gathered up in a wave ; the wave broke ; but other waves would be bound to follow it. It was one of those events, which, viewed gloomily beforehand by nervous souls as an irreparable break with the English tradition, are seen afterwards to fit so well into that tradition that their significance is like to be forgotten. The Duchess found that the tumbril did not call for her. My little business man was not liquidated. There rises up in memory's eye the face of a high Government official with an expression on it of astonishment and jubilation mixed in equal parts. He is saying of Mr. MacDonald's note to the Egyptian Government on the assassination of the Sirdar, ' Oh, it is a great State paper. It is firm and strong. It is worthy of William Pitt.' Outside Parliament there were always long strings of working people waiting to go into the gallery of the House to see ' our people ' in the seats of power.

" One week I saw Lord Curzon in the Secretary of State's room in the Foreign Office ; the next week I saw Mr. MacDonald. That is how English revolutions are achieved.

" This was a period when it seemed as if the last demand of the Chartists—annual Parliaments—had been met. For we had

General Elections in 1922 and 1923, and another in 1924. This last was not to be remembered with much pride. It was the election at which the country was scared by the 'Red Letter', the Zinovieff forgery. The confused explanations given by an overstrained Prime Minister disheartened his supporters. It was a symptom of the instability of the times that so large a part of the nation should believe its institutions were in peril from such a sheet of paper. Again, it was characteristic of the years between the wars, that when the pendulum swung, it should swing violently. The election produced another huge Conservative majority ; the Liberal revival of a year before ended in a Liberal rout ; and Mr. Baldwin sat in Mr. MacDonald's place ; a man who had a greater natural liking for John Keats than for the *Statistical Year Book*, and was not made for the confused times in which he lived.

" With all the zig-zags of politics, all the ups and downs of politicians, and all the gusts of public fancy, there was one thing constant. That was unemployment. It was always there, aching inside the body of the nation and sucking its vitality. It might have been thought that a country which had been robbed by the war of much of its best stock would be lacking enough hands to do all the work that had to be done. Instead, one was presented with the spectacle of the returned soldier become heart-sick from lack of occupation ; of the growing up of a generation of youths with no chance to acquire a trade ; and of inherited skills of high value to the community grown rusty. The pictures of this period that stick in the mind are of cold furnaces, stilled wheels and silent ship-yards ; the listless plodding to and fro of men in search of jobs and—most unhappy sight of all—the youths lounging at street corners in the mining towns, the mill towns, and the Tyneside towns. This spread a greyness over these years. There was a sense of drifting, of pitching and tossing on cheerless waters, with the skies giving no sign. It was a mood immeasurably different from the optimism of our Victorians, who had, above all things, a consciousness of direction and purpose ; who were all either villains, heroes or comic relief in a large, fat Victorian novel, never characters in a Tchekov play.

" Ever since the violent Labour disorders of 1912 and 1913 there had lurked in the back of the collective mind a fear that one day the frightening weapon of the General Strike might be used. Its terrors were shadowy. It was a vague but ill-defined threat, like the bombing of the big cities which was forecast for the next war. Not even the most dogmatic could be sure whether it would be final in its destructiveness, or whether its explosive force might be tempered in the event. The children of Pollyanna declared cheerfully that there could be no General Strike, as the British working man was too sensible a fellow to indulge in such a Continental folly. When it—that terrifying *it*—did come in 1926 it came as most things came in that period, not violently like a thunderbolt, but as a slow, reluctant, half-hearted drifting on to the rocks. There were few level-headed men, even in that gloomy time, who really believed that the men and women who took part in that General Strike were moved by a revolutionary ardour. Their impulse to action was in large part a fraternal one, and, if it was muddle-headed, it was at the same time instinctively generous. It sprang from a sympathy with the miners, traditionally the most ill-starred members of the working masses, not the least of their misfortunes being that physical isolation of their communities which erected the eternal, invisible barrier between them and a crowded world. There was mixed with the confused eagerness to give expression to the fraternal impulse, a desire to make a demonstration against the encircling futility and despair. There was little conscious feeling of provoking a mighty constitutional issue, of defying the lightning of the State. This was an event marked by a singular absence of rhetoric. There were no such tumultuous outpourings as had accompanied the big strikes of 1912-13. Even the somewhat melodramatic circumstances which attended the production of *The British Gazette* aroused smiles rather than passion, as though this were a page from *The Three Musketeers* bound into a volume of George Gissing's drab realism. This should have been—perhaps, indeed, it was—the most formidable test of the political structure of the country in many decades, but, by all accounts, there were two or three Franchise Bills during the century which had brought the people much nearer to mass violence. Nothing was here of the excitement which bubbled in the city on that April morning in 1848 when the old victor of Waterloo stood on guard against the Chartists. There was not even the apprehension that filled respectable bosoms on those three days of the Reform agitation in 1866 when the crowd broke down the Hyde Park railings near Marble Arch and Spencer Walpole, the Home Secretary, burst into tears at the thought of such violence. One remembers a French observer saying, 'The British take their revolutions very sadly.' The Strike had the flatness of anti-climax from the start. It is but half the truth to say of the strikers that their hearts weren't in it. Their hearts were committed to a loyalty for which their actions supplied a most inadequate expression, as though a man should try to rifle the Crown jewels in order to prove how much he loved his mother. On green patches the strikers and the policemen played football. The pickets stood about sadly in the rain, or chatted with the drivers of the ' essential services ' vehicles. Acts of violence or sabotage were relatively few. Volunteers brought up the country trains ; and a peer, photographed smiling benevolently from the footplate, had the ancestral look of all peers opening all village flower shows. The General Strike crumbled away rather than ended—collapsing almost casually, without blood and fire. One day the evening papers reported a High Court judge's ruling that a General Strike was an illegal act. The case had not attracted much attention ; it had not been at all regarded as the test upon whose outcome both sides hung suspended. But that verdict, once given, was decisive. It did not need Sir John Simon's forensic effort in the House of Commons to clinch the effect. Illegality ? Oh, said the strike leaders, in a kind of huff, that was the last thing intended. The profound respect for the Law which quenched the Strike was as touching as the spirit of baffled fraternity which began it. One sees as a picture of that ragged ending a band of railwaymen marching round and round the dreary streets in the neighbourhood of St. Pancras Station—never on the sunniest day a corner of Merrie England—carrying rain-soaked banners, despairing and be-draggled. The Strike was over, but round and round they still went, silent shapes and grey, registering a last mute protest against life's general futility. Like many other people in that time, they could not quite comprehend what had happened.

" It was undoubtedly this failure to understand the inward meaning of events that made Mr. Baldwin, not normally a man who would go out of his way to look for trouble, and not normally a man without perception, decide to bring in the Trade Disputes Bill. Did he really not understand ? Or was the pressure of an indignant Party on an amiable and weak Leader too strong to be withstood ? Here again one touches, as so often in the history of our times, the danger that those two diverse men of genius, Dickens and Disraeli, perceived long ago as being England's greatest danger—the failure of class to speak to class in a common language, clear and true and friendly. It was ironical that in the twilight of the Indus-trial Revolution we had the same problems of misunderstood idiom and bad communications between man and man as in its dawn.

" It would sure have been better had there been a benevolent conspiracy of all parties to forget. Nothing was more certain than that the General Strike would not be attempted again in our time. The resentment aroused by the Trade Disputes Bill seemed dis-proportionate to its provisions. But it was looked at by the Labour people as a punitive expedition into a territory which had already made peace. ' But we had shaken hands on it and said let bygones be bygones.' What affronted them most was the thought that a double standard of honour had been set up. That indignation smouldered for twenty years. One saw its blazing up in Mr. Ernest Bevin's speech in the House of Commons in February 1946 when he vehemently insisted that his union card be cleared. For twenty years at Trade Union meetings they had exhibited the poster, ' Repeal the Act.' And yet the Act could scarcely be proved a disabling and fettering thing. For during the twenty years since its passage the Trade Unions had increased vastly in membership and power, and the Labour Party had grown to such stature that in the summer of 1945 it assumed the government of the nation with the backing of a great majority. No, it was not the physical limitations, it was the implied slur that irked.

" In the backward look, it is never pleasant to see Englishmen at odds when they are in a general hazard. The disputes of those years appear of sorry account compared with the condition of the people and the fortunes of the island. The pulse was slowing ; unemployment had become a pernicious amæmia ; and, outside our stockade, one could hear the first faint beat of the enemy's drums. These were the grey decades. An impalpable dust seemed to settle on everything ; it formed a film over the eyes ; it stopped the ears ; it deadened expression."

III

CHAPTER'S END

In 1931 came the Manchurian incident. That was aggression's first blow. The Black Dragon was out on the prowl. In Germany economic miseries, political weakness and high-placed treachery opened all doors to Hitler. The world watched with dismay, with a frozen foreboding, the irruption of the irrational—almost of the supernatural—into its affairs, for there seemed a black art at the command of this mesmerist who held in thrall a nation of sixty millions. Men in the old time would have called it witchcraft —we found weaker words. We spoke of mass suggestion, herd hypnotism, general somnambulism. In those years of the pagan revival the values which all good Europeans had conserved for centuries were, one by one, cast after the books into the bonfire. The black impulses that man had with painful effort subdued in himself were now set free and put into the seats of Government. Those heavenly twins of the Victorians, Progress and Peace, went into exile together.

The world reflected in the pages of the *News Chronicle* in the
nineteen-thirties' was an increasingly grim and threatening world.
Aggression's appetite grew with feeding. Mussolini, become bold
through other men's weaknesses, pounced on Abyssinia. Under
his rule, the Italy of Mazzini and Garibaldi, which had greatly
stirred the hopes of the Victorians, became perverted to a vulgar
Caesarism. The Japanese war lords stretched out greedy hands.
The British people at the General Election of 1935—the last chance
open to them—made known their will that the League should be
upheld and sanctions be visited upon aggressors. The electors
proposed—but others disposed. In the ensuing years the authority
of the League steadily decayed and the hope of collective security
was a match in the wind. Russia, estranged and aloof, watched,
waited, and pursued in enigmatic silence her own quest for security.
The United States withdrew into a dream of isolation in which
she imagined she was part of another planet. The Spanish Civil War
served as a dress rehearsal for the would-be conquerors of the
world. The Luftwaffe tried out its strength. A polish was put
upon the methods to be employed in blasting Warsaw, Rotterdam,
London and Coventry. The battle of ideas, the struggle for the
soul of Europe, was being fought long before the signal of general
havoc was given. Austria went. Czecho-Slovakia went. The
flickering candle of appeasement, that brief hope of saving peace
in our time, was soon blown out. Meanwhile, in sombre imagery,
Winston Churchill spoke warning wisdom to his countrymen,
over and over and over again. The complacent smiled, and
knowingly quoted the Fat Boy in *Pickwick*.

These years were like the *March to the Scaffold* in Berlioz, the
wildness of a mind in a fever. Europe was on the march to the
scaffold, with old drums from the jungle pounding ; bloodstained
flags in ribbons ; and a rout of apes following.

This was a harsh period for Liberal journalism.* The qualities
and elements in living prized most highly by Western man were
never in worse peril than in these years. Freedoms that our fathers

---

* The fate of John Segrue, who, as correspondent of the *Daily News* had been
the first journalist to enter Berlin after 1918, epitomised the tragedy of many men
of good will. Believing fervently in the ultimate revival of a Liberal Europe, he
remained as Berlin correspondent so long as it was physically possible for him to
do so.

He was taken prisoner by the Nazis in Yugoslavia in 1941, and died in a prison
camp in Upper Silesia in October 1942. Another war correspondent of the newspaper, the gifted Stuart Emeny who was killed with Wingate in Burma in May
1944, had followed the march of aggression in far different corners of the earth.
Emeny had been through the rigours of the Ethiopian campaign and had seen
the over-running of Hailé Selassie's dominions by the triumphant hordes of
Mussolini.

had taken as much for granted as their own bodies were extinguished. The blissful Victorian certainty that progress was automatic was finally trampled down under the march past of the jack-boots. The Victorian belief that European evolution was a broad white road rolling endlessly on into the future proved sadly false, for the road was now seen to describe a violent loop back into the past, sweeping round as far as the mind could reach into the primitive swamps. It was seen, too, that not one of the eternal assumptions was unassailable, that the very ideas of justice, tolerance, mercy and fair dealing had to be battled for all over again as though man were back at his beginnings. Yet if these days represented the sharpest testing to which the tradition had ever been put, they brought in the end its highest vindication. It was the system that hated liberty, flouted justice, annulled toleration and despised mercy that lost the war. What was base in the Victorian tradition had been burned away, but what was fine had passed through the fire and is ours to inherit.

CHAPTER XVII

THE TEMPER OF THE TIMES

LOOKING into these grey old files, one comes slowly to see the changing shapes of the ideas that have governed the Englishman during this century. It is like walking in the country on a misty morning—the nearer trees at first appear larger than nature, and the farther prospect is quite veiled—but, bit by bit, the silvery haze falls away, and the entire landscape unfolds to the traveller's eye.

One of the unifying themes in this loose survey of a century has been the breaking down of fences. Lady Dorothy Nevill, who was 26 in the year 1846, records in her book, *My Own Times* (published in 1912) that " it was not altogether unnatural that, with a view to maintaining the prestige of their class, the aristocracy of the past should have understood that their best policy was to make their offspring believe that they were the finest people ever born into the world. In some cases, indeed, the latter though they were encouraged to see something of the people, were taught to regard them as beings totally apart. Such a thing as living in close contact with those of inferior caste was unheard of. . . ."

Many waters have flowed over those old boundary marks since— often bitter waters. Two great wars, with their acceleration of change ; modern technology and transport ; high taxation and the redistribution of wealth ; the social criticisms of novelists, playwrights and journalists of talent ; the new spirit in the teaching of the churches, have played their part in a revolution without guillotines. In Peel's Conservative Cabinet of 1846 and in Russell's Whig Cabinet that followed it, the aristocratic element was overwhelmingly predominant.* The century saw the shift to middle-class mastery, and, after that, the gradual increase of the political power of the working class. Gladstone in his extreme old age, looking back over more than sixty years of political activity, said, " These years offer us the picture of what the historian will recognise as a great legislative and administrative period—perhaps, on the whole, the greatest in our annals. It has been predominantly a history of emancipation—that is of enabling man to do his work— of emancipation, political, social, moral, intellectual."

The Liberal State came to full stature ; with the sweep of the century it rounded out its accomplishments. One might say, not

* Russell's Cabinet included two commoners—Charles Wood, grandfather of the present Lord Halifax, and Henry Labouchere, afterwards Lord Taunton, who left his great fortune to his nephew, the " Labby " of this record.

only of the Victorians, but of the Edwardians and Georgians as well, " Shut them in—with their triumphs and their glories and the rest ! " The concept of Progress had suffered many changes. It was no longer seen in the image of an express train, thundering into the sunrise with its load of first-class, second-class and third-class passengers. Progress was no longer to be tested simply by the tapping of the wheels at Crewe Station. More subtle instruments were demanded. Or rather, it began to be realised that there was more than one order of Progress, that mechanical achievement was no guarantee of intellectual or moral or cultural growth. The control of Nature was the fulfilment of an old and magnificent dream, but suppose that the command of these limitless powers was exercised by Human Nature *out* of control ?

There had grown up during the century a common acceptance among the heirs of Peel and Palmerston, of Dizzy as well as Gladstone, of a collective social responsibility. Controversy, accepting the obligation, had come to concern itself with defining its limits ; and with reconciling freedom and a planned economy. At the same time, the sensitiveness to human suffering had increased with the increase in the weapons that caused suffering ; the sense of the value of the individual human being was enhanced as individualism in politics and economics decayed. The callous prodigality of Nature was no longer imitated by human society. There was a conserving care for " the least of these creatures," for the once despised and disinherited, which suggested that the principles of the New Testament were being more broadly diffused at a time when the power of the Churches was held to be waning. What was to happen next? Was the Liberal State which had flourished between 1846 and 1946, and had survived fierce tests, to be replaced by the purely Collective State? And just how jejune will this question seem if any eye chances to light on this page in the year 2046 ?

Side by side with the changes in the domestic mood went a steady evolution in the Briton's relationship to the world beyond his islands. In Russell's Government of 1846 Palmerston came back to the Foreign Office. During a large part of the succeeding twenty years he managed our foreign affairs with a liveliness, and at times a jauntiness, that stirred the admiration of his countrymen and often astonished the world. At its worst, his diplomacy became the cavortings of a high-spirited horse in the main street of Europe—a brave, breath-taking show—with head-on smashes avoided by the eagerness of other riders to keep out of the way. At its best it represented a generous sympathy with movements of liberation, a chivalrous taking of sides against tyrants. Palmerston, as Foreign Secretary, receiving deputations from cross-Channel rebels and giving them his blessing, treating the conventions of diplomacy with a gay airiness, was a spectacle that could anger the Queen and Prince Albert beyond measure but it was applauded by the nation at large. Old Pam, this tough evergreen from the eighteenth century, with his dyed whiskers, whom the electors of Tiverton saluted as *Cupid*, became the paragon of the middle-class, and in his speeches in the 'fifties and 'sixties he defined the middle-class attitude to the universe with uncommon pith and saltiness.

Matthew Arnold in one of his assaults on the Philistines (*My Countrymen*, 1866) had sardonically quoted the *Daily News* as saying that "all the world knew that the great middle-class of this country supplies the mind, the will, and the power for all the great and good things that have been done." It was all very fine for the mandarin of culture to gibe at that naïve boast, but the blunt fact was that the triumphant middle-class not only believed it to be so, without a quaver of self-doubting, but acted strongly on its faith.

Again, Arnold had asserted, "Our aristocratical class, the Barbarians have no perception of the real wants of the community at home. Our middle classes, the Philistines, have no perception of our real relation to the world abroad." But was that true? Surely Palmerston was the spear-point of the middle-class thrust in foreign affairs. In resurrecting these files of the 'forties and 'fifties one comes to comprehend why a Liberal newspaper like the *Daily News* could be attached to a statesman who in home affairs remained to the end an old-fashioned Whig save for his un-Whiggish sympathy with factory reform. The records of the newspaper tell of Shaftes-bury—at that time a frequent visitor—striding into the office one morning in 1859 and exclaiming, "Palmerston has been sent for—thank God!" Palmerston gave the manufacturing classes an exhilarating revelation of their own power. In effect, he said to them, "See, you are now so strong you can keep the world in order and your principles are so high that you can always be counted upon to throw that weight on the side of the angels." Their wealth and energy had given them political dominion in their own land—now they felt they were clothing England with the strength of a lion to rule the jungle of the foreign world. The nearest resemblance to that mood which we have witnessed in our times is America waking up to the political power with which its industrial resources has invested it. One surmises there might be considerable scope for a reincarnation of Palmerston in America to-day if there were a man to wear his armour.

In sampling leading articles and the foreign correspondence in the *Daily News* during the Palmerston era, one sees a Britain who is sublimely sure of herself. She plunges this way and that in the affairs of the world, eagerly taking sides, particularly when foreign despotisms were crushing the hopes of free men, but usually behaving as though she herself were invulnerable. " England, queen of the waves, whose green inviolate girdle enrings thee round." If there were bad storms in the Channel, then it was the Continent which was cut off from England ; and it was so much the worse for the Continent. An American writer has said that the world was saved from major wars and achieved unbounded prosperity in the nineteenth century because there were two benevolent policemen on the beat—the Royal Navy and the £ sterling. It was sea power and golden guineas that enabled Palmerston as Foreign Minister to behave like a prefect in a scuffle of small boys. In order to remind the world where ultimate strength resided it was some-times necessary to flex the biceps. So we had the Don Pacifico incident, when the weight of the Royal Navy was brought into play against Greece in defence of a highly dubious moneylender who called for British protection because he had been born in Malta. And Palmerston, challenged in Parliament, won an even more resounding vote of confidence from the middle-classes than from the House with his great *Civis Romanus Sum* speech.

Podsnap declared at the party at which the brow-beaten French-man was present, " We Englishmen are very proud of our constitu-tion, sir. It was bestowed upon us by Providence. No other country is so favoured as this country. This island was blest, sir, to the direct exclusion of such other countries as—as there may happen to be." That emotion to-day is called Blimpery. But Podsnappery was not always a Victorian variety of Blimpery. It was often married to an ardent love of liberty, to a loathing for foreign despots, and to a readiness to use Britain's strength in supporting the extension of democratic reforms in other countries. The notion that Dickens drew Podsnap from the character of his friend, John Forster, the second editor of the *Daily News*, is not ill-founded and not wholly malicious. There are even some students of Dickens who think that he himself grew a shade Podsnappish in his last years.

In one of the early issues of the *Daily News* one comes across a short letter signed Jos. Mazzini dealing with the Italian exiles in London. This shock of historical recognition—it is as difficult to think of that radiant, half-angelic figure as Jos. as of Mr. Gladstone as Willie—brings to mind one of the happiest of Britain's interventions in the Palmerstonian period. The triumph of the Italian struggle for independence and unity owed much to the British Government's skilful and steadfast diplomatic support of the Italian patriots. Here was a cause which the British nation espoused with ardour and even vehemence. The Duchess of Sutherland's reception for Garibaldi at Stafford House was a high-water mark of Victorian liberalism and of Victorian romanticism. The hero appealed to the heart of chivalry that swelled beneath Victorian Paisley shawls and plaids. When Freedom was so picturesquely arrayed as this and spoke with so melting an accent she was irresistible. The liberation of Italy was a cause to make the pulse beat faster, and the *Daily News* took conscious pride in being a leader in it. There was the quickening of high adventure in the smuggling of Mazzini's letters, from his hiding place in Genoa, for publication in the paper. " Let not Ocean's Queen abandon the children of Ocean," was the appeal made to the paper by one of the Italian patriots. The doctrine that Britain's surest defence lay in the creation of a free Europe—that despotism must always be Britain's enemy and liberty be always her friend—took fast root in those years. A Europe composed of free and independent nations, with the thrall of tyranny broken, would surely be a peaceful Europe, never challenging Albion, but seeking her mighty friendship and welcoming her queenship of the seas. There was a disinterested passion for liberty, as well as a response to romance in bondage, in British hearts that made them exult and cheer as the exploits of Garibaldi and the Thousand were recounted, and as the grand design of Italian unity unfolded. The intoxicating music of Swinburne's hymns to Mazzini and Liberty found echoes in most unpoetical bosoms. The dedication of *Songs Before Sunrise* to Mazzini touched chords of revolutionary sentiment in the mansions of respectable merchants in Highgate or on Clapham Common :—

> If a perfume be left, if a bloom,
> Let it live till Italia be risen,
> To be strewn in the dust of her car
> When her voice shall awake from the tomb
> England, and France from her prison,
> Sisters, a star by a star.

It was a time when English Republicanism wore a frock coat and an orchid in its lapel. The passion for Liberty was none the less pure because the political instinct of the British told them that the Europe of Mazzini and Kossuth was the kind of Europe most favourable to the development of their own peaceful arts and the spreading of their Heaven-sent prosperity. Recalling those brave times, Sir John Robinson said in his farewell address to his staff, " The struggle for liberty and unity in Italy is almost forgotten, but not by me. I see again the pale face of Mazzini, the apostle of Italian unity, with eyes that fascinated one, with a voice that

thrilled like the voice of Kean or Kemble, and made one ready to
start for Milan at once should he desire it. . . . Ah ! that shabby
old room in Bouverie Street in the old times glows like a palace in
my thoughts. Garibaldi trod that rickety floor ; Kossuth in his
braided coat did not shrink from the risk of sitting on the cane-
bottomed chairs ; Mazzini leaned on its ink-spotted desk." One
sees again E. H. Vizetelly in his troubadour's costume—an R. L.
Stevenson figure from *Providence and a Guitar*—as the romantic war
correspondent of Italian liberation. There was *panache*—there was
the grandiloquent gesture—but there was also a glorious faith that
did move mountains.

With John Bull growing ever richer and rotunder, there was
no reason apparent to the country why, to put it on the material
level, the role of Leviathan keeping the lesser fishes in order could
not be kept up as far ahead as the mind could reach. Tennyson,
who on one side of him, at least, was the well-tempered laureate
of the middle-classes, expressed the prevailing sentiment :—

> *We sailed wherever ships could sail ;*
> *We founded many a mighty state ;*
> *Pray God our greatness may not fail*
> *Through craven fear of being great.*

But the check came, almost at the end of Palmerston's resplendent
career. In consulting the files at the time of the Schleswig-Holstein
crisis, a modern reader is in danger of being less than fair to his
ancestors. With all the superiority of those who are wise after
the event, the critic is tempted to say, " But surely didn't they see
that this new force rising in European affairs, this steely-bright
Germany, was a very different proposition from everything else
they had been dealing with, the Offenbach empire of Napoleon
the Third, the muzzy, blundering uncertainties of Czarist Russia,
the many-coloured crazy quilt called the Austro-Hungarian
Empire. Here was Prussia, a force as distinct from the old empires
as a railway train was from a stage coach, a purposeful State,
with a religion of pride and a philosophy of conquest, and a new
technique in war which, seventy years later, we were calling the
blitzkrieg." When Prussia glowered at Denmark like a wolf at a
lamb, Britain vibrated with impulses of sympathy for the Danes.
This very year (1863) a Danish princess who was as beautiful as
a fairy-tale princess had married the Prince of Wales. Palmerston
and Gladstone were her friends ; Tennyson saluted the sea-king's
daughter from over the sea ; and all the romantic Liberalism of
Victorian England was engaged by the beauty and the sorrows of
Alexandra. The chivalrous instincts which had been moved by the

victims of Austrian tyranny or Russian tyranny, the emotions which had prompted the London dray-men to assault the Austrian General Haynau* in the streets because he had whipped Hungarian women rebels, or to cheer Garibaldi, now rallied to the side of the Danes. And, inerrantly true as always, in expressing his countryman's emotions, the venerable Palmerston warned Germany that if war came Denmark would not stand alone. Bismarck ignored the warning. War came. And Denmark *did* stand alone. For Palmerston found when it came to the pinch, that Britain did not have the rifles to enforce her word and defend the cause she had espoused. The War Office, having learned little from the scourgings it had received over the Crimea War, was in a state of fine unpreparedness. Prussia had an army of 200,000 equipped with breech-loading rifles. Britain could meet this with an army of no more than 20,000 equipped with muzzle-loading rifles. Palmerston's gay swagger could not make up the difference in fire power. The new force in Europe was telling Britain that her rusty arms invited defiance. Within a few years Lord Salisbury was writing, " It is clear enough that the traditional Palmerston policy is at an end." After Schleswig-Holstein, nothing could be the same again.

Yet Britain was by now too deeply implicated in the world's affairs to withdraw behind her sea walls. Foreign policy became a series of uncertain swervings, and, because the nation was uneasy, it was disputatious.

For many years British public opinion was to be divided by hot disagreement over Russia and Turkey. The illusion that the Victorian age was a ripe age of continuity in foreign policy will not survive an hour's reading of the political speeches and leading articles during the period of Disraeli's 1874-80 Ministry. The Liberals were outraged that the British Government should bolster the odious tyranny of the Turk. The Conservatives, for their part, said they were shocked by the indifference of the Opposition to the menace of Russia, and their recklessness in affronting Turkey. The Conservative Cabinet itself was far from united. The Queen, who had no doubts of her own sentiments, wrote to Disraeli (then become Lord Beaconsfield) in January 1878, " She is utterly ashamed of the Cabinet. Be firm and you will rally your party round you. . . . Oh, if the Queen were a man, she would like to go and give those Russians, whose word one cannot believe, such a beating ! "

One of the longest-rumbling political storms of the century was

* Marshal Haynau, greeted by shouts of " Hyena " by the London mob, was ejected from Messrs. Barclay Perkins' Brewery in Southwark by the draymen in 1850.

AUGUST 1945
The End of the Century.

stirred up by a despatch from Edwin Pears, the Constantinople correspondent of the *Daily News* on 23 June 1876, describing Turkish repression of the Insurrection in Bulgaria. The Bashi-bazouks had ravaged the Bulgarian countryside. Thousands of peasants were killed, girls were burned alive, and a number of villages wiped out as completely as was Lidice years afterwards. The publication of these reports in the *Daily News* struck a chill of horror to the public. Disraeli, in an unhappy moment in the House of Commons dismissed the first reports as "coffee house babble." To his confidant, Lady Bradford, he wrote, "They appear in that journal alone, which is the real Opposition journal, and, I believe, are to a great extent inventions. But their object is to create a cry against the Government" (*Life of Disraeli*, Moneypenny and Buckle). Disraeli was ill-served by the British Ambassador at Constantinople, Sir Henry Elliot, who, bemused by the charm and gentlemanliness of the Turk, had failed to transmit to London intelligence of the atrocities, and by the dilatoriness of the Foreign Office in forwarding the Prime Minister a despatch of the British Consul at Rustchuk which at least partly confirmed the tale of blood. It was that dashing son of Ohio, J. A. MacGahan, famous for his ride of six hundred perilous miles to see the Russian assault on Khiva, who at great risk to himself, travelled through Bulgaria to check these reports. His letters to the *Daily News* convinced even the Foreign Office ; and brought the Under-Secretary of State to his feet in the House to express an indebtedness that politicians seldom feel towards newspapers. In September of that year Gladstone wrote, "It is even possible that but for the courage, determination and ability of this single organ, we might even at this moment have remained in darkness, and Bulgarian wretchedness might have been without its best and brightest hope." Not long afterwards *The Times*, the *Daily Telegraph* and other newspapers brought the powerful reinforcement of their own reports, and anger was soon sweeping the country. To modern readers, knowing only a Turkey, shrunken and poor, it is hard to conceive that so short a time ago she was a formidable power in Europe, sprawling over great territories, and holding many Christian communities in thrall.

The religious sentiment of Britain was deeply moved by the sight of Christian peoples tortured by the great Moslem power. Few words are more fatigued from over-work than crusade, but when Gladstone set out to arouse the nation over Bulgarian atrocities, he was seen as the plumed champion of the Cross against the Crescent. There were Christian slaves to be rescued from the Infidel ; and an old magic quivered in the air. In the earlier decades of our century the British passion for liberty abroad had been a blending of the romantic and the rational. There was nothing of the mystic about Palmerston or *Punch* or the early *Daily News*. Now, with Gladstone at the peak of his more than human energies, the burning force of religious emotions was applied to politics. In Palmerston's time the tyrants and despots, however murky, were like the secular villains of a Lyceum melodrama who would be put in handcuffs and packed off in a Black Maria at the end of Act 5. But here, in the Gladstonian era, there came the recognition of a spiritual evil operating in affairs and transcending them ; and on the stage of foreign politics men saw enacted the eternal conflict between the powers of light and the powers of darkness. In the Bulgarian atrocity campaign, Gladstone came naturally to speak of the " fell, satanic orgies " of the Turks who were " the one great anti-human specimen of humanity." On the lava flow of Gladstone's oratory, the Near Eastern question was carried above considerations of expediency, balance of power, diplomatic adjustment and practical politics and became an issue between the sons of God and the brood of Satan. Gladstone moved about the land like an Old Testament prophet, the falcon head transfigured with wrath, the hypnotic eyes flashing their lightnings, and the canorous voice crying out against wickedness in high places. There are many men and women still living who can testify to the effect which this discharge of electrical energy had upon them. Gladstone communicated to more than his immediate audiences his prophetic ardours, and from this period onwards the identity of politics, particularly foreign policy, with ethical or religious aspirations became increasingly marked among considerable sections of our people. Here again one can identify a new element coming into our national life ; or, rather, the change of direction of an old element. The British habits of political thinking to-day are deeply coloured by the apostolic Gladstone of the Bulgarian atrocities period and of the subsequent (1879) Midlothian campaign, that " pilgrimage of passion."

Disraeli, who belonged to another age and a different tradition, in which politics and morals were kept in separate boxes, could not comprehend the peculiar nature of this quality in Gladstone nor the vibration which it set up among his countrymen. The imaginative power of the " alien patriot," which enabled him to divine many truths about the British, failed him on this side. Gladstone was a phenomenon that puzzled as much as it angered him. Sometimes Disraeli believed he had isolated his antagonist for good as the most consummate hypocrite in history, beside whom Tartuffe and Pecksniff were transparencies. Sometimes he dismissed him as " the sophisticated rhetorician intoxicated by the exuberance of his own verbosity." Sometimes he thought him to be mentally unhinged. In a revealing letter to his Foreign Secretary, Lord Derby, in October, 1876, Disraeli wrote, " Posterity will do justice to that unprincipled maniac Gladstone—extraordinary mixture of envy, vindictiveness, hypocrisy and superstition ; and with one commanding characteristic—whether Prime Minister or Leader of the Opposition, whether preaching, praying, speechifying or scribbling—never a gentleman." (Moneypenny and Buckle).

There is a baffled anti-climax of exasperation in that conclusion. When a statesman dismisses his rival as no gentleman, it is certain that all subtler diagnosis has failed him. But there was a sense in which Disraeli's assessment was accurate. Gladstone was not a gentleman in that traditional eighteenth-century mould which had endured long into the nineteenth century. He was not a gentleman of that school which regarded enthusiasm as vulgar, religion as an embarrassing secret and all passions as purely private. He was not a gentleman in the sense that a prophet, a poet or a rebel could hope to be a gentleman.

What Disraeli never understood was the secret of Gladstone's power over his countrymen—that he had liberated a fresh source of energy in the hidden places of their natures. One measure of that lack of comprehending was the painful surprise which Dizzy experienced when Gladstone so conspicuously triumphed in the 1880 election. So the unbelievable was true. The old maniac, the non-gentleman with his " drenching rhetoric," which Disraeli found unreadable, had spoken for England after all.

Gladstone, for his part, brooding over the problem of sin in politics, came increasingly to conceive of his rival as a diabolical figure, heartless, unprincipled and a-moral. That his policy was false was bad enough. But the man himself, to the smouldering eyes of the watcher on the opposite Front Bench, was false, false beyond redemption, inside. It was his cleverness that was killing us all, this elastic cleverness of wits without conscience, of statecraft without a soul. Few writers, however, partial, would accept that judgment to-day but in 1880 there was no bridging the temperamental gulf.

Gladstone and Disraeli ! Out of the duel of those two beings, both creatures of genius, but in genius as different as a panther and an eagle, was generated much of the emotional force of British politics in the last seventy years. It meant that the Liberalism of modern times would be infused by the particular strength of the Free Churches, gathering up again into political motion the

evangelical forces which Wilberforce had long before drawn upon
in the Abolition movement and Cobden in the Repeal of the Corn
Laws. The religious emotion was to become something far more
widely diffused and less literal than Mr. Gladstone and Professor
Huxley arguing in public over the miracle of the Gadarene swine.
The life history of David Lloyd George exhibits the power of
that political Nonconformity which Gladstone, the devout High
Anglican, conjured to his aid in the last fiery phases of a career
whose influence more than spans our century. Gladstone in
his youth had, like Peel, represented the rise to power of the
mercantile middle-classes who were to make the Victorian Age
a golden age for their sons. But through Gladstone it came about
that the final legacy of that class was this ethical or religious
impulse in politics. However maddening its interventions might
have appeared to the realists, its necessity seemed to grow
increasingly manifest to millions of Britons. In the gathering darkness of the age of machines it was seen to be essential to the survival
of Western man. For as the engines multiplied, and mechanical
progress swept on from one conquest to another, the danger grew
that the spirit of man would be locked up in an iron box—that pity
and compassion would be smothered, that an immense indifference
would deaden the nerves, and that the serfs of the machine,
well fed and secure, would forget the very names of justice and
fraternity. Each in his little cell would be warmly and cosily alone,
the sensibilities withering, the life-giving force of sympathy decaying
in that airless comfort. In the eyes of most Britons, that must have
been the tragedy of numberless Germans deeply committed to
Nazism, and content to exchange their consciences for material
benefits but in the end losing all.

The intelligent men among the early Victorians had been
troubled by the shadow of this doom, but they had counted, too
optimistically, on the natural good sense of mankind to avoid it,
and to use mechanical advance and scientific invention for the
betterment of the human condition. Samuel Butler's *Erewhon* was
published as long ago as 1872. It will be recalled that this brilliant
satire tells how the Erewhonians had ordained the utter destruction
of all machines to save men from their domination, from being
eaten alive by them. In that land of Erewhon it was a crime to
possess even a watch. It is surprising that Butler's chapters on the
abolition of the machines have not been more often quoted during
these past two years when the V weapons and the atom bomb
might seem fierce confirmation of his fears. In 1872, when men
were buoyed up by faith in mechanical progress, Butler was thought
to be either an amusing entertainer or an irritating huckster of

paradoxes. To many he appeared to be perversely providing a philosophy, long after the event, for those poor working men, the Luddites who in the early years of the nineteenth century had gone about in the industrial parts of England breaking up the machines. All such thoughts as these in *Erewhon* were surely black reactions, said an optimistic generation. For was not man a moral being who would subdue the machine to his high purposes as certainly as he would destroy the ape and tiger in himself? The ape and the tiger did not die ; it was they who first became mechanised. The assertion of moral principles in politics and affairs came barely in time to prevent the ape from breaking the atom and blowing up the world. (The tiger had already taken to riding the clouds on rockets.) If one were to try to put into words the attitude of the Briton of today who is steeped in the ethical tradition of his fathers, no matter what his party ties may be, one might phrase it like this : " When our friends abroad say that it is to Britain they look for leadership, it is of the quality of being vividly alive and sensitive that they are thinking. Their hopes reside in Britain's power to resist the exhaustion of ideals among the whirring complexities of the vast machinery of modern existence—of being always aware of the sweep of stars behind the array of the machines. Of that awareness, the issues of justice and injustice and the place a man gives to truth in his schemes is a part. It becomes impossible to eat well, talk about the weather and sleep like a child when wickedness rides high and cruelty is done. The miseries and humiliations of other people cannot be run away from, cannot be shut and put upon the shelf like an old book. All the whispers of self-indulgence are towards forgetfulness, but the deep instinct for life in the British people has made them understand that to be the active participants, the sharers, the committed ones, is the way of survival." Nothing has sharpened the urgency of that belief so much as the making and using of the atom bomb.

This is no over-night conversion, but a steady drift of feeling. There was not a chemical trace of jingoism in the British composition in the 'nineteen-thirties and the war years, but there was a great recognition of the ethical nature of the European struggle. The consciousness of spiritual evil, striving after the mastery of the world, was shared by countless men and women who had become indifferent to creeds. Less than fifty years before, the nation had plunged into the Boer War with cheers and songs. On 3 September 1939, there was no thirst for blood and fire, but a feeling that we could do none other than resist with a steadfast mind the uprushing of evil. If there was no physical exhilaration in the mortal necessity, there developed among ordinary men and women, not given to heroics, a fortitude and constancy in the worst hours that came near to the sublime. The difference between John Bull in 1898 and John Bull in the 'nineteen-forties appears so wide as to make us ask where are the family resemblances. They are there, none the less. Certain characteristics in the national temperament that were then submerged, certain muscles overlaid by the fat of Victorian good living, have since asserted themselves and become the dominant traits.

There is much worth pondering in the lessons of the century that has gone ; in particular, the manner in which certain principles of foreign policy have stood the test of harsh challenges. The Foreign Office memorandum of Sir Eyre Crowe* written nearly forty years ago at a time when Britain's naval supremacy was absolute, and statecraft still retained the magnificent aura of the Victorian age, laid it down that the condition of the continuance of this domination was that it should be used so " as to harmonise with the general desires and ideals common to all mankind, and more particularly that it is closely identified with the primary and vital interests of a majority, or as many as possible, of the other nations. Now, the first interest of all countries is the preservation of national independence." Therefore Britain must always be the protector of small nations and resist any attempt by a single power, or an alliance, to overlordship of the world. In defending that principle Britain has since lost much blood and spent most of the stored treasures of the Victorians. Whatever slurs may be cast upon the British name, this record has given Britain high authority abroad. That order of influence is an asset that cannot be computed by accountants, as they can compute national income, or the balance of trade, but it is as solid as the gold of the Victorians. It is an asset which renews itself by being spent.

The changes that have taken place in the century under review have enriched and subtilised the quality of patriotism. No generation of Britons ever cherished a dearer love for their native earth than the generation which faced the threat of 1940. Never before was every single hill and field, every grass plot and tree gazed upon with such jealous possessiveness as in that falsely smiling summer of 1940 when men and women made ready to die for them. But beyond this dedication to the beloved place, there was a fierce seizing upon the idea of Britain because of the wide trust that was reposed in it ; because of the hopes and dreams of general mankind which were fixed upon it ; because of the flame from the sun that was cherished in the small lamp. These were universal essences

* He was the grandson of Eyre Crowe, third editor of the *Daily News*.

not peculiar to our patriotism. It was not English freedom alone that made this soil sacred. It was freedom's self. The patriot's all-consuming love for his country was an element in which fields and cities became symbols of ideas. " He would rather die than see a spire of English grass trampled down by a foreign trespasser." That was still true, more true than ever. But these spires of grass now stood not only for the love of home and the place of one's birth but had become a local habitation and a name for values that belonged to all men. Thereby the world has been brought sensibly nearer that " more perfect union " of the peoples.

INDEX